About Earth's Child

The Earth Bible Commentary Series, 2

Series Editor
Norman Habel

Editorial Board
Vicky Balabanski, Hilary Marlow, Barbara Rossing, Peter Trudinger,
Elaine Wainwright, Joh Wurst

In Memory of Laurence Michael Trainor

(1919–2011)

About Earth's Child

An Ecological Listening to the Gospel of Luke

Michael Trainor

Sheffield Phoenix Press
2017

Copyright © 2012, 2017 Sheffield Phoenix Press

First published in hardback, 2012
First published in paperback, 2017

Published by Sheffield Phoenix Press
Biblical Studies, University of Sheffield
45 Victoria Street
Sheffield S3 7QB

www.sheffieldphoenix.com

All rights reserved.
No part of this publication may be reproduced or transmitted in any form or by any means, electronic or mechanical, including photocopying, recording or any information storage or retrieval system, without the publisher's permission in writing.

A CIP catalogue record for this book
is available from the British Library

Typeset by ISB Typesetting
Printed by Lightning Source Inc.

ISBN 978-1-907534-64-5 (hardback)
ISBN 978-1-910928-28-8 (paperback)

Contents

Abbreviations	vii
List of Figures	ix
Introduction	1

Part I

Chapter 1
Differing Attitudes to Earth: Luke's Audience 20

Chapter 2
Intertextual Engagement in Luke's Gospel 40

Part II

Chapter 3
Luke 1.1–2.52: Jesus—Earth's Child 64

Chapter 4
Luke 3.1–4.30: Luke's Ecological Principles 96

Chapter 5
Luke 4.14–7.23: Jesus' Ministry in the Garden of God's Earthly Delights ... 118

Chapter 6
Luke 7.24–9.50: Feasting and Fasting in the Paradisiacal Garden 146

Chapter 7
Introducing Luke 9.51–19.27: The Story of Earth's Journey 166

Chapter 8
Luke 9.51–13.22: Earth Matters 169

Chapter 9
Luke 13.23–17.10: Material Freedom; Earth Care 202

Chapter 10
LUKE 17.11–19.27: THE IMMINENCE OF GOD'S BASILEIA–ECOTOPIA   223

Chapter 11
LUKE 19.28–21.38: ECOLOGICAL INTERTWINING WITH JESUS' WORD   245

Chapter 12
LUKE 22.1–24.53: THE SUFFERING, DEATH AND CELEBRATION OF
EARTH'S CHILD   265

PART III

Conclusion
LUKE'S ECOLOGICAL RESONANCES   294

Bibliography   305
Index of References   316
Index of Authors   322

Abbreviations

ABR	*Australian Biblical Review*
AnnStorEseg	*Annali di storia dell'esegesi*
BAR	*Biblical Archaeology Review*
BibInt	*Biblical Interpretation*
BTB	*Biblical Theology Bulletin*
CBQ	*Catholic Biblical Quarterly*
CurrBibRes	*Currents in Biblical Research*
DBI	John. H. Hayes (ed.), *Dictionary of Biblical Interpretation* (2 vols.; Nashville, TN: Abingdon Press, 1999).
EDNT	Horst Balz and Gerhard Schneider (ed.), *Exegetical Dictionary of the New Testament* (3 vols.; Grand Rapids, MI: Wm B. Eerdmans Publishing Co., 1991).
ETL	*Ephemerides Theologicae Lovanienses*
IDB	George Arthur Buttrick (ed.), *The Interpreter's Dictionary of the Bible* (4 vols.; Nashville, TN: Abingdon Press, 1962).
ISBE	Geoffrey Bromiley (ed.), *The International Standard Bible Encyclopedia* (4 vols.; Grand Rapids, MI: Wm B. Eerdmans Publishing Co., rev. edn, 1979–88).
JBL	*Journal of Biblical Literature*
JSNT	*Journal for the Study of the New Testament*
KJB	King James Version
LXX	The Septuagint
NIDNTT	Colin Brown (ed.), *The New International Dictionary of New Testament Theology* (4 vols.; Grand Rapids, MI: Zondervan, 1986).
NIV	New International Version
NJB	New Jerusalem Bible
NJBC	Raymond E. Brown, *et. al.* (ed.), *The New Jerome Biblical Commentary*. (London: Chapman, 1991).
NovT	*Novum Testamentum*
NRSV	New Revised Standard Version
ScrBull	*Scripture Bulletin*
TDNT	Gerhard Kittel and Gerhard Friedrich (eds.), *Theological Dictionary of the New Testament* (trans. Geoffrey W. Bromiley; 10 vols.; Grand Rapids, MI: Wm B. Eerdmans Publishing Co., 1964–1976).
TEV	Today's English Version
TS	*Theological Studies*

List of Figures

Figure 1
The three 'worlds' of gospel engagement — 14

Figure 2
Social stratification in the Herodian period — 28

Figure 3
Different ecological attitudes in Luke's audience — 37

Figure 4
The embedded nature of Luke's four Mediterranean 'worlds' — 38

Figure 5
The contribution of earlier texts and traditions to later texts and meaning — 41

Figure 6
An earlier text as intertext *in a fresh social context* — 42

Figure 7
Luke's gospel as a new intertext *for contemporary ecological concerns* — 43

Figure 8
Intertexts, including Luke's gospel, for engaging present ecological concerns — 44

Figure 9
Social and cultural influences on the meaning of 'text' — 45

Figure 10
The 'reading-listening to' intertextual dynamic — 49

Figure 11
The intertextual approach for an ecological listening to Luke's gospel — 56

Figure 12
The four dimensions of the intertextual approach for engaging Luke's gospel — 59

Figure 13
The inner play of Lk. 1.5–2.52 — 67

Figure 14
The gestational allusions in Lk. 1.5–2.52 — 68

Figure 15 *The literary structure of Lk. 2.14*	87
Figure 16 *The structure of Lk. 19.38*	89
Figure 17 *The chiasmic inner play of Lk. 3.1–4.30*	97
Figure 18 *Redactional comparsion between Mk 1.9-12 and Lk. 3.21-22; 4.1*	102
Figure 19 *Structure of Lk. 4.18-19*	112
Figure 20 *The Word–Deed thematic pattern in Lk. 4.14–7.23*	125
Figure 21 *The Word–Deed thematic pattern in Lk. 5.1–6.16*	131
Figure 22 *Luke's 'sermon on the plain' (Lk. 6.20-49)*	139
Figure 23 *The inner play of Lk. 7.24–9.50*	147
Figure 24 *Division of Lk. 13.6-21*	190
Figure 25 *The structure of the parables of Luke 15*	210
Figure 26 *The parables of Luke 15*	211
Figure 27 *The chiastic literary structure of Lk. 17.22-37*	226
Figure 28 *The inner play of Lk. 19.28–21.38*	246
Figure 29 *The literary structure of Lk. 2.14*	249
Figure 30 *The structure of Lk. 19.38*	250
Figure 31 *Mark's 'fig-tree' scenes (Mk 11.12-26)*	259
Figure 32 *Literary structure of Lk. 21.37-38*	261

Figure 33.
The chiasmic structure of Lk. 22.15-30   269

Figure 34
The trials of Jesus (Lk. 22.54–23.26)   275

Figure 35
Redactional comparison of Mk 15.22-25 and Lk. 23.33-34   281

Introduction

It is early spring.

I am sitting at a desk, tapping away on my laptop keyboard. The sun shines through the large open window before me. I look out through the window on to the world it frames.

My eyes first rest on the grass clasped by the sun's light illuminating it into an almost phosphorescent green. I see three small birds hopping about, two sparrows and a blackbird, thrusting their beaks curiously into the grass at different rates and depths accompanied by their distinctive tones. A little distance further over I notice how the grass is bordered by an aged and weathered wooden fence.

The fence is made of upright palings clasped together by two horizontal rails of thick wood at the fence's top and middle which run its length. These are secured by thicker vertical posts at regular intervals. The fence runs at an angle along this vision of the world permitted by my window, from lower left to midway upper right of the window frame. The sight line of the upper level of fence is broken by a variety of plants of different colours, shapes and contortions.

As my eyes move beyond these and to the left of my window, I notice a forest of trees from what I know to be a recreational park. To the right, above the fence a visual gap forms and I see the blue water of the bay and the gentle swoop of black petrels. I can just hear the rhythm of sound from the waves moving to the beach. A whiff of ocean air passes through my window and enfolds my nostrils releasing memories of family fun at a beach from a different era and place.

I notice a bench on a ledge of land near the water's edge. It faces the sea.

A young woman sits there gazing out across the water.

She notices a four-engine jet plane high in the cloudless sky flying away from her.

I hear a car coming to a halt somewhere beyond the fenced border. A petroleum odour hangs in the air.

What has this scene—on a spring morning in the north eastern part of the North Island of New Zealand, at a beautiful place called Torbay that looks out across the Pacific Ocean—have to do with Luke's gospel?

At first thought there might be little, if any, connection. The link between my window panorama and Luke's world could be even more tenuous given the chronological and cultural distance that separates us, the dissimilarity in flora and fauna, and our different locations. How can I, in my antipodean world, given all that surrounds me and about which I am concerned, create a meaningful dialogue with a story that emerges from a different time and place and is addressed to an audience located somewhere near the Mediterranean Sea?

As I reflect further on the scene before me more emerges than appears at first glance. What I see and hear in this second engagement is a maze of interconnected realities. I recognize that I am linked in some way to all that I hear, see and smell. I notice this particular morning an apparent harmony in the world beyond my desk. And something happens within. It touches my soul. The scene is a gift, unexpected and gratuitous. What I see, hear and smell reveals a world that offers, on this particular morning and for reasons I don't completely understand, the possibility of uplifting my spirits.

From a theological perspective, this unsolicited and unforeseen encounter with creation draws me into myself. It invites me into my memory and my earlier life, as the ocean aroma takes me back to younger years and cricket games on the beach with my brothers scrutinized by Mum and Dad. This is a memory of familial harmony and energy. Such a memory is especially poignant given the deaths of my mother and brother in the past decade and the death of my father exactly two weeks ago to the day as I write these words. This particular scene invites me to remember in a most unexpected way. It also draws me into something beyond myself, to the ultimate Other.

There are other noteworthy dimensions to this scene. It involves objects inanimate (a laptop, window, a wooden fence, bench, plane and car) and animate (plants, birds and a young woman). My focus is captured by the scenery and the prominence which the young woman takes as she looks out on to the ocean. I am curious about the possibility of our connection of being drawn beyond ourselves into an oceanless ocean, a great beyond. Her presence is not a distraction to the interconnected harmony I sense this morning, but a confirmation of the goodness that I experience. My communion with her enhances the enjoyment of the moment.

There is something else that brings realism to what I experience.

The sight of the plane, the sound of the car and the odour of petroleum disturbs the ecological harmony I experience. They remind me of the potential damage that human beings, that I, can cause to creation. I drive a car and I fly in planes. I, too, contribute to the damage caused to our environment.

This awareness brings me to the key question that motivates me to write this book. How can I live authentically—which means for me, spiritually—and respectfully with everything that constitutes my world: creation, the environment, and the people I know?

This question underpins the particular perspective I bring as I begin to engage the *Gospel according to Luke*.[1] Environmental sensitivity has been deepened by the litanies of ecological damage that have become most familiar and are far better catalogued and explained elsewhere.[2]

Christiana Figueres, Executive Secretary for the United Nations Framework Convention on Climate Change (UNFCCC), in her response to a report from the United Nations sponsored Intergovernmental Panel on Climate Control (IPCC), offers a global environmental snapshot and summarizes the environmental and economic challenges facing nations. Her statement also recognizes the particular vulnerability of the poor and marginalized:

> The new IPCC report is a stark reminder of the extent to which rising greenhouse gas concentrations and the ensuing rise in global average temperatures are already leading to increased incidences of floods and heat waves, and that such incidences will become more frequent and severe if the global rise in greenhouse gas emissions is left unchecked. The ability of the world to become more climate-resilient will largely depend on the speed with which emissions can be decreased, and the extent to which the poor and vulnerable populations in developing countries are provided with necessary finance and technology to adapt to the inevitable.[3]

There are several points about Figueres's statement that capture my attention:

---

1. I identify 'Luke' as the human author of the third gospel, without making any assertion as to the writer's biographical identity or gender. I concede that there is a link through the author back to the first generations of Jesus followers. See Richard Bauckham, *Jesus and the Eyewitnesses: The Gospels as Eyewitness Testimony* (Michigan: Wm B. Eerdmans, 2006). I also distinguish between 'Gospel' and 'gospel'. The first is the Good News of God revealed in the historical ministry of Jesus of Nazareth, through his words and deeds. The second, the written expression of this Good News as communicated in story form in the Gospels according to Luke (Lk.), Mark (Mk), Matthew (Mt.) and John (Jn). Finally, I agree with those scholars that hold for Markan priority, that Mark was the earlier narrative basis for Luke and Matthew. These last two gospels were added to by unique material from their households (which we can call 'L' and 'M' respectively) and by 220 verses of common material ('Q') mainly of Jesus sayings independent of Mark. I see this two-source literary hypothesis as the best explanation for the development, structure and redactional differences between Luke and Mark. I also acknowledge the influence of an oral tradition in the development of the gospel and the role which eyewitnesses played in establishing or verifying Jesus material.

2. For example, Joseph F.C. DiMento and Pamela M. Doughman (eds.), *Climate Change: What it Means for Us, our Children, and our Grandchildren* (Cambridge, MA: The Massachusetts Institute of Technology Press, 2007).

3. Media statement of 18 November 2011, in reaction to IPCC Special Report on Managing the Risks of Extreme Events and Disasters to Advance Climate Change Adaptation (SREX), launched in Kampala (http://unfccc.int/2860.php; accessed 23 November 2011).

- The dire consequences of environmental degradation seem unavoidable; it is, as expressed above, 'inevitable'. An overall pessimism about the irreversibility of environmental damage concludes the statement.
- If there is a solution to the ecological crisis it is primarily economic and scientific; with enough money and the right scientific solution, the ecological problem will be overcome.
- The solution also depends on the 'ability of the world to become more climate-resilient'. By this I presume is meant the ability of human beings ('the world') to protect themselves from the negative effects of climatic and environmental degradation.

Missing in the above statement is explicit recognition of human involvement and responsibility for Earth.[4] This recognition invites a response that will raise the level of awareness of personal and communal care for our planet, apart from the economic and scientific strategies that will also help. Theologians and biblical scholars have a vital contribution to make here. Their ecological discourse is founded on appreciation of what we believe. For biblical scholars, this is influenced by an appreciation of the biblical heritage and how it offers insight into the current ecological crisis. For Christians, what the Bible teaches is important. And this brings me back to an earlier question, 'What has the scene that greets me through my window have to do with Luke's gospel?'

Well, everything actually.

The way I engage Luke's gospel reveals my preconceptions about a gospel and the reasons I believe that this engagement is important. I hold that there is something fundamentally truthful about this gospel encounter that can influence the way I live in my world, with creation that surrounds me and the people I meet. As the history of biblical interpretation has shown, it is possible that a particular interpretation of the gospels can reinforce me in a stance that *resists* openness to others and confirms me in a way of life that is self-serving, oppressive and environmentally destructive. It is also possible that gospel encounter can reveal my existential blindness and invite me to *conversion*—a spirit of openness and encounter that leads to ecological communion. It is something of this encounter that I experience as I gaze out upon the scene that unfolds outside my window and take up Luke's gospel.

---

4. Like other authors in the Earth-Bible team, I use 'Earth' to refer to the complex ecological network of interrelationships of humans and non-humans that constitute the planet not anthropologically determined or derivative.

Eco-justice Hermeneutic Principles

The *Preface* to the *Earth Bible Commentary* series summarizes the key hermeneutical principles that will guide my interpretation of Luke's gospel. These principles (intrinsic worth, interconnectedness, voice, purpose, mutual custodianship and resistance) remind me of the cultural limitations and biases I bring as a western interpreter. They offer me a way of engaging the gospel with a hermeneutic of suspicion, identification and retrieval. These invite me to suspect interpretations of the gospel that are exclusively anthropocentric and blind to Earth's presence in the story, to identify Earth and its ecosystems especially even when they seem absent in the story, and to retrieve the gospel's environmental story and ecological presence particularly when these seem not to be the author's explicit narrative focus. This interpretive hermeneutic, of suspicion, identification and retrieval, offers a way of hearing afresh Luke's story of salvation revealed in Jesus. It is a story that involves human and non-human creation—whether it is a story of human-non human inclusivity remains to be seen.

All of the eco-justice principles are important. Three that I find particularly helpful are intrinsic worth, interconnectedness and voice. The world of the gospel into which we are about to enter is preoccupied with relationships based on a Mediterranean dyadic value system. Identity was dependent on the 'dyad', the other. Personal identity was conventionally determined by the 'dyadic' human other.

The principle of intrinsic worth expands this consideration to see how Luke's gospel can include creation and the wider non-human community as authentic contributors to human identity and bearers of intrinsic worth, independent of human assessment or usefulness. This links to the principle of interconnectedness, the recognition that Earth is an interconnected web of relationships and ecological systems, inclusive of all organic and non-organic beings, human and non-human. We, Earth's household, are all linked; we are part of cosmic matter and the dust of stars.[5] This interconnectedness offers another dimension by which to consider the gospel and foreground all the living and material aspects in Luke's story, explicit, implicit and hidden, that bear on the gospel's ecological picture. Human identity in Luke's world was a matter of the dyadic human other; it was also formed by the non-human other. All of Earth's members shape human identity.

These approaches also presume a third eco-justice principle, that of voice. They allow the 'other' silent or unnoticed voice in Luke's story to be

---

5. For a fuller explanation of my preference for the expression 'household', see Chapter 2 where I discuss the 'household of auditors' and acknowledge the household as the primary social unit of the Roman empire and the context for the proclamation of and listening to the gospel.

heard. This is the voice of Earth that speaks alongside and sometimes with the voice of God, Jesus and the gospel's human characters. I am reminded here of the insight which St Bede (c. 672–735 CE) had about Lk. 8.24 when Jesus rebukes the wind and raging waves that threaten to annihilate a boat full of his disciples. The response of the wind and the waves to Jesus comes about for

> every creature senses the Creator, because they are responsive to the majesty of the Creator. And what they sense is insensible to us.[6]

For Bede, a seventh century biblical interpreter, Earth was living and, in some ways, more attuned to God than human beings who seem 'insensible'. It follows, using Bede's logic, that we can learn from Earth as we listen to its voice and deepen our 'sensibility'. How to acknowledge Earth's voice and listen for its ecological resonances in Luke's gospel will be discussed further in Chapter 2.

These eco-justice principles remind us that the writer of the third gospel was not an ecologist. My environmental sensitivity may not be shared by Luke. This does not prevent me from bringing an ecological sensitivity and empathy for Earth with which to engage the gospel. But it does caution me against imposing my worldview and perspective in a unilateral manner on to a text composed in a different time and place. Without nuance, balance, and a sensitivity that recognizes the cultural gap that separates us, I could disengage the gospel rather than *engage* it.[7] If I bring an imperialistic or colonizing attitude, Luke's gospel will have nothing to offer me or my world. Rather, I construct what I think is the gospel that confirms my idiosyncratic, culturally limited, critical imprint. I might even regard my interpretation of the gospel without critique as I presume my world more enlightened and better-informed than that of a first century Mediterranean peasant.

This book falls into three parts.

Part I, made up of the next two chapters, lays the foundation for the approach that will guide me in Part II as I explicitly engage Luke's gospel from an ecological perspective.

In Chapter 1 I explore the background to Luke's gospel and present a brief thematic overview. A closer study of the gospel's prologue, its opening four verses (Lk. 1.1-4), will explicate Luke's sources and aim. From the gospel's first verses I shall also identify the method by which the evangelist draws on earlier texts and traditions and reshapes them in the light of present interest and cultural concerns. Luke's orthopraxis suggests an approach valuable for

---

6. Robert J. Karris (ed.), *Works of St. Bonaventure: Commentary on the Gospel of Luke. Chapters 1–8* (Saint Bonaventure, NY: Franciscan Institute Publications, 2001), p. 693.

7. Michael Trainor, 'Five Ways Australian Christians use the Bible', *Reo: A Journal of Theology and Ministry* 8 (1998), pp. 7-17.

the present project. This method will be explored in Chapter 2 in the light of contemporary insights into the inherent dynamics of literary texts.

The evangelist also identifies in this prologue the gospel's only named addressee ('Theophilus'). I shall suggest that Theophilus and the elite social group he represents are not the gospel's only audience. Social anthropologists recognize the importance of societal stratification dominant in Luke's first century Greco-Roman world.[8] This recognition leads to a possible social reconstruction of Luke's urban addressees and their respective ecological attitudes. These attitudes appear in the gospel and become part of Earth's picture with which I engage. How I do this is also the focus of Chapter 2.

In Chapter 2 I concentrate on the particular approach to Luke's gospel, where I intend to create a balanced interrelating interpretative partnership between my world and that of Luke and the gospel. My concern is to avoid any suggestion of 'eisegesis', of a reading *into* the text, as I come to the gospel in a manner that is respectful and dialogical. This approach allows my ecological interests to interact with but not determine Luke's story and its Earth features. This interaction occurs through an interplay of different worlds, what I call 'texts', that is essentially *intertextual*. The importance of intertextuality has already been introduced in the *Preface* of the *Earth Bible Commentary* series but it deserves fuller treatment. It is an approach that I think can be very useful. In Chapter 2, the book's most theoretical and perhaps dense chapter, I study the contribution to intertextuality by literary critics and conclude by explicating a four dimensional approach to Luke's gospel that I adopt in Part II.

---

8. Chapters 1 and 3 draw upon and modify my earlier sociological and literary ecological reflections of Lk. 2 found in Michael Trainor, '"…And on Earth, Peace…" (Luke 2.14): Luke's Perspectives on the Earth,' in *Readings from the Perspective of the Earth*. Volume 2 (ed. Norman Habel; Sheffield: Sheffield Academic Press, 2000), pp. 174-92, with the permission of the publisher. In the pages that follow I shall use this expression, limited as it is, to describe the cultural and social context of Luke's world and the context of the gospel's auditors. I recognize that the 'Greco' part of the expression is anachronistic, but it seeks to honor the Hellenization that occurred through Alexander the Great's Macedonian cultural and linguistic 'reform' of the Mediterranean in the early fourth century BCE. The 'Roman' part of the expression recognizes the Roman influence on the Mediterranean world that had overthrown all powers and created an imperial Roman dominance over the Mediterranean in the early first century CE. How successful was this dominance and what it actually means are subjects for debate. However, my use of 'Greco-Roman' affirms the coexistence of different cultural expressions in the same locality at the same time, neither specifically Greek, Macedonian nor Roman. Local tribal cultures and languages continued to exist and thrive despite Roman dominance in this 'Greco-Roman' world. This is affirmed particularly in a region like Galilee where Greek language and culture, dominant as it was, did not displace the indigenous languages of Aramaic and Hebrew. See Richard A. Horsley, *Archaeology, History, and Society in Galilee: The Social Context of Jesus and the Rabbis* (Valley Forge, PA: Trinity Press International, 1996), p. 177.

In Part II, the longest of the book, I systematically work through each section of Luke's narrative highlighting its ecological implications. As I shall explain later, I consider Luke's gospel a narrative symphony and I seek to attune my ears to its ecological sounds or notes as they surface. As I discerned the completeness of Luke's symphony I soon came to the conclusion that I could not do justice to the gospel's potential to offer ecological insights if I isolated them from the overall literary pattern and story of the gospel.

For this reason, I have erred on the side of offering a summary of Luke's story while pausing at those moments in the narrative that resonate with ecological and Earth themes, allusions and images. This means sometimes I shall skirt quickly through long passages, at other times pause where Earth images, teachings and stories appear. I therefore have not given each verse, every story and defined gospel pericopes the same attention. I leave that to the classical commentaries of Lukan scholars upon whom I rely and acknowledge in footnotes and the bibliography. My lingering over a text is shaped primarily by the ecological potential which I consider the text holds; only secondarily do I spend time with a text because of its importance for the overall narrative and thematic direction of the gospel which I consider essential for appreciating the evangelist's bigger project. Luke's gospel is, however, the longest of the four which goes towards explaining the challenge involved in attempting even a digest of Luke's succinct and integral narrative.[9]

A final note is also in order. I conclude each chapter of Part II with an imaginative and meditative moment, 'Earth's Voice'. This allows me to suggest a way of listening to Earth revealed through one of its members and suggested by a particular gospel story or passage from the chapter. I offer this imaginative reflection, though, not without a note of caution.[10]

Drawing upon the outline of Luke's narrative found in most commentaries,[11]

---

9. In the Greek text, the statistics run: Lk. 19482 words in 1151 verses; Mt. with 18345 in 1071 verses; Jn with 15635 in 879 verses; Mk with 11304 in 678 verses (http://catholic-resources.org/Bible/NT-Statistics-Greek.htm; accessed 26 October 2011).

10. To presume to give Earth human voice is to again anthropomorphize it and to reinforce, however subtle, an anthropocentric gospels focus. On the other hand, allowing Earth to have voice allows it to speak to contemporary auditors sensitive to the insights that have emerged from our study of Luke's gospel.

11. For example: E. Earle Ellis, *The Gospel of Luke* (London: Marshall, Morgan & Scott, revised edn, 1974), pp. 32-36; I. Howard Marshall, *The Gospel of Luke: A Commentary on the Greek Text* (Grand Rapids, MI: Wm B. Eerdmans Publishing Co., 1978), pp. 7-11; Joseph A. Fitzmyer, *The Gospel according to Luke I–IX* (Garden City, NY: Doubleday & Company, Inc., 1981), pp. xiii-xvi; Christopher Francis Evans, *Saint Luke* (London: SCM Press, 1990), pp. v-vi; Josef Ernst, *Das Evangelium nach Lukas* (Regensburg: Verlag

- Chapter 3 will focus on Luke's story of Jesus' birth and its christological presentation of Jesus as Earth's child (1.1–2.52);
- Chapter 4 spotlights the preparation for Jesus' public ministry (3.1–4.30) where I identify four ecological principles that undergird the rest of the gospel;
- Chapter 5 concerns Jesus' ministry in Galilee, the garden of God's earthly delights (4.14–7.23);
- Chapter 6 continues Jesus' public Galilean ministry (7.24–9.50) as fasting and feasting occur in the paradisiacal garden;
- Chapters 7, 8, 9 and 10 cover Luke's story of Jesus' journey to Jerusalem with his disciples (9.51–19.27). This story comprises almost half of the gospel and one of its principal themes is ecological responsibility and asceticism;
- Chapter 11 brings us into Jerusalem (19.28–21.38) as its topographical setting, Mount Olivet, intertwines Jesus' teaching;
- Chapter 12 is the climax of the gospel in the suffering, death and celebration of God's Earth child (22.1–24.53).

Part III comprises one brief chapter. It summarizes Luke's ecological insights and proposes eight theses which I consider important for contemporary disciples concerned about the planet and the care of Earth.

The Human Presence as Part of Earth's Ecosystem

To return for a brief moment to the scene I see through my window. Evident is the young woman's presence. She adds another dimension to what I see and reflect upon. Though the implicit presence of other human beings (the driver of the car and the people associated with the plane) acts in a way that might be potentially damaging to the ecological balance, the woman's gaze out on to the ocean and her observation of the plane overhead bring a resonance with the surrounding environment with which I connect.

Her presence reminds me that human beings are part of the ecological picture. And they are not necessarily a negative or destructive influence. There remains the possibility of a form of ecological communion that brings grace to both. The woman's personal world could be enlarged by her contemplation of what she sees; the world she looks out upon might be blessed by the prayer she offers in gratitude for a freedom experienced or beauty enjoyed.

Friedrich Pustet, 1993), pp. 5-11; Robert C. Tannehill, *Luke* (Nashville, TN: Abingdon Press, 1996), pp. 7-12; Joel B. Green, *The Gospel of Luke* (Grand Rapids, MI: Wm B. Eerdmans Publishing Co., 1997), pp. v-vi. I draw upon many of these commentaries in the pages ahead. Finally, for a helpful summary on the current state of Lukan scholarship, see Peter Anthony, 'What are They Saying about Luke–Acts?', *ScrBull* 40 (2010), pp. 10-21.

This insight into the mutual benefits and eco-synchronicity between the woman and the beauty that surrounds me highlights the importance of remembering the human community in Earth's household. As I bring an explicitly ecological focus to Luke's story and highlight the gospel's Earth community I shall also include in that community the gospel's human characters. The human and the non-human are part of the created universe. Together they belong to the same environmental and ecological household. How these two—the human and the non-human world—actually interrelate, or are perceived as interrelating, or are believed to interrelate, is important. Luke's gospel will shed light on this.

As I prepare for this ecological study of Luke's gospel, two questions surface:

- Will Luke's gospel reinforce a destructive and utilitarian attitude to the planet that seeks to subjugate creation for selfish reasons?
- Can this gospel contribute to an ecological theology that will encourage a respectful attitude to Earth integral to contemporary discipleship?

Luke's inherited Earth-picture from the First Testament

The relationship which human beings have to Earth in Luke's gospel is partly influenced by the picture created from the evangelist's biblical heritage as discerned in the Old Testament, the Hebrew Bible or, my preferred expression, the First Testament.[12] This inherited tradition that influences Luke's Earth picture I shall call in Chapter 2 a 'text'. The nature of this tradition, whether it is positive, negative or mixed, will emerge more clearly as we engage the gospel. I will suggest that in Luke's story of Jesus, introduced in the story concerned with his birth (2.1-20) and in the narratives surrounding and including the evangelist's construction of Jesus' genealogy (3.21–4.13), there is a return to the Genesis accounts of creation

---

12. My use of 'First Testament' describes the collection of writings gathered by Israelites living in Palestine or the Diaspora over a millennium. The term is inclusive of both Hebrew and Greek writings acknowledged by some Christian traditions as an authentic 'first witness' of God's faithful revelation amongst the Israelite people. The 'second witness' classically called the 'New Testament' is the 'Second Testament' of God's revelation in the person of Jesus of Nazareth and the community of disciples that gathered around him and continued his message and ministry. This community I call 'household' and I prefer to describe the members of Jesus household and subsequent generation as Jesus 'followers', 'disciples' or 'householders'. These descriptors avoid the use of 'Christian' as an epithet for the disciples of Jesus. 'Christian' was a not a self-description used by Jesus followers in the first century CE, but rather a derogatory expression by outsiders, equivalent to 'Christ-lackeys'. Only later, in the fourth century, did 'Christian' become the popular term for those who followed the teachings of Jesus.

and an invitation to human beings to participate in God's creative activity, enjoyment of creation and identity with Earth. These are reflected in Luke's portrait of Jesus.

Earth's Metanarrative

I wish to pause here to consider further Luke's inherited biblical story of creation, Earth and human communion with Earth. This story is foundational, a metanarrative, as it is remembered and shaped by Luke's story of Jesus.

The story begins in the first book of the Bible in the first chapters of Genesis. Gen. 1.26-28 is central. In this story of creation, human beings are created in the 'image of God' and directed to 'rule over' every living creature and to 'subdue' Earth. Upon the interpretation of each of these Hebrew expressions, their meaning within the poetic schema of the Genesis text, their other biblical occurrences, and their meaning in a wider socio-literary milieu hangs so much ecological freight and the perception of the interrelationship between human beings and creation.

There are two different points of view about the meaning of this divinely appointed mandate of human stewardship.[13] Whatever position one takes on this, that humans act with dominion *over* Earth (Habel) or *on behalf of* Earth (Bauckham), this story and all that follow it in the biblical tradition are concerned about Earth, human beings' place with Earth, and God's relationship with both. This first creation story is also the beginning of a continuing creation narrative and part of an eco-theological thread in a larger biblical metanarrative that begins with this Genesis text and continues through to the book of Revelation. To identify this thread is not an attempt to identify a 'canon within the canon', reduce the complexity of

---

13. In this present *Earth Bible Commentary* series, Norman Habel considers the creation of the human being in Gen. 1.1-24 an unambiguous divine endorsement for humans to subdue, devalue and disempower Earth; see Norman Habel, *The Birth, the Curse and the Greening of Earth: An Ecological Reading of Genesis 1–11* (Sheffield: Sheffield Phoenix Press, 2011), Chapter 3. Richard Bauckham, on the other hand, interprets Genesis's story of the creation of humans and the divine mandate to fill and subdue Earth (Gen. 1.27-28) from a different point of view. He considers that the stories of creation in Genesis 1 and 2 reveal how human beings are part of the creation scenario and are invited to live in God's 'ecotopia', not above or beneath it, in solidarity with creation. They are called by God to care for Earth. I shall borrow Bauckham's term 'ecotopia' later in Chapter 5 to explore the meaning of the 'kingdom' or 'reign' of God. See Richard Bauckham, *The Bible and Ecology: Rediscovering the Community of Creation* (Waco, TX: Baylor University Press, 2010). Also helpful, Richard Bauckham, *Living with Other Creatures: Green Exegesis and Theology* (Waco, TX: Baylor University Press, 2010). Bauckham is not without his critics. See the review of *The Bible and Ecology* by Norman Habel, in *Review of Biblical Literature Blog*, 2011.08.11 (http://rblnewsletter.blogspot.com/2011/08/20110811-bauckham-bible-and-ecology.html; accessed 23 November, 2011).

biblical literature into a monochromatic story or eradicate the diversity of Earth's picture found throughout the Bible.

While the human person is unique in Genesis's creation scenarios, there is either communion or the desire for communion with other living Earth creatures.[14] The human person is called in this sense into stewardship. Its exercise is not exclusive of God's activity, seeking simply to repair environmental damage already done in a display of patriarchal domination over creation.[15] In the second creation story in Gen. 2.4-7, in the creation of Earth's creature, *Adam*, ecological communion is presaged. God fashions this creature from Earth's soil, *adamah*, as human creatureliness becomes literally grounded out of Earth. It is in solidarity with Earth that the human person belongs.

Earth's story begun in Genesis continues in various forms and expressions throughout the rest of the Bible. Within a variety of insights in a diverse range of biblical writings there exists an overarching narrative about Earth. This concern is expressed in the biblical writings themselves, in the several summaries found in the range of biblical literature in the First and Second Testaments. These summaries do not attempt to homogenize the whole story into a straitjacketed narrative; they resist completeness.[16] There remains openness for further insights into Earth's story that cannot be controlled by the summaries themselves. This applies even when Earth's human beings seem to dominate and 'subdue' the rest of creation (as in Genesis 1), or when Earth is the victim of control and disempowerment (as when Earth gets destroyed by flood and plagues). Though different forms of biblical narratives and literary expressions of the story exist, this metanarrative continuously appears and finds its way into the Second Testament.[17]

These different expressions of Earth's story are not repeated but presumed by the gospel writers and Luke. As we shall see, they will be given a fresh frame of reference through Luke's story of Jesus. The story of Earth and creation, the eco-metanarrative, will become the backdrop against which Luke's gospel will unfold. At the same time, it might be helpful to remember the limited cultural and ecological world of the biblical writer

---

14. The fact of communion would come from a Bauckham-oriented reading; a *desire* for communion from Habel's interpretation and the tension present in the first creation story created by two myths dealing with *eretz* (Earth) and *tselem* (the creation of humans in the image of God); the identification of this tension is a recognition that this imperialistic domination of the human over Earth should not be.

15. Bauckham, *Bible*, pp. 2-10.

16. Richard Bauckham, 'Reading Scripture as a Coherent Story', in *The Art of Reading Scripture*, (ed. Ellen F. Davis and Richard B. Hays; Grand Rapids, MI: Wm B. Eerdmans Publishing Co., 2003), pp. 38-53 (44).

17. For a helpful overview of this metanarrative in the Second Testament, see Bauckham, *Living*, pp. 1-13.

and the writer's audience. This recognition helps to acknowledge the text's potential to offer negative and devaluing Earth attitudes and identify ways of retrieving them. Some of these have already been acknowledged in the *Preface* in which the presence, action and voice of Earth as an actor in the biblical story is affirmed—Jeremiah's attention to Earth's voice as it mourns what is happening (Jer. 4.28; 12.11) or Amos's recognition of creation's role in the prophetic act.[18] In this open approach, biblical texts can either be 'green' or 'grey', they either affirm Earth and nature ('green') or devalue and deprive them of any intrinsic worth ('grey').[19] As we move into Luke's gospel, Earth will be revealed in a surprising way.

The Three 'Worlds'

As I begin this exploration I will engage in a tripartite dialogue, between my world with its ecological and environmental concerns; Luke's gospel, the story of Jesus and the above eco-narrative; and the social and cultural environment out of which the gospel story came to birth (Figure 1). As one who believes that the stories of Jesus in the gospels are foundational for faith life, and for the growth of the Christian community to be relevant for today's society, and communicate an essential truth about God's presence, such a dialogue is critical.

The first world is Luke's gospel itself with its story of Jesus and his disciples. With the ecological interest that I intentionally bring (the world *in front of* the text—this is *my* world), I will seek to be attentive to the ecological and Earth-related echoes in the unfolding story of Jesus and his household of disciples. My world in front of the gospel provides the listening parameters as I concentrate on this story. The world *behind the text* is the world of Luke's audience, presumed and not explicit. It concerns the social setting and composition of Luke's addressees and the manner by which an ancient audience engaged a proclaimed text. This world acknowledges that Luke's gospel is a *cultural* text.[20]

I intend to converse with each of these worlds using an ecological filter. Such a dialogue will bring me to appreciate Luke's gospel and its promise for contemporary theological meaning. How I do this will be explained in greater detail in Chapter 2. But care is needed because of the gospel's

---

18. See *Preface* to this *Earth Bible Commentary* series and Hilary Marlow 'The Other Prophet! The Voice of the Earth in the Book of Amos', in *Exploring Ecological Hermeneutics* (ed. Norman C. Habel and Peter Trudinger; Atlanta, GA: Society of Biblical Literature, 2008), pp. 75-84 (75).

19. Norman Habel, *An Inconvenient Text; Is Green Reading of the Bible Possible?* (Adelaide: ATF Press, 2009).

20. Green, *Luke*, p. 11.

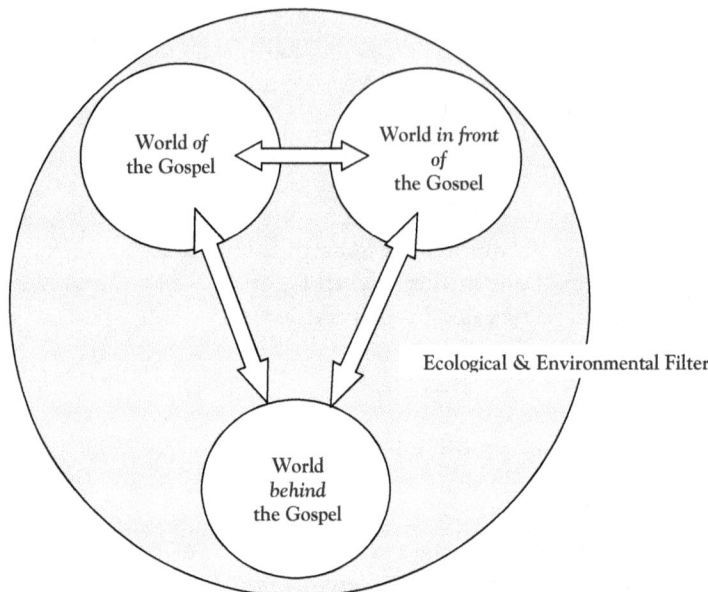

Figure 1. *The three 'worlds' of gospel engagement.*

cultural limitations and the possibility of an androcentric interpretation of the gospel influenced by a patriarchal world view.

An uncritical absorption of Luke's limited worldview, and the values and attitude of an ancient Mediterranean people inscribed or presumed in Luke's gospel, needs constant checking. Such attitudes might influence the way we regard Earth and the environment today. A literal understanding of the gospel leads to fundamentalist attitudes that can be unwittingly absorbed by interpreters. This has ethical and ecological consequences, some of which have been named in the *Preface*. It could lead to treating the Earth as a mere stepping stone to a heavenly utopia. With an anti-Earth attitude, ecological disaster or environmental degradation might be seen as part of a divine plan, a sort of preparation for a divinely programmed eventual cosmic cataclysm. This planetary calamity, so fundamentalists consider, will usher in God's final coming, the salvation of the worthy and the vindication of the righteous. It is important, therefore, to consider first the world *behind* the gospel. This is the focus of the next chapters. The writer of the gospel and the evangelist's audience presume this world but nowhere explicate it—except perhaps in the gospel's opening verses (Lk. 1.1-4).

A couple of things are important to note as I undertake this journey through the gospel.

Unless stated, I offer my own translation of the Greek text. While this translation will at times appear wooden and literal, I attempt to preserve the sense of Luke's authorial intention communicated in the Greek that can get lost in some English translations. For ease of identification and particularly when focus on particular words or phrases is essential to the study, I divide up verses (with a, b, c...). For those who may not be familiar with New Testament Greek, I have transliterated the Greek text into English. But I do this only when a particular word or expression in the original is significant for an understanding of the passage under consideration or for its contribution to an eco-theological perspective that can be gleaned from Luke's gospel.

Ideally, it would have been helpful had I offered a translation of the whole of Luke's gospel and placed it beside each segment, passage, story and teaching that I explore in the pages ahead. Space prevents such a format. I would suggest that readers have the text of Luke's gospel open before them as we move through the gospel together.

Parts of Chapters 1 and 3 have appeared previously.[21] I am grateful for permission from the publishers at Sheffield Phoenix Press for permission to reproduce that work here, though with substantial difference.

I am appreciative for the insights and critical comments offered to earlier drafts of this book by friends and colleagues. In particular I thank Cathy Jenkins, Denis Edwards, Norman Habel, Marie Turner and Alan Cadwallader. Each in their own way helped me sharpen my thoughts, expressions and eliminate some obvious embarrassing infelicities and exegetical inaccuracies. I am especially grateful for the generous editing of my work by the coordinating librarian at the Adelaide Theological Library, Rosemary Hocking. Rosemary read every word of this present text and suggested changes in expression and editing alterations that have added to the quality of this book. Of course, I take full responsibility for any limitations that remain.

I have been aware of the space, support and care offered to me through a residential academic scholarship in 2011 at the Vaughan Park Anglican Retreat and Conference, Torbay, New Zealand. I have been deeply touched by the kindness and hospitality shown me by its director, John Fairbrother, administrator, Marion Nickerson, priest assistant Joy McCormick and other staff members. The environmental beauty of the place provided the perfect setting to reflect ecologically on Luke's gospel.

Three things happened while I was at Vaughan Park that impinged directly on what I wrote.

First, while engaged in writing an initial draft of this ecological commentary, some 150 kilometres away New Zealand suffered its worst ecological calamity. The damage was potentially catastrophic, caused by a cargo vessel running aground on a reef, spilling its oil and affecting seas, fish, bird life and foreshore. While the environmental damage caused may not have been as disastrous as other more famous events in recent years in other parts of the world, it was a timely reminder that human beings will always be the cause of

---

21. Trainor, "'... And on Earth, Peace...'", pp. 174-92.

such damage. How we reflect creatively and carefully for our Earth remains constant.

Second, while writing, the liturgical Feast of Saint Luke, evangelist, occurred (October 18). I was deeply reflective in a way never before of the contribution which this gospel author has made to our appreciation of Earth and the invitation to discipleship. The day after the feast of Saint Luke, the New Zealand Anglican community celebrates a twelve year old Maori girl, Tarore of Waharoa who died tragically in an inter-tribal raid on 19 October 1836. This annual celebration had even more impact on me than that of Saint Luke.

Tarore attended a mission school and was given a copy of Luke's gospel to read, the only gospel that had been translated into her language. Tribal tensions meant that the mission school had to be evacuated and the group was led to a place of apparent safety. Their camp fire attracted the attention of Maori antagonists led by its leader named Uita. Though their raid on the school mission group was unsuccessful, Tarore was found dead where she slept and the copy of Luke's gospel under her pillow was taken by Uita who thought it valuable.

At her funeral the following day, her father spoke against revenge, arguing that too much blood had already been shed and 'that the people should trust in the justice of God'.[22] Uita, unable to read the stolen text, left it unopened until a slave was brought to Uita's place and read the gospel out loud to all the people. This eventually led to reconciliation and forgiveness between Tarore's father and Uita. A reading of the same gospel led others to Christianity and it became the inspiration for the spread of the gospel of peace and reconciliation to New Zealand's South Island.

This story of Tarore and her Maori text of Luke's gospel touched me deeply as I engaged my own study and reading of that same gospel. Her story reflects much of what the gospel is about: peace, reconciliation and communion between peoples and the whole Earth community.

Third, while at Vaughan Park and into the early stages of writing, my father died. Dad was an environmentalist well before his time. He was a passionate ecologist, though he would never describe himself as such or even understand what ecology was about. He grew vegetables in our backyard garden. These vegetables became part of the family meals which he cooked. He never got rid of anything if he felt he could use it at a later date. His recycling spirit meant that his backyard shed became for him, as it does for many Australian males, a place of hoarding, design, recreation, male bonding and retreat. Dad was family chef and, due to reasons of ill

---

22. Ken Booth (ed.), *For All the Saints: A Resource for the Commemorations of the Calendar* (Hastings, NZ: Anglican Church in Aotearoa, New Zealand and Polynesia, 1996), p. 394.

health, house-husband and father. My earliest memories are of him looking after me and my older siblings at home, while Mum went off to teach at a local school.

In essence, he walked lightly on this planet leaving, if anything, a barely noticeable carbon footprint. It is to the memory of *Laurence Michael Trainor* that this book is dedicated. And I shall always wonder what he will think of it.

PART I

Chapter 1

DIFFERING ATTITUDES TO EARTH: LUKE'S AUDIENCE

Luke's gospel emerges out of a particular cultural and social world, addressed to a specific community of Jesus followers. It is a community that I shall call, for the present, a 'household', and I shall explain in the next chapter why I favour this expression. Nowhere does Luke clearly identify the gospel's audience, though, as we shall see, a suggestion comes in the opening four verses (1.1-4). But this hint will need to be filled out with other data. By sleuthing behind some of the themes in the gospel narrative, drawing on the work of anthropologists and social researchers, and through a closer investigation of these opening verses, a fuller social picture will emerge.

Recognition of the kind of stratified society of Luke's day will also help us suggest various ecological attitudes to Earth. It is a complex picture, one that is not easy to depict. For this reason, part of what I offer here is a hypothetical reconstruction of Luke's audience; for some, perhaps beyond the evidence. However I think it best explains some of the depictions of Luke's characters. They appear as 'windows' on to the characters that compose Luke's actual social landscape and stratified world.

Whatever the judgment on my social analysis, two things are clear which form the heart of this chapter. First, Luke's audience had attitudes to Earth and its environment that cannot be simply or monochromatically described. These attitudes affect the environmental memory as it is captured in the gospel.[1] Second and more pertinent to the ecological approach that I shall use in interpreting the gospel, the evangelist employs a method engaging the issues of the addressees' own day with the story of Jesus. This method is explicated in the prologue and filters throughout the narrative. I hope to show in the next chapter how I complement Luke's method. This second concern I consider first before moving towards identifying Luke's social

---

1. Sean Freyne critiques biblical approaches to gospel interpretation that hitherto have concentrated only on economic and social factors without appreciation of the ecological and environmental contexts of Jesus, his disciples and gospel audiences, in *Jesus, a Jewish Galilean: A New Reading of the Jesus-Story* (London: T. & T. Clark International, 2004), esp. pp. 24-27.

stratification and the various ecological attitudes present in the gospel's audience. Central to both concerns is the gospel's prologue, Lk. 1.1-4.

The Nature of the Gospel and Luke's Method

The Gospel according to Luke was written for a Greco-Roman audience in the latter part of the first century CE. From this point of view, there is already an anthropocentric *Tendenz*; the gospel's audience are human beings and they are directly addressed by it. This does not automatically mean that Earth's other members are not present in the gospel. As we shall see later, integral to the story of Jesus is the story of Earth; attitudes, responses to, and stories about Earth will be part of the gospel narrative symphony.

Scholars date the gospel somewhere between the 80s and 90s and locate it either in Antioch in Syria (present day Antakya in south east Turkey), Macedonia or even Rome.[2] Luke's penchant for highlighting Greco-Roman cities in the gospel, and especially in Acts with the missionary journeys of Paul, reinforces the view that Luke wrote more for an urban rather than rural audience. I shall presume Luke's urban context as I engage the gospel and, where appropriate, Acts.

The pastoral situation of the gospel's urban audience located in a Greco-Roman city of the Mediterranean world shapes the memory and meaning of the events recounted in Luke. It is not intended for a peasant Israelite audience located in Galilee or Judea during the time of Jesus' ministry in the 30s. This reminder prevents us from accidentally or unwittingly slipping from Luke's world into that of the historical Jesus in an attempt to recreate the actual events and peasant social setting at the time of Jesus.[3] This also

---

2. Helpful introductions to Luke which present detailed arguments for the material I summarize here and below include Henry J. Cadbury, *The Style and Literary Method of Luke* (Cambridge, MA: Harvard University Press, 1920); Henry J. Cadbury, *The Making of Luke–Acts* (New York: Macmillan & Co., 1927); Hans Conzelmann, *The Theology of St. Luke* (New York: Harper and Row, 1961); Richard J. Dillon, *From Eyewitnesses to Ministers of the Word: Tradition and Composition in Luke 24* (Rome: Biblical Institute, 1978); Robert J. Karris, 'Missionary Communities: A New Paradigm for the Study of Luke–Acts', CBQ 41 (1979), pp. 80-97; Fitzmyer, *Luke I–IX*, pp. 3-283; Robert Maddox, *The Purpose of Luke–Acts* (Göttingen: Vandenhoeck & Ruprecht, 1982); Tannehill, *Narrative Unity*; François Bovon, *Luke 1: A Commentary on the Gospel of Luke 1:1–9:50* (Minneapolis, MN: Augsburg Fortress Press, 2002), pp. 1-12; Luke Timothy Johnson, *The Gospel of Luke* (Collegeville, MN: Liturgical Press, 1991), pp. 2-26; Raymond E. Brown, *An Introduction to the New Testament* (Garden City, NY: Doubleday, 1997), p. 226. For the Roman setting for Luke–Acts, see Barbara Shellard, *New Light on Luke: Its Purpose, Sources and Literary Context* (Sheffield: Sheffield Academic Press, 2002), pp. 34-36.

3. Although helpful for a discussion of Jesus' peasant background, this influence in his teaching and its relationship to the gospels, especially Luke, see Douglas E. Oakman, 'Was Jesus a Peasant? Implications for Reading the Jesus Tradition (Luke 10:30-35)', in

cautions us against using Luke's gospel as a fundamentalist blueprint for living in the twenty first century—as though we were living in the exact same social, cultural and ecological world as Luke's.

Whatever the gospel's dating and provenance, its prologue (1.1-4), portrait of Jesus and his interaction with its characters, especially his disciples, reveal the author's interest in presenting Jesus as a cultured and lettered figure. Luke's portrait of Jesus affirms the Greco-Roman environment of the gospel's addressees. Rather than encouraging a sectarian response to their world from which the followers of Jesus seclude themselves, the evangelist encourages cultural engagement. For Luke, the world is a good place. This includes the gospel's social and cultural context and, as we shall see, its physical or ecological environment. Jesus followers addressed by the gospel are encouraged to interact creatively and positively, yet subversively, within their world. This eco-socio-cultural agenda shapes the narrative and the characterization of its key figures.

Leaving aside for the moment the ecological implications of Luke's gospel which hitherto have not been generally acknowledged by commentators, clues to this positive cultural interaction are dotted throughout the narrative. They are found in Luke's presentation of Jesus and the gospel's character cast supporting his ministry, especially though not exclusively in stories concerning Mary and Simon Peter.

In summary, Luke's Jesus reveals God. Jesus' teaching, meal ministry and healing deeds reveal a welcoming and delighted God. God's gladness is shed upon those who unexpectedly find themselves members of his entourage of disciples. They are healed of diseases and included at his table. No one, whatever their social class or degree of social purity, is excluded from his household. Luke's Jesus reveals a God delighted by human beings. This extends to non-human beings and all of creation. How this is present in the gospel, albeit sometimes in subtle, unnoticed or subversive ways, is the principal preoccupation of this book.

In the initial presentation of Mary (1.26-38) and Simon (5.1-11), Luke holds up for later Jesus followers ways of engaging their present confrontational perplexing realities. Mary is to be the mother of Jesus under impossible circumstances. Luke's story of her is a reminder of how Jesus' divinely initiated birth will inaugurate a new moment in Roman history and redescribe human interaction within the conventional domestic and imperial structures (2.1-3). Simon is called out on to the Sea of Galilee while Jesus preaches to the crowd (5.1-3) and then later asked to fish in waters that seem to be barren (5.4-5). The size of the catch that almost sinks his boat (5.6b, 7b), the response by his fishing partners to his plight

The Social World of the New Testament: Insights and Models (ed. Jerome H. Neyrey and Eric C. Stewart; Peabody, MA: Hendrickson, 2008), pp. 125-40.

(5.7), his overwhelming recognition of his unworthiness before Jesus (5.8) and the invitation to 'catch alive human beings' (5.10), flag Simon's future ministry and status in Luke's story of Jesus and his followers. They also indicate the style of missionary activity in which the followers of Jesus in the Book of Acts, especially the reconstituted Twelve, Peter and Paul, will engage. This fishing story is a metaphor for the potential fruitfulness of the life of the Lukan audience as they confront what seem socio-culturally barren and impossible realities in their world.

The above summary offers a conventional anthropocentric interpretation of Luke's story, as it focuses on some of the key *human* figures important for the gospel's narrative. This anthropological emphasis common in Lukan commentaries highlights only one member of Earth's household, the human. I shall seek to address this imbalance by also listening for other ecological tones from forgotten non-human members of the Earth community. They are also part of the narrative symphony, albeit members whose tones or melodies have been somewhat muted in conventional gospel commentaries.[4]

Such a reclaimed perspective allows Luke's gospel to become an ecological symphony essentially *theo*centric and *christo*centric. It presents a story about God revealed through Jesus that can impact on the way we see and treat Earth. Luke refashions the inherited story of the Galilean Jesus for a particular audience geographically and chronologically separated from the originating story. This refashioning is set within particular Earth perspectives held by the gospel's audience. An acknowledgment and identification of these different perspectives, on the one hand, and an awareness of Earth-related potential which the gospel bears for contemporary interpreters on the other, can offer fresh and stimulating insights in our quest to respond to the ecological challenges summarized in Christiana Figueres's global environmental snapshot from the last chapter.

Luke's theocentric and christological emphases become paradigmatic for future generations, especially our present as we engage serious environmental issues upon which the future and survival of our planet depends. The gospel thus becomes a privileged, ritually oriented, divinely inspired sacred text that shapes and transforms. It enables future Jesus followers to engage new cultural, social, political and ecological realities as it guides their lives into an unknown future.[5]

---

4. Freyne, *Jesus*, pp. 24-25.
5. Robert W. Jenson, 'Scripture's Authority in the Church', in *The Art of Reading Scripture* (ed. Ellen F. Davis and Richard B. Hays; Grand Rapids, MI: Wm. B. Eerdmans Publishing Co., 2003), pp. 27-37 (36). Also, Robert Detweiler, 'What is a sacred text?', in *Reader-Response Approaches to Biblical and Secular Texts*, (Semeia, 31; Decatur: Scholars Press, 1985), pp. 213-30 (223).

Luke's Prologue and Orthopraxis (Lk. 1.1-4)

In a carefully crafted and repeated orthopraxis, first flagged in the prologue and then enacted in the commissioning or call narratives of the gospel's central characters (such as Mary, Simon and Paul), Luke offers a way of bringing new eco-cultural and political realities into dialogue with the theological conviction of God's faithful ongoing presence.[6] For the evangelist, this presence continues in Luke's day and is revealed through the story of Jesus. The writer's ancient orthopraxis mirrors and confirms the approach which I shall adopt as I engage Luke's gospel with a new concern—the ecological and environmental issues important for the future of this planet.

Luke's agenda and orthopraxis are clearly articulated in the gospel's opening four verses (1.1-4) and deserve closer scrutiny.

> [1] In as much as many have undertaken to compose a narrative of things which have been brought to fruition among us [2] just as they were handed down to us by those who were from the beginning eyewitnesses and became servants of the word, [3] it seemed opportune for me also, having followed everything closely from the very beginning, to write an orderly account for your most excellent (*kratistos*) Theophilus, [4] so that you may know about those matters with which you have been catechized, with certainty (*asphaleia*).

These four verses are a translator's challenge, given the elegant Greek style of this single sentence and the number of words that appear nowhere else in the Second Testament.[7] These opening verses present to the gospel's addressees the author's sources, content, method and fundamental purpose. The writer acknowledges the written and human sources upon which the present narrative is based. The written sources include Mark, Q and the Greek or Septuagintal version of the Bible.[8] The human witnesses are those upon which the Lukan household is founded—Mary, the twelve and other characters who appear in the gospel. They are the ones who have been eyewitnesses to the ministry of Jesus and later became communicators of his message and presence to the next generation of Jesus followers.[9] These are

---

6. For a fuller treatment of Luke's orthopraxis, see Michael Trainor, *According to Luke: Insights for Contemporary Pastoral Practice* (North Blackburn, Vic: Collins Dove, 1992).

7. Helpful for the study of the preface is Loveday C. Alexander, *The Preface to Luke's Gospel: Literary Convention and Social Context in Luke 1.1–4 and Acts 1.1* (Cambridge: Cambridge University Press, 1993).

8. Fitzmyer, *Luke I–IX*, pp. 109-25; Alexander, *Preface*, pp. 114-15.

9. This two-stage movement of these human witnesses from being eyewitnesses to communicators of the meaning of Jesus' mission and ministry is subtly inscribed in

the foundational witnesses of God's action in Jesus for Luke's householders. What they (the written and oral sources) witness to are the fruits of God's salvific activity throughout history—what has been 'brought to fruition among us' (1.1b).

These fruits are God's actions of divine communion, liberation and inclusivity revealed in history, in the people of Israel, continued in the story of Jesus and now bearing fruit among 'us', the household of Luke's own day. What is past continues into the present and, by implication, into the future. Luke explicitly affirms a theocentric view of history, creation and the world to which the gospel's audience is intimately linked.[10] The Greek verbal passive voice in these two verbs ('...been brought to fruition among us...', '...as they were handed down to us...') confirms this. It is God acting and God is faithful.

For a contemporary listener to this verse, the expression about 'bearing fruit' registers an ecological note. God's action 'bears fruit'; but this also presages fructive and maternal dimensions of God's activity which will be explicated in the fruit-bearing ministry of Jesus. In other words, God's action is not all concerned with human salvation. Earth, too, is involved.

Luke also reveals the manner, which I have called 'orthopraxis', by which the story of God revealed in Jesus and in Luke's present will unfold. The author writes in the style of a Jewish or Greek historiographer, not recording sequential historical facts, but bringing a narrative together in a certain order to communicate a particular point of view. This point of view is explicated in the prologue's final verse—it is concerned with the reception of the audience's inherited theological tradition, which I have translated as 'those matters [they] have been catechized' about and symbolically focused in the character of Theophilus.

The final word in Luke's linguistically and theologically dense sentence is emphatic. It concerns 'certainty' or 'assurance' (*asphaleia*, 1.4c).[11] Luke is concerned about ensuring that the story of Jesus and his followers, in Jerusalem, Judea, Samaria, Asia Minor, Greece and 'Earth's end' (Acts 1.9), is trustworthy, reliable and can offer confidence to Theophilus and those whom he socially represents. Luke's 'orderly account' has come about because of a crisis. It is a crisis of credibility. Can gospel householders be confident that the way the story of Jesus has been interpreted in Luke's

---

the Greek sentence of v. 2, though most English translations do not distinguish it. For example, NRSV: 'just as they were handed on to us by those who from the beginning were eyewitnesses and servants of the word...' See Fitzmyer, *Luke I–IX*, p. 294. Alexander (*Preface*, p. 120) offers an alternative translation for 'eyewitnesses' as 'those with personal / first-hand experience: those who know the facts at first hand.'

10. Alexander, *Preface*, p. 113.
11. Alexander, *Preface*, pp. 140-41.

day and expressed in liturgical, ethical and moral practices is authentic and trustworthy?

Important background for the world *behind* the gospel is an evaluation of the social composition of Luke's addressees and the explicit address in 1.3b of 'most excellent Theophilus'. This analysis is important. Later it will be used to show how their appreciation of Earth was differently understood by each of these groups.

The Social Composition of Luke's Audience and their Respective Earth Stances

Taking Lk. 1.3b into consideration, it would seem that Luke's intended audience comes from a high or elite social status. This is suggested by Luke's elevated literary style in the prologue, reflecting a desire to address those more familiar with the Attic prose of classical Greek.[12] The audience presumed in the first instance by the prologue might further be identified through the designation which Luke gives Theophilus as 'most excellent' (*kratistos*). This title certainly does not place Theophilus among the peasant majority of Luke's world. It indicates rather his elevated social rank, perhaps a *patronus* of the evangelist. At a more symbolic level, Theophilus could represent all in Luke's household that would be 'God-lovers' or at least 'God-fearers' attracted to Judaism and open to God and God's story revealed in Jesus.[13]

If we had only the prologue to go by then it would seem that the primary, and perhaps only, audience for the gospel would be those of elite social standing. However, a linguistic and narrative analysis of the whole Lukan corpus enables us to identify better the intended audience of the writing and the social composition of its author.[14] This information, coupled with the author's narrative frame—where scenes are set and people located—offers a hypothetical social snapshot.[15]

---

12. Bovon, *Luke 1*, p. 4; also Cadbury, *Style*, pp. 4-39; Fitzmyer, *Luke I–IX*, p. 113.

13. On the discussion of Theophilus, see Fitzmyer, *Luke I–IX*, pp. 299-300, who unequivocally denies that 'Theophilus' is a symbolic name for the gospel's audience.

14. Vernon K. Robbins, 'The Social Location of the Implied Author of Luke–Acts', in *The Social World of Luke–Acts: Models for Interpretation* (ed. Jerome H. Neyrey; Peabody, MA: Hendrickson, 1991), pp. 305-32.

15. As I acknowledge the tentative nature of my attempt to delineate the social composition of Luke's audience, I draw on the work of social anthropologists and suggest that my conjectural social picture best explains the evidence found in the Lukan text when considered as a 'window' on to Luke's social landscape. See also Richard L. Rohrbaugh, 'The Pre-industrial City in Luke–Acts', in *The Social World of Luke–Acts: Models for Interpretation* (ed. Jerome H. Neyrey; Peabody, MA: Hendrickson, 1991), pp. 125-50; Douglas E Oakman, 'The Countryside in Luke–Acts', in *The Social World of Luke–Acts Models for Interpretation* (ed. Jerome H. Neyrey; Peabody, MA: Hendrickson, 1991), pp. 151-80; John H. Elliott, 'Temple versus Household in Luke–Acts: A Contrast

The flask-shaped social grid below (Figure 2) visually presents the stratification of Mediterranean society in the Herodian period.[16] This stratification would have, with slight adaptation, its parallel in Luke's Greco-Roman world.[17] All these identified social groups are characterized in Luke's gospel—from the most powerful to the 'expendables'. Commentators on the gospel's provenance suggest that the Lukan household is composed of a cross-section of the social strata of Mediterranean society that would be found on the edge or outskirts of the pre-industrial city or village of the ancient world. Generally, this consisted of four social groups: peasants, dispossessed peasants, urban workers including artisans and slaves, and the social elite. These are located in the diagram below within the oval-shape perforation located across the grid's middle.

In terms of power, prestige and privilege, the social stratification grid suggests that Luke's household consisted of people drawn from both the elite, or socially elevated sections of Greco-Roman society ('Theophilus') and its lower rungs. It did not include those from the highest and lowest. In terms of social representation, we find a broad cross section, including those identified in the grid as 'lay aristocrats'. This is Theophilus and others in Luke's gospel identified as having wealthy status and being aligned to the royal household. This elite group, socially the most powerful and numerically the smallest (being 1-2 per cent of the population), were proportionally more dominant in the evangelist's household. For this reason, they are the explicit addressees of the gospel.

Within the wider society, these elites exercised control over the peasant majority through a process of redistributive economic exchange.[18] This meant

---

in Social Institutions', in *The Social World of Luke–Acts: Models for Interpretation* (ed. Jerome H. Neyrey; Peabody, MA: Hendrickson, 1991), pp. 211-40.

16. Richard L. Rohrbaugh, 'The Social Location of the Markan Audience', in *The Social World of the New Testament: Insights and Models* (ed. Jerome H. Neyrey and Eric C. Stewart; Peabody, MA: Hendrickson Publishers, 2008), pp. 143-62 (146). Rohrbaugh's stratification grid draws on the work of Dennis Duling, *The New Testament: An Introduction* (New York: Harcourt, Brace, Jovanovich, 1993), Chapter 2; Richard L. Rohrbaugh, 'The Social Location of the Marcan Audience', *BTB* 23 (1993), pp. 114-27 (23); Gerhard E. Lenski and Jeanne Lenski, *Human Societies: An Introduction to Macrosociology* (New York, NY: McGraw-Hill, 1974), pp. 207-62.

17. First developed by Gerhard E. Lenski [*Power and Privilege: A Theory of Social Stratification* (New York, NY: McGraw-Hill, 1966), pp. 215-90] and further summarized by John Dominic Crossan, *The Historical Jesus: The Life of a Mediterranean Jewish Peasant* (San Francisco: HarperCollins, 1991), pp. 45-46. The slight modification I suggest would be the labelling of those who hold political power. In Luke's world this would be the Roman emperor. The value of social-stratification and its application to Luke's audience is a hallmark of Green's commentary (*Luke*, pp. 56-62).

18. Thomas F. Carney, *The Shape of the Past: Models of Antiquity* (Lawrence, KA: Coronado Press, 1975), p. 182.

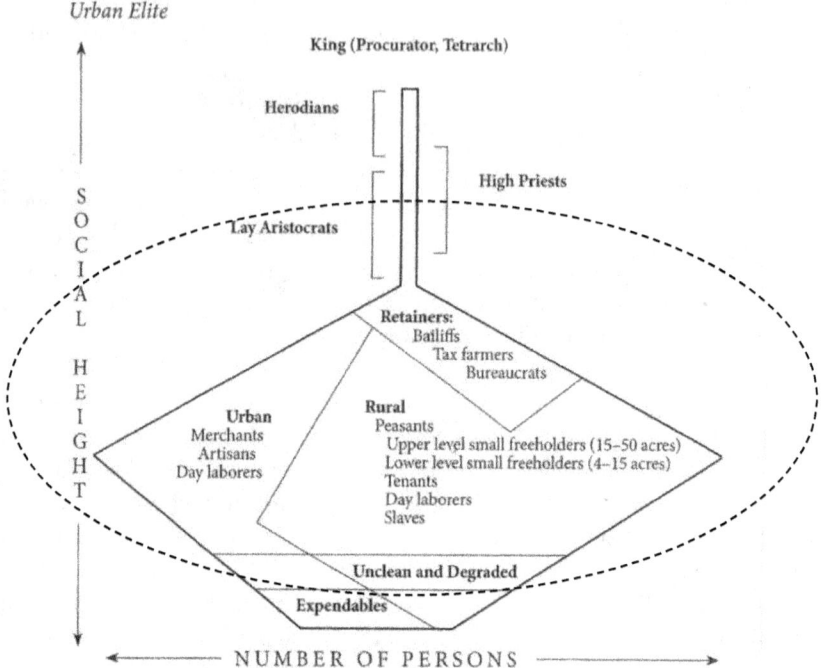

Figure 2. *Social stratification in the Herodian period.*

that they extracted the produce of local peasant farmers through taxation or temple tithing, which they stored and later redistributed for political or religious reasons.[19] Their predilection towards redistribution as an economic practice and the temptation for peasant exploitation laid the foundations for what developed later as a free-market economy and the potential for revolt and social unrest.

> The economic integration of the society under consideration into a larger, possibly international market; the consequent drive to commercialize agriculture and the subsequent encroachment on peasant lands and peasant rights and status in general; this sequence is certainly the most promising candidate for the position of 'universal ultimate cause [of agrarian discontent and revolt]'.[20]

The elites represented the interests of those who held religious and political power in the cities, and had the economic base and initiative to confiscate

---

19. On this see Oakman 'Countryside', p. 129.
20. Henry Landsberger, 'Peasant Unrest: Themes and Variations', in *Rural Protest: Peasant Movements and Social Change* (ed. Henry Landsberger; New York: Barnes & Noble, 1973), as quoted by Oakman, 'Was Jesus a Peasant?', p. 128.

and control the lands of the peasant farmers when they became debt-ridden.[21] Alongside this power to control wealth, the elites would have viewed Earth and its fruits as a commodity that could be accumulated, bartered and dispensed with. For them, land symbolized power and wealth. This attitude is not lost on the evangelist and finds its way into the gospel story.

The penchant by the elite for social power and economic control would not have evaporated in their membership of Luke's household. This is the reason I suggest they are explicitly identified through Theophilus in the prologue and are later addressed by other teachings and stories, especially in the journey narrative (Lk. chs. 9-19). They are encouraged to re-evaluate all socially acceptable practices that would have kept them removed from those of lower socio-economic status: their use of power and wealth and reciprocal exchange. They are invited to reconsider their dining companions and to offer hospitality to all, even those outside their own social class. In short, they are challenged to reform their friendship allegiances protected by the classical purity standards familiar in the Greco-Roman world.[22]

Their discipleship in Luke's household would have encouraged them to reconsider their use of patronage, the importance of status and, more practically, their demand to extract debts from peasant farmers and even to return lands that had been previously confiscated. This invitation would have included a reform in their attitude to Earth's household. Of all groups in Luke's audience, the elite had the most opportunity to bring about social change, economic reform and environmental respect. They would have had to deal with economic disadvantage and a decline in social status and honour as they gathered with non-elites, artisans, merchants, retainers and some peasants in the inclusive gathering that featured around Luke's table of the Lord.[23] Their persistence with the kind of social and ecological reform envisaged in the gospel would have contributed towards a new or renewed social design in the Greco-Roman world in the late first century CE.

The elites exercised social control through their use of money and confiscation of land and its produce. They were supported in this control by the other socially identifiable groups more directly involved in the life of

---

21. On the issue of peasant debt, especially in Galilee, see Horsley, *Archaeology*, pp. 84, 89, 181; Bruce J. Malina and Richard L. Rohrbaugh, *Social-Science Commentary on the Synoptic Gospels* (Minneapolis, MN: Fortress Press, 1992), pp. 332-33.

22. On purity see Mary T. Douglas, *Purity and Danger: An Analysis of Concepts of Pollution and Taboo* (New York: Praeger, 1966); Jacob Neusner, *The Idea of Purity in Ancient Judaism* (Leiden: Brill, 1973); Neyrey, *The Social World*, pp. 103-104.

23. See Jerome H. Neyrey, 'Loss of Wealth, Loss of Family, Loss of Honor: The Cultural Context of the Original Makarisms in Q', in *The Social World of the New Testament: Insights and Models* (ed. Jerome H. Neyrey and Eric C. Stewart; Peabody, MA: Hendrickson Publishers, 2008), pp. 87-102.

the urban centre. This broad ranging group of urbanites is identified in the mid-section of the social stratification grid. These are the urban merchants and artisans (who produced and sold the goods necessary for the day-to-day life of the elites), and retainers (bailiffs, tax farmers and other bureaucrats) who enacted the social (taxation) control of the elites. I would also add into this mix slaves, owned or rented by the elite for their service and comfort. Though curiously absent in the stratification analysis, they constituted about a third of the population in some urban centres of the Mediterranean.[24]

Differing Attitudes to Earth

Members of this non-elite urban group would have had differing attitudes to Earth. Some, especially the skilled artisan or craftsperson, who ensured the generational survival of their trade and acted as 'mediators' of nature, would have looked upon creation with respect. For merchants, potters, tent-makers, carpenters and other crafts-people, the natural world would have been a source of economy but treated with esteem.[25] Without Earth's goods, they would not have been able to survive. These groups would have also been part of Luke's world and members of the gospel household. Their encouragement to work fairly and with diligence finds an echo in the gospel. Their presence in the gospel household and their response to the story of Jesus would have enabled them to invite the elites to a greater awareness of those who were socially excluded and, in terms of Earth, to an appreciation of the fruits of the land and its produce to sustain elite needs at the urban centre.

A third group, representative of the majority in Luke's audience, were the 'peasants'. The peasants in Luke's world figure in the gospel. They represented the powerless majority in the ancient world. Their livelihood in the countryside depended on their agricultural skills for the survival of their family and kinship group connected to nearby villages.[26] Through the technology of plough and harnessed animals, peasants sought to produce food for their own sustenance, and have enough left over to pay the necessary taxes. Their survival depended on a good harvest and the natural support

---

24. While the literature on slavery in the ancient world is enormous, for an overview of slavery in the Greco-Roman world consult Keith Bradley and Paul Cartledge (eds.), *The Cambridge World History of Slavery. Volume 1. The Ancient Mediterranean World* (Cambridge: Cambridge University Press, 2011).

25. For a helpful critique of my sociological analyses of Luke's audience and their respective Earth relationships, see Anne Elvey, *An Ecological Feminist Reading of the Gospel of Luke: A Gestational Paradigm* (Lewiston, NY: Edwin Mellen Press, 2005), p. 62.

26. On kinship, see K.C. Hanson, 'All in the Family: Kinship in Agrarian Roman Palestine', in *The Social World of the New Testament: Insights and Models* (ed. Jerome H. Neyrey and Eric C. Stewart; Peabody, MA: Hendrickson Publishers, 2008), pp. 25-46. Hanson's appreciation of kinship in the Roman Palestine setting would also echo Luke's context.

from strong familial and kinship networks. These family links allowed for reciprocal exchange, gift giving and non-competitiveness. In Luke's peasant-based society, reciprocal exchange was based on a barter or gift exchange. In peasant clans knit closely together, subsistence or survival was crucial. They 'lived by subsistence farming, employing agricultural produce as a form of money and wrapped in an intricate network of reciprocal exchange.'[27]

The respectful working of the land became their means of life and survival. Rather than seeing the land as a commodity to be exploited as did the elites and bureaucrats, the peasant farmer saw the need to attend to and work in synchronicity with the land.

> The typical peasant's socialization and life is molded by the agricultural year. Mediterranean peasants have devoted the majority of their energies towards viticulture, arboriculture, and agriculture. Vines and orchards, as well as grain and vegetable production, provide their staples. Animals supplemented the vegetable diet. Inanimate energy sources are rarely tapped, and productivity is relatively low. Excess peasant labour may be devoted to craft specialization if agricultural opportunities dwindle and tax pressures are high.[28]

The peasants' respectful attention to the ecological features of their world encouraged mutual exchange of Earth's produce through balanced reciprocity. They were able to support one another and obtain a livelihood. Their agricultural endeavours were not intended to make a profit, for to do so would be at the expense of one of their number going without. The accumulation of wealth was considered an evil because it created division and greater poverty for others. Within the village-peasant world, systems were created to ensure that any excess produce was redistributed in the form of gifts to fellow peasants, a loan to a member in need, or an offering at a local village festival.[29] From a modern perspective, peasants were the better ecologists who respected their Earth and relied upon sustainable farming.

Luke's urban location is confirmed through a study of the gospel's stated metropolitan language and explicated through a redactional study of Mark—where Luke deliberately changes Mark's village or country allusions to a city thematic. The peasants were the majority in Lukan society, about 75 per cent of the population. They were, however, proportionally underrepresented in the gospel household, especially if we envisage its urban setting. If peasants were members of Luke's household, their very presence would have invited those from higher social ranks (elites, bureaucrats, artisans) to reconsider their attitude to their civic status, the impoverished and the land. Table communion at the Lord's Supper would have further meant for the elites compromised family status and honour. They ate with

---

27. Carney, *Shape*, p. 199.
28. Oakman, 'Was Jesus a Peasant?', p. 127.
29. Carney, *Shape*, p. 198.

landless peasants whom they considered responsible for their own ongoing impoverishment and debt-ridden farm holdings. In this same setting, from the peasant perspective, social involvement and table communion with the elites would have invited peasants to real forgiveness, maintenance of harmonious relationships and resistance to vengeance.

This same invitation of openness towards the elite would have been present for another land aligned peasant-based group but whose representation within the Lukan household would have been much higher than their rural-based peasant counterparts. These are those who were drawn to the outskirts of the ancient city because of social disruption and economic need. They continued to be sympathetic to the interests and environmental perspective and practices of their country kin.

Like the rural farmers, these urban peasants were originally owners of ancestral lands, but years of increasing taxation demands and seasons of harvest drought prevented them from harvesting enough crops to provide food and pay debt. Economic inability gradually forced them to become more financially dependent on others, especially their own more successful kin in the same village area or geographical region. Eventually, unable to repay even these loans, they sold their ancestral lands, often to absentee landlords, the equivalent to Luke's elites. These peasants became tenant farmers on the lands they once owned or became entirely dispossessed and landless. In this second scenario, deprived of any family and kinship network of support, judged as inferior to all other social groups except perhaps the 'expendables' in the stratification grid, they sought out employment in the cities to keep them and their families alive.[30] If they found work as hired day labourers, they became dependent on the patronage of the elite. Some would have even sold themselves and their families into slavery to serve the needs of the elite and to ensure their survival.

This description of the dispossessed peasant in the late first century was applicable not to an isolated or single person. It affected whole farming communities and was a social reality brought about by the booming growth in international trade in the first century determined by the agrarian needs in the Mediterranean societies of Egypt, Palestine, Syria, Asia Minor, Macedonia and Italy. This dramatic societal change influenced by trading demands forced peasant farmers into poly-cropping and away from their traditional practice of mono-cropping, the ancient basis of peasant-village reciprocal exchange and support. The pressure placed on farmers to adopt newer forms of technology to produce different abundant crops at times resulted in production failure, exacerbated by poor seasonal conditions.

---

30. Richard L. Rohrbaugh (ed.), *The Social Sciences and New Testament Interpretation* (Peabody, MA: Hendrickson, 1996), p. 110; Rohrbaugh, 'The Pre-industrial City', pp. 128-29.

This move away from a peasant-based socially determined economy to an international market would have been felt in Luke's gospel household. Its urban setting meant that more dispossessed peasant families were attracted to the kind of membership offered by the fictive kinship gospel community. Luke's inclusive and hospitable household, founded on the ministry of Jesus, would have been an obvious attraction to these landless urban peasants and their families. They now had a new household to which they could belong and with which they could identify. It was one in which the social and economic structures of the Greco-Roman world were reconfigured.

This identifiable group in the overall social composition of Luke's gospel audience would have gathered weekly at the celebration of the Lord's Supper with others from different social groupings—the elite, artisans, retainers, slaves and merchants. Their earlier memory of the importance of Earth for their livelihood would have continued into their new urban context now forced upon them by circumstances out of their control.

The above social picture of Luke's world and the gospel household, though conjectural, is a fair explanation of the data gleaned from social anthropologists and the narrative world presumed by the gospel. The gospel text provides us with a 'window' on to Luke's social world—elite, artisans, urban workers, retainers, bailiffs, slaves, peasants, and the dispossessed. All find their characterization in Luke's story.

I suggest that the richness and diversity of the gospel's social world bring also a complexity with regard to attitudes, social scenarios and themes that cannot easily be homogenized or reduced into monochromatic sketches. This principle also applies when seeking to engage the gospel with an ecological hermeneutic. For example, in terms of the principle of intrinsic worth, each group saw Earth from a different point of view—something essential for living, to be respected and treated respectfully, or as a commodity and object of exploitation. In the light of the hermeneutical principle of interconnectedness and honouring Earth as integral to community, attitudes here would also vary, given the social status of the groups identified and their connectedness to Earth. In the Mediterranean dyadic value system that shaped interfamilial and tribal relationship, people found their identity through the other.

Thomas Carney offers an insight of urban life in first century Rome. While his description is explicit of Rome itself, it would apply to most of the large cities in the Roman empire and arguably to the kind of urban setting envisaged for Luke's household. Carney's depiction is particularly pertinent for envisaging typical relationships in Luke's social and urban world between the elite and the urban poor, the city workers, artisans and dispossessed peasants, whose livelihood depended on their patronage. Carney shows how a person's social status determined their view of the city. I would add that their social status also determined their perception of Earth's environment and the fruits produced.

Carney's first description focuses on the elite and underscores the importance placed on their privilege, prestige and honour. The social deference paid to them, and the extravagance of their country villas and urban houses, reinforced this honour. Implicit in his description is an elite attitude to Earth's soil and land.

> Our image of a city of antiquity, however, would be very different according to our status. If we were a member of the Roman elite, for instance, we would leave our country house—spacious, centrally heated, with a swimming bath, library, works of art, etc—and estate, and drive, ride or be carried in a litter to the city. We would pass the tombs of the great along the highway nearer to the city. Our entourage would make a way for us through the teeming city streets. We would thus make our way through the city centre, past splendid theatres, amphitheatres, public halls and baths and parks. Eventually we would be welcomed by yet more attendants in our town house, which would be almost as elegant as our country house—and largely supplied with foodstuffs by our country estate. There our clients would be waiting to dance attendance upon us.[31]

Carney's implicit disclosure of the elites' rapacious ecological attitude confirms the picture already established from the social analysis of Luke's audience. For the elites in Carney's Roman city, Earth was a commodity from which they were able to extract more than simply the necessities for the livelihood of those who belonged to their *domus*. It confirmed the kind of honour they regarded as their due. The soil and its production reinforced their social status and display of wealth in their urban setting and the honourable attention that this attracted.

For those who belonged to the inferior levels of urban Roman society, represented by the middle and lower sections of Rohrbaugh's social stratification grid, urban life would have been far different. Carney describes them as 'the poor'. These would be Luke's urban non-elite and the majority in the gospel household.

> If we were poor…our day in Rome would start in a noisome tenement. There would be no central heating; possibly a charcoal brazier (chimneys had not yet been invented). There would be no running water, no toilet (slops were tossed from the window—for which glass panes had yet to be invented). An oil lamp would light our room, sparsely furnished for want of money and for fear of wall-breakers (as burglars were known). We would don our dirty, louse-ridden outer clothing and plunge down as many as six flights of stairs into the teeming mass of humanity outside. A meal from a street vendor whose stall obstructed the press of human traffic in the street might follow, if we had time and money a wheaten cake or some fruit, maybe. Then a drink from a fountain—tea, coffee and chocolate were as yet unknown.

---

31. Carney, *Shape*, p. 85.

> Then to our day's work. This might be labor in a brick-works, or running errands for some dignitary or other or some such, if we were fortunate enough to have a job currently. Or it might merely be visiting the homes of those of the great by whose arrogant slave flunkeys we would be grudgingly recognized. We would accordingly push through the throng, probably with running nose or hacking cough if it were winter, or feeling slightly aguish if it were summer. The noisome twisting streets between the tall tenements of the slums would give way to broader streets flanked by the windowless exteriors of the one-storey houses of the wealthy or the shop fronts of the two-storey houses of the moderately well-to-do. We might catch a preoccupied glimpse of some of 'their' big, important public buildings, or even jostle our way along a portico or two. But we probably would not move out of 'our' quarter of the city—'our' section of the slums plus their adjacent good residential area and well-appointed public places. A man had to be careful in this violent city world of tough soldiers, sneaky cutpurses and other desperate, poor.[32]

Carney's graphic description of the world of the urban poor, their living situation, health conditions, means of subsistence and employment situation, imaginatively reinforces the challenge that would have faced the Lukan writer. This concerned the evangelist's attempt to reconfigure social status and the politically determined circles of friendship which structure status, honour and well-being. The gospel becomes a window into this kind of world and a mirror by which Luke's audience is invited to engage those from different social groups. This would have become more emphatic within a household setting (probably for one of higher social status who could accommodate a large gathering of the gospel household). The gospel narrative, its story of Jesus' ministry, his outreach to the socially disenfranchised and his engagement with the urban well-to-do would have been Luke's manner for addressing the unrest growing within the gospel household and needing response. This is the *asphāleia* or 'assurance' that Luke's socially diverse audience seeks.

From an ecological perspective, Carney's description of the day-to-day life of the urban poor implicitly offers an insight into their attitude to their physical and earthly environment. The elite were, to a certain extent, shielded from negative environmental conditions or the demands of caring for Earth and directly benefiting from its fruits—they had slaves to do that. The poor, on the other hand, were subject to the environmental conditions that surrounded them in their urban setting. These conditions included living in close quartered rented tenement situations exposed to 'the teeming mass of humanity'. It also meant more direct exposure to the weather and their gradual dependency on access to the actual fruits of Earth with which they would have been in greater resonance. Synchronicity with their ecological world would have brought them greater health and well-

---

32. Carney, *Shape*, pp. 85-86.

being. For those landless urban peasants the memory of their respect for Earth and what its environment could do for them would have only been more exacerbated or palpable in an urban setting of greater physical and economic hardship.

Carney's lively depiction of urban life for the elite and poor adds another level of reflection on to Luke's world and the kind of community or household addressed by the gospel. It further helps to isolate the different though subtle differences shared by each social group in relation to its appreciation of the physical environment and Earth-related aspects of their lives.

While I have sought to reconstruct a plausible picture of Luke's social stratification I have also suggested ecological attitudes that would have also differed according to the particular relationship which each social group had with the Earth and their immediate contact with the soil of the land. This immediacy, I suggest, was shaped by their working focus and dependency on the land.

For the rural peasants and the urban dispossessed, their tie to the land and the appreciation of their ecological environment would have been greater than the urban elite. This appreciation would have been tempered by their need to overly cultivate and work the land to pay Rome's tribute.[33] The elite, on the other hand, would have had some appreciation of their links with the Earth—and more so than the kind of removed or isolated individualism typical in western societies today. But their attachment to the land was more tenuous than those whose livelihoods were dependent on it. Successful cropping came out of an attitude of ecological synchronicity. For the elites this was unimportant. Power and honour were the social values that determined their urban location and social interaction. The land and its environment were irrelevant. They were more a commodity:

> Human as well as natural resources, including, or especially the water, were required to maintain the luxurious and decorative lifestyle of the urban elites, with their fine garments and royal palaces, adorned with fountains and bath houses.[34]

The urban workers and urban non-elites but non-poor—the bailiffs, tax officers, artisans, bureaucrats and merchants, and slaves located in the social grid—would have reflected a variety of attitudes to the physical and ecological world. These would have come out of their needs to work with Earth's products (like carpenters and stone masons), sell its fruits (like merchants) or tax those who benefited from what Earth produced (bailiffs, tax agents, food suppliers and fishers). The variations in ecological attitudes to Earth in Luke's gospel audience might be depicted as a perforated vector

---

33. Freyne, *Jesus*, p. 45.
34. Freyne, *Jesus*, p. 45.

1. *Differing Attitudes to Earth*

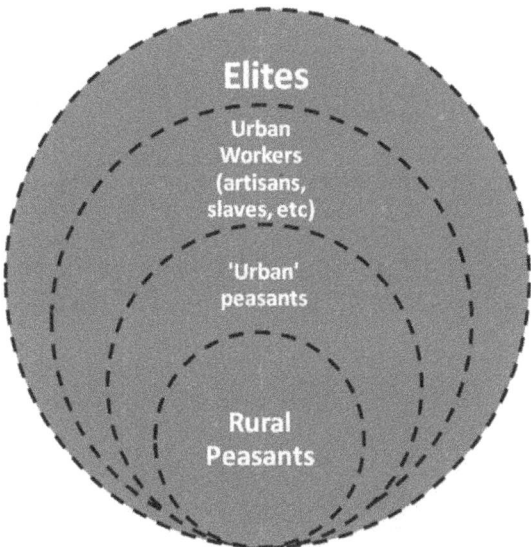

Figure 3. *Different ecological attitudes in Luke's audience.*

stack (Figure 3): the closer to the top of the stack, the higher the social status; the nearer to the bottom the greater the ecological appreciation. The perforation in each circle is an acknowledgement of an attitudinal fluidity between social groups and the size of each inversely proportional to the size of each group in the wider Greco-Roman world.

Whatever judgment one might offer of the hypothetical variations of ecological attitudes in Luke's household depicted above, the main point would be unquestionable. Various social groups would have a variety of attitudes to Earth. To use contemporary language, each of their ecological dispositions would be different. I have tried to offer a plausible reconstruction of these variations. I also suggest that these differences find their way into Luke's gospel narrative.

There is a further point that bears on the ecological focus that I seek to bring to Luke's story. If the gospel is primarily, though not exclusively, addressed to the elite inviting them to conversion, this would have enormous consequences socially. It would invite them into a spirit of conversion towards other social groups present in Luke's household. This conversion would be not only religious or theological. It would also be economic, political and ecological. That is, the elites would be invited to consider the Greco-Roman world and the structure of urban society that impact on other urban non-elite members. The elite would be invited to 'stand in the sandals' of these others. Accompanying this spirit of theological, economic and political conversation in the spirit of Jesus communicated through Luke's gospel would have been an ecological conversion. Such

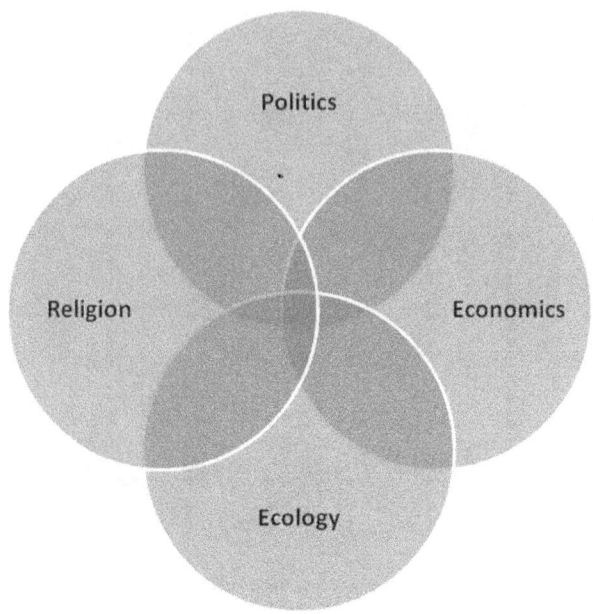

Figure 4. *The embedded nature of Luke's four Mediterranean 'worlds'.*

consideration would be even clearer given the dyadic nature of Luke's world and the interrelationship of these different social values or 'worlds'. The political, theological and economic worlds are well acknowledged in social anthropological literature of ancient Mediterranean societies. I now wish to add a fourth, the ecological or environmental world (Figure 4).

Conclusion

Luke realistically acknowledged that the radical social renewal envisaged in the early Jesus movement had not happened and the evangelist had to live within the realities of social strata and hierarchy as promoted in the Greco-Roman world of the late first century CE. The evangelist sought to address those on the lower and middle rungs of the socio-economic hierarchy—some peasants, urban landless peasants, urban workers, artisans, slaves (Figure 2). As reflected in society generally, these were numerically the larger group of the gospel household. Luke particularly wanted to address the 'Theophiluses' of the Jesus household: the wealthy social elites. They were, I suggest, a minority but most influential and powerful. I have argued that this principal audience resided in a town or city somewhere in the Roman empire. Such a city had a variety of elite who held high social positions and controlled spaces within the city and countryside. Country control happened through taxation and land confiscation.

Luke's household also embraced peasants; some were rural-based but most of Luke's peasants were those who had been affected by the manipulative control of the urban elite. They had gone into debt, borrowed from fellow peasants and kin, were eventually forced to sell inherited lands to the elites and absentee landlords, and moved into the city.

From this social scenario with its complex attitudes to Earth, we sense the delicacy of Luke's situation. A more difficult pastoral challenge would be harder to imagine. I have suggested that Luke's audience mirrored the power structures of the Roman empire.[35] This meant that the gospel's addressees had the potential to split along economic and geographical lines, dividing into social camps with little desire for forming the one household with those who came from different social strata. Luke wrote for different social groups, included household members from a rural background but now urban based and without social voice or influence; and for elite urban dwellers with status and wealth. Luke sought to address all the social groups that were members of the Jesus household, but mainly this last group. This focus means that the gospel is *anthropocentric*; it is addressed to human beings. It is not, however, exclusively anthropocentric. Listened to from another perspective, Luke's gospel concerns the *whole* Earth household, its fruits and creatures, human and non-human.

A focus on the social context of Luke's gospel reveals that different members of the gospel's audience had a variety of complex attitudes towards Earth (Figure 3). Our western penchant to segregate or individualize societal values needs to be critiqued as we consider Luke's first century Mediterranean world. If one thing is certain from this social reconstruction it is that we cannot expect a simple or homogenised Earth-picture to be revealed. I have described a complex social picture in Luke's world, one that was embedded with politics, religion, economics and—I would add—ecology (Figure 4). How I go about bringing the ecological concern of Luke's world and my own to the fore is the focus of the next chapter.

---

35. Rohrbaugh, 'The Pre-industrial City', pp. 125-50.

Chapter 2

INTERTEXTUAL ENGAGEMENT IN LUKE'S GOSPEL

In the previous chapter I offered a summary of conventional Lukan scholarship. This included a study of Luke's social context, theology, christology and narrative strategy. I also offered a hypothetical reconstruction of the social stratification of Luke's audience and their attitudes to Earth. I now return to the key question. How can we engage Luke's gospel afresh in the light of our ecological concerns?

As we have seen, the problem that faced the evangelist—in seeking to straddle the chronological and cultural gap between Jesus of Nazareth and Luke's later householders—is the same that faces us. I have suggested that the methodological key in responding to our question is found in Luke's strategy. Inherent in Luke's approach was a refashioning of the gospel tradition, of formulating a new gospel 'text' (1.3) for new times (1.4), by drawing on earlier literary and personal sources (1.1-2) upon which Luke's gospel and its householders depended. For reasons that I shall soon explain, these literary and human sources I call 'texts'.

Luke's methodological strategy was to address new concerns while remaining faithful to the inherited tradition ('brought to fruition among us', 1.1b). This strategy, in contemporary textual studies, is ultimately 'intertextual'. As Luke demonstrated for a first century audience, an engagement between two 'texts' defined in a particular way not exclusively linguistic can lead to fresh insights for a later household of believers. This same approach can be most helpful as we engage Luke's gospel from a contemporary ecological perspective and as we appreciate better the nature of a text—including an ancient gospel text. Helpful for this is the work of textual and literary critics who have formulated an approach to textual study called 'intertextuality'. This study can help us deepen the appreciation of a text's dynamic and, with modification of its methodology, provide the interpretative strategy for an intentional ecological study of Luke's gospel.

Intertextuality

Amongst contemporary literary critics, intertextuality is an approach to literary composition that respects the metaphoric, imaginative and symbolic

2. *Intertextual Engagement in Luke's Gospel* 41

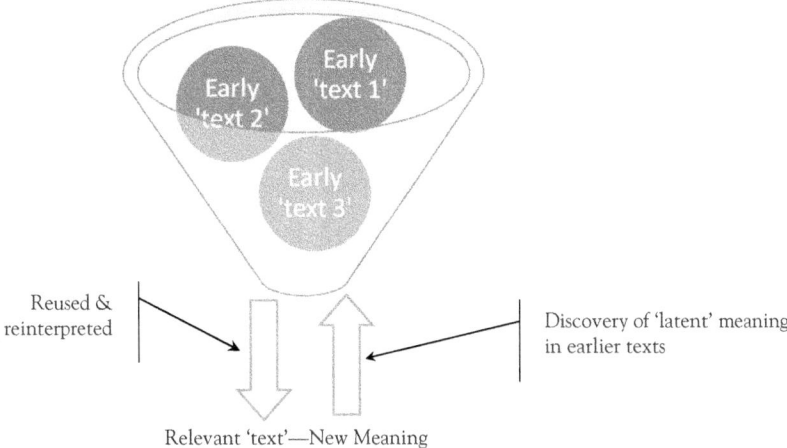

Figure 5. *The contribution of earlier texts and traditions to later texts and meaning.*

worlds of its textual predecessors.[1] In a literary sense, intertextuality allows an interpreter to identify those texts and traditions (the 'Early texts' 1, 2 and 3 in Figure 5 above) that are later re-used and reinterpreted to offer people new understandings in changing contexts. They esteem these newer texts as critically relevant for helping elucidate, encourage, challenge and critique what is happening in their lives. The interpreting community in a later period of time can draw forth from these texts and traditions meanings hitherto unsuspected and latent but now perceived as relevant for its present situation.[2]

Thus, a text of an earlier period can offer fresh substantive meaning when drawn upon in a new social setting, unforeseen by its original author. The earlier text ('intertext' 1, 2 and 3 in Figure 6 below) becomes an 'intertext' to the newly created text.

The parallel between this appreciation of intertextuality and the approach already discerned in Lk. 1.1-4 could not be clearer.

Intertextuality is a neologism credited to Julia Kristeva who recognized the influence of different texts on writing, reading and literary interpretation.[3]

---

1. See for example Gail R. O'Day, 'Jeremiah 9:22-23 and 1 Corinthians 1:26-31: A study of Intertextuality', *JBL* 109 (1990), pp. 259-67, who describes intertextuality as 'a literary and hermeneutical category…[which]…refers to the ways a new text is created from the metaphors, images, and symbolic world of an earlier text or tradition.' (p. 259).

2. Pertinent here is Michael Fishbane, *Biblical Interpretation in Ancient Israel* (Oxford: Clarendon Press, 1985).

3. On Julia Kristeva's contribution to the understanding of intertextuality, see Morny Joy, Kathleen O'Grady and Judith L. Poxon (eds.), *French Feminists on Religion: A Reader* (London: Routledge, 2002), pp. 83-91. For a helpful overview of the use of intertextuality by biblical commentators, consult the chapters in George Aichele and

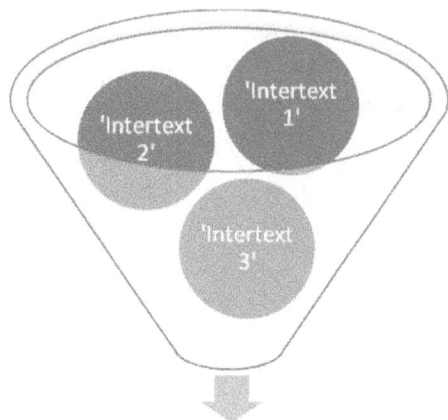

Newly-created 'text'—New Social Context

Figure 6. *An earlier text as* intertext *in a fresh social context.*

She was concerned with the relationship of the classical literary tradition to contemporary works of literature and the role that culture and society played in the construction of literary meaning and expression. By the later part of the twentieth century, biblical interpreters recognized the importance of the work of Kristeva and other intertextual scholars (Harold Bloom, John Hollander, Michael Riffaterre, Gerard Genette, Manfred R. Jacobson, Mikhail M. Bakhtin, Roland Barthes, Jonathan Culler and Jacques Derrida). They appreciated the contribution which intertextuality could make to literary criticism and the 'texts' of biblical texts.[4]

As I understand Kristeva, intertextuality focuses on the literary text and its synchronic dynamic. She is particularly interested in the text's antecedents, and semiotic and symbolic aspects.[5] Intertextuality allows an interpreter to discern the relationship between tradition and texts and the manner by which social context and cultural settings further shape texts.

All these aspects concerned with textual formation and meaning find an echo in Luke's prologue. Luke's attempt to reformulate Mark's gospel and other sources can be understood in terms of this appreciation of intertextuality. It also affirms our engagement of the gospel 'text' in the

---

Gary Allen Phillips (eds.), *Intertextuality and the Bible* (Semeia, 69/70; Atlanta: Scholars Press, 1995).

4. Gail R. O'Day, 'Intertextuality', *DBI*, I (ed. J.H. Hayes; Nashville: Abingdon Press, 1999), pp. 546-48 (546).

5. Kristeva called the rhythm and tone of language with its cadence and measure its 'semiotic' aspect. This gave language its non-linear quality of incongruity and unpredictability (Joy, *French Feminists*, pp. 84-85).

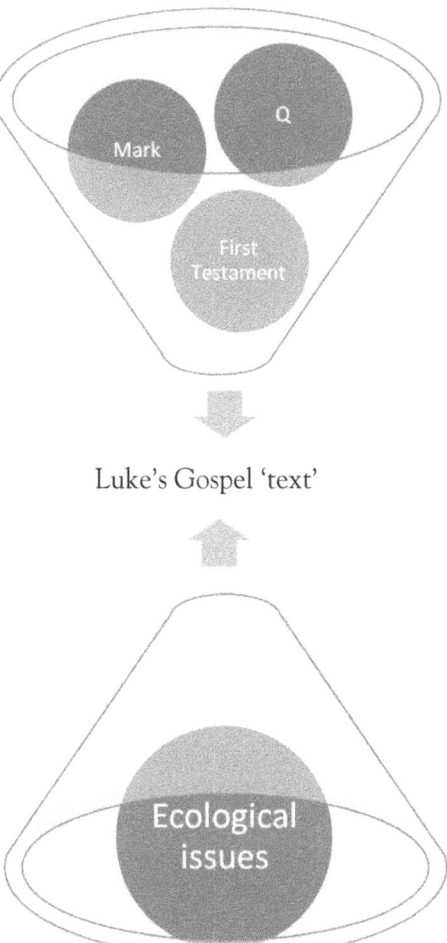

Figure 7. *Luke's gospel, influenced by earlier intertexts, becomes a new intertext for contemporary ecological concerns.*

light of a new 'text' concerned about Earth and its environment. As Mark's gospel is Luke's 'intertext' so too our ecological interests are a new 'intertext' for engaging Luke's gospel afresh (Figure 7).

Or, Luke's gospel, with its earlier intertexts (Mark, Q, First Testament etc.) offers the 'text' with which to engage our present concerns about the environment.[6] Luke's gospel now becomes a *new* intertext for us (Figure 8).

---

6. On Luke's use of the First Testament see Richard B. Hays and Joel B. Green, 'The Use of the Old Testament by New Testament Writers', in *Hearing the New Testament: Strategies for Interpretation* (ed. Joel B. Green; Grand Rapids, MI: Wm B. Eerdmans Publishing Co., 2010), pp. 122-39.

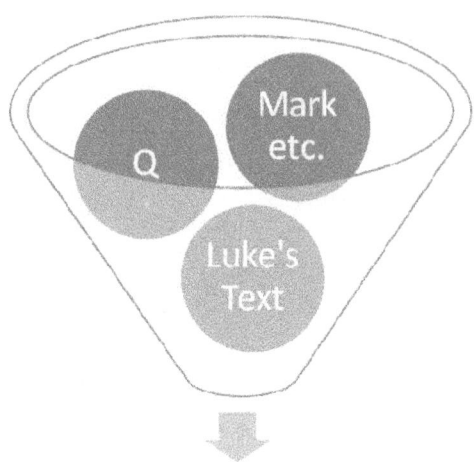

Contemporary Ecological Concerns

Figure 8. *Intertexts, including Luke's gospel, for engaging present ecological concerns.*

This contemporary intertextual dialogue illustrated in Figure 7 parallels Luke's approach in the first century which, from our perspective, is also intertextual. Intertextuality builds upon and complements the conventional diachronic or historically critical approaches that have dominated Lukan studies in the last part of the twentieth century found in more classical commentaries. Intertextual appreciation affirms the evolution of the faith tradition in textual expression, in this case Luke's 'gospel', for a new historical moment and different cultural contexts. It affirms the evangelist's concern to ensure the continuity of the *traditioning* process through the act of writing.[7] Our brief study of Luke's prologue identified the evangelist's agenda and intention. We see clearly in this how earlier 'texts' (understood as written and oral sources) influence and shape later texts, in this case, Luke's gospel.

So far we have considered intertextuality primarily, though not exclusively, from the perspective of the formation and antecedents that structure and give meaning to a 'text'. I have called this the 'traditioning process' and shown how Luke goes about this. Implicit in this process is the cultural and social context in which the text is received and the manner in which 'I' as interpreting subject encounter this 'text'.

A comprehensive understanding of intertextuality moves beyond a concern only about the literary nature of texts. It must also include an awareness of the role that culture plays in a text's formation. That is to say,

---

7. O'Day, 'Intertextuality', p. 547.

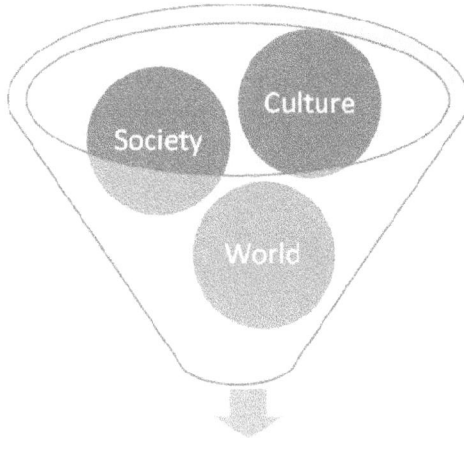

Present 'text'

Figure 9. *Social and cultural influences on the meaning of 'text'.*

society and culture are intertexts that influence the meaning of literary texts.[8] Insights into society help us to understand how these texts might have been understood in earlier settings, and how they might be freshly appreciated today. We have seen, for example, the contribution which an awareness of Luke's social world and cultural context has helped appreciate the gospel, particularly how Earth and the environment were perceived by the author and the gospel's diversely structured audience. This has allowed us to begin to consider the ecological implications of Luke's gospel from the perspective of the addressees themselves. Luke's potential ecological story can become in turn another intertext for subsequent Jesus followers—ourselves.

Cultural and social influence on a text's construction and meaning (Figure 9) leads us to explore further the social dynamic that interplays and undergirds a text's meaning. It also invites us to consider the role played by the interpreting subject. These are particularly important later when 'I' as the interpreter bring my social concerns, namely about the natural world and the environment, into dialogue with Luke's gospel.

Helpful for understanding the social contribution to a text's meaning are T.S. Eliot's insights into poetry and Julia Kristeva's definition of 'text'. Both confirm the importance of the social nature of a text. They also offer

---

8. On the influence of ancient texts and cultures on biblical texts see Loveday C. Alexander, 'The Relevance of Greco-Roman Literature and Culture to New Testament Study,' in *Hearing the New Testament: Strategies for Interpretation* (ed. Joel B. Green; Grand Rapids, MI: Wm B. Eerdmans Publishing Co., 2010), pp. 85-101.

an entrée into considering the oral-aural features of Luke's gospel and its manner of proclamation within a setting of the Greco-Roman household. This will be important background later as we seek to 'listen to' the ecological sounds within Luke's gospel considered as a narrative symphony.

T.S. Eliot on Poetry

In the early twentieth century, Eliot explored the relationship between society and culture and the appreciation of a text. For Eliot, this text was the poem. He considered that the relevance of a poem emerged out of the 'interplay' between interpreter, culture, and literary texts.[9] In a 1919 essay, 'Tradition and the Individual Talent', Eliot challenged the assumption that poetic inspiration was solely the fruit of the poet's genius and inspiration. For him, poetic meaning was a communal rather than private enterprise. It relied on its poetic forebears and a community of culturally influenced interpreters. For these reasons, meaning must be set 'among the dead'. 'We shall often find,' he wrote,

> that not only the best, but the most individual parts of [the poet's] work may be those in which the dead poets, [the] ancestors, assert their immortality most vigorously.[10]

Eliot's point is that the meaning of a poem is influenced by the writer's predecessors, and that the later meaning that the poem receives is not determined by the poet at the time of its creation. Its meaning continues and expands beyond the writer's lifetime. The poem as a text is not an isolated cultural artefact that stands alone. It is interrelated to other texts. It is a 'living whole' that depends on what precedes it and the contexts in which the text (the poem) is received or heard.

To summarize Eliot, the interpretation of poetic literature is the fruit of interrelated texts—earlier generational insights, cultural factors that influence the writer, the social world of the text's original audience, previous texts and traditions, and the world which the interpreter brings

---

9. I like the expression 'interplay' for a number of reasons. It suggests a more-than-cognitive interaction between aspects under consideration (in this case, interpreter, culture and text). It acknowledges the playfulness of an open-ended enterprise not cerebrally controlled and influenced by affective dimensions of engagement. It is this spirit that lies behind Elaine Wainwright's acknowledgement of 'the dialogic interplay between the questions each interpreter brings to the biblical text and the questions the biblical text asks of the interpreter in each creative act of interpretation' in Elaine Wainwright, *Shall We Look for Another: A Feminist Rereading of the Matthean Jesus* (Maryknoll, NY: Orbis Books, 1998), p. 119.

10. Eliot, *Selected*, p. 4 as quoted by O'Day, 'Intertextuality', p. 546.

to the text.[11] It is this confluence of literary, cultural, social and personal intertexts that I seek to keep before me as I engage Luke's gospel.

Speaking and Listening

Before I turn to Kristeva and her definition of 'text' that underscores more fully, though somewhat technically, the social influence on textual meaning, there is something further in Eliot's exploration of poetic appreciation that I find very helpful for the ecological engagement with Luke's gospel that I envisage. This concerns the essential oral-aural quality of texts exemplified in poetry that become suppressed in highly literate or digitally oriented cultures. This particular quality of poetry promotes the view that the poem is spoken, enacted and memorized, while it is listened to by an audience. Eliot's study of the intertextual nature of the poem reinforces its oral-aural dynamic. This dynamic requires, perhaps even demands, performance, proclamation and an audience. This is because a poem is a product of literary intricacy with an attractive auditory quality that captures the attention of its auditors. The auditors engage the poem through its speaker and become an intimate community of listeners.

A consideration of Eliot's appreciation of poetic communication recalls elements of textual energy more familiar to Luke's audience. These concern the social nature of the text, that is, the communal context for its reception and understanding. A text, in Eliot's estimation which would find resonance in Luke's world, is essentially proclamatory; it is meant to be spoken out loud and listened to rather than quietly studied or read. This oral-aural connection is important for considering Luke's audience and the manner and setting of the gospel's proclamation. Eliot's study of the intertextual nature of the poem reinforces its oral-aural dynamic, the process of communal formation through the group listening.

This oral-aural appreciation of a poem as text is further enhanced by a consideration of what intertextual critics call 'semiotics'. This reinforces what we have already seen, the relationship between text and culture and the acknowledgment that a text cannot be reduced to a single rhetorical or literary piece by an individual author. The 'text' is a whole system of social signification, more comprehensive than the original intended meaning. Nor is its meaning derived solely through a systematic reading and study as simple literary artefacts.[12] Meaning emerges from the interrelationship

---

11. O'Day, 'Intertextuality', p. 546.
12. Further to this introductory and limited discussion offered here, semiotics recognizes that social meaning and communication derive from a variety of signs and signifiers culturally interpreted. Literature is one expression of this as we have seen in considering the manner of proclamation and engagement of Luke's gospel above;

of a number of factors: previous or antecedent texts, the cultural system in which the original text was created, the intention of the author, the current social 'intertext' into which the text is received, and the perspective which the interpreter brings to the intertextual engagement. All these elements at work in deciding a text's present meaning are cryptically summed up in Eliot's declaration that the 'best'...[and]... the 'most individual parts' of a text (the poem) are those in which his poetic forebears, those 'dead poets... assert their immortality most vigorously.'

Listening to the Gospel as a 'Household' of Auditors

This discussion about the auditory quality of text of a poem and text and their communal aspect leads to a consideration of the addressees of Luke's gospel. They are 'listeners' or 'auditors' not 'readers'—as we tend to be. We engage the gospel better as *hearers* rather than readers. This respects the original context in which Luke's gospel would have been heard or, perhaps more accurately, 'performed' among a people who are anachronistically called illiterate. To speak of 'hearing' the gospel in preference to reading also honours the dynamic by which Luke's original audience encountered the gospel within a domestic setting.[13]

'Hearing' rather than 'reading' the gospel, particularly in engaging an ecological hermeneutic, is a more 'environmentally friendly' approach. To 'listen to' the gospel reflects a stance of openness and receptive encounter that listens *for* the ecological sounds inherent in Luke's text. Reading is a first step. It allows me as interpreter to bring my world to the text. Listening is a second part of the movement as my encounter and imposition of an initial understanding pauses to allow the text to engage my world in the intertextual dynamic that we have explored through Kristeva and Eliot. The 'listening to' also returns me, as a contemporary western interpreter with a penchant for reading and writing (as I do now), to the stance of Luke's original audience, as auditors of the text and their predilection for *orality* (speaking) and *aurality* (listening).

The 'reading-listening to' is an ongoing intertextual dynamic that allows me as interpreter to be shaped by the world of the text and its earlier

---

oral performance and attentive listening is another. R. Jacobson and C. Lévi-Strauss identified the structures and elements that give a text consistency and stability in meaning. Their semiotic approach presumed that communication was unambiguous and stable. Other practitioners of semiotics and intertextuality have been more aware of the instability and ambiguity of a text's meaning (see O'Day, 'Intertextuality', pp. 546-47).

13. On orality and written languages in the ancient world, see Horsley, *Archaeology*, pp. 156-71; also, Pieter J.J. Botha, 'Cognition, Orality-Literacy, and Approaches to First-Century Writings,' in *Orality, Literacy, and Colonialism* (ed. Jonathan A. Draper; Atlanta, G: Society of Biblical Literature, 2004), pp. 37-64, esp. p. 38 n. 1.

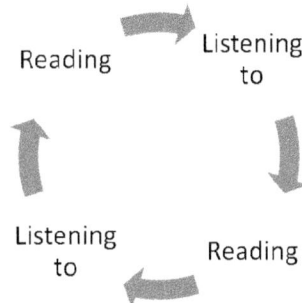

Figure 10. *The 'reading-listening to' intertextual dynamic.*

intexts (Figure 10). At the same time, 'listening to' the world of this text invites me into new considerations that refresh my reading/listening perspective. I then come to the intertextual engagement with fresh insights and openness that deepen over time in the light of new information, either from my world (the world *in front of* the text) or from the worlds *in* the text or *behind* the text.

The invitation in the chapters ahead as we engage Luke's gospel is to *listen to* the text, like listening to music, especially for its ecological and environmental melodies. For this reason I consider Luke's gospel a narrative symphony and recognize the importance of allowing its ecological tones and melodies to surface.

This appreciation of the oral-aural nature of Luke's audience might lead us to think that the addressees were illiterate given their inability to read and write. But to speak of illiteracy in the ancient world is anachronistic that needs critique. At the same time we acknowledge the literary quality of Luke's prologue and presumed literacy level of the gospel's explicit addressee ('Theophilus').[14] From a perspective more culturally sensitive to Luke's Mediterranean context, literacy was the ability to listen, remember and vocally recall—with appropriate adaptations—what was first spoken. Luke's explicit elite audience is presumed to be able to read, but this audience was not the only group addressed by the gospel. As we have seen, it included others of lower social status who, presumably, were unable to read Latin or Greek. They were, from a culturally sensitive perspective, highly literate with a honed ability to remember, repeat and interpret what they heard.[15]

Let me push the implications of this oral-aural dynamic operating in Luke's household a little further. Conceivably, a 'minister of the word' (Lk.

---

14. On literacy in the ancient world, Roman society and Galilee, see Horsley, *Archaeology*, pp. 156-58.

15. This appreciation of ancient literacy explains the repetition of 'remember' either linguistically or thematically in Lk. 24 (vv. 6, 8, 25-27, 32, 45-47). Remembrance leads to action.

1.2b) entrusted with the gospel text would have proclaimed it within the liturgical domestic setting of the Lord's Supper. The narrative structure of the gospel, particularly its use of chiasm, would have assisted the minister to commit the story to memory and retell it.[16] The proclamation would have taken the style of 'performance'. By this, I do not mean that the minister would be like a Greek actor on a stage presenting a flamboyant or dramatic rendition of Luke's gospel, although elements of Greek drama and chorus participation would have been clearly present. Rather, the minister would offer an interpretation of the particular gospel story or teaching, proclaimed from memory, stressing certain aspects through cadence, vocal control and gesture, and suggesting what we could name today as a hermeneutic—how the gospel informs the auditors' present social or cultural realities. The minister was for later gospel auditors what Luke was for an earlier audience. The minister of the word was, in contemporary parlance, an 'intertextual critic'. Intertextuality was at the heart of the gospel's performance.

There is a further point suggested by this consideration of the communal setting of the text's oral-aural performance. This has to do with the household. Up until now I have been using the language of 'household' without explanation. The household was the primary social unit of the Greco-Roman world and the Roman Empire.[17] Its stability and order assured social and civic security. The imperial household was the model on which smaller household units in Luke's day were structured, along clearly delineated lines

---

16. The chiasm literary structure thematically follows an A–B–C–B1–A1 layout, where C is the centrepiece surrounded or framed by A–A1 and B–B1. The legitimate recognition of chiasm in biblical literature in general, and Luke in particular, is argued by Augustine Stock, 'Chiastic Awareness and Education in Antiquity', *Biblical Theological Bulletin* 14 (1984), pp. 23-27; and John Breck, 'Biblical Chiasmus: Exploring Structure for Meaning', *BTB* 17 (1987), pp. 70-74. While I see the chiasm as a popular Lukan literary structure, I am also aware that it does not dominate the entire gospel. This is seen especially in the gospel journey narrative (chapters 9–19).

17. For a summary of the importance, function and nature of the household in the ancient world see Michael Trainor, *The Quest for Home: The Household in Mark's Community* (Collegeville, MN: Liturgical Press, 2001), pp. 15-68; and Santiago Guijarro, 'The Family in First-Century Galilee', in *Constructing Early Christian Families: Family as Social Reality and Metaphor* (ed. Halvor Moxnes; London: Routledge, 1997), pp. 42-65. A helpful summary of Second Testament period household archaeology is offered in Carolyn Osiek and David L. Balch, *Families in the New Testament World: Households and House Churches* (Louisville, KY: Westminster / John Knox Press, 1997), pp. 5-35, who study excavations in Palestine, Syria, Italy and Ephesus; also, Kathryn A. Kamp, 'Towards an Archaeology of Architecture: Clues from a Modern Syrian Village', *Journal of Anthropological Research* 49 (1993), pp. 293-318; S.M. Foster, 'Analysis of Spatial Patterns in Buildings (Access Analysis) as an Insight into the Social Structure: Examples from the Scottish Atlantic Iron Age', *Antiquity* 63 (1989), pp. 40-51. For the peasant domestic context in first century CE Galilee, see Horsley, *Archaeology*, pp.73-75.

of hierarchical, patriarchal and androcentric authority. This was Luke's world. In the gospel we shall see how these conventional lines of authority change and subtly destabilize. This is evident in Luke's story of Jesus and his concern about familial relationships, table hospitality, social structures and the emphasis on friendship that embraces all, especially those outside conventionally defined social groups.

Julia Kristeva on 'Text'

There is a final consideration about 'text' and its communal setting that I would like to explore from Julia Kristeva's work.

Kristeva recognizes that in the intentional engagement of a text by an interpreter, writer, community or audience two aspects must be taken into account that concern what she calls 'intertextual relations'.[18] She names these two aspects as the 'inner play' and 'outer play'.[19] The inner play is 'the web of relationships which produce the structure of the text (or subject).' The outer play is the 'web of relationships linking the text (subject) with other discourses.' Kristeva systematically develops both 'plays' in considering literature in general and 'text' in particular. They have implications for a broader appreciation of texts as auditory encounters in a social setting. Her definition of text further highlights the linguistic-auditory aspect of language upon which communication depends. We have already noted this in thinking about the setting and process of proclamation of Luke's gospel.[20]

Kristeva defines 'text' as a 'trans-linguistic apparatus that redistributes the order of language by relating communicative speech...to different kinds of anterior or synchronic utterances.'[21] This technical definition of 'text' offers key insights valuable for the ecological hermeneutic with which I intend to engage Luke's gospel. Kristeva does not believe that a text is static with its meaning immediately transparent and applicable to every culture, time and place. For her, a 'text' can only communicate across several social contexts and language situations because of certain malleability in the text's meaning. This is what makes a text a 'trans-linguistic apparatus'. But 'text' can only communicate by linking past meanings to the present. These past

---

18. Shuli Barzilai, 'Borders of Language: Kristeva's Critique of Lacan', *Publications of the Modern Language Association of America* 106 (March 1991), pp. 294-305 (297).

19. These are terms which Barzilai explains in her essay drawing on Kristeva's intertextual approach ('Borders', p. 297).

20. See Julia Kristeva, *Desire in Language: A Semiotic Approach to Literature and Art* (ed. L. S. Roudiez; New York: Columbia University Press, 1980); Julia Kristeva, *Revolution in Poetic Language* (New York: Columbia University Press, 1984). For a reproduction of the theoretical chapters of *Revolution*, see Toril Moi (ed.), *The Kristeva Reader* (Oxford: Basil Blackwell Ltd, 1986), pp. 89-136.

21. Kristeva, *Desire*, p. 36.

meanings of the text are the 'anterior utterances.' They are the meanings that have been attributed or assigned to a text in history and preceded this present moment of textual or verbal expression in the text's 'redistribution'. Kristeva also affirms that a text can only be understood and communicated in the present through the interpreting subject who gathers meaning together (what Kristeva calls 'synchronic utterances') to make sense of a text in a socially constructed present.[22] This 'interpreting subject' is the evangelist, the 'minister of the word' in Lk. 1.2, and the gospel's auditors.

The Subject as Interpreter

It is obvious that no meaning or interpretation of a text can exist without an interpreter. There is always the subject, the 'I' (in our contemporary setting) or the 'we' (in Luke's world). We who hear the text use interpretative strategies to unfold the text's meaning which, as we have seen through Kristeva's definition of 'text', is socially constructed, not frozen in time. The truth is truth for the 'subject' or 'subjects' who belong to a listening household engaged in dialogue with the text, its author, the authorial community and world. From this point of view, truth is subjective and relative to the listening context.[23]

---

22. Kristeva explores the process of arriving at meaning, which she names as "the signifying process." The process consists of an identification of the deep structures of language that are historical, semantic, logical and inter-communicational, and opened to other social and philosophical categories (*Revolution*, pp. 90-93). She also identifies the cross-roads at which the theory of meaning has arrived and articulates two characteristic approaches. One is logical, mechanistic or mathematical. This approach, she assesses, formulates "models on the basis of a conception (already dated) of meaning as an act of a transcendental ego, cut off from its body, its unconscious and also its history" (Moi, *Kristeva*, p. 28). This approach to meaning divorced from the real, material and historical world of the text's subject is a notable gap. A second approach Kristeva gleans from her psychoanalytical work and reading of Freud. She recognizes that the speaking subject is divided between the conscious and unconscious and seeks to participate in the signifying process that is bio-physiological and influenced by social constraints and codes (Moi, *Kristeva*, pp. 28-31). Kristeva affirms that the discovery of meaning (called 'semiotics') is necessarily linked to the social, political and historical context of the interpreting subject. This connection 'rends and renews the social code' (Moi, *Kristeva*, p. 33).

23. On various perspectives on the importance and role of the reader who engages the biblical text, see Ingrid R. Kitzberger (ed.), *The Personal Voice in Biblical Interpretation*, (London: Routledge, 1999). See also the discussion about subjectivity in gospel reading in Dale C. Allison, *Jesus of Nazareth: Millenarian Prophet* (Minneapolis, MN: Fortress Press, 1998), pp. 34-37, and his response to John D. Crossan, *Who Killed Jesus? Exposing the roots of Anti-Semitism in the Gospel Story of the Death of Jesus* (San Francisco: HarperCollins, 1995). For a restatement of the need to honour the interpreting subject of a biblical text, especially in the development of a relevant biblical theology, see Virginia Wiles, 'On Transforming New Testament Theology: (Re)Claiming Subjectivity', in *Putting Body and*

In biblical studies, this appreciation coheres with reader-response criticism, socio-linguistics, cultural studies, and autobiographical criticism. These can be clustered under the general category of *personal voice criticism*.[24] They all recognize that the personal voice of the auditor is an essential and legitimate contributor to interpreting a text.[25] For the contemporary Jesus follower, the ecclesial community is the context in which the interpreter's personal voice is expressed. This context cautions against the personal voice of the interpreter overruling other ways the text can be heard authentically.[26] It relativizes the personal voice and guards against imperialistic or hegemonic presentations that exclude other voices or texts.

This means that as an interpreter and auditor of the biblical text I am not a mere passive receptor of its meaning. I come to its meaning through engaging it sympathetically. I recognize that the meaning I arrive at may not be the only meaning, but polyvalent, historically conditioned and limited. Future research on the text, and further cultural insights about the world from which the text comes, can open up other possible insights. Fresh or different questions that surface from life experience will also bring a different valid perspective to my hearing of these texts. As Kristeva suggests in her discussion on intertextuality, every discourse (whether vocal or written)

Soul Together: Essays in Honour of Robin Scroggs (ed. Virginia Wiles, Alexandra Brown and Graydon F. Snyder; Valley Forge, PA: Trinity Press International, 1997), pp. 311-35.

24. Kitzberger, *Personal Voice*, p. 4. For other essays that acknowledge the legitimacy of the personal stance or voice of the interpreter in biblical exegesis, see Janice C. Anderson and Jeffrey L. Staley, *Taking it Personally: Autobiographical Biblical Criticism* (Semeia, 72; Atlanta: Scholars Press, 1995).

25. See Fernando F. Segovia's journey of critique and divestiture of the sacred goal of historical criticism in 'My Personal Voice: The Making of a Postcolonial Critic', in *The Personal Voice in Biblical Interpretation*, (ed. Ingrid R. Kitzberger; London: Routledge, 1999), pp. 25-37; Fernando F. Segovia, 'The Text as Other: Towards a Hispanic American Hermeneutic', in *Text & Experience: Towards a Cultural Exegesis of the Bible* (ed. D. Smith-Christopher; Sheffield: Sheffield Academic Press, 1995), pp. 276-98. For Segovia's recognition of the importance of the personal voice in biblical interpretation see Fernando F. Segovia, 'Towards a Hermeneutics of the Diaspora: A Hermeneutics of Otherness and Engagement', in *Reading from this Place. Volume 1: Social Location and Biblical Interpretation in the United States* (ed. F.F. Segovia and M.A. Tolbert; Minneapolis, MN: Fortress, 1995), pp. 57-73; Fernando F. Segovia, 'Towards Intercultural Criticism: A Reading Strategy from the Diaspora', in *Reading from this Place. Volume 2: Social Location and Biblical Interpretation in Global Perspective* (ed. F.F. Segovia and M.A. Tolbert; Minneapolis, MN: Fortress Press, 1995), pp. 303-30.

26. Daniel Patte, 'The Guarded Personal Voice of a Male European American Biblical Scholar', in *The Personal Voice in Biblical Interpretation*, (ed. Ingrid R. Kitzberger; London: Routledge, 1999), pp. 12-23.

consists of 'an intersection of textual surfaces rather than a point (a fixed meaning).'[27]

Kristeva urges that a text is the fruit of *productivity*. As 'I', the text's interpreting subject, 'redistribute' language through an act of destructing and constructing, I come to a new meaning of the text. This results from my interpenetration ('permutation') of texts, of utterances, that influence each other.[28] My renewed appreciation of a text's meaning becomes a complex process in Kristeva's semiotic analysis; it is shaped by the text's position within the 'general text' of culture as I understand this. Textual meaning results from the symbiotic relationship between text, culture and interpreter. Each shapes and is shaped by the other. From this perspective, 'studying the text as intertextuality, considers [the text] as such with (the text of) society and history'.[29] From another angle, a text becomes 'a tissue of quotations drawn from innumerable centers of culture.'[30] One such centre is the subject who shapes the way the text has been considered in the past ('history') and in the present ('social') and makes the text the fruit of 'various cultural discourses' dependent on what 'I' as interpreting subject bring to that discourse.[31]

Summary and Approach

Let me summarize where we have come from so far, and the contribution which intertextuality makes to an ecological listening to Luke's gospel.

In the last chapter I offered a brief summary of Luke's gospel, its narrative framework and missionary interests. A study of the prologue allowed me to identify Luke's approach in writing a new gospel and the nature of the audience addressed. This introduced us to a brief consideration of the social groupings that constituted the gospel's addressees—and some consideration of their attitude to Earth and their environment.

More pertinently, in Chapter 1 I considered Luke's use of prior sources or 'texts' (written and personal) in this new formulation. I identified the explicit method that the evangelist employed in the writing of the gospel. Borrowing language from contemporary literary critics and a study of intertextuality, the focus of the present chapter, I see that the evangelist's

27. Kristeva, *Desire*, p. 65.
28. Kristeva, *Desire*, p. 36.
29. Kristeva, *Desire*, p. 37.
30. James W. Voelz, 'Multiple Signs, Levels of Meaning and Self as Text: Elements of Intertextuality', in *Intertextuality and the Bible* (Semeia 69/70; Atlanta: Scholars Press, 1995), pp. 149-64 (149), quoting Roland Barthes, *Image, Music, Text* (New York: Hill & Wang, 1977), p. 146.
31. Voelz, 'Multiple', p. 149, quoting Jonathan D. Culler, *On Deconstruction: Theory and Criticism after Structuralism* (Ithaca, NY: Cornell University Press, 1982), p. 149.

approach was essentially *intertextual*. The evangelist refashioned earlier texts (especially Mark, Q and the First Testament with its ecological tradition identified in the Introduction) to shape a new text, a gospel story, to address unforeseen and unpredictable pastoral circumstances facing the gospel's auditors. Luke's method parallels the approach which I shall employ.

This present chapter has presented a deeper exploration of 'text' recognizing that its meaning depends on the cultural setting. A study of intertextuality, the implications of Eliot's affirmation of his poetic ancestors who 'continue to assert their immortality most vigorously', and Kristeva's recognition of the social-cultural-historical relationship which texts have in a symbiotic relationship with an interpreting subject—all these aspects further affirm the approach I take to Luke's gospel in bringing a contemporary 'cultural discourse' concerned about the ecological world.[32] Luke's first century approach and the practice of those today who explore intertextuality legitimate the intertextual dialogue I envisage (Figure 11).

Applying the intertextual approach explicated in this chapter (Figure 11), I consider two worlds as 'texts': the world of Luke's gospel, and the 'cultural text' of my present experience. To these central texts I bring others: the biblical tradition that Luke absorbed in constructing the gospel; previous narratives about Jesus; the eye-witness memories of those who became 'servants of the word'; the theological appreciation of the world and its environment; Earth's story that the gospel writer inherited from the Hebrew Scriptures; the cultural world presumed by Luke; and the social values and culturally delineated interactions of the gospel's addressees. These are filtered and absorbed by the evangelist and appear in the gospel narrative. These texts together represent Kristeva's 'anterior utterances.' Their study through a closer reading of Luke's gospel represents Kristeva's 'inner play'. They allow for the second movement in this intertextual dialogue, as 'I', the interpreting subject, link these anterior utterances to the 'text' of my world, with its specific cultural and unique environmental focus.

As I engage Luke's gospel in an authentic legitimated intertextual dialogue I read the story of Jesus and listen for its ecological sounds. What I listen for is the text's 'outer play'. While such an intertextual approach is not unique amongst biblical scholars, attending to Luke's story by listening for its ecological tones in the light of present concerns is.[33] It is here, in this

---

32. See George Aichele and Gary Allen Phillips, 'Introduction: Exegesis, Eisegesis, and Intergesis', in *Intertextuality and the Bible* (Semeia 69/70; Atlanta: Scholars Press, 1995), pp. 8-9; and Timothy K. Beal, 'Ideology and Intertextuality: Surplus of Meaning and Controlling the Means of Production', in *Reading Between Texts: Intertextuality and the Hebrew Bible* (ed. D.N. Fewell; Louisville, KY: Westminster/John Knox Press, 1992), pp. 27-40.

33. The intertextual approach that I draw on here has been employed in different ways by other, mainly feminist, scholars, either implicitly or explicitly. They have developed

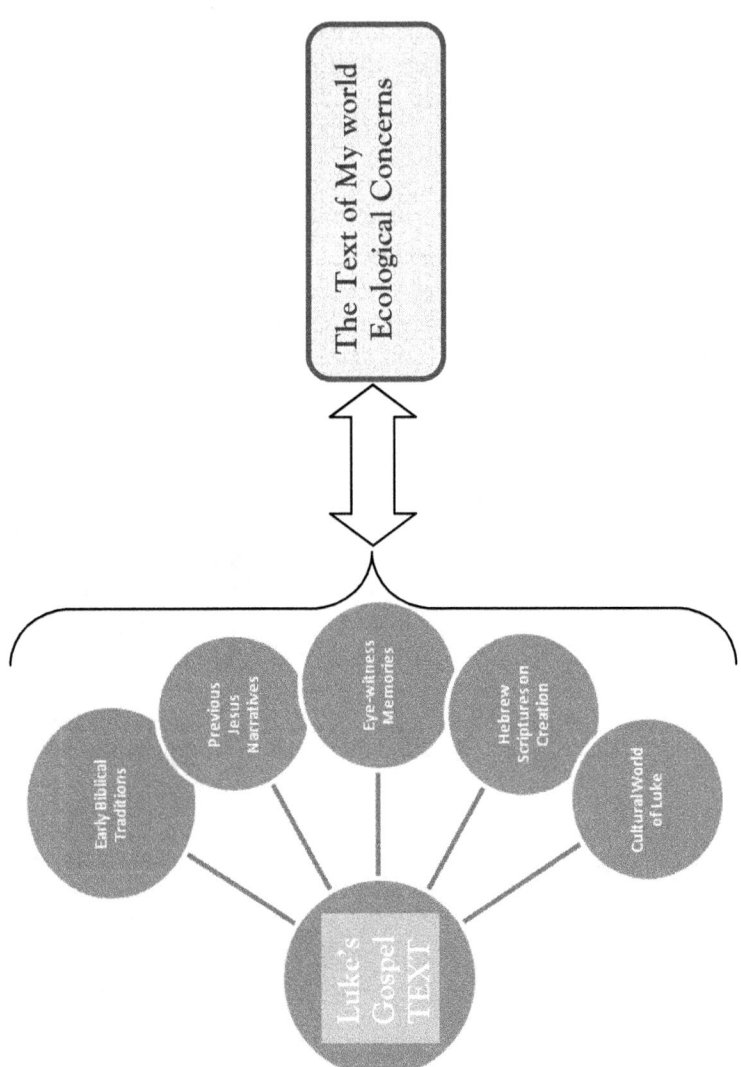

Figure 11. *The intertextual approach for an ecological listening to Luke's gospel.*

engagement with a multiplicity of texts, as I bring my texts to Luke's, that I encounter, in classic theological language, the 'Word of God'.

Luke's Gospel as 'Word of God'

Luke's gospel is not God's word literally understood. This is especially so given the limited cultural and environmental perspectives of Luke and the gospel's audience. Otherwise, the attitude that biblical authors express about creation could be interpreted by some as God's definitive word about creation. The introductory chapter has highlighted the limitations of this approach. What I am interested in is recovering how Luke's gospel and its Earth story might be God's Word in another sense.

This sense is helped by considering 'Word' as a root metaphor essential for human conduct that points to reality inaccessible to ordinary human experience.[34] This concerns the experience of the transcendent, of God. Language about the transcendent can only occur through our limited experience mediated by the created world around us; Earth mediates God's word. For this reason, it is important to listen to Earth's voice which can communicate the 'Word of God' and affirm for us the conviction that God desires communion with human beings and non-human creation.

This divine self-communication, spoken of in theological terms as revelation, allows us to encounter God and to know, at the core of our being and in creation, of God's desire for intimacy and communion with us and creation. In this sense, God's 'Word', is a *root* metaphor and the most essential basis for religious experience and encountering our world. Without this 'word', God would be anonymous and silent. We would be locked in a meaningless universe in which creation is a utilitarian commodity for human

---

a feminist hermeneutic to enable marginalized and oppressed auditors to engage biblical texts that are essentially androcentric and patriarchal. Ground breaking in this has been Elisabeth Schüssler Fiorenza, *In Memory of Her: A Feminist Theological Reconstruction of Christian Origins* (New York: Crossroad, 1983). Of particular interest to me is the work of the Australian scholar Elaine Wainwright, who explores the poetics, rhetorics and politics of engendered reading to interpret a gospel for women and men readers today. She also adopts an explicitly inter-textual and intra-textual approach in interpreting sections of Matthew's Gospel. See Wainwright, *Shall we Look for Another?* pp. 9-32. For a study of the influence of society and culture in shaping the meaning of language see Michael Alexander Kirkwood Halliday, *Language as Social Semiotic: The Social Interpretation of Language and Meaning* (London: Edward Arnold, 1978). The cultural and social contexts as influential in arriving at biblical meaning are also explored in Daniel L. Smith-Christopher (ed.), *Text and Experience: Cultural Exegesis of the Bible* (Sheffield: Sheffield Academic Press, 1995), and Paul R. House, *Beyond Form Criticism: Essays in Old Testament Literary Criticism* (Winona Lake, IN: Eisenbrauns, 1992).

34. Sandra Schneiders, *Beyond Patching: Faith and Feminism in the Catholic Church* (New York: Paulist Press, 1991).

abuse or consumption. We would ultimately resign ourselves to a form of existential silence in which we would not be able to communicate beyond that which we experience in the present or appreciate the beauty of creation.

To speak of Luke's gospel as God's Word is to recognize it, like all modalities of communication, as symbolic. And like all symbols, always open for misunderstanding and in need of constant interpretation and reinterpretation. It is this need that confirms the present quest to consider the gospel from an ecological point of view and draw out contemporary implications. Without pre-empting what Luke's gospel will reveal in the pages that follow, a fresh listening for the ecological notes in the gospel will remind us that the gospel's symbols can never be eternally defined. I shall be looking for how an ecological openness to the gospel will critique an anthropocentrism that excludes God's communion with creation and allows Earth's story to be heard. What we shall discover is that God's word expressed in Luke's gospel is addressed to all creation—human and non-human. This has moral consequences for auditors who seek to belong to a Jesus household whose members are also human and non-human.

The declaration that Luke's gospel is the 'Word of God' is a conviction that it has something to communicate about Jesus, the true Word of God, which is eternally significant. Jesus is God's word addressed to human and non-human beings; it is also a word addressed to all of creation. I described earlier that Luke's gospel is theocentric and christocentric. As the Word of God it speaks about God's self-revelation revealed in creation and humanity. How this occurs in Luke remains to be explored.

Sandra Schneiders names this encounter with God's self-revelation, the Word of God, very clearly when she writes:

> 'Word of God'...is a metaphor for the totality of divine revelation, especially as it is expressed in Jesus. The Bible is a witness to the human experience of divine revelation. In other words, it is a limited, biased, human testimony to a limited experience of God's self-gift. The Bible is not divine revelation nor does it contain divine revelation. It contains the necessarily inadequate, sometimes even erroneous, verbal expression of the experience of divine revelation of those who are privileged subjects of that gift of God...The Bible is literally the word of human beings about their experience of God.[35]

From an ecological perspective, the biblical word also points to the divine word echoing in creation. As we shall see, Luke has a particular angle on this. We shall see that its implications for contemporary Jesus householders will be challenging, affirming and spiritually invigorating.

In conclusion, let me outline the intertextual approach in which I shall engage as I seek to listen for the ecological sounds in Luke's symphonic gospel (Figure 12). The approach is made up of four dimensions that see-

---

35. Schneiders, *Beyond*, p. 50.

2. *Intertextual Engagement in Luke's Gospel*   59

saw between themselves, engaging with different 'texts' in a reading-listening dynamic.

1. I shall read Luke's gospel closely, looking for the 'inner play' of the text, its structural and thematic features that will help delineate the structural composition of the gospel and points of focus. But I suggest this inner play with a word of caution. I am aware that the identification of the gospel's inner play is *my* construction. It may or may not reveal the author's original intention, though I hope it would help to accentuate key themes and interests that are authentic to the Lukan author. In this respect I find the comment Elizabeth Struthers Malbon offers in her discussion on the construction of an outline for Mark's gospel pertinent to my effort here:

   > In my view, it is not necessarily Mark's Gospel that *has* an outline, certainly not a single, simple outline; it is Markan interpreters who *offer* multiple outlines as they pick up different threads of the interwoven tapestry or listen to different strains of the fugue that is Mark's Gospel. Making an outline of a narrative is a heuristic task—first for the maker herself or himself and then for anyone else who reads it; a thoughtfully constructed outline can

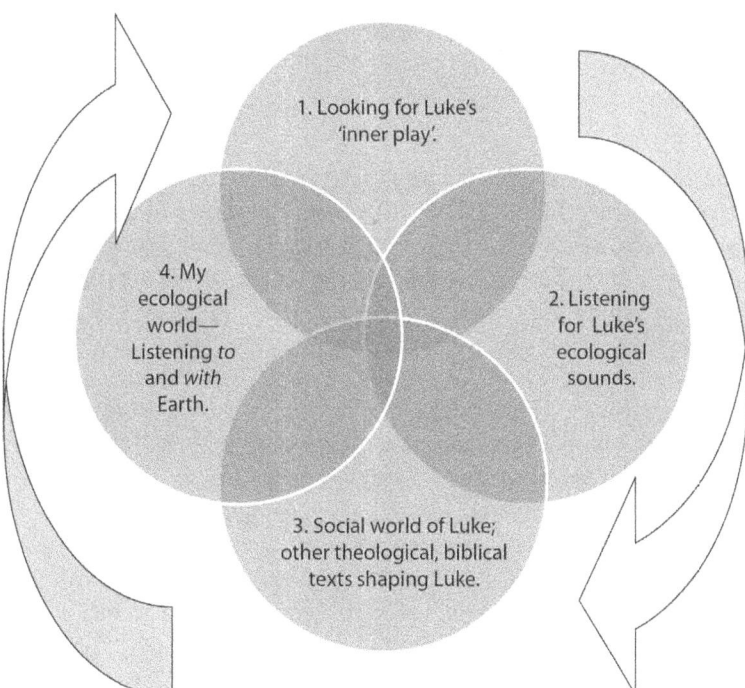

Figure 12. *The four dimensions of the intertextual approach for engaging Luke's gospel.*

    help interpreters appreciate various dimensions of the narrative and its interpretation. Yet the goal of the procedure is to reveal something about the narrative even as it reveals something about the interpreter of the narrative.[36]

2. After I read the text in each section I shall listen for the ecological sounds that emerge from the story and characters of Luke's narrative symphony. My focus here is to summarize some of the key elements of the narrative as I understand them, and see how these interact with or are interpreted by the ecological or environmental elements that I identify.
3. The identification of Earth in Luke's story will be determined by several 'intertexts' that I bring to this engagement. Two of them will be what I have called earlier, the world *of* the text and the world *behind* the text (Figure 1). These include theological, biblical and gospel traditions that pre-date Luke's composition, and the cultural, social and ecological script or text that the evangelist and gospel audience presume. Here I draw on the insights of Lukan commentators, other biblical scholars and social anthropologists.
4. There is a final intertext necessary for the attentive listening to Luke's story. This intertext is the one that I bring myself as interpreter with my ecological concerns. The engagement that results will allow me to offer hermeneutical insights from the gospel into the present and draw out its implications for contemporary Jesus followers. These will be summarized in a final chapter.

Let me clarify further this final and important intertextual step that I take as a contemporary auditor of Luke's gospel. The writer of the third gospel was not an ecologist. However as I listen to Luke's narrative symphony it is legitimate for me to hear ecological tones in the gospel perhaps either muted or not intended by the evangelist. These tones are suggested by my present stance context. What I hear is formed by the world and ecological context that I bring to this fresh encounter with Luke's gospel. In this engagement a fresh *word* arises that is legitimate for me and the interpreting community that hears the gospel. This dynamic undergirds my interpretation of the gospel and fresh listening that I seek to identify in Part II. It is presumed, though it may not be explicitly stated in every chapter.

As mentioned in the introductory chapter with an accompanying cautionary note, I shall conclude each chapter of Part II with *Earth's Voice*. This is my attempt to allow Earth's voice to speak to me, a member

---

36. Elizabeth Struthers Malbon, *Mark's Jesus: Characterization as Narrative Christology* (Waco, TX: Baylor University Press, 2009), p. 27. Emphasis original.

of its household. Even as early as the fifth century CE, Christian writers acknowledged the importance of listening to this voice. Pope Leo the Great (391/400–461 CE), for example, celebrated Earth's voice to instruct human beings:

> Earth is always filled with the mercy of the Lord. For every one of us Christians nature is full of instruction that we should worship God. The heavens and Earth, the sea and all within them, proclaim the goodness and the almighty power of their maker.[37]

If I identify *with* Earth and listen *to* Earth, what do I hear?

---

37. Pope St Leo the Great, *Sermon 6 on Lent*, in *The Divine Office: The Liturgy of the Hours According to the Roman Rite*, volume II (London: Collins, 1974), p.13.

Part II

Chapter 3

LUKE 1.1–2.52

JESUS—EARTH'S CHILD

As noted in Chapter 1, Luke's gospel begins with a prologue (1.1-4) and introduces us to the evangelist's explicit audience, aim and method in writing a new gospel. We also saw in Chapter 2 that Luke's method was intertextual, relying upon and adapting earlier witnesses and literary and theological traditions, including the First Testament. These were Luke's 'intertexts'.

'…brought to fruition among us' (1.1b)

In the gospel's opening verse Luke builds upon a narrative that has already been composed (1.1a, *anataxasthai diēgēsin*), which has 'been brought to fruition among us' (1.1b). This narrative is the story of God revealed among the Israelites and Jesus and now communicated by those who were first eyewitnesses and then became ministers of the word for the Lukan household. A foundational 'narrative', one of Luke's intertexts, is Earth's story. This story is an ecological *metanarrative* of God's communion with creation; it is one to which the evangelist will return frequently. Luke receives this eco-metanarrative from two sources: the written traditions found in other gospels and particularly the First Testament, and from those who have been personal observers of the ministry of Jesus and his teaching about creation. These are Luke's 'ministers of the word' who communicate, amongst many other stories and traditions, God's story of Earth's household to Luke. Clearly, Luke is dissatisfied with earlier efforts to narrate this story, other stories linked to the First Testament, and the story of Jesus, otherwise there would be no reason for this new composition.[1]

The evangelist affirms that this story of divine Earth-inclusive communion has 'been brought to fruition (*plērophoreō*) among us' (1.1b). The word that I have translated here as 'brought to fruition' is regularly translated as 'fulfilled' (NRSV). The meaning of this second translation is

1. Johnson, *Luke*, pp. 29-30.

that God's actions announced and revealed in the First Testament have their completion or fulfilment in Luke's present. Luke's statement of 1.1b also affirms that what is happening in the present is indeed God's act (the divine passive of the original Greek verb underscores this); but is also a story that is ecologically sensitive and inclusive. God's action is essentially 'fruit bearing' within the Lukan household ('us'). This household is being 'filled' by God. In this sense, God's story that Luke has received from textual and personal sources is 'full filled'; it is *fully filling* Luke's gospel household. And, as we shall see in our consideration of Luke's story of Jesus' birth, God is also *fully filling* Earth's household.

This divine Earth centredness is further confirmed in the prologue by the link that Philo and Rabbinic traditions make between the verbal root of *plērophoreō* (*pleorō*) and God's 'filling' activity in creation.[2] God's action is neither anthropologically driven nor cosmologically exclusive. It embraces the all Earth's human and non-human members. God's accomplishment in Luke's world and the Earth household, what is 'bearing fruit,' reflects God's story in creation, Israel and Jesus. This creation connected story of God's intimacy is also being 'filled' in Luke's own day among gospel auditors. They are now being 'fully filled' with the cosmological implications of God's creative action revealed in Jesus.

As we also saw from the earlier consideration of the prologue, Luke intends to write a new account of God's story for Theophilus. This new narrative emerges from Luke's scrutiny of what has been received. As stated in the prologue, the evangelist writes 'having followed everything closely from the very beginning' (1.3). The language here is deliberate and intriguing. In what sense do we hear 'the beginning'? Is Luke's scrutiny on 'the beginning' about the foundational narrative that gave birth to Luke's household, the story of Jesus and his ministry (the gospel) and continued in the life of subsequent generations of Jesus followers (Acts)? Is 'the beginning' the first stories about Israel's formation in the Abrahamic and Exodus traditions? Is 'the beginning' the real beginning found in God's first act of creative love in the stories of creation as encapsulated in Genesis? It is all these. Commentators have focused on the first two, though mainly the second.[3] But the third, the beginning linked to creation, seems unrecognized. I suggest it must be

---

2. The cosmological sense of the root verb *pleorō* in *plērophoreō* occurs approximately 70 times in the LXX. Its literal use frequently refers to Earth elements (filling with drink, water, sacrifice, moon). In Jer. 23.24 God 'fills' heaven and Earth. God is conjoined to creation and upholds creation. Philo continues this understanding of God filling all things; God is distinct from Earth, yet omnipresent. The rabbinic tradition continues to see God's glory 'filling' all creation by God's grace. (Gerhard Delling, 'πληρόω', *TDNT*, VI [ed. Gerhard Kittel and Gerhard Friedrich; Grand Rapids, MI: Wm B. Eerdmans Publishing Co., 1964], pp. 286-311.)

3. Bovon, *Luke 1*, p. 22; Fitzmyer, *Luke I–IX*, p. 298.

present, for this is the real 'beginning'. Luke takes us back to this beginning in Jesus' genealogy (3.23-38). Located between his baptism (3.21-22) and encounter with Satan (4.1-13), the genealogy confirms his ecological and earthly identity established in creation. Jesus is explicitly linked to Adam (1.38c), that creature of Earth (*adamah*) and offspring of God (1.38d).

The prologue establishes the Lukan strategy in what is about to unfold in the gospel. It is prefigured by those intertexts that affirm that God's action of salvation and liberation, acting in the story of Israel, revealed in the First Testament, and the story of Jesus, witnessed to and spoken about by human beings. But this story is also the story of Earth. God is bound up in Earth's story 'from the beginning' and will continue to be so in Luke's own day. This story will also unfold now as Luke begins to tell it freshly, of God's creative involvement through the ministry of Jesus, beginning with his birth, the focus of 1.5–2.52.

The Birth Stories (1.5–2.52)

As is well known, Luke structures the birth narrative of Jesus around a contrasting and explicitly parallel account of the birth of John the Baptizer (Figure 13). The story of John prepares for and contrasts with that of Jesus. Involved in the literary and narrative construction of these parallels are those to whom the birth of each child is announced (Zechariah in 1.5-25 and Mary in 1.26-38), the meeting of the two mothers (Elizabeth and Mary in 1.39-56), the birth of John (1.57-79) and Jesus (2.1-20) and their aftermath (1.80; 2.21-39). Two notes about the growth of Jesus and his maturation in wisdom (2.40, 52) frame a story of his presence in the Jerusalem temple (2.41-51). The temple account completes this section of Luke's gospel and leads to John the Baptizer's ministry (3.1-20). This prepares for Jesus' public ministry (3.21–4.30) and the continuity of the gospel as Luke picks up where the Markan gospel tradition also begins.

The literary design and thematic emphasis that Luke gives to the events that surround Jesus, his birth, its aftermath and the temple scene underscore the evangelist's primary focus: the introduction of Jesus to Luke's audience as God's intimate holy presence to humanity and creation. The apparent literary complexity of the gospel's opening chapters, the *inner play*, belies a simpler configuration (Figure 13). This centres on the meeting of two pregnant women, Elizabeth and Mary (1.39-56). Around this scene is a balanced harmony of other parallel narratives about Jesus and John that prepare for and lead away from it. The gospel's opening chapters begin in the temple of Solomon and conclude with a number of events located in the temple. The temple offers an overarching thematic perspective that attunes us to ecological and creation oriented motifs that will unfold. Green remarks in reference to these opening chapters, that the focal point is

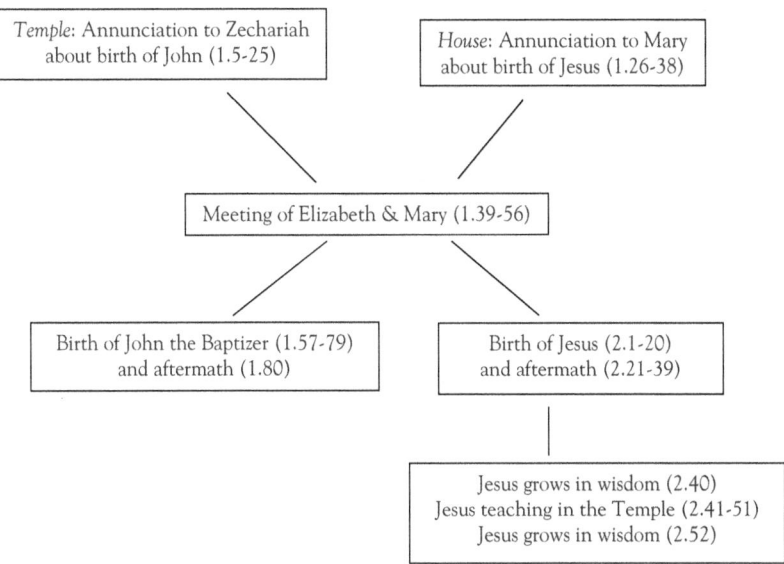

Figure 13. *The inner play of Lk. 1.5–2.52.*

the centrality of the Jerusalem temple. This is indicated above all by…the fact that approximately 40 per cent of the story itself is set within the walls of the temple. Here the temple's function as a 'cultural centre'—the divinely legitimated, sacred point around which life is oriented and from which emanates the contours of the social dynamics with which life in this world is occupied—has already begun to be clarified.[4]

The whole section offers an overture to the rest of the gospel, an opening movement in the gospel's symphony. Themes announced here continue throughout Luke's narrative. One of them concerns the relationship which the child-to-be-born has to Earth. As I hear these opening chapters of the gospel, this relationship will continue to be celebrated in the subsequent ministry of Jesus as it unfolds through the rest of Luke's gospel. How Luke establishes this christological portrait is the focus of the present chapter.

The shape of this section, the *inner play*, reveals something important. So often the focus of interpretation is about the call of Mary, the birth of Jesus and his identity revealed in the angelic annunciation. This is appropriate given the christological concern of the gospel's author to reveal Jesus to Lukan householders to offer them 'assurance' (1.4) in their present. But listening to the story from another perspective, ecological sounds pervade the narrative. Some of these are alluded to, others are clear.

The story is essentially about barrenness and virginity, fertility and pregnancy, birth and afterbirth—literally and metaphorically, anthropologically

---

4. Green, *Luke*, p. 61. Emphasis original.

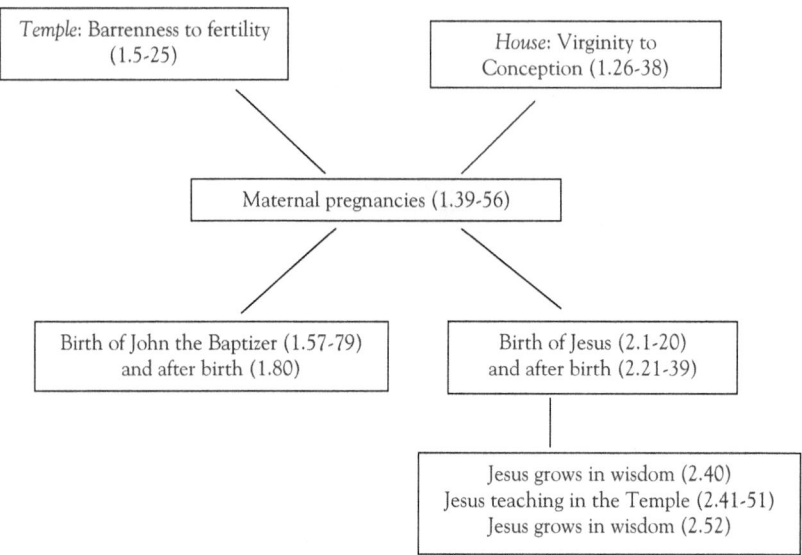

Figure 14. *The gestational allusions in Lk. 1.5–2.52.*

and ecologically (Figure 14). There is Earth rootedness in the narratives that need to be, literally, unearthed. In this perspective the literary structure and inner play appear differently nuanced with 'gestational' allusions.[5]

The gospel story begins under the rule of Herod as king of Judea with the introductions of Zechariah, village priest, and Elizabeth, descendent from the priestly tribe of Aaron. Their introduction, character descriptions ('righteous' and 'blameless', 1.6) and Zechariah's location in the inner temple sanctuary (1.9) links us to the piety and world of the First Testament. We are in a setting of holiness. This is God's world symbolized in the temple sanctuary, juxtaposed to the world constructed by Herod. We learn that both Zechariah and Elizabeth are childless (1.7). Elizabeth is 'sterile' (*steira*) and they are both aged. Barrenness and sterility permeate the scene.[6] These themes are anticipated by Herod's mention and the memory of his economic, political and religious program; they are palpably felt in the childlessness of this religiously pious priestly couple. Fruitlessness dominates; the scene's setting says something else.

Though no explicit mention is made of the temple or Jerusalem as the setting of this opening scene, it is assumed: a village priest chosen by lot to

---

5. I am grateful here and for what follows for the insights of Elvey, *Ecological*. Her work exposed me to a fresh view of Luke's infancy narrative that helped link me more coherently to the ecological allusions present in the birth ('gestational') paradigm present in the gospel. Elvey also gave me an insight into pregnancy, birth and its aftermath, currently beyond my (male) experience!

6. About barrenness, see Malina, *Social-Science*, p. 287.

offer incense at the altar of incense (1.9) and an assembly of people outside the sanctuary area, while Zechariah is inside, presumably in the area just before the Holy of Holies (1.10). The barren one, representative of family, kin and nation, is in the temple, the location of potential divine fruitfulness, though even this sacred building might be considered barren, too.

Herod's reconstruction of the temple came at the expense of a certain pillaging of Earth's gifts. Herod's temple is the quintessential setting of sacrifice and death of Earth's animals. From this perspective, the temple itself needs to be returned to innocence, where life can be celebrated and Earth's gifts restored. The ecological potential for the temple's restoration and earthly return richly symbolized in the earlier Solomonic structure into which Zechariah enters will be reflected upon shortly. But to return for a moment to Zechariah himself.

Zechariah's name in Hebrew means 'the Lord has remembered'.[7] In this setting, God will indeed remember. The presence of Zechariah in the temple's holy sanctuary is a symbolic reminder that the gospel begins with the memory of God, in the named 'Zechariah' as the God who *remembers*. This divine memory encompasses Earth's story, including Israel's. Another story is about to unfold in which the Lord will remember. This is the story of Jesus who will be the memory of God and bring people to remember God. They will re-*member* God and God will re-*member* them in Earth's household. This reconnection begins now.

There is something further about the site of this scene that links the opening of the gospel to the Earth story and to the eco-metanarrative. Zechariah is present in a place of ideal sacred memory that is also about remembering Earth. Though the Herodian temple can be seen as a negative ecological symbol, from another ideal perspective, and one that surrounds the scene with Zechariah, it is the nexus between heaven and Earth, God and humanity.[8] These links are symbolically established through the images of creation, flowers and fruits of the Earth that surround the temple beautified with cedar. Before its entrance is an altar, two large stands of light and a huge bronze basin of water that, as we shall see, recall the stories of creation and the exodus.

Solomon's Temple

Solomon sought to centralize all the smaller local post-nomadic temples of the Israelites in a magnificent temple, the 'first temple' in Jerusalem that he built in 957 BCE. It is in the postexilic temple, the 'second temple' rebuilt by Zerubbabel over the years 538 to 515 BCE and refashioned by Herod (c. 20

---

7. Fitzmyer, *Luke I–IX*, p. 322.
8. Green, *Luke*, p. 62.

CE), that Zechariah is depicted as now standing. By the time Luke writes it is destroyed but its memory, an intertext, lingers and will recur at key points in the gospel.

The structure and style of Solomon's first temple essentially continued through to the Herodian period though with a less than honourable intent from its second builder. 1 Kings 5–8 describes its layout and design.[9] Cedar covered its interior walls and floor (1 Kgs 6.14-18) with gold or ivory inlay. The cedar panels on the walls were decorated with artwork of plants, palm trees, open flowers and cherubim (1 Kgs 6.18, 29). The olivewood double door (later replaced by a curtain) leading to the holy of holies, the inner sanctum and holiest place of the temple, before which Zechariah is depicted as standing, were decorated with similar artwork. In the Holy of Holies were two huge cherubim fashioned from gold-trimmed olivewood with their wings touching the edges of the room and beneath them, the Ark of the Covenant. The Ark was reverenced as the very extension or material embodiment of God's presence and 'counterpart to the divine soul' (Num. 10.35-36; 1 Sam. 6.3-20).[10] It was the sacred navel, Earth's centre, the nexus between heaven and Earth. It was here that God's presence was tangibly encountered. Only the high priest could enter before this presence, and then only once a year on the Day of Atonement. The doors to the nave of the temple were decorated with creation inspired artwork similar to those at the entrance of the Holy of Holies and on the temple's panelling and floors. The inner court in front of the temple consisted of 'three courses of dressed stone to one course of cedar beams' (1 Kgs 6.36).

Solomon also had two great hollow bronze pillars cast and placed at the vestibule's entrance (1 Kgs 7.15, 19, 21; 2 Chron. 3.15). They may have been filled with fire to give off flames by night and smoke during the day—evocative of the Exodus story and God's accompaniment of the Israelites.[11] The biblical texts emphasize the pillars' size and their lily and pomegranate decoration (1 Kgs 7.15-22). In the southeast corner of the inner court stood a spectacularly large bronze circular basin topped with a lily-shaped brim and decorated with rows of fruits. It was supported by four groups of bronze bulls, each group of three facing the points of the compass (1 Kgs 7.23-26, 39, 44).[12] The basin held around 40,000 litres of water. This basin with its water

---

9. 2 Chron. 2–7 parallels the description of 1 Kgs. Ezek. 40–43 also offers a reference to the temple which, though future oriented, reflects authentic memory of Solomon's first temple. See William Franklin Stinespring, 'Temple, Jerusalem', in *IDB*, IV (ed. George A. Buttrick; Nashville, TN: Abingdon Press, 1962), pp. 534-60 (534), for this reference and what follows.

10. Gwynne Henton Davies, 'Ark of the Covenant', in *IDB*, I (ed. George A. Buttrick; Nashville, TN: Abingdon Press, 1962), pp. 222-26 (222).

11. Stinespring, 'Temple', p. 537.

12. Stinespring, 'Temple', p. 538.

was called the 'sea', and symbolized the cosmic primeval watery matter from which creation unfolded and life and fertility first came (Genesis 1).[13]

Solomon's temple was an ecological map of the universe, evocative of God's action revealed in the Genesis story of creation. Into this religiously symbolic womb Luke has Zechariah step before the presence of God. Barrenness and infertility are about to be reversed.

All these images that surround this opening scene of Luke's gospel and introduced by Zechariah's presence before the temple's altar of incense will echo several times throughout the gospel. Its memory will be recalled when Jesus enters the temple for the first time as a baby (2.22-38) and young lad (2.41-51), then later in his public ministry (19.45; 20.1) when he laments its destruction (21.5). The memory and symbolism of the temple will also be evoked when its curtain is torn at his death (23.45) and, as I shall suggest then, divine communion with creation is permanently restored.

Finally, the Solomonic temple with its rich creation-inspired fructive imagery linked to stories in Genesis and Exodus will be the definitive powerful symbol heard by Luke's auditors in the last verse of the gospel. On the day of Easter, after Jesus ascends to God, the disciples joyfully return to Jerusalem 'and were continually in the temple praising God' (24.53). The imagery of creation, Earth's story and fertility, what I have called the eco-metanarrative and now evoked by the temple, Luke's intertext, thus frames the whole of the gospel.

In this metaphorically fertile setting, a theologically symbolic womb, Zechariah encounters God's presence. His prayer is heard. We learn that the prayer is ultimately but unwittingly a prayer for fertility conceived in terms of national liberation that parallels the prayer of the people outside the sanctuary. But this liberation will begin through the birth of John (Hebrew, 'grace'), the explicit presence of God's grace breaking into the scene and now announced by the angel. This is the 'gospel', the 'good news' of God's intimate involvement in the cosmos, including human affairs.

Zechariah is made literally speechless about the possibility of his fertility and Elizabeth's pregnancy which belie the ultimate fruitfulness of God's presence within a story of creation and salvation about to unfold. Only later, when Zechariah engages the actual materiality of Earth and inscribes on a small wooden-based bees-waxed writing tablet (*pinakidion*, 1.63) and connects to his own adamic or Earth-bound relationship to God, is his speech restored.[14] Luke's introductory story ends with the note of Elizabeth's

---

13. Stinespring, 'Temple', p. 538.
14. Examples of ancient waxed writing tablets abound, archaeologically and in literature. See, for example, Homer, *Iliad* 6.168, 155-203; Herodotus 7.239; Dionysius of Halicarnassus, *On Literary Composition* 25; Pliny the Elder, *Natural History* 13.69. There is an image of a sixth-century BCE Greek vase painter, Douris, and his tablet writer with

pregnancy and her praise for God acting to release her from shame among humans (1.24-25).

Mary Encounters God (1.26-38)

Mary's initial encounter with God through her angelic visitor reveals a perplexed and struggling woman. The language which the evangelist uses of Mary to describe her initial meeting reveals her confusion over what comes to her through the angel's greeting. She was,

> deeply disturbed/confused (*dietrassomai*) by his words and wondered/dialogued about (*dielogizomai*) what sort of greeting this might be… (1.29).

The awkwardness of the English translation here communicates two rich Greek verbs, *dietrassomai* and *dielogizomai*. Taken together they express Mary's interior dialogue with a perplexing human impossibility happening in and around her. Luke's imperfect verbal use *dielogizomai* means that this an ongoing essential disposition in Mary and for the gospel's auditors as they, too, confront seemingly impossible situations and realities that affect themselves within Earth's household.

The angel's response to Mary's struggle reassures her as one graced by God. She will be the active agent of what will unfold. The angel tells Mary,

> '..you will conceive in the womb and give birth to a son and you will call his name Jesus' (1.31).

Then we are introduced to the qualities of the child-to-be-born. He will be from God, as 'son', will reign in the spirit of his ancestor David, 'will reign over the house of Jacob and his kingdom will have no end' (1.33). The regal nature of the child is emphasized in terms that echo the idyllic kingship of David over God's people. The First Testament interprets David's reign as one of peace and idyllic communion, though not without its difficulties.[15] We also learn how God's spirit will 'come upon' Mary and 'the power of the Highest One' (*hupsistos*) will 'overshadow' (*episkiatzo*) her (1.35).[16] Two features here are noteworthy.

---

stylus and folding wax board in Berlin's *Egyptian Museum and Papyrus collection*. See Jocelyn Penny Small, *Wax Tablets of the Mind: Cognitive Studies of Memory and Literacy in Classical Antiquity* (Abingdon, Oxford: Routledge, 1997), pp. 146, 150, 154. For the composition of the tablet, see Small, *Wax*, p. 297 n. 30.

15. For example, 2 Sam. 8.6, 14; 1 Kgs 2.33; 1 Chron. 11.14; Isa. 9.7.

16. For an overview of the narrative function and characterization of the spirit in Luke–Acts , see Ju Hur, *A Dynamic Reading of the Holy Spirit in Luke–Acts* (Sheffield: Sheffield Academic Press, 2001).

First, the association of God with the cosmic realm, as the 'Highest One', recurs through the gospel and at significant points in Acts.[17] It is a Lukan favourite in associating God with the cosmic abode and celestial regions within Earth's household, the household not made by 'human hands' (Acts 7.48). God's relationship is not determined by what humans do, think or construct. Luke's designation for God and for the divine dwelling place not of human construction is a reminder that this celestial divine being has a care for all creation that is not exclusively anthropocentric. Mary's child is the 'son of the *hupsistos*' (1.32b). He will share in this divine participation with creation in a ministry inclusive of all God's creatures.

Second, this relationship between a God inclusive of all creation and Jesus is confirmed in Luke's description of Mary being 'overshadowed' (*episkiatzo*). This will also happen to Jesus and his disciples on the mountain in their journey to Jerusalem as they, too, are 'overshadowed' (*episkiatzo*) by a cloud (9.34). The action of this physical, natural, meteorological phenomenon, the cloud, in the middle of the gospel echoes God's presence over Mary at the gospel's beginning. God's overshadowing deed is the reason that Mary's child will be called holy and 'Son of *hupsistos*' (1.35c). Luke's acknowledgment of the spirit's presence and action over Mary recalls God's same spirit in a similar action at the beginning of time, as it hovered over the primordial waters of creation (Gen. 1.2). For those in Luke's household who know the temple and its forecourt, the spirit's action over the primeval waters is also memorialized by the great bronze 'sea' basin. God's creation-oriented spirit now hovers over Mary. Jesus, like creation, will be the fruit of God's creative act.

Rhēma—God's 'Word-Event'

Luke builds upon this creation association by what the angel says further: Mary's pregnancy is God's work that will make her child holy, 'because every "word-event" (*rhēma*) is possible to God' (1.37). *Rhēma* is frequently translated here as 'thing' or 'word' as in the next verse where Mary responds to the angel,

> 'Behold the servant of the Lord. May it be done to me according to your word (*rhēma*)' (1.38).

Mary's response introduces us to an important Lukan term that echoes through the gospel; it has deep ecological resonances. This is the Greek word

---

17. Besides here at Lk. 1.35, *hupsistos* has already been used three verses earlier to refer to Jesus as 'Son of *hupsistos*' (1.32). It also occurs in Lk. 1.76; 6.35; 8.28; 19.38; Acts 7.48; 16.17. As a reference to the abode of God, it occurs in Lk. 2.14; 19.38. There are only four Second Testament instances of *hupsistos* as a reference to God or the divine abode outside of Luke–Acts.

rhēma. This term and its associate expression, *logos*, will recur frequently. Luke's Semitic intertextual appreciation of *rhēma* is better translated as 'word-deed.' This reflects more properly the ancient sense of the Hebrew *dabar*, God's word that speaks and brings about in material form what is spoken.[18] More is implied here than a simple philological nicety. How *rhēma* is used here and appreciated by Luke's audience will help foreground ecological insights later.[19]

Dabar/rhēma is essentially linked to Earth. This is confirmed in the Genesis story of creation (when God speaks, creation happens) and repeated in the words of God's prophets. Their prophetic action expresses God's *dabar*, word-event. They speak in what they enact, and they act in what they say. For Luke, the angel witnesses to Mary that what is about to happen is an act of God's *rhēma*, of word-event. God's announcement (the word) will be fruitful in the birth of her child (the event). Mary's gestation is God's word-deed, like the original divine act of creation in Genesis. The story concludes as Mary assents to God's *rhēma* acting in her. Thus, the eco-metanarrative continues to disclose itself in Mary's pregnancy.

The link to creation and Earth in Mary's pregnancy is also confirmed from another point of view. This comes from considering the ancient understanding of the pregnant body and its links to life-giving Earth.[20] Ancient Mediterranean understandings in agriculture and animal husbandry associated the pregnant body with its capacity to transform natural creation and mediate nature. In such a body God's spirit was felt to be deeply earthed and materially connected.[21] Pregnancy was not the product of male activity or ownership.[22] This is clearly the point that Luke expresses in attesting Mary's agency in the gestation and birth process (1.31). Further, 'the pregnant body', avers Elvey, 'reflects the state of divine-human relationship. It is a metaphor for the intimacy of divine concern for humankind, an assurance of divine faithfulness and power'.[23] It is the work of God's presence in creation through the enlivening, fruit-bearing spirit—allusions already prompted from the gospel's opening scene in the temple. Jesus, the fruit of Mary's pregnant womb, is linked through birth to the spirit and Earth, a connection we will explore later in this chapter as we ponder Luke's story of the child's

---

18. Albert Debrunner, 'ῥῆμα', *TDNT*, IV (ed. Gerhard Kittel and Gerhard Friedrich; Grand Rapids, MI: Wm B. Eerdmans Publishing Co., 1964), pp. 69-77 (75-76).

19. For more on Luke's use of the 'word' in *Acts* see Jerome Kodell, 'The Word of God Grew: The Ecclesial Tendency of *Logos* in Acts 1:7; 12:24; 19:20', *Biblica* 55 (1974), pp. 505-19.

20. For this and what follows, I am indebted to the insights of Elvey, *Ecological*, pp. 37-39.

21. Elvey, *Ecological*, pp. 82-83.

22. Elvey, *Ecological*, pp. 77-78.

23. Elvey, *Ecological*, p. 50.

birth (2.1-7). But this link is further reinforced in the household gathering of the two pregnant women in the Judean hills (1.39-56).

Two Pregnant Women Meet (1.39-56)

This setting is significant. The house in which the two women meet is identified as Zechariah's, recalling his earlier appearance in the temple and everything associated with it. The women meet in the 'hill country' and in a city of Judah (1.39). The hillside and city are not opposites but complementary sites of divine encounter. Earth's hills provide the means or pathway for communion between these two maternal figures and a luxuriant setting for what is about to unfold. Their meeting is replete with themes of joy, delight, divine blessing and fruitfulness associated with the womb mentioned three times in the scene (1.41, 42, 44). Mary is blessed by Elizabeth because of her belief 'that there would be a completion of what was spoken to her by the Lord' (1.45). She is blessed because of her commitment to God's action within her, reflecting God's *rhēma* within human history and Earth's community.

Mary's gestation is the fruit of the action of a God intimately concerned about creation and humanity. This is the real fruit of Mary's womb and for which Elizabeth blesses and praises God (1.41). It is not only for the presence of the child growing within her that Mary is blessed. Her womb is the tangible expression of God's presence and action, as the spirit shapes the materiality of her body in an act of creative love similar to God's deed in the Genesis story of creation. Mary is acclaimed for her conviction that God will continue to act this way until it is 'complete'. God's fulfilling and completing *rhēma* will unfold in the ministry of Jesus. It is celebrated in Luke's song placed on Mary's lips (1.46-55). This pulls together threads of the First Testament narrative remembering God's mercy revealed in Israel's story, where expectations are reversed. The story of creation is indirectly part of this narrative recall and the heritage of Israel's encounter with God's mercy.

The Birth of John the Baptizer (1.57-80)

At the end of her encounter with Elizabeth, Mary returns to *her own* home (1.56). This little detail reminds auditors that there is something subversive at work in the narrative. Mary should be returning to the house of *Joseph*, the conventionally expected owner of the house and with whom the household identifies.[24] Mary is presented by Luke as independent of such male reference and alliance. She is her own person. Luke then moves to the story of the birth of John the Baptizer (1.57-80).

---

24. Malina, *Social-Science*, pp. 289-90.

This narrative is a companion piece to the story that immediately follows, the birth of Jesus (2.1-21). The nativity of Elizabeth's child is a kinship and household event (1.58) surrounded by joy. Elizabeth names the child 'John' (1.60). When this is confirmed by Zechariah (1.63), he is able to speak and blesses the God who has enabled this miraculous event of fruitfulness to take place (1.64).

The song of Zechariah which follows (1.67-80) is a masterful tissue of First Testament allusions that emphasize God's salvific deeds of deliverance, visitation and redemption. For Luke, God's actions continue into the present and future. They will be revealed more tangibly in the ministry of Jesus. The song is initially concerned about recalling God's saving actions among the Israelite community demonstrated through David, the prophets and formalized initially in the covenant with Abraham (1.69-73). The middle section of the song (1.74-75) highlights the human benefits that come from God's action—deliverance from enemies, serving God without fear, holiness and righteousness; classical First Testament themes and desires that will be more firmly manifested in John's ministry.

Up to this point in the song, anthropocentrism seems evident. Zechariah rejoices in God's deliverance of human beings revealed in Israel's story and its ancestors. He affirms that what had been evident in the First Testament story of humanity and its relationship to God will find its expression in the story of John and the future ministry of Jesus. But it is in the song's final section (1.76-79), as it celebrates the child just born and discloses his ministry, that an ecological undercurrent surfaces. As Jesus is the 'son of *hupsistos*' (1.35c), John is 'prophet of *hupsistos*' (1.76b). John's identity first as 'prophet' and then as prophet of the 'Highest One' recall creation-cosmic and Earth-related associations found earlier in Luke's gospel.

The prophet is the authorized advocate and executioner of God's *dabar / rhēma*, that *word-deed* that enacts God's creative expression as found in the Book of Genesis. John will continue to remind people about this expansive God. Further, John belongs to the 'Highest One', the divine title that is reminiscent of God's ecological and creation orientated status in an Earth household not constructed by human beings. If there were some in John's future audience who thought that they were the exclusive recipients of God's merciful deeds, his ministry will prepare them for a God of largesse, inclusive of everything, human and non-human (1.76). This is what Luke calls the 'knowledge of salvation' and 'forgiveness of sins' (1.77). John will minister these divine gifts and they will be encountered through creation. This is the experience of light in the midst of darkness and death (1.79)—images drawn from the creation story in Genesis as God fashions light out of primordial darkness (Gen. 1.2-5).

Finally, Zechariah identifies John's definitive ministerial deed in the last words of the song. These encapsulate his vocation for the whole Earth community. He is called 'to guide our feet along the way (*hodos*) of peace (*eirēnē*)' (1.79). In other words, his ministry invites the human household ('us') on to a path ('way'— *hodos*) of ongoing conversion open to a divine intimacy that brings total restoration and restored communion ('peace'— *eirēnē*). Luke's word for journey (*hodos*) will occur several times throughout the gospel. Its first appearance here sets the tone for its subsequent use in the gospel's major section, the journey narrative (9.51–19.27). *Hodos* identifies the cosmological journey which the Jesus household must undertake. This is the journey of peace, by ending strife between warring people, overcoming social divisions that segregate, and orchestrating cosmic and universal peace. Towards this global and universal mission, ushered through John's ministry, the Jesus household journeys.

Luke finally locates John in the desert or wilderness (1.80), a homeless setting away from the urban centre of power and manipulation. This is the place of Earth, where potential communion with creation and non-human creatures can occur. John becomes the quintessential figure of humanity in communion with creation. This wilderness location will later become the place from which his ministry will begin as he calls all those familiar in Luke's household to conversion at all kinds of levels, not the least ecologically (3.1-20).

As we look back on Luke's first chapter, we encounter rural based characters associated with urban centres. Though Zechariah is in the most prominent urban centre of religious, economic and political power, he is a village priest. Elizabeth and Mary are rural-peasant characters, though they both live in what Luke calls 'cities' (1.26, 39).[25] By contrast, John lives in the wilderness away from urban power or association, though aligned in upbringing and social allegiance with the peasant world. All Luke's characters and their location become the means by which the gospel's auditors identify themselves in the story. They, too, are urban located but there are some more able to identify with the rural-peasant characterizations implicit in Luke's narrative. Their unstated identity with Earth emerges in the gestational and birth paradigms that permeate the chapter. This establishes the background for the birth of Jesus and, like John, his identification with nature, creation and the non-human world.

---

25. Although Luke describes Nazareth, the place where Zechariah's house is located, and Bethlehem as 'cities', the author uses terminology for village and city interchangeably—perhaps underscoring the urban setting of the gospel household with its close affiliation through some members with the peasant-rural world and their villages. 'City' occurs 164 times in the Second Testament; at least half of these are in Luke–Acts. On this point, see Oakman, 'Countryside', pp. 151-52.

The Birth of Jesus (2.1-20)

We know the story of Jesus' birth so well. It is a familiar story repeated each year at Christmas. We grew up with it and we repeat it to our children. Practically, though, many adults today only know the hybrid story—a combination of elements from Luke and Matthew, as Luke's shepherds and angels congregate with Matthew's magi around a stable filled with straw. All the attention of these gospel characters is transfixed on the child Jesus lying in a crib of straw with his adoring parents kneeling either side with hands joined in prayerful doting attention. This scenario gets repeated throughout the years supplemented by picture books and the crib scene in our local churches. As we extract Luke's characters from this scene and begin to listen for ecological sounds in the gospel, different and more helpful insights emerge for a world faced with potential environmental disaster.

Luke's story unfolds in the geo-political setting of Roman hegemony and imperial elitism. Mary and Joseph are forced by imperial decree and for economic reasons to travel from their rural village ('city') of Nazareth in southern Galilee to the *city* of David in Judea, Bethlehem (2.1-6). While they are in this city and the conventional setting of the urban elite, Mary gives birth to their son, 'wraps him bands of cloth' and lays him in a manger (2.7), important birth details to which I shall return shortly. An angel announces to shepherds in the countryside the birth of the child and reminds them of a 'sign' of 'a baby wrapped in bands of cloth and lying in a manger' (2.8-12). The announcement is accompanied by an angelic chorus singing a liturgical hymn celebrating God (2.13-14). The shepherds go to Bethlehem, see this *rhēma*—God's word-deed (2.15)—and find Mary and Joseph with 'the baby laid in the manger' (2.16). On seeing this sign, they repeat the *rhēma* about the child communicated to them by the angel (2.17). Everyone is in awe at the shepherd's words (2.18). Mary ponders them (2.19) and the shepherds return to their flocks glorifying God (2.20).

As we reflect on this story, I focus on three narrative details, the 'inn', the 'manger', and 'the bands of cloth' placed around the child.

The 'Inn'

Highly imaginative reasons have been offered for the location of Jesus' birth and his placement in the manger. However our imaginations have reconstructed the story to make an innkeeper a central figure, Luke's story mentions nothing about such a person. The emphasis is on 'place': 'there was no *place* for them in the guest house (*kataluma*)' (2.7). Interpreted against the social world familiar to Luke's auditors, it is all too clear: the guest house is under the control of the elite and is a *place* where peasants do not belong socially.[26] Luke's audience would be too familiar with this scene: peasant travellers journeying to a village or town for economic or political reasons. In the case of Mary and Joseph, Luke has them travel to Joseph's family city of Bethlehem to be counted in a census that would determine taxation imposed upon them by the imperial representatives. If kin lived in the town, and with Joseph this would be presumed, they would find welcome and accommodation. There would be no reason for them to stay at one of the traveller's caravansary strategically located on the major trade routes.[27] If family were living in the town then the public accommodation of kin arriving from elsewhere would be inconceivable. This would be *no place* for them to stay.[28]

Perhaps underlying Luke's recognition of the inn as an unsuitable place for the birth of the child is a subtle message addressed to the gospel's elite members. If it is subtle here, it becomes clearer as the gospel progresses. These powerful and wealthy members—absentee farm owners, claimants of debts and owners of urban dwellings rented to travelling peasants—will be invited to conversion. Luke's Jesus will ask them to renounce every one of their possessions, offer gracious and generous hospitality to all, irrespective of social standing, and to release the debts owed by poverty-ridden peasant farmers forced to come to the city. Mary and Joseph could well represent such people. Luke wants gospel addressees to move their gaze away from what is owned and controlled by the elite. This is the 'guest house' or 'inn' (*kataluma*). Their gaze is to be on the peasant household or farm. From this kind of dwelling the poorer members of the Lukan household come. From this place people are looked after and domestic animals housed and fed. This is also the place where the manger is located.[29]

The Manger

Luke refers to the manger three times (2.7, 12, 16) so it is not missed. Along with the twice-mentioned wrappings that surround the child (2.7, 12), it is

---

26. Malina, *Social-Science*, p. 297.

27. On the caravansary, see Robert Karris, 'The Gospel According to Luke', in *NJBC* (ed. Raymond E. Brown, *et al.*; London: Geoffrey Chapman, 1991), pp. 675-721 (683). On other possible meanings of Luke's guest house, see Raymond E. Brown, *The Birth of the Messiah: A Commentary on the Infancy Narratives in Matthew and Luke* (Garden City, NY: Doubleday, 1977), pp. 400-401.

28. 'The fact that Joseph comes to Bethlehem to be enrolled may imply that he had land (hence family) there, since the census or enrollment was for land taxation purposes. If so, he would have been obligated to stay with family, not in a commercial inn' (Malina, *Social-Science*, p. 297).

29. For more on the location of the manger in a peasant household, see Guijarro, 'The Family', pp. 42-65; Malina, *Social-Science*, p. 296.

an obvious narrative clue to which the auditor is invited to listen. These two clues, the manger and the wrapping cloths, resonate with surprising ecological sounds.

There are two insights that come from Luke's reference to the manger, one christological and the other ecological; both are linked. Christologically, the manger is a place of food, nurture and life. It prepares for a dominant theme in Luke–Acts. In Jesus' future public ministry, food, meals and the place of eating will play an important part. Ecologically, the manger affirms Jesus' connection to the land, the human community and non-human creatures. The manger is an important intertext for Luke. From Isa. 1.3 we learn that servile animals were intimately bonded or, literally, tied to it.[30]

The manger was also positioned relative to the sleeping quarters and domestic space of the peasant household, either at the entrance of the lower level of the one-room peasant dwelling or in a natural cave on which the house was built.[31] The specific location of the manger and the animals it fed connected the manger and its animals to the members of the peasant household. At a symbolic level the manger is, like the temple earlier, the nexus between the human and non-human world; it is a symbol of ecological communion. Into it the child is laid. His presence in this place binds him to the worlds with which the manger is associated. He becomes the locus of communion of these worlds and is at home with them. This imagery alludes to an important First Testament intertext from the prophet Jeremiah:

> O hope of Israel, its saviour in time of trouble, why should you be like a stranger in the land, like a traveller seeking lodgings for the night? (Jer. 14.8).

In Jer. 14.8 God is addressed as Israel's hope and saviour. According to the prophet, God seems like an alien or stranger amongst the very people that God has formed and looked after. God is like a stranger in the land and, as a travelling stranger, looks for accommodation in travellers' lodgings. In Luke, Jesus, God's agent and revealer, is not found in travellers' lodgings; the reason: Jesus is *not* an alien in the land. He belongs to Earth, is part of it; he is the fruit of divine activity in the maternal womb, the place where earthed-materiality and God's creatively active spirit combine. Jesus' placement in the manger testifies to this.

The christological aspect of the manger links Jesus to his future meal ministry of hospitality. Through this ministry Jesus welcomes the socially strange and isolated. The 'strange' also includes those aspects of creation

---

30. See Brown, *Birth*, p. 419, who also shows how the Isaiah text and its link between the manger and the domestic, servile animal is paralleled with a Midrash on Gen. 3.18, 'Shall I be tied to the manger to eat with my donkey…?'

31. S. Vernon Fawcett, 'Manger', *IDB*, III (ed. George Arthur Buttrick; Nashville, TN: Abingdon Press, 1962), p. 257.

that have become isolated from the human community. The manger is the place where the wider human world gathers, represented by the shepherds. It is also the place of receptivity and welcome for non-human creatures, for animals where food is placed.

The manger also acts in a similar fashion to Mary's womb.[32] It is the place of receptivity for the body of the child, from which growth, strength, security and mission will emerge and from where God's identity will be revealed. The manger is a sign that unequivocally points to Jesus' present and future identity: he is Earth-bound and cosmically connected; the fruit of human gestation from the maternal womb by God's quickening spirit. He is primarily a nurturer and identified with the place of sustenance for the wider non-human Earth household. Luke's association of Jesus with the manger attests to his future maternal ministry of nurture and inclusivity that embraces all creation and Earth's household. This embrace is further symbolized by Jesus' association with the 'womb-like' manger. The placement of the wrapped living child in the manger early in the gospel will have its counterpart in the deposition of the wrapped body of the dead Jesus in the tomb towards the gospel's end. Both the manger and the tomb are wombs from which, each in their own way, new life emerges.

'Wrapped in Bands of Cloth'

The second sign to which Luke points in the birth story is the wrapping of the child. It is referred to twice. In the first (2.7), Luke uses the active voice of the Greek verbal form for the act of 'wrapping' the child. It is that act that Mary does to the child. The focus is on Mary as she completes all that is traditionally associated with immediate after-birth care.

In Ezekiel the prophet speaks of God's maternal care of Jerusalem. God laments the lack of attention shown to Jerusalem. God, in the words of the prophet, speaks of this in terms of neglect shown to a child immediately after birth:

> As for your birth, on the day you were born your navel cord was not cut, nor were you washed with water to cleanse you, nor rubbed with salt, nor wrapped in cloths (Ezek. 16.4).

Ezekiel identifies the conventional post-natal practice for every newborn child in the ancient Mediterranean world. This was to have the umbilical cord cut and tied, and the child to be washed and rubbed with salt, and finally wrapped in bands of linen cloth.[33] These post-natal procedures would

---

32. Elvey, *Ecological*, p. 125.
33. David E. Garland, 'Swaddling', *ISBE*, IV (ed. Geoffrey W. Bromiley; Grand Rapids: Wm B. Eerdmans. 1995), p. 670.

have been well known to Luke and the gospel's auditors. They are summed up in the last act, the wrapping of the child in bands of cloth. All this suggests that Jesus would have been treated like any other new-born child. He is one with, not above or different to, other members of the *human* household.[34]

If the after-birth procedures involved a number of maternal acts, then Luke's focus on only one of them, the wrapping of the child, must be especially significant. While the evangelist's initial reason for naming this specific act may be considered part of the post-birth process, mention of Jesus' clothing recurs in other parts of the gospel: a haemorrhaging woman touches his clothing for healing (8.44); his clothing becomes luminescent in a moment of transfigured glory on a mountain with his disciples (9.29); Herod clothes him with 'transparent apparel' during his trial (23.11), a garment which Luke implies he retains for his death; after death, Joseph from Arimathea clothes the body of Jesus in a linen shroud (23.53) which Peter discovers in the tomb on the day of Jesus' resurrection (24.12).[35]

The nature of the linen or cloth material in which Jesus is wrapped at birth further confirms his communion with *Earth's* household. Unlike our synthetic clothes, clothing in the ancient world came from natural products, flax (from which linen was made), wool, silk, shell, cashmere, goat hair and cotton.[36] Clothing provided identity, warmth and, in the case of the

---

34. Elvey, *Ecological*, p. 124. For a study of Luke's Jesus as a 'human being', see Robert F. O'Toole, *Luke's Presentation of Jesus: A Christology* (Rome: Pontificio Istituto Biblico, 2008), pp. 7-28.

35. On the nature of linen and the shroud, see Raymond Brown, *The Death of the Messiah: From Gethsemane to the Grave: A Commentary on the Passion Narratives of the Four Gospels. Volume 2* (New York: Doubleday, 1994), pp. 1244-45; Raymond E. Brown, 'Brief Observations on the Shroud of Turin', *BTB* 14 (1984), pp. 145-48.

36. On the composition of the material of ancient fabrics, see Glennda Susan Marsh-Letts, 'Ancient Egyptian Linen: The Role of Natron and other Salts in the Preservation and Conservation of Archaeological Textiles—A Pilot Study', BA *(Hon) Thesis* (Sydney: University of Western Sydney, 2002); Eve Cockburn and Mary W. Ballard, 'Cotton in Ancient Egypt: A Unique Find', *Proceedings of the First World Congress on Mummy Studies, Puerto de la Cruz, Tenerife, Canary Islands, February 3-6, 1992* (Santa Cruz, Tenerife: Archeological Museum of Tenerife, 1996), pp. 625-31; Sheila Landi and Rosalind M. Hall, 'The discovery and conservation of an ancient Egyptian linen tunic', *Studies in Conservation* 24 (1979), pp. 141-52. On the use of silk and shell for material see Peter Sroka, 'Kostbare Faserstoffe aus der Antike: handelt es sich beim biblischen Byssus um Muschelseide?' ('Precious Fibre used in Antiquity: Is the Biblical Byssus Shell Silk?'), *Restauro: Zeitschrift für Kunsttechniken, Restaurierung und Museumsfragen* 101 (1995), pp. 338-42. On goat hair and cashmere, see Harald Böhmer and Recep Karadag, 'New dye research on Palmyra textiles', *Dyes in History and Archaeology: Papers Presented at the Annual Meetings of Dyes in History and Archaeology* 19 (2003), pp. 88-93.

newly born wrapped child, security.³⁷ The wrapping of Jesus at birth in 'bands of cloth' might well symbolize his being wrapped by Earth in natural linen. If this is the case, and it is certainly implied from what we know of birth and burial practices of the ancient world, then it underscores Luke's christology.³⁸ His cloth wrapping connects him to Earth as he is, at the same time, surrounded by Earth symbolized in the stone manger.³⁹ The double symbolic 'womb', the manger and the linen wrapping, is the sign to which Luke is keen to point gospel auditors.

The Nature of Jesus' Birth Cloths

The exact nature of the material in which Jesus is wrapped or clothed throughout the gospel remains unidentified—except in the final chapters, where it is explicitly linen (23.53; 24.12). In Luke's world, linen symbolized immortality.⁴⁰

Plutarch (46–120 CE), discussing the reason that the priests wore linen and not wool, reminds his readers that 'flax springs from Earth which is immortal; it yields edible seeds, and supplies a plain and cleanly clothing'.⁴¹ Linen was judged differently to wool, 'the hair of domestic animals' that perished and was mortal.⁴² For these reasons linen was considered the most appropriate clothing for priests and royals, and according to Ovid, anything made of animal skins and reminded worshippers of death was excluded from a temple.⁴³ Later, when discussing Luke 24, I shall explore the theological symbolism behind the linen garment in which Jesus is wrapped for burial and which is left in the tomb after his resurrection. The parallels between the placement and wrapping of Jesus' body at the beginning of the gospel, in the manger after his birth, and at the end of the gospel, after his death in the

---

37. Malina, *Social-Science*, pp. 296-97.

38. Linen is implied, not explicit. The only time the Greek word for 'linen' (*bússos*) is explicitly used is to describe the rich person in Jesus' story about the poor Lazarus in Luke's travel section of the gospel (16.19-31).

39. On the manger, Martin Hengel, 'φάτνη', TDNT, IX (ed. Gerhard Kittel and Gerhard Friedrich; Grand Rapids, MI: Wm B. Eerdmans Publishing Co., 1964), pp. 49-55. On its stone structure, see L.G. Herr, 'Stall', *ISBE*, IV (ed. Geoffrey W. Bromiley; Grand Rapids, MI: Wm B. Eerdmans Publishing Co., 1995), pp. 609-10. The only archaeological evidence of mangers from the period under consideration is stone. To my knowledge, no wooden mangers have been noted, though our creative and childhood imagination would like a wooden manger!

40. Johannes Quasten, 'A Pythagorean Idea in Jerome', *American Journal of Philology* 63 (1942), pp. 207-15.

41. Plutarch, *De Iside et Osiride* 4.

42. Ovid, 1. 629.

43. Ovid, 1. 629.

tomb, are very close.[44] Linen explicit in his burial can arguably be implicit in the birth narrative. If linen is the garment in which Jesus is wrapped at birth, this further corroborates his elevated status already confirmed by the angel to Mary. His eminence as God's representative and spirit's agent will unfold in the gospel's remaining chapters.

The second mention of the child being wrapped in bands of cloth is part of the sign which the angel points out to the shepherds (2.12). This second reference concerns what is *done* to Jesus. The use of the Greek verbal passive voice here suggests that this cloth wrapping is what God does to Jesus. This connects him spatially and theologically beyond the human household, to the heavens and cosmos, the home of Wisdom (Sophia). This same swaddling act happens to Solomon, Luke's presumed author of the Book of Wisdom and earthly representative of regal wisdom:

> ...I was nursed with care in swaddling clothes. For no king has had a different beginning of existence... (Wis. 7.4-5).

If this is one of Luke's intertexts, then the evangelist sees Jesus as a regal figure and the personification of Wisdom, prefigured in the Book of Wisdom and in the swaddling act done to him.

In summary, an ecological focus on this most beloved of Christmas stories takes us beyond a child-centred biblical literalism. The gospel offers a narrative that moves us into a depth of theological and christological appreciation that connects with Earth's household. Luke envisions a social harmony in the peasant world and Luke's urban audience brought about by the birth of Jesus. His birth outside the conventional place of hospitality run by the elite landlords emphasizes his connection with the land and its people. He finds a welcome among those who rely on Earth for sustenance: those in Luke's audience who would identify themselves as peasants. In other words, in Luke's story, Jesus is the child of a peasant-village couple, the victims of taxation and economic hardship from a system imposed by the urban elite. He finds hospitality and communion among those whose livelihood is connected to Earth's soil.

The evangelist also envisions that Jesus' birth and his presence will also bring about cosmic and environmental harmony. The images that surround Jesus' birth, especially the inn, manger and swaddling clothes, present an important ecological message: Jesus is Wisdom's heavenly-focused and Earth-centred child. In him divine communion with the whole of creation

---

44. Johnson, *Luke*, p. 53. J. Duncan M. Derrett, 'The Manger at Bethlehem: Light on St. Luke's Technique from Contemporary Jewish Religious Law', in *Studies in the New Testament, volume 2* (Leiden: E. J. Brill, 1978), pp. 39-47; J. Duncan M. Derrett, 'The Manger: Ritual Law and Soteriology', *Studies in the New Testament: Midrash in Action and as a Literary Device, volume 2* (Leiden: E.J. Brill, 1978), pp. 48-53.

and Earth household occurs and is identified. This idyllic communion connects to and is confirmed by the second part of Luke's birth story of Jesus (2.8-20), a scene filled with political, economic and ecological intrigue.

The Shepherds

Luke's story shifts to the countryside, to shepherds out on the rural landscape 'keeping watch over their flocks by night' (2.8). They, like Mary, experience an angelic announcer who declares to them a message of good news,

> [10]Do not fear; behold, I proclaim to you good news of great joy which is for all the people, [11]because there is born this day a saviour who is Christ the Lord in the city of David. [12]And this is a sign for you: You will find a baby wrapped in bands of cloth and lying in a manger. [13]And suddenly there was with the angel a great throng of the heavenly host praising God and singing:
>
>> [14]Glory
>> among the highest to God,
>> and upon Earth, peace
>> among human beings
>> of good will.' (2.10-14)[45]

The angelic message has five elements:

- it is a message of universal joy (2.10);
- the reason for the joy is the birth of the Saviour (2.11a);
- this Saviour is the awaited Messiah who is in the 'city' of David (2.11b);
- the sign of this urban, salvific figure is found in the 'baby wrapped in bands of cloth and lying in a manger' (2.12);
- because of this birth, glory redounds to God and peace will come upon Earth (2.14).

We have traditionally interpreted the shepherds as the 'first poor' to receive the good news of Jesus' birth and respond to it. They are instructed by the heavenly messenger about Jesus' birth and the signs that accompany it (the cloth wrapping and the manger) and they go to 'see this *rhēma* that has occurred' (2.15). Already the attentive auditor would hear the ecological tones present in the early part of the narrative repeated here (the bands of cloth, manger and *rhēma*). But from a level of social interaction reflective of the constituted social groups in Luke's audience more is implied in the shepherds' acquiescence.

The relationship between shepherds and peasant farmers was mixed. In some cases, in situations where land was precious and its fruitfulness limited,

---

45. The layout of v. 14 here reflects a discernible hymnic structure which we shall investigate in greater detail below.

the relationship would have been strained, if not violent. In other situations, where land was plentiful and its harvest bountiful, their relationship more accommodating. Sheep could easily graze on such lands without hindrance or competition. Both farmer and shepherd held the land with respect; for both it was a source of nurture, support and sustenance. But how one lived in symbiotic and open relationship to the other was determined by the availability of land, the fruitfulness of the soil and the communal-village spirit that shaped their interactions. The sheep of the shepherds produced a commodity needed for the village and peasant households.

From Israel's nomadic period onwards (twelfth century BCE) sheep were valuable for many reasons. They provided food (1 Sam. 14.32), milk (Isa. 7.21-22), wool for weaving (Lev. 13.47-48; Job 31.20; Ezek. 34.3), and tent covering (Exod. 26.4); facilitated economic reciprocity (2 Kgs 3.4; Ezek. 27.18-19) and were an important part of the religious sacrificial system (Exod. 20.24; Num. 22.40). In reality, sheep symbolized wealth, livelihood and security.[46] Given the generally affectionate, docile, unaggressive, and defenceless nature of sheep and the shepherd's attentive, caring relationship to them, 'it is not at all surprising that in figurative-theological language the sheep and shepherd are repeatedly, and often movingly, employed.'[47] Their appearance at this point in the Lukan narrative is not without significance.

Rather than being seen as 'sinners' or violent aggressors, disrespectful of the rights and properties of others, shepherds were representative of those in Luke's audience who were of lower social status. They were on a similar level to the peasant farmers or homeless urban peasants of the gospel household and could identify with the transient peasants represented in Mary and Joseph.[48] They represent the symbiotic and necessary dependent relationship between the human and creaturely world. This spirit of potential harmony for all creation becomes an overarching theme encapsulated in the birth of Jesus and sung in the angelic chorus (2.14). This contrasts sharply to Luke's world. The countryside was not a place of ideal tranquillity but rather disturbance and social upheaval. The resulting tension affected the relations between urban residents and country dwellers, a tension that Luke is keen to address within the gospel household.[49] It is against this background, the social reality of the addressees with its divisions and tensions, and the pastoral ideal represented in the sheep-shepherd relationship, that Luke's Christmas story is staged.

---

46. B. Davie Napier, 'Sheep', *IDB*, IV (ed. George Arthur Buttrick; Nashville, TN: Abingdon Press, 1962), pp. 315-16.

47. Napier, 'Sheep', p. 316.

48. In this description of shepherds I move away from my earlier social evaluation in Trainor, '"And on Earth, Peace..." (Luke 2.14)', p. 184. See Johnson, *Luke*, p. 52.

49. Oakman, 'Countryside', p. 171 discusses the social disorder in the countryside.

The Angelic Song (2.14)

The heavenly song which accompanies the birth of Jesus and the revelation to the shepherds also sounds ecological tones. Luke's angelic visitors announce that Jesus' birth will bring joy to all, not constrained by economic or social status and environmental locality. The birth will bring together the urban elite (it takes place in a 'city') and rural poor (the birth is in a manger associated with a peasant farming household) and landless (represented in the figures of Mary, Joseph and the shepherds). The birth will also bring together heaven and Earth. These two cosmological spheres, familiar to Luke's audience, will be totally affected by the birth of this Saviour. These two spheres do not remain separate from each other, but coalesce. This point is particularly emphasized in the angelic sung refrain of 2.14 reminiscent of liturgical hymns familiar in Luke's household.[50]

The structure of the refrain in the Greek text is carefully balanced (Figure 15).[51] Literally, it can be translated:

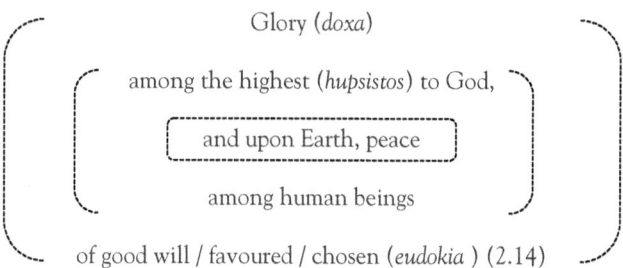

Figure 15. *The literary structure of Lk. 2.14.*

---

50. Otherwise, why do the angels 'sing' when a spoken chorus or refrain similar to the classical Greek plays and familiar to Luke's Greco-Roman audience would have served the same purpose? On the liturgical association of the heavenly refrain, see Bovon, *Luke 1*, p. 90.

51. Brown (*Birth*, pp. 404-405) presents the respective scholarly arguments for the hymn's structure as a bicolon (two-line structure) or tricolon (three-line). Good reasons are given for both. My proposal advances the tricolon proposal to a five-line structure. This places more weight on the first and last expressions that have 'glory' as their Greek root and the 'among' (*en*, in Greek) which marks off two key phrases—one referring to God, the other to human beings. The final and central element of the canticle's structure concerns Earth. Whatever structure is finally chosen, Brown's verdict that the structure is 'fiercely debated' (Brown, *Birth*, p. 426, n. 56) holds true! My point simply is that a five-line structure is defensible.

The structure of this liturgical heavenly song reflects Luke's theological cosmology.[52] It is a chiasmic structure focused on 'and upon Earth, peace'.[53] Leading to this is Luke's appreciation of the heavens, the uppermost level of the cosmos, the abode of God and the heavenly powers. This is the *hupsistos* that we have noted earlier. Beneath this abode is the realm of the spirits. It is God who dwells in the highest level of this cosmic hierarchy.[54]

Beneath the spirit world is the abode of human beings, and beneath them, the underworld. In the structure of the canticle, 'Earth' is located midpoint between the divine realm in the first part of the song and the abode of human beings in the final part. As the connecting sphere between the heavenly and human Earth is blessed with peace. Peace is 'upon' (*epi*) Earth. The whole unit is framed by the Greek terms that at their root refer to 'glory', 'splendour' or 'grandeur' (*doxa, eudokia*). The first refers to the praise or glory that is due to God. The second is the 'glory' or 'splendour' that comes to human beings from God's 'favour'.

Significantly, God's favour comes upon human beings through *Earth's* mediation. Earth reflects the relationship between humans and God, and carries the divine beneficence that comes down to human beings from God. The tangible arena for the reception of this divine blessing is 'Earth'. In other words, the hymn is not a celebration of an exclusive anthropologically centred act of divine graciousness. Rather, it celebrates the inclusivity of God's act for all of Earth's human and non-human participants. Earth, centrally located in Luke's chiasmic structure, is the medium through which God's divine blessing is communicated and experienced.

This theological truth literally 'grounds' the human household within Earth, not apart from it. The interconnection between the two is fundamental to the gospel story of Jesus. While his ministry is taken up with people's plight and their need for release and healing, this can only happen, according to the divine schema perceived in 2.14, because of the human bond to Earth. Jesus' healing and ministry amongst human beings is also a ministry with Earth. In his baptism (3.22), Luke will present Jesus specifically as *eudokia*, declared by God as the 'favoured one'. He becomes the representative of all human beings similarly declared favoured and graced by God. God's declaration of Jesus and his representation of humanity finds its anticipation here in 2.14 which celebrates human solidarity with Earth who mediates divine blessing and *shalom*. As we already know earlier in the gospel, Jesus is God's chosen one and the bearer of God's glory. The angelic choristers singing to the shepherds prepare for the full public disclosure of

---

52. See Brown, *Birth*, pp. 401-406, 420-29. Echoes of some of the themes or motifs of the angelic canticle are found in Ps. Sol. 18.10; Isa. 57.19; Ezek. 6.15 and Ps. 51.20.

53. On the chiasm, refer to footnote 73, Chapter 2.

54. Malina, *Social-Science*, pp. 182-83.

Jesus' status and mission. This will occur at his baptism (3.21-22) and in the synagogue at Nazareth (4.16-22a).

The angelic song also presents gospel auditors with a symphony of possibilities for the human household. Irrespective of social class and economic standing, the human household and by association and its mediation, the whole Earth community, are graced or 'favoured' by God. This reveals an ultimate truth for Luke's world, that if human beings and Earth are so favoured and blessed, God's glory also shines upon the Greco-Roman world. Jesus' birth brings 'favour' to human beings and communion with Earth, as the bearer and intermediary of God's peace to the human and non-human world. Through his birth, geographical, social and cosmological division can be overcome and competition healed. Earth and those who live on it are blessed with peace.

All this explains the essential optimism that pervades Luke's gospel and the Book of Acts. The world is a good place, already blessed by God confirmed in the birth of Jesus. Earth is the fruit of divine blessing that brings harmony and communion to all who depend on it and openly relate to it. This is not to deny that suffering, disharmony and sin are realistically part of the social and ecological milieu in which Luke writes. But God's act in Jesus' birth transforms Earth from a place of rivalry, violence and rapaciousness, to an abode of total earthly communion inclusive of the human and non-human household. This peace identified in this early chapter of the gospel is celebrated towards the gospel's end in 19.38 (Figure 16). There, the disciples welcome Jesus into the outskirts of Jerusalem. Their hymn is a response to the mighty works they had seen Jesus perform in his ministry.

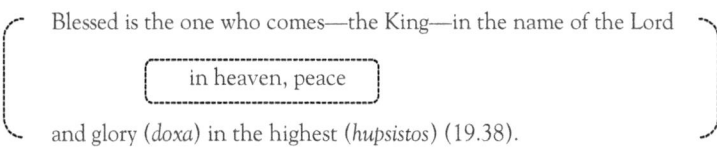

Figure 16. *The structure of Lk. 19.38.*

The disciples' hymn of praise to the king Jesus is a reversed mirror image of the angels' canticle in 2.14. In both canticles, peace is central, found in Earth in one, and in heaven in the other. As Jesus comes into Jerusalem towards the end of his public ministry, his deeds and the disciples' response to his powerful deeds bring about harmony ('peace') celebrated with God in the heavenly realm. While the heavenly and earthly arena of this experience of peace might be seen as separated cosmic spheres in line of the Mediterranean appreciation of the cosmic social hierarchy, as we shall see, they come together in the future ministry of Jesus. This Earth child is also God's child.

Luke's cosmic and earthly vision revealed in the angel's song to the shepherds has profound ecological consequences. The angelic canticle celebrates the communion that humans share with God through Jesus' birth. The birth reveals God's glory and blesses Earth with peace. This reflects the primordial vision expressed in the first creation story of Genesis and the cosmic harmony described in Isaiah (Isa. 9.6-7; 32.17-20). This harmony, initiated through God's creative act, is now renewed through the birth and presence of Earth's saviour, Jesus. All this is confirmed in what follows after the angelic song.

The shepherds go to Bethlehem and, as we have already noted, 'see this "word-deed" (*rhēma*) which has happened' (2.15). When they see the 'sign' they speak about the *rhēma* about which the angel/s told them. This is the angelic, and Luke's, vision of social and cosmic harmony that results from Jesus' birth. This vision brings wonder to all to whom the shepherds speak (2.18). Logically, the only other people present are Joseph and Mary and the newly born child. However, the evangelist envisages that the angelic declaration revealed through the shepherds confirms for the gospel's auditors the universal implications and public application of this event. It affects all who are open to the message of a social renewal now manifest through the birth of this child.

The birth narrative concludes on a final ecological note. We hear that Mary 'kept all these "word-events" (*rhēmata*) going over them in her heart' (2.19). And the shepherds return to the countryside praising God and presumably to again keep watch over or 'guard' their flocks (1.20). Elvey convincingly argues that the expression of 'keeping' for Mary and 'guarding' for the shepherds are both gestational expressions linked to nurturing and sustaining life.[55] They are also associated with storing, 'an activity of both the human heart and [E]arth'.[56] This image of nurture and care, associated with 'keeping' and 'watching' for the human and non-human world, is the final note which concludes Luke's birth story of Jesus proper. Mary and the shepherds are both mothers. A final post-natal act, faithful to the Israelite tradition, is performed on Jesus. This binds him definitively to his people. He is now circumcised (2.21), defining his identity and future ministry amongst the gospel's Israelite people as he receives for the first time the name of 'Jesus' originally spoken by the angel to Mary (1.31). In Jesus, defined by his circumcision and in the name given him, God is about to 'save' and liberate Earth's community.

The Return to Solomon's Temple (2.22-52)

The theme of maternal and environmental nurture of the total Earth household found in Jesus' birth story and celebrated through the angelic

---

55. Elvey, *Ecological*, pp. 145-49.
56. Elvey, *Ecological*, p. 149.

canticle continues as the narrative returns to the location of the opening scene—the temple (2.22-52). Jesus' identification with the Israelite people illustrated in his circumcision is further confirmed in the legal purification observations of his parents. He is presented and dedicated to the God of Israel in the temple, surrounded by life-giving images of nature and memories of the story of Israel and the meta-econarrative reflected in the architecture of the temple. In the temple, the prophets Simeon and Anna confirm his identity with God's people and his mission of God's Earth saving action (2.31-32). The words that Simeon speaks (2.30, 34-35) sum up the future ministry of Jesus in the gospel and the mission of the Lukan household in the Greco-Roman world in Acts. Simeon thanks God,

> because my eyes have seen your salvation which you have prepared in the presence of all the people, a light for revelation to the nations and for the glory of your people Israel (2.30-31).

As Simeon addresses Mary (2.34-35) he also anticipates the gospel's final chapters as Jesus enters into his passion accompanied by those closest to him. His ministry will not be without suffering. It will bring about division and suffering, even to those closest to him.

A final temple scene (2.41-51), framed by notes of Jesus' growth in maturity, wisdom and God's grace (2.40, 51-52), rounds off the gospel opening chapters. He is found sitting amongst the temple teachers, 'listening to them and questioning them' (2.46). There is apparently no supernatural knowledge operating here, only Luke's recognition of Jesus being 'Son of God, and a human being'.[57] Luke then allows us to hear Jesus' voice for the first time. After being questioned by his parents about his actions, he responds,

> Why were you seeking me? Did you not know that I must be [...about the affairs / in the house...] of my father?' (2.49).

Jesus' response, his first words, is rich, enigmatic, confirming and inclusive. The first part of his response ('Why were you seeking me?') is the question addressed to all who seek Jesus. His parents seek him because they are anxious (2.48). Is this the same case with Luke's audience, anxious about what is happening around them and desire to seek Jesus? Is this the *asphelaia* (1.4) about which Luke seeks to reassure Theophilus?

The second part of Jesus' response is a particular interrogative Greek construction that expects a positive response. This implies that Joseph and Mary had no need to look for him.[58] It should be no mystery to them and gospel auditors where Jesus is, in a teaching setting, in the building to which Israel's theological (and ecological) story points, surrounded by all the

---

57. Bovon, *Luke 1*, p. 115; O'Toole, *Luke's Presentation*, pp. 11-12.
58. Bovon, *Luke 1*, p. 114.

images to which we were first introduced with Zechariah. Arguably, 'house' or 'business' have equal interpretative weight, and whatever translation one chooses, they both sum up Jesus' future ministerial activity.[59] It will be about God, the affairs of God, reflected in the temple-setting symbolic of the story of God's household from the beginning of creation. As we have already heard in the birth story, God is concerned about the healing of and communion with Earth's household. This is inclusive of humanity. These are the 'affairs' of God that will preoccupy Jesus. These belong to the *rhēma* Luke notes as the story concludes and as Mary '*kept* all these word-deeds (*rhēma*) in her heart' (2.51c)—with all the maternal, gestational and Earth-connected imagery implied by Luke's deliberate use of *rhēma* and 'kept'. These creation-orientated aspects that reflect God's concern will be revealed in Jesus' public ministry, about to commence.

Conclusion

While I consider Lk. 1.1-4 a prologue and an initial overture to the gospel, Luke's birth story with its concluding temple scenes offers a fuller symphonic overture. It initiates thematic melodies that will emerge through the gospel; it introduces us to Luke's Jesus, Son of God, child of Earth's household and peasant world, beloved of God; it invites us to consider some of the essential qualities that Jesus householders must develop. These include a spirit of hospitality to those from other social groups, openness to the alien and foreign, and a respectful attitude to Earth. There is also present a critique of dominant anthropocentric, androcentric and patriarchal imperial values. These are offset by the pervasiveness of maternal, gestational, nurturing and birthing paradigms that surround the characterization of the two most important female figures, Mary and Elizabeth. Their presence and actions are not determined by their male counterparts (Joseph and Zechariah). They act as important grounding characters for Luke's householders shaped by the conventional domestic structures of Greco-Roman society.

Elizabeth's pregnancy establishes a connection to Luke's next diptych-like scene, the angelic annunciation to Mary of her pregnancy and the promised birth of Jesus, 'the Lord's salvation' (1.26-38). The concluding verses of the annunciation of the birth of John (1.24-25), Mary's encounter with the angel (1.26-38) and all that surrounds the meeting of the two pregnant women (1.39-56) offer the major hermeneutical keys by which the rest of the gospel is heard. They are filled with allusions to life, creation and Earth connectedness (Figure 14). They present two women who are agent subjects in God's plan and act in ways that subvert Luke's social

---

59. On the translation of 'house' or 'business', see Bovon, *Luke 1*, p. 114; Johnson, *Luke*, pp. 59, 61.

convention: both Mary and Elizabeth name their respective children. The final little detail that concludes this section, after Mary and Elizabeth complete their visit, is important. We hear that Mary 'returned to *her* home' (1.56). Conventionally, this would be the house of the husband, of Joseph. Instead this is Mary's house. She, together with Elizabeth, shape the manner by which humans are invited to consider their response to God, to allow God to act within human barrenness and virginity to bring about grace (John) and salvation for Earth's household (Jesus). This household is also Mary's household. Their story and Mary's household will subvert the traditional Greco-Roman patriarchal paradigm, focused on the male and on an anthropologically centred universe.

These hermeneutical keys—divine fertility before apparent barrenness, the earthly association with gestation, and the subversion of anthropocentrism—must continue to be remembered as the gospel story unfolds and Luke's conventional pre-disposition for male dominance occasionally appears.[60] This undercurrent of feminine subversion that conflicts with an androcentric world-view potentially dismissive of any ecological sensitivity is identified again by the evangelist. It will make its appearance in the gospel's final chapter.

A study of the inner play of this opening section of Luke's gospel (Figure 13) helps to define the manner by which the evangelist parallels and contrasts the stories of John and Jesus and everything that surrounds their births and what follows. The juxtaposition of their two stories is complemented by the images aligned to Elizabeth and Mary. Our focus on the birth images—a focus not easy for this writer, a childless male—and female ownership and participation in the process allowed for eco-theological insights to emerge. The centrality of Earth-connectedness and materiality through a consideration of the double wombs of the mothers and manger support this. The other central sign to which Luke wants gospel auditors to attend, the baby wrapped in 'bands of cloth', is also evocative of nurture and human embeddedness within Earth's household. Finally, a reflection on the shepherds' encounter with the hymn from angelic choristers (Figure 15) confirms God's vision of communion celebrated in the birth of Jesus expressed in terms of a universal *shalom* mediated by Earth.

While it is tempting to repeat the traditional story of Christmas as a narrative exclusively focused on human beings and the birth of a child in a peasant household, Luke's story offers illuminating insights when approached from an ecological and Earth-oriented angle. Certainly, the

---

60. See a summary of feminist scholarship on Luke in Robert Karris, 'Women and Discipleship in Luke', *CBQ* 56 (1994), pp. 1-20. See also, Amy-Jill Levine and Marianne Blickenstaff (eds.), *A Feminist Companion to Luke* (London: Sheffield Academic Press, 2002).

emphasis placed on the narrative on God's communion with humanity through the birth of a child wrapped in bands of cloth and lying in a manger is a central truth. But the story is also replete with other fructive images that evoke consideration of the wider Earth community and God's desire to include this fuller community as part of the divine vision. This is supported by a consideration of Luke's intertexts, those textual and cultural precursors that have helped to enhance the interpretation of this section. These include the dominance of the Genesis eco-narrative, other creation-related First Testament texts and especially the allusions to nature, creation and the stories from the Books of Genesis and Exodus that would have been evoked by the memory of Solomon's temple, a setting that frames these first chapters.

As we enter into the world behind the gospel, we explored the implications of hearing the story from the point of view of the social groups represented in Luke's household, in so far as these can be discerned. With the best available knowledge of ancient economic and social stratification, we can judiciously plot the representation of these social groups in the narrative—whether in the couple who travel from the rural countryside of southern Galilee to a city in Judea, or the urban dwellers implicit owners of inns, or urban peasant dwellers who insist that their kin travellers have *no place* in public urban accommodation, or the landless and artisans who could identify with the shepherds as they come and go from the city of David. Whatever the accuracy of this social construction, clearly Luke is making a point about economic renewal and social cohesion. The elite are encouraged to consider their relationships to the poorer and socially more fractured members of the Lukan household. They are invited to conversion through reconsideration of friendship, benefaction and debt release. This will have social and ecological consequences. Not only will people be freed; they will also be celebrated upon Earth because of God's blessing upon an Earth that mediates peace for those who are favoured.

The final point that emerges from the gospel's first two chapters is christological. Luke's birth story of Jesus presents him as a child of Earth and a member of its household. As his ministry unfolds in the gospel the implications of this identity will be revealed, in his gesture of hospitality, healing, teaching and in his maternal nurturing disposition that offers a household of communion for all, human and non-human.

Earth's Voice

The angel said to the shepherds, 'You will find a baby wrapped in bands of cloth and lying in a manger' (Lk. 2.12).

Earth speaks:

> I wrap him, this new born child,
>
> Saviour and God's gift to humanity.
>
> I surround him with gifts that I treasure,
>
> I wrap him in cloth of eternity's flax, fruit of my seed.
>
> I have him placed in a manger fashioned from my body.
>
> I want to surround this child with myself, to protect him.
>
> I love him.
>
> He is mine and I am his.
>
> He is my child.

Chapter 4

Luke 3.1–4.30

Luke's Ecological Principles

In the previous chapter we identified the ecological insights present to the contemporary auditor in Luke's opening chapter. We now see how the evangelist continues the story of Jesus and takes up the gospel from the Markan source, one of the foundational intertexts indicated in Lk. 1.1. As in the birth narrative, Luke introduces us to John the Baptizer in the context of the socio-political imperial world (3.1-2a). What is about to happen will take place in an apparently domestic and environmentally controlled arena. However, the gospel has universal and cosmic implications that will usurp the supremacy wielded by political, economic and religious power-brokers.

> In the fifteenth year of the reign of Tiberius Caesar, Pontius Pilate governor of Judea, Herod tetrarch of Galilee…in the high-priesthood of Annas and Caiaphas, the *rhēma* of God came to John son of Zechariah in the wilderness (3.1-2).

On to the politically and religiously hegemonic stage of the Roman and Israelite world, God's word-deed (*rhēma*) explicitly appears (3.1b). We have already been introduced to the divine *rhēma*. All the creative and empowering aspects of God's *rhēma* as the fruit of God's spirit noted previously apply here. What is about to unfold concerns the whole Earth household, not just an isolated, secluded or exclusive part of it. The presence of the *rhēma* and its alliance with the spirit, God's creative life-giving and gestational energy, continue into this section of the gospel, the second movement in Luke's gospel symphony.

The association between *rhēma* and God's spirit appears in the opening scenes of Luke 3 and in Jesus' programmatic announcement in the synagogue at Nazareth (4.16-30). Between these two literary and thematic bookends we learn how God's spirit acts. The spirit comes down upon Jesus at his baptism (3.21-22), leads him into the wilderness where he is tempted by Satan (4.1-13), and ushers him into his public ministry in Galilee (4.14-15). Jesus' temptation is the centrepiece of this section where the spirit, God's *rhēma* and creation images come together.

The Inner Play of Lk. 3.2–4.18

The discernible chiasmic inner play in Lk. 3.2–4.18 (Figure 17) allows us to identify the important role which Luke sees the story of Jesus' temptation playing. Through the way Jesus responds to the devil (in Greek, *diabolos*), the traditional biblical tempter, tester and accuser, Jesus' identity as God's loyal and covenantal son is confirmed and assured. This central story (C: 4.1-13) is framed by two outer frames. The first (A: 3.1-20; 4.16-30) concerns Jesus' ministry; the second (B: 3.21-38) by the action of God's spirit upon and with Jesus. While the inner play revolves around the temptation story, this overall section of the gospel is progressive. One scene leads to the next, moving forward to the moment that concludes the section, Jesus' announcement in the Nazareth synagogue (4.16-30). The declaration of Luke's Jesus draws on the First Testament prophet Isaiah to say something important about his future ministry. Listening to this declaration, filtered through the evangelist's agenda, gospel auditors are able to attend to the rest of Luke's narrative. The contemporary attentive auditor will also hear discernible ecological undercurrents.

We hear how God's *rhēma* comes to John 'son of Zechariah in the wilderness' (3.2b-c). These echoes from the gospel's opening chapters associated with Zechariah—the Solomonic temple with its rich intricate symbolism and associations, the encounter with God's angelic announcer, and the promise of a child—are remembered here, as God's word-deed is about to manifest itself in the ministry of John in anticipation of the public ministry of Earth's child, Jesus. God's dynamic creation centred *rhēma* moves out of Israel's past and the heavenly sphere into present time geographically

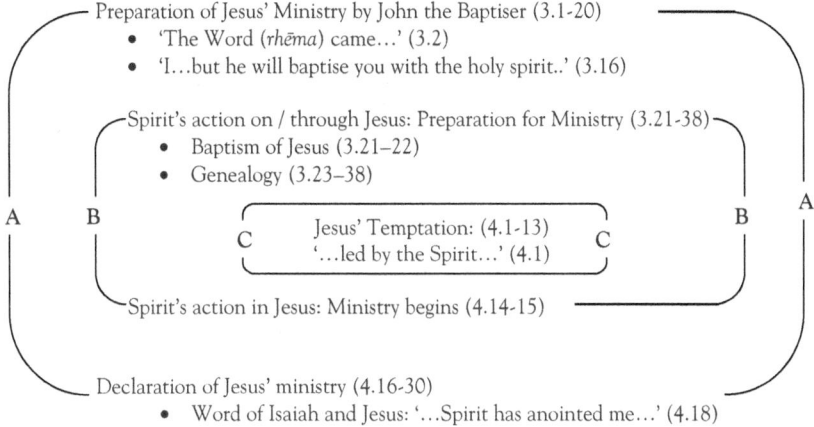

Figure 17. *The chiasmic inner play of Lk. 3.1–4.30.*

fixed. It begins in the *wilderness*, the place of Israel's formative memory and the manifestation of Earth's rawness.

> Then, as now, the desert, though threatening in terms of human survival, was a place that facilitated a deeper encounter with the self and the discovery of a new purpose, freed as one was from the encumbrance of life as lived in 'the real world'. It was natural, therefore, that various Jewish dissidents are to be found in the desert as part of their protest against the existing religious establishment.[1]

From this setting John's ministry begins; to this setting Jesus will return. John's movement from the wilderness is described in geographical and Earth-related terms. He goes *into* all the 'the surrounding area' (*perichōros*) about the river Jordan (2.3). He, like Jesus, is Earth centred, away from the urban attraction of power and control;[2] his initial ministry is linked to the waters of the river Jordan. The imagery of wilderness and waters evokes the creation story when God's spirit hovered over the watery wilderness in preparation for God's creative act. Another beginning now occurs with the opening ministry of John.

John in the Wilderness (3.1-20)

John's first invitation to his audience is for a 'baptism of repentance for the forgiveness of sins' (3.3). Two key images here further the story of creation. These concern 'baptism-repentance' and 'forgiveness of sins'. The act of baptismal washing drawn from Israelite purification or Essene washing rituals symbolizes the desire for moral living and 'repentance' (*metanoia*).[3] John's use of water, Earth's primordial substance, becomes the means of this 'repentance'. Into this ancient Earth element of creation John's audience will be immersed. Their conversion will be confirmed through their immersion into the waters of Earth. The Greek *metanoia* literally means 'change the way one thinks'. It is essentially an attitudinal change. In Luke's day this would imply a moral and social change; in ours, we can add, an explicitly ecological one. In whatever way one hears *metanoia*, it affects and influences relationships within the eco-system of the ancient world familiar to Luke's addressees. This links to the second key image of John's opening proclamation.

The kind of forgiveness that Luke envisages, which *metanoia* and baptism reflect and John urges, is fundamentally communal. It is neither individually nor anthropologically centred; rather social and environmental. 'Forgiveness

---

1. Freyne, *Jesus*, p. 41.
2. Green, *Luke*, p. 170.
3. It is conceivable that John was originally a member of the desert based Essenes. See Fitzmyer, *Luke I–IX*, pp. 452-53.

of sin' concerns restoring the whole gamut of relationships that involve John's audience. It gets to the heart of all relationships with which the world is bound. It is about the deeper spirit of *shalom* that is at the same time, personal, communal and environmental. To Luke's contemporary auditors, John summons the same invitation for a change of attitude to the universe and its people that establishes, heals or restores relationships. Ecological commitment through immersion in water will be the sign.

From the wilderness of John and the wilderness of Luke's compiled Isaiah intertext, auditors are invited to prepare for Jesus ('the Lord', 3.4b). Luke uses a double intertext—the Markan gospel and Mark's use of Isaiah—to prepare for the coming of Jesus:

> ⁴As it is written in the book of the prophet Isaiah, 'The voice of one crying in the wilderness: Prepare the way of the Lord, make straight his paths. ⁵Every ravine shall be filled in and every mountain and hill shall be humbled, and the crooked straightened and the rough smoothed. ⁶And all flesh shall see the salvation of God.' (3.4-6).

What are we to make of Luke's use of a First Testament intertext that seems to denigrate the environmental features of the land in an apparent act of violence in order to elevate God? It would seem that this is a clear example of environmental damage for a divine or anthropological purpose. If so, it needs to be acknowledged. Valleys are filled in and mountains levelled to enable a metaphorically easy access for God's coming. The natural landscape of Earth is drastically altered in preparation for God's coming. This geographical alteration mirrors for Luke and for the textual sources (originally LXX Isa. 40.3, then Mk 1.3) the human effort supposedly needed for God to access the chosen community.[4]

A Text of 'Earth Terror'?

The text of Isa. 40.3 has the potential to be a text of 'Earth terror'. The voice of Earth would cry out in pain at the violence done to it. The recognition of the potential which this text has for creating environmental abuse becomes even more important in contemporary worship situations, especially in Advent time, when the equivalent synoptic stories about John the Baptizer (Mk 1.2-4; Lk. 3.1-18; Mt. 3.1-12) and their Isaiah source are the focus of liturgy. The concern expressed here links back to the *Preface* for the Earth Bible commentary series and the acknowledgment that there are biblical texts that are 'grey'. Unwitting repetition or uncritical use of these biblical texts cements attitudes to creation and our environment that are literally unsustainable.

---

4. The LXX is the Greek version of the First Testament.

Luke's use of the Isaiah text is influenced by its integration already in the Markan source gospel. The Isaiah text was also familiar to the Qumran-Essene community in the Judean wilderness on the edge of the Dead Sea.[5] Its *Manual of Discipline* appropriated this particular reference from Isaiah to affirm the role of Qumran's wilderness community as an alternative voice to the moral corruption and religious vacuum that seemed apparent in Jerusalem.[6] John was arguably a member of the Essene community. His introduction into the synoptic gospels as a baptizer and user of the Isaiah passage would reflect an historical memory of his connection to the Essene community, its practice of ritual purification and the eschatological insight which Isaiah offered them. It is conceivable that John left the Essenes after he was called into the wilderness to prepare for Jesus' coming.[7]

Besides drawing on the historical background to the Isaiah text and John's baptismal practice, Luke makes two redactional changes to Mark's use of Isaiah. These changes ameliorate the potential negative ecological impact of Isa. 40.3.

First, Luke adds to Mark's text 'and the crooked straightened and the rough smoothed' (3.5c). If this expression is applied to what happens to Earth it is possible to hear this act as a deed of violence upon it; physical paths and highways need to be straightened and smoothed. However, a negative environmental application is not entirely clear either in Luke's text or in LXX Isaiah upon which the evangelist draws. Linguistic clarity would have been possible if Isaiah (and Luke) were appropriating these images of straightening and smoothing Earth's environment specifically. Their generic nature implies a wider household inclusive of human beings and not primarily or exclusively to the geological formation that typifies the Jordan valley region.

From this point of view, while the images are ecologically violent—and again, this should not be overlooked or easily dismissed—the intention is to invite the human auditors of the text to conversion, to offer a spiritual 'filling in' of what is empty or a 'levelling off' of what seems arrogant, to 'straighten' and 'smooth' hearts in preparation for the gospel soon to be proclaimed by Jesus. If the author's appropriation of Earth images is intended to bring about conversion amongst the gospel's addressees, then Earth (the valleys and hills)

---

5. The debate remains as to the nature of the membership of the Qumran community. While Roland de Vaux's Essene position still holds sway (*Archaeology and the Dead Sea Scrolls* [Oxford: Oxford University Press, 1973]) more recent publications continue to explore the identity of Qumran's membership. See, for example, Robert R. Cargill, *Qumran through (Real) Time: A Virtual Reconstruction of Qumran and the Dead Sea Scrolls* (Piscataway, NJ: Gorgias, 2009) and Alison Schofield, *From Qumran to the Yahad: A New Paradigm of Textual Development for* The Community Rule, Studies on the Texts of the Desert of Judah 77 (Leiden: Brill, 2009).

6. Fitzmyer, *Luke I–IX*, pp. 454, 460-61.

7. Fitzmyer, *Luke I–IX*, p. 453.

becomes the mediator of this call to conversion and forgiveness. This is an Earth ministry and intercession already witnessed at the birth of Jesus in the angelic chorus to the shepherds. There Earth mediated peace, here it mediates conversion.

A second detail in Luke's reworking of the Markan source is also important. Luke adds LXX Isa. 40.5 to Mark:

> And all flesh shall see the salvation of God (3.6).

Of interest here is the phrase 'all flesh' (*pasa sarx*). This confirms Luke's penchant for the universality of the gospel message, the invitation to conversion and the experience of God's salvation. 'All flesh' not only refers to human beings. As witnessed in a non-canonical biblical intertext and Josephus, 'all flesh' can include the whole of the non-human world'.[8] This appreciation further helps to ameliorate the potential ecological destruction communicated in LXX Isaiah and by Luke's Markan source.

The whole purpose of the ecological changes envisioned in the Isaiah text and used by the synoptic gospel writers is to encourage human readiness for the call to conversion and the gospel soon to be publicly announced by Jesus. Luke's adjustments to Mark through additions made from LXX Isaiah caution us against too readily condemning Luke for what seems to be an anti-ecological stance revealed at this point of the gospel. It is possible that Earth and its geological features could be mediators of conversion for Luke's human household anticipated in the preaching of John. This is designed to bring God's salvation to the whole Earth, to 'all flesh'.

God's salvation intended for all is preceded by John's call to conversion. The next scene in John's ministry spells this out in practical and social terms (3.7-14). Practitioners of religious privilege (3.7-9), material greed (3.10-11, 14c) and violent conduct (3.13-14b) are all called to conversion. In a final act of preaching in *word-deed* before he leaves the gospel to reappear later, John announces the coming of one more worthy than he, who will baptize the people with the Holy Spirit and bring about eschatological judgment (3.15-18). John's preaching concludes as he is incarcerated for his socially radical call to conversion that reaches even the ears of the political establishment in Herod (3.20).

---

8. Alexander Sand, 'σάρξ', *EDNT*, III (ed. Horst Balz and Gerhard Schneider; Grand Rapids, MI: Wm B. Eerdmans Publishing Co., 1991), pp. 230-33; Eduard Schweizer, 'σάρξ', *TDNT*, VII (ed. Gerhard Kittel and Gerhard Friedrich; Grand Rapids, MI: Wm B. Eerdmans Publishing Co., 1964), pp. 98-151.

Jesus Anointed with the Spirit in his Baptism (3.21-22)

The next scene, the second in Luke's development of the *word-spirit* motif, is the baptism of Jesus (3.21-22). This is Luke's first episode of Jesus in his public ministry in the gospel. It is highly significant. Luke deliberately constructs links back to themes from the birth: Jesus, Earth-related and heavenly blessed from birth, is confirmed for his public ministry. The scene of his baptism, without the expected presence of John, indicates that this is God's initiated deed upon Jesus as Luke adapts again imagery taken from the Markan source. A redactional comparison between the two gospel scenes (Figure 18) highlights Luke's emphasis and Earth connection which Luke adds to Mark's narrative.

Mk 1.9-12	Lk. 3.21-22; 4.1
[9] In those days Jesus came from Nazareth of Galilee and was baptized by John in the Jordan.	[21] Now when all the people were baptized, and when Jesus also had been baptized and was praying, the heaven was opened,
[10] And just as he was coming up out of the water, he saw the heavens torn apart and the Spirit descending like a dove on him.	[22] and the Holy Spirit descended upon him in bodily form (*sōmatikos*) like a dove.
[11] And a voice came from heaven, 'You are my Son, the Beloved; with you I am well pleased.'	And a voice came from heaven, 'You are my Son, the Beloved; with you I am well pleased.' [Genealogy]
[12] The Spirit immediately drove him out into the wilderness…	[4.1] and Jesus, full of the Holy Spirit returned from the Jordan, and was led by the Spirit…

Figure 18. *Redactional comparison between Mk 1.9-12 and Lk. 3.21-22; 4.1.*

Luke's reworking of Mark's story adds a number of important features that contribute to Jesus' mission and ministry. He is found to be with those who belong to the human household, who, like him, are baptized (Lk. 3.21). The passive form of the verb referring to Jesus' baptism ('and had been baptized', Lk. 3.21b) highlights the action of God. John is not present (as in Mark) and Luke's Jesus is baptized in a moment of prayer (Lk. 3.21c). Prayer confirms his belovedness before God. For Luke, Jesus' prayer becomes the occasion of his communion with God which also initiates the opening of the heavens, God's traditional abode.

The heavens' opening in Luke (Lk. 3.21d) seems less violent and more revelatory than Mark's 'torn apart' (Mk 1.10b). For Luke the heavens become accessible through Jesus and the divine voice and physical disposition of the spirit's presence upon him. Within the Lukan structure of the scene, the heavens' opening, the spirit's descent and the heavenly voice are centre-stage (Lk. 3.21d-22c). The divine communion with humanity and Earth represented in Jesus is emphatic. The spirit of God, emphasized by Luke as 'holy', recalls the action of the spirit on Mary in Luke 1 and the accompanying reminder that her child will be called 'holy'. The spirit's action coming down upon Jesus also recalls the spirit's presence in the beginning of Genesis in the story of creation.

The Spirit's Bodiliness and 'Bird' Shape (3.22)

The spirit comes upon Jesus in 'bodily form' (3.22) anointing him for ministry. The corporeality (*sōmatikos*) of the spirit, 'like a dove', underscores the materiality of the spirit's presence and link with a world more-than-human. God's spirit is now indeed capable of being experienced within the context of the physical world of Luke's audience.[9] The spirit's corporeal presence means that it is intended to be seen and noticed externally. Luke accentuates this external identification through the adjective *sōmatikos*, an editorial addition to Mark's narrative. God's spirit now manifest beyond the heavens, on Earth, renews Earth's members with holiness through sanctifying the waters into which Jesus is baptized.[10] As Ephrem (c. 306–373 CE) celebrated in song, 'The spirit descended from on high and sanctified the water by her hovering'.[11]

The spirit's corporeality further enables God's creative and prophetic spirit to be manifest.[12] The manifestation is not restricted only to the ones with whom Jesus is baptized, but is for the whole Earth eco-system, human and non-human.

Jesus' link to the wider Earth household is affirmed first through his insertion or immersion into Earth's water. This primordial being, the watery substance at creation's beginning, surrounds him like a womb. From Earth's water he is born into ministry.

---

9. Green, *Luke*, p. 187. Fitzmyer suggests that the 'bodily' form stresses the spirit's reality in *Luke I–IX*, p. 481.

10. On the Earth connection to spirit's bodiliness, see Karl Hermann Schelkle, 'σωματικός', *EDNT*, III (ed. Horst Balz and Gerhard Schneider; Grand Rapids, MI: Wm B. Eerdmans Publishing Co., 1991), p. 325.

11. Ephrem, *Hymns on Epiphany* 6.1, as quoted by Killian McDonnell, 'Jesus' Baptism in the Jordan', *TS* 56 (1995), pp. 209-36 (220). It is noteworthy that Ephrem associates the spirit with the feminine.

12. Fitzmyer, *Luke I–IX*, p. 484: 'Since in the OT the "Spirit" of God is usually a manifestation of his [sic] creative or prophetic presence to human beings, it should be so understood here.' I would not restrict this manifestation just to human beings, but to the whole Earth community.

Further, the spirit is described as descending with a somatic shape 'like a dove'.[13] Not much thought has been given to the spirit's association with a 'dove', other than to First Testament allusions (Gen. 1.2; 8.8; Deut. 32.11; Joel 3.1-5).[14] The evangelist's relationship of the spirit with the physical identity of a bird, while it could conceivably become part of a modern day comedy skit or bible play ('Did you hear the one about the Holy Spirit being seen as a bird?'), connects God's spirit to the non-human and animal world. This association was first recognized by John Chrysostom (c. 347–407) whom the Franciscan, St Bonaventure (1217–74) later quotes. In his commentary on Luke's gospel, Bonaventure writes:

> Now the Holy Spirit descends on [Jesus] in the form of a *dove* because of its signification, because, as Chrysostom says, 'this bird above all others is the cultivator of greatest love'. Thus, the Holy Spirit appeared to Christ in *full animal form*.[15]

In the light of the contemporary ecological hermeneutic with which I engage the story of Jesus' baptism, Bonaventure offers a most relevant insight. The spirit, intimately connected to God's presence and sanctity of being, has now moved beyond the heavenly abode into Earth's total household—human and animal—through alighting upon Jesus in 'full animal form' *in the form of a dove*.[16]

Parenthetically but significantly, the link between womb and Jesus' watery plunging and release by God's spirit, accompanied by his explicit identification from the heavenly voice, does not go unnoticed by early Christian writers and theologians.[17] They interpret Jesus' baptism as a *birth event*. They explicitly acknowledge the cosmic significance of his baptism which 'restores a wounded cosmos' and, according to Philoxenus (d. 523 CE), renews creation.[18] As McDonnell notes:

> In an extensive section on the baptism of Jesus, the *Teaching of St Gregory* [5th century CE] places the Jordan event in the context of the Genesis account of the creation of the world. In the beginning the Spirit transformed chaos into cosmos, 'moving over the waters, and thence set out the order of the creatures', including the ornamenting of the heavens where the angels dwell. The Spirit transforms chaos into cosmos. But there is a larger, cosmic role of the Spirit at creation '[who] came down to the waters and sanctified

---

13. Harrington translates the pertinent section of the Greek text as 'and the Holy Spirit descended on him with the physical shape of a dove' (*Luke*, p. 68).
14. Harrington, *Luke*, p. 69; Fitzmyer, *Luke I–IX*, pp. 483-84.
15. Karris, *Bonaventure 1–8*, p. 270. Emphasis original to translated text.
16. Bonaventure also links the spirit to other Earth features in Luke's gospel, to a cloud and fire; Karris, *Bonaventure 1–8*, p. 271.
17. See McDonnell, 'Baptism', pp. 209-36.
18. McDonnell, 'Baptism', p. 217-18.

the lower waters of the earth'. What happened at creation is echoed at baptism.[19]

In hindsight, we find in the writings of these early theologians a surprisingly clear ecological appreciation of the baptism of Jesus.

The second Earth link in the scene comes from the presence of the corporeal spirit and the words of God. These heavenly words spoken upon and over Earth's household ('You are my Son, the Beloved; with you I am well pleased') attest Jesus' belovedness before God; God delights in him. Luke depicts God speaking these words directly to Jesus. They confirm his identity and intimacy with God. Whatever Jesus now does in the gospel, he will bring joy to God. Furthermore, God's voice is not silent or only heard by Jesus. The gospel's auditors and Earth also hear them. They include Earth's household because Jesus is its member; he is literally *grounded* in Earth and formed from it. This is clear from the genealogy which Luke inserts before Mark's final verse of the equivalent baptismal story (3.23-38). As in Matthew's genealogy (Mt. 1.1-17), Luke affirms Jesus' Israelite heritage. Unlike Matthew, Luke explicitly links Jesus to the very beginning of creation, to *Adam*, Earth creature from *adamah*, the soil. As Jerome (c. 347–420 CE) points out, *Adam* can be associated with *homo siue terrenus aut indigena vel terra rubra* ('humanity or earthly or native or red Earth').[20] The genealogy frames Jesus with the title of 'Son':

> He was the son (as was supposed) of Joseph…[the rest of the genealogy, then concludes]….son of Adam, son of God (3.23, 37).

The auditor already knows Jesus' kinship and lineage from the birth narrative, and does not need a genealogy to determine these. Jesus is already God's son and connected to Earth's household. Luke's genealogy links Jesus' birth and the early childhood temple event to his public ministry. It also serves a literary and theological function, locating him with the story of Israel, confirming his status with God and his readiness for his public ministry. Luke introduces the genealogy with a small biographical detail placing Jesus at 'about thirty years of age', the conventional age for public service.[21] The genealogy's repetition of 'son of' links him to the historical and narrative memory of his Israelite ancestry and covenantal relationship with God. It also highlights Jesus' filial loyalty as 'son' of God, prefigured in his birth and confirmed in his baptism. As Luke returns to Mark's storyline, Jesus' covenantal loyalty and filial intimacy with God is about to be scrutinized in an encounter with the cosmic adversary, the devil (*diabolos*).

---

19. McDonnell, 'Baptism', p. 217.
20. Karris, *Bonaventure 1–8*, p. 285 n. 100.
21. Green, *Luke*, p. 188.

Jesus' Testing—Three Ecological Principles (4.1-13)

Luke's story of the temptation of Jesus (4.1-13) is the centre of this gospel's symphonic movement in which the *word-spirit* dynamic melody thematically unfolds. Of significance again is the considerable expansion which Luke makes to Mark, bringing additions from the Q intertext, a hypothetical Jesus sayings-source common to Matthew and Luke. Luke returns us to the wilderness, the ecologically untainted and testing environment from where John's ministry began. We are reminded of the spirit's presence. Jesus, 'full of the Holy Spirit' (4.1a), comes into the wilderness because of the action of the spirit. Ecological nuances are implicit in the language and description which Luke employs.

The link between Jesus' encounter with temptation and Israel's similar experience in the wilderness is unmistakable. The theological symbolism behind the number 40, the wilderness setting and the engagement which Jesus has with the devil (*diabolos*) parallels Israel in the wilderness of Zin in the First Testament. It is recounted in Exodus and gets further reflection in *Deuteronomy*. Luke draws on these intertexts to illustrate how Israel's testing in the wilderness finds its response in the story of Jesus. The heart of each temptation, as with Israel, is fundamentally relational. It concerns Jesus' relationship with the God of creation and the covenant. Beneath the surface of Luke's narrative lie environmental and Earth-related themes present in Jesus' three temptations. At stake is his communion with God and his attitude to Earth. Will Jesus act as one dependent on God, as God's beloved one? Or will he compromise his covenantal and filial relationship? Will he forget his genealogical link to *Adam* and his communion with Earth's household? These questions prompted by the story are pertinent to all disciples in history concerned with their relationship to God and Earth.

The story begins and ends with the mention of 'stone' (4.3, 11). After its last mention, the final words that Luke's Jesus speaks are addressed to the devil. They draw upon LXX Deut. 6.16 'You shall not tempt the Lord your God'. The ecological frame I see created by the repetition of 'stone' is not coincidental. Any visit to the place where Luke sets the scene for Jesus' temptation will highlight how prevalent stones are in the wilderness. This is not an Australian desert or a treeless plain. This is a place where food and water are also scarce. It is the place where one's humanity is tested and dependency on the fruits of Earth deeply realized. Humiliation, in the rooted meaning of this word in English, is what the temptations are about. They are intended to allow the Lukan audience know its *'humilis'*-ation— Earth (Lat. *humus*) connectedness as modelled through the action of Jesus.

The first temptation occurs after Jesus' forty day fasting and he is naturally 'hungry' (4.2c). The hunger at one level is for physical food, at another level, the hunger that has emerged for Jesus is about his desire for communion with God. The wilderness motif and the memory of Israel would suggest this deeper more metaphorical and less physical level of hunger engrosses Jesus' spirit. It is at the physical level that the devil enters the scene.

The *diabolos* was traditionally the adversary or seducer.[22] Originally part of the heavenly court who tests the integrity of God's faithful ones (e.g. Job 1.6), by Luke's day and under the influence of ancient Near Eastern traditions the *diabolos* came to be seen independent of God's heavenly court and an adversarial agent exposing people to evil. The *diabolos* became the explanation in Jewish intertestamental literature for the evil impulse in the world. It acts to sever the faithful one's relationship with God and God's world. With this in mind, the *diabolos* seeks to disrupt and unhinge Jesus' relationship with God.

Three Ecological Principles

The *diabolos* poses Jesus' first test, 'If you are the son of God, tell this stone to become bread'(4.3). Jesus is the son of God. There is no doubt about this and it has been underscored in Luke's gospel from the opening chapters. The real test concerns Jesus' relationship to the elements of Earth symbolized in the stone. The *diabolos* wants Jesus to prove his filial relationship by a manipulation of Earth, to convert stone into bread for eating. The real test is about Jesus' relationship to God mirrored in his treatment of Earth. Manipulation and abuse of Earth would 'prove' to the *diabolos* that Jesus is God's son. But Jesus does not have to prove it. He is unwilling to compromise the intimate kinship he shares with Earth already attested in the gospel. For Luke's Jesus, there is more to life than physical bread (4.4). Jesus refuses self-satiation that would manipulate Earth and damage it through greed. Luke presents us with what might be considered, albeit anachronistically, the first of three ecological ethical principles: *Earth is to be cared for and treated respectfully, not ravaged through covetousness.*

The second temptation is definitively set on Earth's stage as the *diabolos* shows Jesus a snapshot of all the kingdoms of Earth (*oikoumenē*) (4.5). The *oikoumenē* can refer to the imperial world as Luke's auditors would understand this. But in the LXX it has a wider, more comprehensive and less politically or socially defined inference. In this case it refers to Earth. It is Earth's household, not just individual empires or kingdoms.[23] In 2.1 it

---

22. Gerhard von Rad, 'The OT View of Satan', TDNT, II (ed. Gerhard Kittel and Gerhard Friedrich; Grand Rapids, MI: Wm B. Eerdmans Publishing Co., 1964), pp. 73-75 (73).

23. Horst Balz, 'οἰκουμένη', *EDNT*, II (ed. Horst Balz and Gerhard Schneider; Grand Rapids, MI: Wm B. Eerdmans Publishing Co., 1991), pp. 503-504, shows how the LXX

appeared that Caesar Augustus had jurisdiction over Earth, but by the time the auditor has engaged the ecological sounds out of Jesus' birth story, the *oikoumenē* is linked to God's authority. Jesus is part of this and, as God's 'son', has authentic communion with Earth; he is Earth's child. The devil deceptively attempts to falsify this relationship and bequeath the *oikoumenē* to Jesus if only he will falsely worship (4.6-7).

Jesus' response with LXX Deut. 6.13 ('You shall worship the Lord your God and serve only God') brings us to discern an important ethical insight from Luke's story: *Hegemony over Earth is a false relationship that usurps one's relationship with God.* This links to the function of stewardship from Genesis explored earlier. Stewardship is not a divine right by which human beings possess and control Earth. It is a divine privilege in which human beings share as they recognize their creatureliness and act sensitively in solidarity with creation. This is the appropriate disposition towards the *oikoumenē* reflected in Jesus' response to the *diabolos*. This brings us to what might be perceived as Luke's second ecological principle: *All ecological and environmental engagement is grounded in and enhanced by one's communion with God.*

The third temptation (4.9-11) occurs at the temple in Jerusalem on its pinnacle. 'Pinnacle' translates the Greek *pterugion* which literally means 'wing'. As discussed earlier, the temple was Earth's navel, the meeting point between the human and the divine, the secular and sacred, heaven and Earth. It symbolized Earth's household and was the localization of God's presence. One feature we have not discussed are its 'wings'.

Two symbolic wings were set above the temple's entrance reminiscent of the eagle's wings from the First Testament (Deut. 32.11; Isa. 40.31) and reminders of God's covenantal care of the Israelites. Symbolically, this is where Luke has the devil set Jesus. It is from here—before the images of God's care and on the building that most represented the creation-narrative and Earth's household—that the *diabolos* tempts Jesus. Borrowing from LXX Psalm 91, the devil entices Jesus to throw himself from these wings, assuring him that God will protect him. Returning to the original image of 'stone' with which the temptations began, the devil quotes LXX Ps. 91.12 'On their [the angels'] hands they will raise you up, lest you strike your foot against a stone.' In this context, Earth's image of stone is no longer a metaphor for food; it is now a negative symbol for harm. The devil seeks to manipulate this Earth-related image as a way of controlling Jesus' response to God. Jesus is firm about his communion with God that will not be compromised, no

---

translation into *oikonmen*, translates as the Earth as a whole, including its inhabitants, kingdoms and all that God has created to bring about the world. In secular Greek it was a geographical term, to distinguish habitable from inhabitable lands (Herodotus, 3. 114; 4. 10) or the cultured from the barbaric peoples.

matter the cost. He responds with LXX Deut. 6.16: 'You shall not test the Lord your God.'

In Jesus' response to the devil we find a third Lukan ecological principle: *Earth's resources are to be respected by all and not usurped as a means of power and control by one over another.* Jesus' response returns to the heart of what Luke's temptation narrative seeks: to remind gospel auditors that everything, human and non-human, is *theo*-logically referred and not used to commandeer God's presence and authority.

Luke Timothy Johnson sums up Luke's teaching found in the story of Jesus' testings. Johnson, coming to his interpretation of the story from a different angle, reflects a similar insight to that which I have proposed here. A subtle Earth connected insight surfaces for him as he reflects on how Jesus treats nature:

> We can read this entire account against the backdrop of first-century Palestinian political upheaval and popular messianic expectation, and recognize that, in Luke's understanding, Jesus eschewed the option of a violent, military, zealot vision of God's kingdom in Israel. But the meaning of the testings go far deeper for Luke's Christian readers, who learn something of their own path from the conscious decision of the 'Lord Christ' to choose another than violent way to be Messiah, *who rejected power over nature* to serve his appetite, over humans for the sake of glory, over God for his own survival, in favor of the 'path of peace' (1:79; 2:14, 29; Acts 10:36) of the Isaianic servant/prophet, as his first words to the people next reveal.[24]

The temptation scene concludes with the devil departing 'until an opportune time' (4.13b). The opportune time will recur in the passion. Between then and this scene, the *diabolos* continues to operate subtly in the background. This is obvious in the resistance that Jesus meets from his opponents, the suffering experienced by those who seek healing, and the cosmic upheaval represented by the evil spirits which need exorcising.

The story of Jesus' temptation occurs at a critical point in the gospel's early chapters. It links the portrait of Jesus from his birth to his future ministry; it cements his fidelity to God and confirms his attitude to Earth's household in which he lives. The scene also connects to his baptism by which he is fully immersed into Earth's womb. He is God's beloved one, the agent of God's spirit which fully possesses him. Jesus' encounter with Satan confirms for Luke's audience how to live as disciples open to God's grace and sensitive to Earth in which one lives. As God's faithful one, Jesus' fidelity is confirmed through the presence of the spirit which has endowed him with holiness, strength, divine communion and respect for Earth's household. This same spirit is also expressly behind Jesus' *rhēma*, the *word-deed* that now publicly takes shape in his ministry. The spirit empowers Jesus

---

24. Johnson, *Luke*, p. 77. My emphasis.

as he commences his ministry of *deed* in Galilee and begins his teaching of *word* in its synagogues (4.14-15). God's *rhēma* is now tangibly enacted through Jesus. He first reveals its true meaning in his home-town synagogue at Nazareth (4.16-30).

Jesus in the Nazareth Synagogue (4.16-30)

Jesus' presence in the Nazareth synagogue is his customary place for the Sabbath (4.16). This first mention of the Sabbath will not be Luke's last.[25] The day memorializes God's rest after the work of creation in Genesis 1. Consequently, the biblical eco-metanarrative still lingers in the background as Jesus stands up to read from the First Testament (4.16). The book of the prophet Isaiah is placed into his hands, Luke tells us (4.17a-b). This book is also Earth's matter that he holds in his hands. It is more than a text from which he will shortly read; it is Earth's being that he embraces evidenced in the physical material (whether it is vellum or parchment) that is a fruit of Earth's work and upon which the text is written and he looks.[26] As he 'opens the book' (4.17b) (or, as the NRSV has 'unrolls the scroll'), Earth reveals to Luke's Jesus what is important and what needs to be proclaimed to gospel auditors that will shape the rest of the gospel. In the hands of Jesus and through his voice, Earth acts prophetically.

The christologically selected scripture, a compilation of two texts from LXX Isa. 61.1 and 58.6, explicate Luke's portrait of Jesus and his future mission. Jesus reads:

> [18a] The spirit of the Lord is upon me, because [the spirit] has anointed me,
> [b] to preach good news to the poor [the spirit] has sent me,
> [c] to proclaim to the captives *release*,
> [d] and to the blind, recovery of sight,
> [e] to send the oppressed *released*,
> [19] to proclaim the year of the Lord's favour (4.18-19).[27]

---

25. Sabbath is most favoured by Luke. It appears 19 times in the gospel and 9 times in Acts (with 10 in Mt. 12 in Mk and 11 in Jn).

26. Anne Elvey, 'Earthing the Text?', *ABR* 52 (2004), pp. 64-79.

27. My translation here keeps the Greek text more literal and adds micro divisions (a-e) to v.18 for ease of identification. I have also explicated and square bracketed 'the spirit' as the subject implied to the verbs 'anointed' and 'sent'. This is to prevent genderizing God's spirit. Linguistically the Hebrew equivalent to the English 'spirit' (*ruah*) is feminine and the LXX alternative is neuter (*pneuma*). On balance, if any gender pronoun were to be associated with the spirit it would be feminine, 'she'. Hur (*Dynamic*, pp. 37-73) offers a helpful analysis of the use of *pneuma* and *ruah* in the extra-Lukan biblical tradition. However, absent in the study and in the monograph generally is any link between spirit and creation. The study is unambiguously anthropocentric.

This First Testament collation is Luke's programmatic announcement of Jesus' future ministry.[28] The evangelist's integration of the Isaiah intertext emphasizes that the action of God's spirit affirmed in the First Testament continues now in Jesus and the Lukan householders.[29] They are the recipients of the spirit's action in Jesus continued through the eyewitnesses and ministers of the *word-deed*, the foundational generation upon which Luke's household is dependent.

The text affirms that Jesus is the agent of God's anointing spirit (4.18a). Auditors would remember that his spirit anointment first occurred at the moment of his conception and was confirmed later in his baptism. Borrowing images from Luke's Isaian intertext, the spirit's anointing empowers Jesus to activate God's vision for creation inclusive of humanity. While it is tempting to make Jesus' ministry anthropologically exclusive, the Isaian vision summed up in the intertext that Luke places on Jesus' lips can also be heard ecologically. This is important, especially when we move towards reflecting on Luke's portrait of Jesus in his Galilean ministry (Luke chs. 4–9). In this ministry, as Jesus heals, dines and teaches, God's *rhēma* is tangibly unfolding. While it seems that Jesus' deeds and words are oriented to human beings within households and meal environments, his ministry is not exclusively anthropocentric. It is concerned about the total Earth household, as our ecologically sensitive listening to Luke's use of the Isaiah intertext will now make clear.

The wooden translation that I offer attempts to honour the Greek text and highlight its main thematic links. Important is Luke's textual inner play. Its pattern is discerned in the evangelist's addition of LXX Isa. 58.6 at the end of the original LXX Isa. 61.1. This addition that forms the last line of Jesus' announcement is out of sequence from the original intertext. This means that Luke's construction is deliberate rather than haphazard. It creates an overall literary and aural balance.

---

28. That this text is a heuristic for Jesus' future ministry in Lk. is attested almost unanimously by Lukan scholars. See for example, Fitzmyer, *Luke II–IX*, p. 529; Tannehill, *Narrative Unity*, p. 61; John Nolland, *Luke 1–9:20* (Dallas, TX: Word Books, 1989), p. 195.

29. 'Of the 525 quotations, references and allusions found in the gospel of Luke, more than one fifth of them are from Isaiah. Of forty five explicit OT references introduced by formulas in Lucan writings, ten are from Isaiah.' (Raymond Joseph Irudhayasamy, *A Prophet in the Making: A Christological Study on Lk 4, 16-30: In the Background of the Isaianic Mix Citation and the Elijah-Elisha Reference* [Frankfurt: Peter Lang, 2002], p. 46). Isaiah provides Luke with an important intertext that shapes the framework and contributes to a discernible ecological gospel theology. On Isaiah's influence on the shape of Luke's gospel, see Michael Prior, *Jesus the Liberator: Nazareth Liberation Theology (Lk. 16–30)* (Sheffield: Sheffield Academic Press, 1995).

18a"The spirit of the Lord is upon me, because [the spirit] has anointed me,

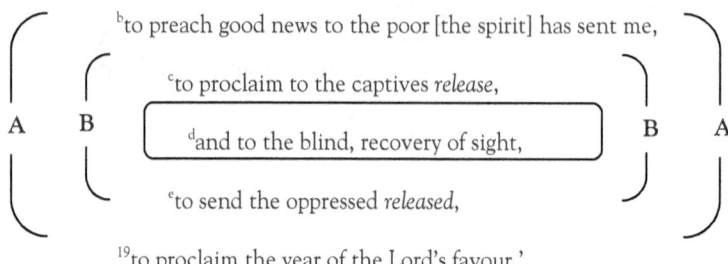

19to proclaim the year of the Lord's favour.'

Figure 19. *Structure of Lk. 4.18-19.*

Jesus' speech begins with v. 18a. Heard from a christological perspective, it sums up Jesus' spirit-filled story so far. The next part of Luke's structure (v. 18b-19), connects to this introductory v. 18a and expands on its christology. It is framed by v. 18b and 19, with the intervening subsections of the verse thematically balanced by an inner frame designated by 'release' (18c, e). The chiasmic structure is centred on 18d, Jesus' ministry of sight recovery. The overall literary pattern of 4.18b-19 is finely balanced, headed by the announcement in v.18a as the summary of Jesus' empowerment already identified in the gospel (Figure 19).

The outer frame (A) identifies the overall focus of Jesus' ministry. It concerns his preaching the 'gospel' (v. 18b) in a way that proclaims God's bounteous deeds in creation and human history. This is the 'year of the Lord's favour' (v. 19), a sacred time every seventh year for debt and land release prescribed by the Torah. The social importance of this practice for Luke's audience of landless peasants and urban elite landlords would be obvious. At an ecological level, Jesus' proclamation of the sabbatical year would have Earth implications. Earth becomes 'released' (v. 18e) from the rhythm of oppression forced upon it as its soil gets overworked to produce crops.

The preaching announced in v. 18b has further ecological implications when considered from the point of view of those to whom the good news is preached, namely the 'poor'. These are the explicit focus of Jesus' spirit-filled mission. They are the members of Luke's household victimized by social structures, taxation demands and marketing pressures who have had their ancestral lands confiscated because of unproductivity. Removed from their farms, barely surviving, they have come to the city and are now the urban peasant landless. Indirectly, their existence and livelihood have been affected by the way Earth has been agriculturally maltreated and over-harvested because of polycropping demands from an international market.

In this scenario, Earth, too, is poor. It, too, is the focus of Jesus' liberating ministry.

Sociologically, the poor includes all regarded as being of 'diminished status'.[30] Luke's concern would be for those members of the gospel household who have experienced this, and for those of elite status who share responsibility for the plight of the poor. This same Lukan insight will occur more explicitly in Jesus' beatitude teaching (6.20-26). The presence of landless peasants in the gospel household is a reminder of the way Earth has been treated. Earth is also of 'diminished status'. The ecological link to the poor is further substantiated by the one who is to announce this good news. Jesus is Earth's child and a member of Earth's household. His ministry would be inclusive of all to whom he belongs and all with whom he identifies. This includes every being, human and non-human, within this household.

This ecological consideration of the outer frame (A) moves us to reflect upon the next inner structure (B) of Jesus' gospel announcement from a similar perspective. This part of the linguistic frame, like the outer one, is theologically balanced. It concerns liberation and release. The recognition of Earth as a living being in symbiotic relationship with humanity is an insight gained earlier from a consideration of the First Testament. It is well formulated in the hermeneutical principle of voice summarized in the Earth Bible commentary *Preface* and echoed in Plato's appreciation of Earth's living interconnectivity. In this context, the release which Jesus' ministry seeks to bring affects humanity and Earth. His mission is to enable release from what incarcerates and oppresses (v. 18c, e). This is global, universal and Earth inclusive.

Listening to this major gospel scene from the perspective of the social groups that constitute Luke's household, Jesus appears elite, with an ability to read from Scripture and interpret it. The Isaiah text which Luke's Jesus quotes, though, preferentially aligns him with the marginalized and disempowered. Something else is also noticeable in the scene. Jesus speaks and announces the meaning of what he has read: 'Today this scripture has been fulfilled in your hearing' (4.21). Luke allows us to hear how the text that has been read by Jesus is linked to his ministry. It is being fulfilled *now*, in Luke's day. The Greek construction of Jesus' statement, connecting 'today' to the perfect passive tense of the verb 'has been fulfilled', makes present that which was past. This concerns the action of God's spirit, present from the beginning of creation, reaffirmed by the prophet Isaiah in the First Testament, materialized hundreds of years later in Jesus of Nazareth, and now demonstrably existent in Luke's household. The present gospel is the fruit of the spirit's agency that removes the chronological and geographical barrier separating Luke's audience from the first witnesses of Jesus' ministry.

---

30. Green, *Luke*, p. 211.

The passive verbal sense ('has been fulfilled') further confirms that this is ultimately God's act.

The whole spirit-inspired inclusive ministry of Jesus is summarized at the chiasm's centre. This concerns recovery of sight to the blind (v. 18d), the hermeneutical centre and key to Jesus' mission.[31] Sight recovery is a healing act that enables people to see; Luke will pick this up later, especially in 18.35-43. However, the kind of seeing intended in Jesus' healing ministry is not simply about human convenience, of enabling people to see and negotiate the physical visible features that surround them; it is not exclusively about a better human lifestyle. At a symbolic deeper level Jesus' healing of blindness is concerned with providing people with something more than a better visual or religiously secure life. It is about deeply seeing all that happens, to interpret, understand and respond. This invitation to a more profound level of reflection and critical scrutiny is also one that is not anthropocentrically driven. It is an invitation to look at and see everyone and everything.

From a contemporary perspective, Jesus' mission can bring ecological openness, study and scrutiny. Such openness results in conversion, ultimately, a capacity for environmental engagement. However, as Jesus' mission and ministry unfold, he will meet resistance. The resistance to this kind of healing is demonstrated in what happens after his Nazareth proclamation (4.22-30). His own townspeople oppose his message that affirms God's universal and non-selective openness, a feature of Jesus' future table ministry. They seek his death for what they consider heresy.

The action of Jesus' home-town opponents anticipates what will happen at the end of the gospel, when his death is finally obtained. Their antipathy also serves to contrast the very point of Jesus' synagogue sermon. His healing act specified at the heart of Luke's programmatic declaration concerns chronic spiritual blindness that prevents potential disciples from seeing, understanding, and analysing the realities of life. It is the kind of blindness that brings oppression on to / in to Earth's household. Jesus is now a victim of this, reflected in the antagonism of his Nazareth compatriots.

Conclusion

What has guided our consideration of an ecological and Earth picture in this part of the gospel is the inner play of Lk. 3.1–4.30 (Figure 17). This is discerned in the framing *word-spirit* dynamic. Both the *word* and *spirit* elements of this dynamic have ecological tones heard against the backdrop of the major symphonic score which Luke composes.

---

31. Chad Hartsock, *Sight and Blindness in Luke–Acts: The use of Physical Features in Characterization* (Leiden: E.J. Brill, 2008), pp. 177-79.

Gospel auditors first hear Luke's ecological tones in John's wilderness location and ministry (3.1-20), and the ameliorating changes which the evangelist makes to the Isaiah intertext received from Mark (3.4-6). As we saw, this text, traditionally associated with John's ministry, has the potential to be a text of 'Earth terror' canonizing its destruction. Luke's additions from LXX Isaiah soften this potential and convert the image of Earth from being a potential victim of human destruction to a mediator of conversion. John's ministry prepares for Jesus. He is baptized in a scene ecologically resonant as the spirit descends upon him and manifests itself 'bodily' (3.21-22). God's spirit is now physically and tangibly upon Earth affirmed in Jesus who, as the genealogy attests, is from Earth, being 'son of Adam, son of God' (3.37). This same spirit, associated with the eco-metanarrative of creation, brings Jesus to encounter the devil at the discernible centrepiece of the inner play in this section of the gospel (4.1-13). In the temptation scenes contemporary auditors can discern three fundamental ecological principles from Luke's story:

- Earth is to be cared for by human beings, not the subject of human greed;
- Communion with God helps deepen communion with Earth;
- Earth's resources are for the good of all and not for manipulation or control over others.

The final scene (4.16-30) set in Jesus' hometown synagogue completes the inner play and presents the essence of Jesus' future ministry. Again, Luke borrows from an Isaiah intertext to craft Jesus' spirit inspired declaration (Figure 19). His future ministry will be concerned about announcing the gospel to 'the poor', a theological symbol that could be interpreted as including all within Earth's household that are marginalized and disrespected by the powerful urban elite. This includes not only the urban poor, but also Earth, a victim of poverty. Jesus' mission concerns all Earth's poor, human and non-human. His ministry is about liberation and salvation that reactivates the Sabbath year and brings salvation to everything. Of importance is Jesus' mission to bring sight to the blind.

At a deeper symbolic and ecological level, the restoration of sight concerns bringing the gospel's human household to social alertness and environmental astuteness. Its members have the power to come to a perceptive level of seeing that will help them interpret the social and ecological issues intrinsic to the Greco-Roman world. This new capacity 'to see' will bring about a release from the existential blindness envisaged by Luke. It will further the healing of the social and ecological fracture in Earth's household caused by political and religious powerbrokers represented in the urban elite. At this deep ecological level of healing, Luke invites the gospel's original audience including ourselves 'to see' and attend; this is essentially about *metanoia*.

For potential disciples, ancient and new, Jesus' central ministry is about healing chronic blindness that prevents people from seeing their link with and responsibility towards Earth's household. How this healing and Jesus' invitation to ecological conversion unfold moves us to the next symphonic movement in Luke's score.

Earth's Voice

The *rhēma* of God came to John son of Zechariah in the wilderness (Lk. 3.2).

Jesus, full of the Holy Spirit, returned from the Jordan and was led by the Spirit in the wilderness, where for forty days he was tempted by the devil (Lk. 4.1-2).

Earth speaks:

> I bring John into my wilderness.
>
> In its stillness and in solitude he touches me and learns from me.
> Like generations earlier, especially the Israelite people who wandered in me, he meets God and learns his calling.
>
> Living in my wilderness, John learns the meaning of *metanoia* and teaches others.
>
> Into my wilderness, God's spirit also brings my child.
>
> Here he confronts and defeats Satan.
>
> In my wilderness, as with John, my child deepens how to be with God
>
> And seeks to protect me, keep me safe,
> and allow my fruits to be for the good of all in my household.

Chapter 5

LUKE 4.14–7.23

JESUS' MINISTRY IN THE GARDEN OF GOD'S EARTHLY DELIGHTS

In the early chapters of the gospel we are introduced to Luke's Jesus. He is Earth's child, faithful and intimate, beloved of God, and empowered by God's spirit to proclaim release and bring about sight to the blind. We have seen that his relationship to God is tangibly experienced in the corporeal descent of God's spirit upon him at his baptism and strengthened in his encounter with the diabolical adversary. As we have attended to Luke's overall narrative and discerned its inner play, we have also been able to perceive its ecological tones. These tones confirm Earth's relationship which Jesus carries forward in his ministry, expressed through the Isaiah intertext that defines his ministry and proclaimed amongst his home-town people. The ecological notes underpinning the main narrative score are not noticed in a casual engagement with Luke's gospel. They have surfaced by attuning our ears to aspects in the gospel charged with environmental overtones. We have noticed this in the temple scenes that surround Luke's story of Jesus' birth (1.8-23; 2.37, 46-49), the Earth-related allusions in the 'womb' theme (1.41-42), pregnancy (1.24, 31, 34, 36) and births of John and Jesus (1.57-60; 2.6-7), the symbolic signs emphasized in the birth of Jesus (manger, 2.7, 12, 16; cloth wrappings, 2.7, 12; and 'no place', 2.7), John's wilderness setting (3.1-6), Jesus' baptism (3.21-22) and genealogy (3.23-38), and the Nazareth synagogue proclamation (4.16-21) in which Luke draws on an Isaiah intertext that will define his future ministry. This ministry is essentially about releasing the oppressed and healing blindness. I have suggested that Jesus' ministry is not anthropologically driven or exclusive. It includes all Earth's human and non-human beings. How Jesus' ministry is pragmatically expressed is the focus of this next major movement in Luke's gospel symphony (Lk. 4.31–9.50).

There are four recurring features in Luke 4–9 that offer a way of highlighting and noticing the gospel's ecological melodies over these chapters. These concern the *word-deed* dynamic (which already defined Luke's inner play in the gospel's last section), the Galilean setting of Jesus' public ministry, the ancient appreciation of the human body as the focus of Jesus' healings, and Jesus' confrontation and defeat of the *diabolos* in the way he heals and feeds.

1. *The* Word-Deed, *God's* rhēma, *Unfolds*

As we move into the heart of the gospel it is important to recall what we have already noted about the divine *word-deed*, expressed in the opening chapters as *rhēma*. This is God's creative dynamism found in the First Testament, especially in Genesis, and experienced in what God says and does. It is vitally linked to God's creative act. God speaks and the Earth comes into being. The divine *dabar* (Heb.) is essentially an act of birthing. The prophets reinforce the ongoing presence of God's *dabar* in the way they confront and confound the religio-political systems of their day and seek Israel's conversion back to the Torah.

As we saw, Luke also witnesses to God's creation-bearing *dabar/rhēma* in the gospel's opening chapters. Mary encounters this *rhēma* through the words of the angelic announcer (1.28-29); she believes in it and acts upon it (1.38). It gestates in her womb. Similar to *dabar* in the First Testament and the Genesis account of creation, God's *rhēma* births the child. Luke's portrait of Mary in these opening chapters concludes as she continues to ponder the implications of the *rhēma* spoken to her and acting within her and whose servant she now is (2.19).

Mary's welcome of the divine *rhēma* encourages Luke's auditors to grasp its centrality in their world, as God continues to act and create. The action of the creation-oriented, Earth-linked *rhēma* continues to filter through Luke 4–9. God's *word-deed* is present in Jesus' spirit-enabled Galilean ministry reflected in what he says and does, in his teaching, healing and table communion (4.31–7.50). These are the concrete manifestations of God's *rhēma*. As Jesus teaches, touches and shares food with people, environmental sounds of God's word-deed surface in his ministry.

2. *The Galilean 'Garden' of Jesus' Public Ministry*

Earth's link to God's *rhēma* is further heightened by the location of the scenes of Luke 4–9 explicitly set within the region of Galilee. For Luke this is more than a geographical setting inherited from Mark's gospel. It is an eco-social symbol for Luke's audience. Galilee is about to become the setting for the unfolding of an eco-socio-political drama.

Jesus' parables, images, and aphorisms first originated in a Galilean context at least three generations prior to Luke's present audience. Jesus' sensitivity for his rural world found in his original teaching was absorbed by subsequent generations of his followers and communicated through Luke's sources. These original teachings with their ecological nuances also made their way into Mark's gospel and would have been remembered by Luke's 'eyewitnesses' and 'ministers of the word' (1.2). Luke shapes these memories into the gospel's story of Jesus' Galilean ministry.

Ecologically, Galilee was a rich rural area. Josephus eulogizes its fertility, agricultural productivity and the variety of crops and fruits that the soil produced. Describing Galilee, Josephus writes:

> ... The land is everywhere so rich in soil and pasturage and produces such a variety of trees, that even the most indolent are tempted by these facilities to devote themselves to agriculture. In fact, every inch of the soil has been cultivated by the inhabitants... In short, Galilee...is entirely under cultivation and produces crops from one end to the other.[1]

As we follow Jesus' ministry into this geographical arena, we also move into an ecologically paradisiacal world. Galilee is the mirror of the original biblical garden of paradise, albeit a struggling one in Luke's gospel. In Gen. 2.4b-25 God creates the harmonious garden environment in which Adam is to live. This is 'an environment of peace and harmony with all God's creations and nature: an eco-balance in a state of symbiosis'.[2] The symbiotic relationship which the Earth shares with the human household has already been identified in earlier chapters, especially as we considered the implications of the future ministry of Earth's child. What happens to this child and all human beings affects Earth. Earth is a mediator of God's goodness to humanity; it, too, is affected by that same presence of evil that influences humans. Jesus' healing acts confront and overcome the evil that human beings experience. Their subjugation to the diabolical influence of evil and their experience of healing and release experienced through Jesus has cosmic implications. His deeds also bring wider environmental healing. They counteract the work of the *diabolos* that affects Earth's household, human and non-human. Galilee is the setting in which this conflict with and defeat of the devil is played out. The ecologically rich geographical setting is the arena in which this diabolical and cosmic struggle takes place.

From the cultural-social context of Luke's audience, the rural context and the topics of Jesus' teaching in Luke 4–9 further suggest a peasant audience. Luke's presentation of Jesus' teaching is geared for a Greco-Roman audience stratified along conventional social lines. The mode of socially expected material exchange shaped the patron-client system controlled by the wealthy elite who kept the poor disempowered. This form of exchange would have been felt more in Galilee, especially when the rural poor were

---

1. Josephus, *Jewish War*, 3.41-44.
2. Renethy Keitzar, 'Creation and Restoration: Three Biblical Reflections,' in *Ecotheology: Voices from South and North* (ed. David G. Hallman; New York: Orbis Books, 1994), p. 53.

beholden to the urban elite for support and sustenance in times of hardship, famine and crop failure.

In sum, Galilee is a rich metaphor in Luke's gospel: evocative of creation's goodness, the importance of Earth, its lands, and the way its soil is treated and cultivated. It is also the setting in which typical relationships and interactions of the Greco-Roman world are played out. Importantly, Galilee offers Luke a metaphor of God's original paradisiacal garden in which human beings are invited to live in right relationship with each other within Earth's household. Galilee also represents a world in need of healing, liberation and restoration.

3. The Human Body

At the heart of Jesus' healing ministry is the human body. Luke's audience would have known that the body implied more than a physical human body. It concerned the world, universe and creation. The ancients believed that this body was symbolically linked to Earth and cosmic bodies. The ancient Greek appreciation of the human body acted as another gospel intertext upon which Luke draws; it influences the appreciation of the gospel healing stories of people's bodies. Of particular relevance are the insights of Plato (427–c. 328 BCE) and Aristotle (384–322 BCE).

Plato on the Body
Plato regarded the body as mortal and the abode for the immortal soul distinct from the body. Only death freed the soul from the restraint caused by its bodily connection.[3] Building upon Homer's anthropology, Plato regarded the totality of the body as an object of contemplation. Together with the soul, it made the person whole. The entire reality of body and soul constituted a living, mortal being. Plato located the immortal soul in the head. This positioning of the soul enabled a person to be drawn upright towards the heavens, to that which the soul belonged and was attracted.[4]

Plato's affirmation of the celestial attraction of the body's soul came from his appreciation of the relationship between the body and the cosmos. This intimate connection between the body and the cosmos, almost like a kinship, had also been explored by other writers of the period. Democritus (c. 460–370 BCE) for example, writing just before Plato, described the human person as a miniature cosmos.[5] Plato expanded on Democritus'

---

3. Plato, *Phaedrus* 64c, 67a; Plato, *Gorgias* 524b.
4. Plato, *Timaeus* 90a b; Eduard Schweizer, 'σῶμα', *TDNT*, VII (ed. Gerhard Kittel and Gerhard Friedrich; Grand Rapids, MI: Wm B. Eerdmans Publishing Co., 1964), pp. 1024-44 (1029).
5. Schweizer, 'σῶμα', p. 1029.

insight and considered the reciprocal relationship between the body and the cosmos. Plato averred that the body was a cosmos and the cosmos a body, a 'single living being'.[6] The body was a *microcosm* of the cosmos; the cosmos a *macrocosm* of the body. This cosmic-body reciprocity meant that the human body was composed of the same elements of the universe: air, Earth, water and fire. For both Plato and his predecessor Democritus, the body was definitively and essentially linked to Earth. What happened to one affected the other.

Aristotle on the Body
Aristotle drew upon Plato's hierarchical distinction between body and soul, placing greater importance on the soul's cognitive faculty of knowing. Like Plato, he affirmed the concord between body and soul, though he developed a philosophy of the body defined by matter and form. Aristotle considered that the soul gave the body particularity because of its indissoluble bond to the body. The soul moulded the body into a piece of art. This was the living person, microcosmically related to the heavenly body, as Plato had earlier affirmed.

Aristotle explored further the political implications of his anthropology. He viewed the body as a physiological parallel to the political structure of the city-state.[7] He used this socio-political reference to the human body to support the social structures of his day, especially society's elitist and hierarchical arrangement. Whatever critique we may make of Aristotle's philosophical argument, he continued to affirm the relationship of the body to the cosmos, Earth and human society. Like Plato, he regarded the body as a social and cosmic map that reflected the universe and Earth in which it existed. In this respect, Aristotle and Plato provided a way of moving beyond an attitude to the body that saw it in purely material or mechanistic terms. It had a value that was essentially symbolic; it was capable of being interpreted as a metaphor for society, Earth's household and the cosmos.

This fruit of Hellenistic corporeal understanding found in Plato and Aristotle was available to Luke. How much of their thought influenced the evangelist is, of course, hard to assess. However, Platonic and Aristotelian approaches to human cognition helped to support a social hierarchy and elitism evident in the Greco-Roman world of Luke's day. Their insights into the human body attest to a holistic anthropology that affirmed the

---

6. See Dale B. Martin, *The Corinthian Body* (Yale, CN: Yale University Press, 1995), pp. 14-16.
7. See Plato, *Demodocus* Frag. 34; Aristotle, *Politics* 1.2; 5,2; *De Anima* 2.1. See also Colin Brown (ed.) *NIDNTT*, I (Grand Rapids: Zondervan, 1986), p. 232; Schweizer, 'σῶμα', p. 1031.

connection of the human person to the social, environmental and cosmic universe. Their recognition of the body's micro and macrocosmic qualities identifies a potential Greek philosophical gospel intertext that was part of the cultural, literary and philosophical landscape available to Luke. If this was a gospel intertext then its reception into Luke's story of Jesus would further help auditors appreciate more fully Jesus' healing ministry. His healing of the physical ailments of people's bodies would imply a broader macro-cosmic healing of Earth and the social body.

4. Confrontation and Defeat of the Diabolos—Jesus Heals and Feeds

In Luke's day, evil spirits were considered the cause of sickness and disease. We already know that the devil left Jesus to 'return at an opportune time' (4.13) in anticipation of his passion. The intervening time is not diabolically free as Luke makes clear in Luke 4–9. Jesus continues to confront the powers of evil still at work in the lives of people. He confronts and defeats these powers through his ministry of healing. An important aspect of this ministry of healing is his table communion, a theme prominent throughout Luke–Acts.[8]

The meals that Jesus provided or at which he was a guest at a deeper, symbolic level spoke about the nature of Jesus' God, God's intention to defeat the diabolical powers at work in the Earth household, and the kind of Earth community God desired. Jesus' meal practice was such a powerful and confronting action that it eventually led to his death. As Robert Karris suggests,

> Jesus got himself crucified because of the way he ate. The religious leaders could not tolerate this prophet of good news to the poor who not only in word, but especially at meals criticized their way of life…Jesus was, for them, a spokesperson for an alien God…Jesus was leading the people astray.[9]

Jesus' healing deeds and his table practice reveal God's desire for humanity and creation: to be released from any form of oppression. Jesus' meal ministry, a key theme that permeates this section of Luke's gospel, is related to his deeds of healing. When we focus on Jesus' meal gathering we will see how important hospitality and welcome are. While these stories are usually interpreted as Jesus' concern for the human household, there is a broader, richer environmental perspective to be considered. The gospel's food stories concern hungry people and demonstrate the kind of hospitality that Jesus

---

8. John P. Heil, *The Meal Scenes in Luke–Acts: An Audience-Oriented Approach* (Atlanta, GA: Society of Biblical Literature, 1999).

9. Robert J. Karris, *Luke: Artist and Theologian: Luke's Passion Account as Literature* (New York: Paulist Press, 1985), p. 70.

models for Luke's audience. They are also stories about the Earth. Jesus dines and reveals the God of delight by the kinds of meals that he celebrates with others. Jesus' God is enchanted with the whole of creation; food is the fruit of God's earthly delight. Jesus' open table communion with all, especially those considered social pariahs is a prominent theme in Luke. Karris asks,

> And why does Luke's kerygmatic story depict Jesus as enjoying life so much? Luke's view of God is the answer. And as his narrative goes, Jesus is the revealer of this God, the faithful God who *feeds hungry creation*, rectifies the ills that plague it, and rejoices to sup with sinners. Can the [auditor] believe this God?[10]

Jesus' table ministry practically expresses the meaning of the 'Lord's year of favour', a time of bounteous giving and debt release according to the Jubilee prescription of Leviticus 25: freedom to slaves, release of accumulated debt, allowing the land to remain fallow. The Jubilee year, now reiterated in the ministry of Jesus, had consequences for the entire Earth household, for human relationships and for the Earth itself. The year had environmental and ecological implications. This Jubilee release from oppression is tangibly expressed through Luke 4–9. It finds its most pragmatic expression in Jesus' deeds of exorcism, in his confrontation with the *diabolos*. Exorcism is not a private affair or a secret healing of a single person. It is essentially a communal and ecologically pertinent act which involves the entire household. Not only are human beings affected and influenced by the diabolic spirits. These invade Earth, too, that is in need of exorcism; Earth's healing will become clearer as Luke's story of Jesus unfolds.

In summary, Jesus is God's Earth child. He delights in the fruits of the Earth, particularly bread. These become the media by which human beings celebrate with each other, in communion with God and God's creation. How the fruits of Earth are received determine authentic discipleship. For this reason, the accumulation of wealth, the elite confiscation of peasant lands, the selfish gathering and storage of Earth's crops, the maintenance of the patronage-client system that keeps people locked into debt and dependency, and the type of economic exchange that expects balanced return—all these practices and socio-cultural mores come under close scrutiny from Luke's Jesus. While they concern human interaction, they are attached to attitudes to Earth and the appreciation of goods and fruits. Luke's Jesus will show potential disciples paths to renewal, conversion, hospitality and Earth-care through his healing, teaching (especially his teaching on enemy love in the 'Sermon on the Plain', 6.27-36), and table ministry. God's *rhēma* continues to unfold in Jesus' life-giving and healing actions.

---

10. Karris, *Luke: Artist*, p. 70. My emphasis.

5. Luke 4.14–7.23

Inner play of Lk. 4.14–7.23

The above four features of Luke 4–9—of the ongoing progress of God's word-deed (*rhēma*), the potentially paradisiacal and environmentally evocative Galilean setting, Jesus' healing of the human and Earth body, and his confrontation with the *diabolos*—offer a way of exploring the Earth-saturated dimensions of Luke's story of Jesus. The ongoing presence of the *rhēma* in Jesus' words and deeds, especially his healing acts and table practice also present us with a means of identifying more clearly Luke's inner play. These five chapters can be divided into two smaller sections, 4.14–7.23 and 7.24–9.51, defined by subunits that focus on Jesus' teaching and deeds of healing and his feasting with others. These are further surrounded by call stories (of the twelve, Levi, others) and reactions to Jesus' public teaching. In what follows I shall first focus on Lk. 4.14–7.23 and its Earth-related stories. The next chapter shall concentrate on Lk. 7.24–9.51. There I shall discuss Luke's inner play in those chapters and reflect on their key Earth-related stories.

The first section, 4.14–7.23, is designated by the interaction of Jesus' *word-deed* (Figure 20). His words (A) and deeds (B) interlock each other in an A–B–A–B–A–A+B–A pattern. Summaries about the success or effect of his words create the skeletal frame in which deeds of healing, exorcisms, table communion and the calling of his disciples are inserted. The centre of the inner play revolves around Jesus' deeds of healing, table communion and calling Simon and the twelve to discipleship (5.1–6.16).

The section begins and ends with programmatic statements about Jesus' ministry announced and accomplished with descriptions that echo each other: 'release…sight to the blind' (4.18, 7.22-23). The opening scene in Jesus' hometown synagogue (4.14-30) defines his liberating and healing activity which has ecological implications. The closing scene (7.18-23) tells

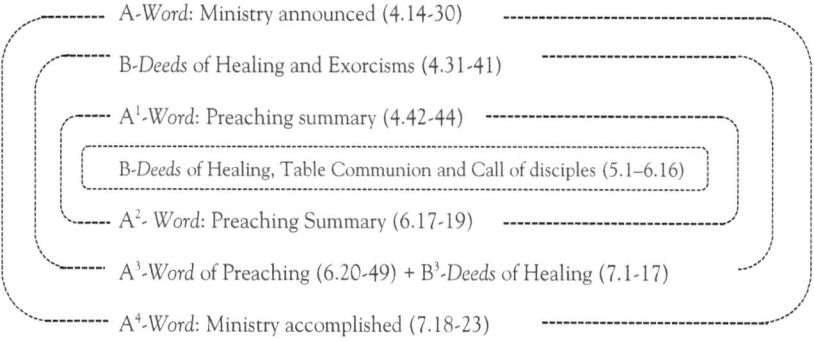

Figure 20. *The* Word-Deed *thematic pattern in Lk. 4.14–7.23*

John the Baptizer's disciples and reminds Luke's auditors how Jesus' ministry has been accomplished. Both scenes also deal with the offending responses to Jesus' ministry. In the Nazareth synagogue his listeners are offended by his explication of the Isaiah intertext, that God's salvific concern is universal, non-sectarian and socially inclusive. To his listeners this seems to deny their prior privilege and divine right as God's foremost people; they seek to kill him for this apparent heresy (4.23-30). In the concluding scene of this subsection, Jesus praises those who take 'no offense' at him (7.23). Both scenes can be heard with ecological 'ears'. In the synagogue teaching, Jesus' liberating ministry applies to Earth and the way it is treated. To John's disciples, Jesus responds in *deed* and *word* to their question about whether he is the one to come or whether they should they wait for another (7.20).

> In that hour he healed many with diseases, plagues and evil spirits, and he released many blind to see. And he answered them, 'Go and announce to John what you have seen and heard: the blind see, the lame walk, lepers are cleansed, and the deaf hear, the dead are raised, the poor are evangelized.' (7.21-23)[11]

The healing of people, by association and macrocosmic symbiosis, is a healing of Earth. Demonic release is explicit as Jesus' deeds and words in these verses reflect, echo and balance each other. The actions of Jesus speak to his statement addressed to John's disciples; his words to John's disciples reflect and summarize his deeds of release for Earth's household; he is literally rectifying the ills 'that plague' God's hungry creation (Karris).

Jesus' healing of Earth's body (4.14-37)

After Jesus' synagogue announcement of his ministry and its reaction by his hometown kin (4.14-30), his first public act of healing occurs in Capernaum (4.31-37), described as a 'city of Galilee' (4.31). This first healing-exorcism sets the parameters for subsequent healings: the confrontation with evil in the diabolic form, the need for release of the person, and the response by those who witness the healing. 'In Luke's presentation, healing is portrayed along similar lines as exorcism,' writes Joel Green,

> with comparable language employed in both cases ('rebuke' + 'come out/ leave'—vv. 35, 39, 41). This is not to interpret illness as necessarily a

---

11. The association of the captive and shattered, blind, mute, lepers and poor together represents a set of types and function 'rhetorically in Luke's narrative to make the christological point that Jesus is God's unique eschatological agent of salvation', according to S. John Roth, *The Blind, the Lame, and the Poor* (Sheffield: Sheffield Academic Press, 1997), p. 23.

consequence of demon possession. Rather, it is to recognize Luke's view that people who 'have a demon' and those who suffer from illness are both oppressed by diabolic forces and both in need of 'release'.[12]

The urban setting of the story focuses on Jesus' word. The people are astonished at 'his teaching, for his word has authority' (4.32). At the forefront of Jesus' ministry is the presence of his word, which has a power to save, heal and defeat evil. In this context, the first exorcism takes place in a religious institutional setting, the synagogue.

Possessed with an evil spirit is a human being (*anthrōpos*), not a gender specific character (a 'male'—*anēr*, in Greek) as all translations would suggest.

There will be other times in the gospel when the evangelist employs the universalising designation *anthrōpos* in preference to the gender specific male term *anēr* that was available. And I shall highlight them when they occur. The point I make here, though, is that Luke's preference for *anthrōpos* underscores the universality of the possessed experience. The person is representative of humanity in a state of oppression and caught by demonic and cosmic evil forces that threaten to annihilate. The words that come from the demonically possessed human being with its use of single and plural references ('Let us alone! What have you to do with us, Jesus of Nazareth? Have you come to destroy us? I know who you are, the Holy One of God', 4.34) reflects a cosmic social hierarchy.[13] This recognizes the power of God and God's agents over the spirit-world, which in turn has power over human beings to make them ill.

The one possessed by several evil spirits ('us', 4.34a) can only be released by a power greater than them. This is the 'holy one of God' (4.34b) that they acknowledge. Jesus rebukes, confronts the evil spirits, and releases the human being from their possession. The reaction of the onlookers praises the power of Jesus' word and the effect of his word, of release. They say,

> What kind of word is this that by authority and power he commands unclean spirits and they come out? (4.36)

Noticeable is that the place or arena *out of which* the release of these evil spirits comes. They 'come out', but the onlookers leave undetermined, unspecified and open ended from where the evil spirits are exorcised. If we were hearing this statement anthropocentrically then the unclean spirits would be exorcised from the human being only. But this is not stated explicitly, though it is implied. This release could conceivably be from anyone or *thing* that is affected; this includes from Earth's body. This wider reference

---

12. Green, *Luke*, pp. 220-21.
13. Malina, *Social-Science*, pp. 312-23.

is confirmed by the last verse of the scene. Jesus' fame spreads into every place and 'surrounding land' (*perichōros*) (4.37) and is not restricted to the adjoining places where only human beings exist. It includes every one, everything, every part of Earth's environs. In other words, hearing the story with ecological sensitivity, Earth's body is healed and affected by Jesus' deed of power. We shall see another Earth parallel towards the end of this subunit after Jesus has restored a dead young man into the care of his mother (7.17).

Healing a Member of Earth's household (4.38-41)

Jesus' exorcisms continue in Simon's house (4.38-41). This domestic scene is a first where Jesus gathers in a household of the prime disciple, Simon. What happens here is significant and, like its predecessor, is an exorcism event. It speaks into the kind of symbolic world represented by this household in need of exorcism. The woman here, like the demonically possessed person in the previous scene, is representative of those who are ostracized from household and communion. Conventionally, she would be expected to reside in the house of her spouse or eldest son. But she is in the house of her daughter. Perhaps for Luke she represents those in the gospel audience widowed, divorced or diseased in need of special care. Perhaps she is symbolically representative of all who are unclean or maltreated. Nevertheless she is present in the house of her son-in-law, Simon. Whatever the reason for her presence, she is seriously ill with a 'high fever' (4.38b). Death seems imminent.

While the woman and Simon are the two key characters that Luke frames, something else is clear. Jesus' act of exorcising the evil that will reveal itself in the woman's sickness is precipitated by the prayer of a number of people: '*they* besought him for her' (4.38c). As a result of communal intercession, her healing is instantaneous. She, a fractured member of Earth's family is, literally, 'resurrected' (*anistēmi*) and 'ministers' (*diakoneō*) to 'them', to the gathered household. Jesus' healing deed in Simon's house becomes a moment of resurrection, release and ministry to be celebrated.

The household of disciples reflected in this scene is paradigmatic for Luke's auditors and their household: it is a place where resurrection is tangibly experienced, people restored and liberated for ministry, and intercession provided on behalf of all within Earth's household in need of healing. Importantly, it is also the place of prayer where Jesus is 'besought' to bring about healing and release for everyone and every place bound by the presence of evil. Reflected upon in concert with the immediately preceding exorcism and Jesus' healing ministry that continues after this scene and concludes his day (4.40-41), such prayer would focus on any aspect of Earth's body known to be in need of healing; it would be ecologically determined.

Summary of Jesus' First Day of Public Ministry—Revelation of the 'Basileia-Ecotopia' *(4.42-44)*

Luke then offers a summary of the first day of Jesus' active ministry and his preaching focus, to the 'cities' and synagogues of Judea (4.42-44). Noteworthy here is how the summary begins as Jesus first enters into the wilderness, a residence for all untamed and undomesticated Earth creatures, and from the First Testament, the place of divine communion. The wilderness has already figured in the gospel. From here John the Baptizer began his preaching and Jesus encountered the *diabolos*. It is an explicitly rich ecological and rural environment far removed from the towns, cities or villages from which Jesus is able to return to the gospel's urban setting. It is as though the wilderness is able to strengthen and nurture Jesus who is then able to declare his real purpose in ministry: 'To these other cities I must proclaim the gospel of the reign (*basileia*) of God, because for this I was sent' (4.43).

Apart from its mention by the angel to Mary in reference to Jesus' future ministry in 1.33, this is the first time since then that 'reign' (*basileia*) is mentioned by Luke. It will recur over forty more times in the gospel. Here it occurs in Jesus' words as a summary of his mission and an echo of the Isaiah text earlier that first flagged his ministry which we have now seen unfolding in this first day of his public ministry.

Basileia is the non-hierarchical, inclusive 'cosmic symbol that invoked creation and the eschatological "new creation"'.[14] It is Earth's idyllic experience of justice, peace and harmony and an ecologically loaded expression.[15] *Basileia* expresses God's liberating presence to release humanity and creation from evil and bring about healing and reconciliation.[16] As Walter Kasper says,

> This thing which God alone can provide, which God ultimately...is, is what is meant by the [*basileia*] of God. It involves the meaning of God's being God and Lord, which at the same time means the humanity of human beings and the salvation of the world because it means *liberation from the forces of evil which are hostile to creation*, and reconciliation in place of the implacable

---

14. Elisabeth Schüssler Fiorenza, *Jesus: Miriam's Child, Sophia's Prophet: Critical Issues in Feminist Christology* (London: SCM Press, 1993), pp. 110-11; Bauckham, *Living*, pp. 70-75.

15. Gordon Zerbe, 'Ecology according to the New Testament', *Direction* 21 (1992), pp. 15-26 (16).

16. For a study on the relationship between the *basileia* and Jesus in Luke–Acts, see Costantino Antonio Ziccardi, *The Relationship of Jesus and the Kingdom of God According to Luke–Acts* (Roma: Pontificia Università Gregoriana, 2008).

antagonism of the present world. That is the fundamental theme of Jesus' message.[17]

The *basileia*, then, is the arena of God's saving action culturally and historically located. It is God's demonstrable deed that liberates Earth and its members and overcomes any evil that prevents this.

Before continuing, let me offer a brief word about the expression I shall use when the Greek *basileia* appears in the gospel. Given the inclusive nature of the *basileia*, the common English translations 'kingdom' or 'reign' are unhelpful, if not misleading. For this reason, I prefer to retain the Greek *basileia*. This expresses the theological reality that Jesus seeks to make tangible by his presence and ministry narrated throughout the rest of Luke's gospel. His mission is to ensure that God's *basileia* is realized in the lives of human beings and the whole created world. As I seek to honour this wider inclusive ecological dimension implicit in the rich appreciation of *basileia* at times I shall add '*ecotopia*' to *basileia*.[18]

My adoption of this expression '*basileia-ecotopia*', therefore, acknowledges the fullness of God's ecological intention present in the *basileia* revealed in Jesus. It also acts as a reminder that God's *basileia* is not exclusively anthropocentric but inclusive of all creation.[19] Ecological reverberations, therefore, lie at the heart of Jesus' explicit mission. This is the 'gospel', the 'good news' of God's encounter with humanity and creation through Jesus' preaching as we now move towards the centrepiece of Lk. 4.14–7.23.

The 'Word-Deed' Pattern in 5.1–6.16

The heart of the developing *word-deed* pattern (5.1–6.16) is an act of meal sharing (5.29-39) that emerges from his call to discipleship of Levi (5.27-28). But this central scene is surrounded by healing and feeding stories (5.12-26; 6.1-11), which in turn are surrounded by the calling of the Twelve (5.1-11; 6.12-16), especially Simon Peter. The whole subunit seems carefully constructed to reinforce Luke's portrait of Jesus as healer, liberator, and revealer of God's abundant joy. This joy gets expressed through the kinds of meals that he celebrates with others as he feeds God's hungry creation. The maternal fructive imagery that surrounded Jesus in his birth story finds its ongoing manifestation here in Luke 5.

---

17. Walter Kasper, *Jesus the Christ* (New York: Paulist Press, 1976), pp. 73-74. My emphasis.

18. I borrow the term 'ecotopia' from Bauckham (*The Bible and Ecology*, pp. 25, 175-77) who in turn borrows it from Bill Deval, *Simple in Means, Deep in Ends: Practising Deep Ecology* (London: Green Print, 1990), p. 34 (*The Bible and Ecology*, p. 184, n. 58).

19. Bauckham, *Living*, pp. 63-64.

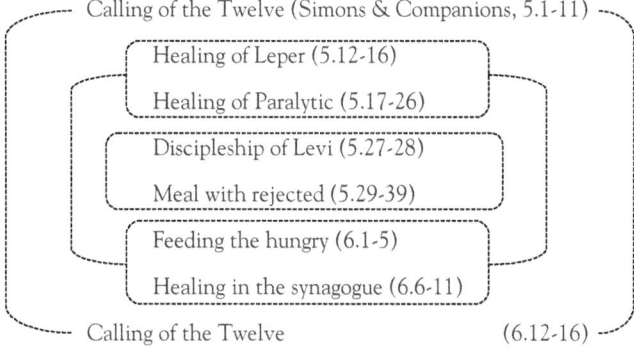

Figure 21. *The* Word-Deed *thematic pattern in Lk. 5.1–6.16.*

This central piece of this opening section of Jesus' public ministry is ecologically framed by Earth images. In the opening scene *water* is central; in the closing one, a *mountain*. In both, disciples are called and the elements of water and Earth are the bearers and contexts for their respective calls. They are, as it were, active participants in the meaning of the calls to discipleship. They offer the context, setting and means by which Jesus' invitation to the disciples becomes clearer.[20]

Jesus Calls his First Disciples from Earth's Elements (5.1-11)

Lk. 5.1-11 is a wonderful story that breaks open with fresh meaning when listened to ecologically. Luke has drawn on Mark's similar intertext (Mk 1.16-20), significantly refashioning it. The evangelist alters Mark's story concerned with the call of the first four of Jesus' disciples (Simon, Andrew, James and John), into a call primarily of one, Simon, and then of those associated with him. The effect is to introduce and heighten Simon's call and prepare for the role he will play in the gospel and the early chapters of Acts. Luke also emphasizes the role played by Earth's primordial substance, water, potentially though not explicitly present in Mark's story.

Water and Earth, the most fundamental universal elements, are characters in the story as significant as Simon and his companions—on whom the story is focused. 'Earth' frames the story: the people are described as being on Earth listening to the 'Word of God' (5.1-3); the disciples literally *Earth* their boats at the story's conclusion; they bring their boats back to 'Earth', leave everything to follow Jesus (5.11). Jesus sits on the water in Simon's boat a 'little from Earth' (5.3b) to preach the word to the people on the Earth. The relationship between Earth and water is noted. Jesus speaks

---

20. For more on the prominence of water in Galilee, the explicit setting for the stories in this part of Luke's gospel, see Freyne, *Jesus*, pp. 49-53.

the 'Word of God' to the people (5.1). The word (*rhēma*) comes to them from the *water*, the element last imaginatively associated in Luke's gospel with Jesus' baptism in 3.21. There Jesus heard God's word to him; here the people also hear God's word now spoken through Jesus. This 'word' turns out later to be explicitly God's *rhēma*. The boat in which Jesus sits with Peter and from which he speaks to the people on the land is fashioned from Earth.[21] Constructed of wood, it becomes the context for a new fashioning of the household of disciples, symbolically represented by the boat in which Jesus and Peter are present.

Jesus finishes preaching. He invites Simon to

> put out into the deep (*bathos*) and let down your nets for a catch (5.4).

The *bathos* expresses the *depth* of water into which Peter's nets will be lowered. It also expresses cosmological aspects not lost on an auditor whose ears are attuned to ecological sounds. The *bathos* and its association with one of the four elements of creation represent the possibilities of 'catch' that are found in the universal depths, the depths of creation, represented in Jesus' invitation to Peter. Without communion with Jesus, fishing has been fruitless. Now in Simon's clear response to Jesus' *rhēma* ('…on your *rhēma*, I shall let down the nets', 5.5b), a fruitless sea becomes fruitful as Peter, 'those with him' and later his 'partners' (James and John, described as *koinōnoi*) are overwhelmed by the catch. This 'catch' is not about a successful fishing expedition under the direction of Jesus. It concerns the act of liberation of the *bathos* of creation, of bringing to life that which is found in the *bathos* and has, up until now, remained dormant. In response to the divine *rhēma* revealed through Jesus, Simon and the household of disciples with him are able to enact God's liberation for humanity and creation.

The liberation of creation (the huge catch of fish) becomes the symbol for the liberation of humanity. This is expressed in Jesus' words, '…from now on you will be catching alive human beings' (5.10). This injunction enables these newly called disciples to be released materially from all that holds them bound from following Jesus. From this point on, the fish no longer feature in the story. In a sense they, too, have been released. They are not described as a commodity for market. Given the generous proportion of the number caught, a lucrative catch they would be indeed. But this is not their purpose. They serve to enable the disciples to be freed, too. These disciples no longer need to use the fruits of the sea for their livelihood. For Luke, Jesus' disciples let go of their possessions, Earth's materials they once owned and its fruits from the sea they sought to harvest, at times unsuccessfully.

---

21. For evidence of the construction of a first century CE Galilean fishing vessel and its significance, see Shelly Waschmann, 'The Galilee Boat: 2000-Year-Old Hull Recovered Intact', *BAR* 14 (1988), pp. 18-33.

Discipleship, for contemporary auditors, is thus a call to ecological freedom and non-possessiveness, a clear pragmatic enactment of the ethical ecological principles identified in Jesus' testing (4.1-13). Communion with Jesus is the heart of all life now for those whom he calls. This is illustrated in the gospel as the first-called disciples 'brought their boats to the Earth left everything and followed him' (5.11). Released from a spirit of possessing Earth and bringing a humanly constructed object manufactured from Earth's trees back to where they belong, to the Earth, they are now free to follow Jesus.

The boat, the symbolic image of the household of disciples, is now linked to the Earth and returned to the matter from which it was first formed. This cosmological harmony is established through the call of Jesus from the watery and apparently fruitless chaos of primeval creation.[22] Their communion with Jesus' *rhēma* enacted through Simon allows for freedom from oppression to be experienced in creation and on the waters. This prefigures what is about to happen in the human household as the disciples begin to 'catch alive human beings' (5.10). As Jesus' ministry begins, the whole Earth affected by the presence of evil is healed and restored.

Earth's Healing and Celebration—Levi's 'Great Feast' (5.12-32)

This restoration is demonstrated in the next two healing stories (5.12-16, 17-26), the call of Levi to discipleship (5.27-28) and the feast that he and other tax collectors and sinners share with Jesus (5.29-32). All that happens over these verses concerns human beings—their healing and forgiveness, an invitation to discipleship and a celebratory meal. They are stories about the restoration of human wholeness and the tangible realization of God's *basileia-ecotopia*. As Brendan Byrne eloquently puts it,

> The miracles are signs pointing to a more complete wholeness that is God's ultimate intent for humanity. They disclose God's purpose here and now, even if the full realization of that purpose must await the final arrival of the kingdom. Moreover, they are not simply acts of great kindness Jesus performed for certain individuals 'back there' (during his historical life). As told in the gospels they are 'our story' as well, invitations to us to enter into the narrative, identify with the characters, and see whether the transforming power of the Risen Lord cannot also be at work within our own bodies, including our wounded, alienated, and indeed 'leprous' parts.'[23]

At another level these verses also concern Earth and the transforming power of the Risen Jesus at work within creation. The symbiotic relationship that exists between the human, cosmic and Earth bodies means that the total

---

22. On the association of water with chaos, see Bauckham, *Living*, pp. 76-77.
23. Brendan Byrne, *Lifting the Burden*, p. 75.

household is healed, liberated from the evil that affects Earth's environment, and is involved in celebrating the presence of a joyous God delighted by human beings and creation. This is the reason for the 'great feast' (5.29) with which Levi celebrates his colleagues, fellow sinners and Jesus. This feast of hospitality is the figurative celebration of the God of earthly delights who entertains and celebrates the stranger and alienated. It is typified by food and drink, Earth's fruits. These mediate and bring restoration, communion, celebration and joy into the lives of human beings ostracized by social and religious structures. Karris describes this story in 5.27-32 as a highlight. It celebrates God's communion with creation.

> Luke's theme of food, which runs throughout his gospel, surfaces here [5:27-32]. God's desire to be with…creation is symbolized by a feast with all its joy, celebration, friendship, and merriment.'[24]

The setting in which this feast takes place is explicitly the house belonging to Jesus' latest disciple Levi (5.29). The identification of the house with Levi is a clarification which Luke makes to the Markan intertext in which the celebratory meal occurs in 'his house' (Mk 2.15). Mark's text is ambiguous as to the one to whom the house belongs. It could belong either to Jesus or Levi; though all English translations presume it is Levi's.[25] For Luke, there is no ambiguity. It is clearly the house of Levi. Emphatic is the nature of the household gathering in Levi's house, a conceivably wealthy environment given the economic status of but social disrespect for taxation agents in Luke's world. It is the guest list rather than the menu that matters for Luke.[26] This is a gathering of taxation collectors associated with sinners. The religious officials criticize Jesus to his disciples for his friendship with such unwholesome people (5.16).

We have already come across taxation issues and people in the gospel: taxation is implied in the census which Caesar Augustus orders that brings the pregnant Mary and Joseph to Bethlehem (2.1-3); taxation officers are attracted to John the Baptizer's message of repentance (3.12-13). Such people would have conceivably been part of Luke's auditors who represented the wealthy elite. Tax or toll collectors were unequivocally judged as dishonest exploiters who abused the Roman taxation system for gain.[27] They bid for the contract to extract the required tolls, and engineered strategies that would cover the cost of their bid and make a hefty profit at

---

24. Karris, 'Luke', p. 693.
25. See Trainor, *Quest*, pp. 97-98.
26. Eugene LaVerdiere, *Dining in the Kingdom of God: Origins of the Eucharist* (Chicago, IN: Liturgy Training Publications, 1994), p. vii.
27. Green, *Luke*, pp. 178-79; John R. Donahue, 'Tax Collectors and Sinners: An Attempt at Identification', *CBQ* 33 (1971), pp. 39-61.

the same time. The toll extraction pressures placed on their targets would have forced these to eke out more produce from Earth and seas. Over-farming and over-fishing would have resulted. Thus, toll collectors could be considered environmental brigands through a chain of economic control that they wielded in forcing peasants into difficult economic situations that had ecological consequences.

Levi's call to discipleship and the celebratory feast that he throws for Jesus, his taxation colleagues and other sinners is also a celebration of creation. Their invitation to this meal results from their conversion to the kind of hospitality that welcomes others, releases the unfairly taxed from debt and frees up the need to pillage Earth for economic and taxation benefit. The feast in Levi's house is therefore a celebration of Earth.

A final point in this rich central scene is the tension between the call of Levi to discipleship which is to leave everything to follow Jesus, and the resources Levi has available to put on such a great festive gathering. As we saw in reflecting on 5.11, Jesus' disciples let go of their possessiveness and dependency on Earth's materials. Discipleship is a life focused on Jesus, open to God and accompanied by ecological release and non-possessiveness. With Levi, Earth's goods he obviously has available to him are no longer for self-aggrandizement. Rather, his life and those of his meal compatriots has been turned around in a spirit of conversion, openness to others and respect for creation. Earth's gifts become the medium through which new relationships are created and community restored. This feast with its delightful earthly fruits helps restore the network and pattern of relationship broken through the presence of evil and the kind of human conduct that toll collectors are judged as exemplifying. These are the ones that Jesus calls to conversion, his table and feast with Earth's fruits.

> I have not come to call righteous people but sinners to conversion (*metanoia*) (5.32).

This call has ecological implications for a household in tune with Earth; the call is an invitation to abundant merriment. Jesus' feasting attitude is criticized by the religious authorities who expect him to fast (5.33-35). His response to their accusation takes the form of aphorisms drawn from the material world and Earth's products, garments, wineskins and wine. These Earth materials become the means by which Jesus affirms his present 'new' (the word occurs seven times in three verses) celebratory and inclusive hospitality brought about through his ministry. The last words that Jesus speaks in response to his antagonists sum up the importance of food and wine, the goodness of creation and the centrality of celebrating.

> New wine must be put into fresh wineskins. And no one after tasting old wine desires new. For one says, 'The old is good.' (5.38-39).

Jesus Chooses the Twelve from Earth's Mountain (6.12-16)

For Jesus, life is good, people are beloved and creation is to be celebrated. Earth is, in a word, delightful. This theme continues into the next two episodes (6.1-5, 6-11) that lead to the scene in which Jesus selects twelve disciples 'whom he names apostles' (6.12-16). This episode concludes the first of the two subunits in Luke 5–9.

The twelve whom Jesus calls are named 'apostles', literally, the ones who are sent on mission. They reflect the leaders of Luke's explicitly mission-orientated household. The attitudes and responses of the twelve will flag for gospel auditors some of the issues and concerns which Luke's householders will meet as they, too, engage in mission. This mission is concerned about the proclamation and enculturation of the gospel in a non-Israelite and Gentile, Greco-Roman world. The twelve are 'windows' and 'mirrors' for Luke's householders; they will show how to act as authentic disciples in a new acculturating era; they will also reflect back to them behaviours and practices that need emulation or critique.

Noteworthy is the way that Luke begins this story of Jesus' selection of the twelve. The scene begins with reference to an Earth image, a mountain.

> It happened in those days, he went on to the mountain [*horos*] to pray and he spent the whole night in prayer to God (6.12).

Environmental elements, water and Earth, feature in stories that frame 5.1–6.16. As water became the means of discipleship in 5.1-11, 'the' mountain becomes the means for Jesus' communion with God in preparation for the selection of the twelve apostles. Here, the mountain is the classic biblical site for divine communion, extraordinary phenomena and revelation.[28] Of the nine occurrences of *horos* in Luke, six come from the Markan intertext.[29] As the prophet Moses encountered God on the mountain, so too, does the mountain set within the Galilean paradisiacal garden provide the means for Jesus' communion with God.

Jesus' mountainous solitude reveals a pattern that Luke uses in relation to Jesus' prayer life and intimacy with God. Luke's Jesus needs to be with nature and Earth before the next stage of his ministry unfolds. Earlier his baptism and wilderness experience prepared him for his encounter with the *diabolos* (3.21; 4.2). Afterwards, Jesus returned to the wilderness before his first public action of preaching and calling his first disciples (4.42). In this scene he is on a mountain to pray 'the whole night in prayer to God' (6.12). This is an experience that will repeat itself two more times, in 9.28

---

28. Heribert Kleine, 'ὄρος', *EDNT*, II (ed. Horst Balz and Gerhard Schneider; Grand Rapids, MI: Wm B. Eerdmans Publishing Co., 1991), pp. 533-34.

29. The three unique uses make the mountain a place of prayer for Luke, as we shall see.

when Jesus is transfigured in prayer, and as he prays with his disciples on the Mount of Olivet just before his passion and death (22.39-46).

For Luke, the mountain is an important intertext. In antiquity, mountains were the abode of the gods and linked to the whole of life and nature. Life and light were associated with mountain peaks, death and darkness with their inner parts or mountain deserts and woods.[30] In the ancient Near East, the primal mountain was common as a figure of power which connected heaven to Earth, its peaks reaching to the gods and its base touching the seas. In Asia Minor, the mountains were associated with the worship of Cybele, the great Earth mother and goddess. In Greece, the soaring mountain of Olympus, identified with the pantheon of the gods, came to symbolize ethical and natural perfection.[31] This appreciation about mountains drawn from the ancient world is further expanded upon in the First Testament; they become the abode of God's proximity and, as Jesus goes on to the mountain to pray all night, allow ecological resonances to surface for the auditor.

Jesus Heals and Preaches on the 'Level Plain' (6.17-49)

After Jesus' night-time mountain prayer and the selection of the twelve, he comes down with them and stands on a 'level plain' (6.17). Earth's 'the level plain' is a place of gathering for all attracted to Jesus. He stands *with* them, not above them. Earth's plain thus provides the platform as the gathering place symbolic of humanity and creation, of the human and non-human. This symbolic setting, Earth's gathering place, ushers in the next moment in Jesus' ministry.

God's *rhēma* again becomes evident in what Jesus says and does. This is the enactment of Jesus' *deeds* of healing and exorcism of those diseased from the whole Mediterranean region (6.17-18). It is followed by his *words* in his teaching on the plain (6.20-49). Luke notes how people sought to 'touch' him to find their healing (6.19). This image of 'touching' evokes the necessity of corporeal interconnection. It is not healing 'from afar' or through a spiritual mechanism that does not require materiality. The touch evokes the need for human contact that links people together in the one household bonded to Earth, the setting and its 'plain' upon which the healing takes place. The crowd seeks to touch Jesus, to initiate their own healing. Jesus allows himself to be touched, to communicate a desire to heal and love that brings about wholeness which has influence within the Earth community. For contemporary auditors, Jesus' teaching has universal implications. As

---

30. Werner Foerster, 'ὄρος', *TDNT*, V (ed. Gerhard Kittel and Gerhard Friedrich; Grand Rapids, MI: Wm B. Eerdmans Publishing Co., 1964), pp. 475-87.

31. Foerster, 'ὄρος', pp. 475-87.

Bovon notes in reflection on the earlier scene where Jesus 'touches' to heal the leper (5.13),

> Every culture, generation, and individual understands something different by 'touching'. The signification and perception depend on the contact and the type of gesture. One touches people to arouse their attention, to make a request that they move, to care for them, and to express love. The analysis of such elementary actions is decisive. Luke intends to say: Jesus took a risk, he came into direct contact with the individual, not in the attitude of a doctor, but in that of a divine helper. His gesture says to the eyes what his voice says to the ears: 'I do choose. Be made clean.'[32]

Jesus then begins to speak the word that people have just witnessed in action (6.20-49). This 'sermon on the plain', as it is often called to distinguish it from Matthew's more famous 'Sermon on the Mount', encapsulates the central truths that Luke's Jesus wants to communicate to potential disciples (Figure 22). The sermon begins explicitly addressing those who are poor and rich, *now* (6.20-26).[33] These are Luke's auditors who are rich and poor. Jesus then speaks about enemy love (6.27-36), anticipating what will be dramatically acted out on the Mount of Olivet when he is arrested by the religious and political leaders (22.47-51), the importance of self-scrutiny (6.37-42), commitment to right action (6.43-45) and the foundation for discipleship, Jesus' words (6.46-49).

The chiastic structure of the sermon is balanced around Jesus' aphorism concerning the relationship between disciple and teacher (D: 6.40) surrounded by layers that express foundational teaching on discipleship (A: 6.20-26, 46-49), the expressed fruits of discipleship (B: 6.27-36, 43-45) and the importance of self-judgment and scrutiny (C: 6.37-39, 40-42).[34]

The layer of the sermon concerned about the fruit of discipleship in action (B) has ecological images used by Luke's Jesus to press home the main point of the teaching. His teaching on enemy love comes from the Q source and encourages disciples to subvert the culturally acceptable mechanism of violent reprisal and a preoccupation with self-protection.[35] Jesus tells his disciples 'To the one who strikes you on the cheek offer the other also' (6.29a). But there are several other features that surround this statement that radicalize Luke's teaching even further, particularly in relation to the care of Earth's resources.

---

32. Bovon, *Luke 1*, p. 175.

33. My position is contra David Peter Seccombe, *Possessions and the Poor in Luke–Acts* (Linz: A. Fuchs, 1982), 'There is nothing socio-economic or socio-religious about Luke's use of the "poor" ... The poor are Israel and the answer to their poverty is the messianic Kingdom' (p. 95).

34. This structure would suggest an order and theological coherence, contra Fitzmyer's comment, 'the Lucan sermon is loose and rambling' (*Luke I–IX*, p. 628).

35. Karris, 'Luke', p. 695.

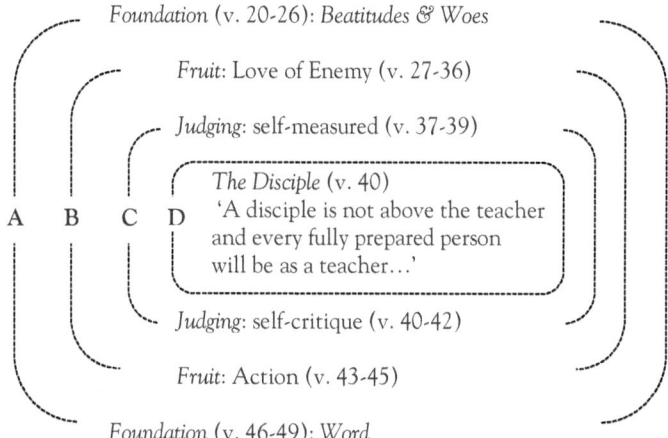

Figure 22. Luke's 'sermon on the plain' (Lk. 6.20-49).

The sermon is addressed to disciples who are called 'blessed' (6.20-23) and invited to ongoing conversion (6.24-26). Their blessedness is God's act when particular circumstances (material poverty, hunger, pain, sadness and persecution) cause them to acknowledge their need for God. In such situations God is their focus. In the final beatitude (6.22-23) Jesus addresses disciples who experience various forms of maltreatment. They, like Earth, experience suffering even though they are beneficiaries of God's loving kindness. Luke's teaching acknowledges the social experience of those who suffer. They are not isolated by the suffering; they belong to Earth which, because of its association with Jesus, will also encounter social stigmatization. What disciples suffer, Earth suffers.

Luke further affirms that all who struggle and experience rejection are not excluded or rejected by God; they are God's beloved, good and holy and living examples of God's capacity to undermine the insults heaped upon them by their antagonists. They are able to reflect the goodness of a God who continues to act beneficently upon the arrogant who exhibit social attitudes that denigrate Earth and its members. Luke names these as 'ungrateful and selfish' (6.35). They make themselves the centre of their world; everything and everyone is to focus on them.

Jesus' Teaching on Enemy Love

Jesus' final beatitude in the sermon connects to Luke's further teaching on retaliation. Mt.'s parallel teaching leads into the 'turning-the-other-cheek' saying with the injunction 'Do not resist the evil doer' (Mt. 5.39a). Luke's teaching is more radical and pervasive and draws on the way one uses Earth's resources.³⁶ Luke makes Jesus' instruction about enemy love the precursor to non-retaliatory action and is most explicit on how such love can be actualized:

> But I say to you who hear, love your enemies, do good to those who hate you, bless those who curse you, pray for those who abuse (*epēreazō*) you. To the one who strikes you on the cheek, offer the other also; and from the one who takes away your coat do not withhold even your shirt. Give to everyone who begs you, and of the one who takes away your possessions do not ask them again (6.27-30).

The enemies are those already identified in the beatitude. They hate and act contemptuously towards the gospel's auditors; they are also explicitly 'abusive' (*epēreazō*).³⁷ Given the symbiotic connection between the human, sacred and ecological network, the enemy's abuse of human beings reflects their abuse of Earth. Luke offers practical advice as to how disciples might show love to their enemies and bring about human and ecological conversion. They are to 'do good', 'bless' and 'pray' for them. Disciples are encouraged to 'love' the enemy. This teaching calls for a proactive agential response to the enemy, not an impossible form of emotional communion that results from affection.³⁸ The abused one is encouraged to *will* the good of their enemies, to act well towards them. This is practical advice, not psychological counsel. The disciples are to *act*, which doesn't equate to 'feeling good' about the enemy or what they have done. The point made here is practically demonstrated in Luke's subtle saying about 'offering' (*parechō*) the other cheek.

Offering the cheek is more than passive resistance from the disciple expecting to be thumped and physically beaten. It is an actively initiated response designed to contain the violence perpetrated and bring the perpetrator to an ecological sensitivity for all Earth's members. This response by the aggrieved disciple would be so culturally unexpected and radically non-retaliatory that the 'offering' would have the potential power to disarm the enemy. In other words, those who are targeted by the

---

36. See Lk. 9.51-56; 10.25-37; 17.11-17; Acts 8.4-25. On enemy love, see Josephine M. Ford, *My Enemy is my Guest: Jesus and Violence in Luke* (Maryknoll, NY: Orbis Books, 1984); William Klassen, 'The Authenticity of the Command: "Love your Enemies"', in *Authenticating the Words of Jesus* (ed. B.D. Chilton and C.A. Evans; Leiden: E. Brill, 1999), pp. 385-407; John Piper, '*Love your enemies*'. *Jesus' Love Command in the Synoptic Gospels and in the Early Christian Paraenesis: A History of the Tradition and Interpretation of its Uses* (New York: Cambridge University Press, 1979), pp. 157-62; William Klassen, *Love of Enemies: The Way to Peace* (Minneapolis, MN: Fortress Press, 1984).

37. This is the only place in the gospels where *epēreazō* appears. Its only other occurrence is in 1 Pet. 3.16.

38. Green comments, 'Love is expressed in doing good—that is, not by passivity in the face of opposition but in proactivity: doing good, blessing, praying, and offering the second cheek and the shirt along with the coat' (*Luke*, p. 272).

violent are not helpless; they can reveal God to them, place them in God's presence and sensitize them to all Earth's members who do not deserve such treatment. All this undergirds disciples' encouragement to 'bless' and 'pray'. It is confirmed by the sayings in 6.35-36 which conclude this section:

> But love your enemies, and do good, and lend expecting nothing in return, and your reward will be much, and you will be children of the most high who is kind (*chrestos*) to the ungrateful (*acharistoi*) and evil. Be compassionate (*oiktirmos*) as your father is compassionate (6.35-36).

The response to the enemy also reflects the disciple's attitude to the material Earth by which goods are lent without expecting return. Open generosity and respect for Earth's gifts devoid of any sense of possessiveness or greed will disarm, liberate and offer the possibility of conversion. Most importantly, it will show God's 'compassion' or 'mercy'. This is substantially an attitude of maternal love that emerges from the depths of the female womb. Luke's use of the Greek *oiktirmos* here (and *splagnizomai* in Luke's next scene at 7.13; at 10.33 and 15.20) is a translation in the LXX for the Hebrew *rachem* whose root is 'womb'. The invitation is for the disciple to reveal and participate in God's generative care abundantly available for the human and non-human household.

Whatever the outcome of the interaction between the disciple and the enemy, Luke recognizes that disciples have a power that can subvert, convert, and reveal God.[39] This is the creator God of 'kindness' (*chrestos*) who acts graciously even to those who are 'ungrateful' (*acharistoi*); this play on words in 6.35 is unmistakable. Situations where the disciple is targeted and maltreated have the potential to be moments of divine action and healing grace, revelatory of God's action in creation for the care and protection of Earth.

Jesus' teaching would encourage those targeted to act constructively towards their enemies. They have a power that could potentially enable their aggressors and revilers to encounter God and practice ecological generosity. Action rather than passivity is the Lukan injunction; it encourages the disciple out of a 'door-mat' disposition of victimization. This attitude spills over into a form of unexpected non-reciprocal generosity and exchange that reveals the very heart of God (6.29-34) found in the goodness of creation and a generous sharing of Earth's resources, themes that will be picked up and reinforced later in the gospel.

The disciple's sensitive and respectful appreciation of Earth's goods is symbolized in the way the disciple gives over a coat, shirt or possessions

---

39. '[Jesus] is asking people to accept an inversion of the world order, to agree with him that the world order has been inverted, and to act accordingly' (Green, *Luke*, p. 272).

(6.29b-30a). These gifts formed from Earth are not to be selfishly sequestered but enjoyed by all. In this case, Earth's goods are also for the benefit of the enemy who needs exposure to a spirit of ecological generosity and open conversion. The practical expression of God's compassion and kindness in the disciples' release of clothing can disarm and subvert: such reverential appreciation of Earth's gifts can reveal goodness and compassion, totally unexpected in a world where the perpetuation of violence and Earth's abuse would be the cultural norm. In this culture, retaliation in kind would be the usual defence mechanism to reclaim lost honour and protect oneself from further hostility.

In sum, the sermon's teaching on enemy love is profoundly radical and startling. For contemporary auditors whose ears are sensitive to the ecological tones that surface out of Luke's symphony, enemy violence is not an act that affects only human beings; it ricochets throughout Earth. It, too, is affected. Luke's sermon affirms how Earth is not a passive victim to such violence; it, too, can be a collaborator in discipleship and an agent in the enemy's conversion.

Final Scenes and a Summary (7.1-23)

Luke's sermon leads to Jesus' action of healing, first of a centurion's servant through the word that Jesus speaks (7.1-10) and his exercise of compassion to the widow of Nain whose son has died (7.11-17). The act of resuscitation reveals God's care for the lonely, widowed and poor. Jesus' act also materializes God's compassion (here translating the Hebrew *rachem* by the Greek, *splagnizomai*) identified in the sermon that the disciple is encouraged to reveal to the enemy. The scene ends with people's amazement at Jesus' action, and his identification as God's prophet and revealer of God's visitation upon Earth's household (7.16). Again, as with the opening healing story of this subunit (4.37), so here at the last of Jesus' healings, Earth's landscape joins in this recognition of Jesus and merriment about him:

> And this word about him went around the whole of Judea and all the surrounding land (*perichōros*) (7.17).

The story of God's Earth child continues to be celebrated, as Luke concludes this subunit by a summary of Jesus' ministry that has taken place over these early chapters of the gospel. This summary echoes his hometown reading of the Isaiah intertext. The Isaiah reading opened up this section of Luke's gospel and created part of the frame for the inner play which this present summary concludes. John's disciples enquire about Jesus' status, whether he is the one to come or should they wait for another (7.20): Luke answers their enquiry by returning to the theme of deed and word, thus rounding off the activity of God's *rhēma*. Jesus heals, exorcises and cures blindness. As Luke concludes this section, the evangelist has Jesus summarize the implications of his ministry now experienced over these chapters using phrases that echo his sermon in the Nazareth synagogue:

> The blind receive sight, the lame walk, lepers are cleansed, the dead are raised to life and the poor have the good news preached to them (7.22).

This ministry, as we have seen, has implications for the way Earth is perceived and respected.

Conclusion

As we have attuned ourselves to listen to Luke's next movement in this ecological symphony, we have identified the focus of Jesus' ministry. Conventional commentaries on this section of the gospel have interpreted Jesus' mission exclusively in anthropocentric terms; he seems only concerned about humans. However as we listen to the gospel from a different perspective, we hear other clear ecological melodies across these chapters that invite a different consideration of his ministry. His public ministry has ecological implications for Earth and the disciple's relationship with it. Earth's household, living and inanimate, human and non-human, is the beneficiary of God's compassionate, maternal care revealed in Jesus' words and deeds. These reflect the way God's *rhēma* unfolds in this section of the gospel. The prominence of *rhēma* helps to identify Luke's inner play (Figure 20).

The enactment of God's *rhēma* is one of four thematic features that assists contemporary gospel auditors to appreciate the ecological consequences of Luke's portrait of Jesus. The other three concern the setting of his ministry, the role of the human body as the focus of his healings and its interconnectivity with the total cosmos and eco-system, and the way Jesus confronts the *diabolos* through his healing ministry and table communion. All four will continue to be important as we move into the next section of the gospel.

In these early chapters, as Jesus begins his public ministry, he reveals God's desire to liberate the oppressed. His liberating ministry is set specifically within Galilee which, I have suggested, is a fruitful, ecologically rich environment that mirrors something of the original Genesis paradisiacal garden. The fruitful potential symbolized in Luke's Galilean setting starkly spotlights damaged and broken human beings that Jesus encounters in these chapters. They are in need of healing and exorcism as he releases them from the evil that handicaps them.

Jesus' ministry of healing and release further reveals the *basileia-ectopia*, God's intention for all Earth's members, not just its human ones. The several stories of healing and exorcisms that dot this section reveal a compassionate God who feels for weakened and struggling human beings and seeks to release them from the powers that entrap them. Their disorder symbolizes something more cosmic and universal that Jesus too heals. Caught up with human entrapment is Earth. The environment too is affected by the *diabolos*, the ever-present power of evil that Luke's Jesus will defeat. His ultimate victory, though, will not come until the gospel's final chapters.

In the meantime, this evil manifests itself in several ways: in physical and spiritual signs that disempower and the way Earth is treated by those whose wealth and status seek to control and ravage for selfish ends. This results in peasant poverty, excessive taxation and disrespect for Earth forced to produce beyond its capacity. The gospel's counteraction to this approach of ecological and human abuse and degradation is Jesus' table communion with the alien and rejected.

Earth's fruits become the means by which the human beings are restored, know that they belong and encounter a delightful God who seeks to feed them and the rest of hungry creation. This God celebrates Earth in meals inclusive of human and non-human beings. In these meals Jesus gathers with the wealthy elite, converted toll agents, and publicly recognized sinners. This is Levi's 'great feast' (5.29), the decisive symbolic occasion where this festive and delightful God dines with every member of creation.

Permeating this narrative of a God who celebrates in a garden of earthly delights are other Earth images. The wilderness (4.42), water (5.1-2, 4), land (4.37; 5.3, 11; 6.17; 7.17) and mountain (6.12) are central to Luke's symphony; they are not passive geographical locations or stage props for Jesus' 'real' ministry perceived as centred solely on human beings; they are active participants in a story concerned about Earth; they reveal aspects of a deeper ecological narrative that involves the disciples' call and formation, the healing of Earth's community, God's communion with creation and, surprisingly in the *Sermon on the Plain* (6.29-49), the redemption of enemies.

As we noted, Earth's elements are an essential part of this sermon. Disciples who have been harshly treated can reveal to their enemies the maternal, gestational image of an embracing God through prayer and enemy forgiveness, especially in their care of Earth's gifts. Through disciples' non-possessive manner, enemy conversion is possible (6.27-36). This image of selfless discipleship can encourage Luke's wealthy householders selfishly controlling Earth's goods. Release from a spirit of possessiveness of its fruits typifies Jesus' disciples who have already 'left everything to follow him' (5.11). Rather being possessed by humans, Earth's resources can participate in a strategy of conversion and discipleship. They can be agents of liberation and offer a voice to those open to listen. They can be the means of releasing enemies from hatred and the wealthy from oppressive behaviour. How this continues is central to the next movement in Luke's symphony, Lk. 7.24–9.50.

5. Luke 4.14–7.23

Earth's Voice

It happened in those days, he went on to the mountain to pray and he spent the whole night in prayer to God (Lk. 6.12).

Earth's Mountain speaks:

> You, Earth's child, climb up upon me.
> We are one, together, for a whole night.
> I provide the space and support for your communion with God.
> With me, you speak to God.
> I listen to your prayer.
> I feel blessed because of you and your prayer
> I protect you throughout the night.
> You pray and ponder about those whom you will call as 'apostles'.
> I am the setting for this important moment.
> You are one with me.
> In the morning, you walk down from me,
> to my level plain at my base.
> Here, within earshot, you teach.
> You are at peace. You know God is with you.

Chapter 6

Luke 7.24–9.50

Feasting and Fasting in the Paradisiacal Garden

The story of God's *rhēma* in the garden of earthly delights continues through Luke 7 to 9 in the words and deeds of Jesus. Themes present in the previous chapters continue to make their appearance: Jesus' healings and meal ministry, the action of the *diabolos*, Jesus' teaching to his disciples as he continues to identify for Luke the inclusive nature of the true household of disciples. Women figure prominently in this section of the gospel as Jesus instructs his disciples, women and men. Stories of fasting contrast with moments of feasting as the God of creation continues to be celebrated in feeding stories. Luke also introduces sayings that anticipate Jesus' passion and death. These chapters and themes prepare us for the next major movement in Luke's gospel symphony, the journey narrative that begins at 9.51.

Inner Play of Lk. 7.24–9.50

Two summaries of Jesus' ministry (7.24-35; 9.1-17) commence and are central to Lk. 7.24–9.50 and prepare for the journey narrative (Figure 23). Contrasting stories of fasting and feasting accompany the summaries. Between them are stories about women (7.36-8.3; 8.40-56). These surround Jesus' meta-parable of the sowing seed, a parable rich with ecological symbolism, and other parables concerned about Earth. The parables alert the auditor to what follows, especially the crises which the disciples experience in their boat on the Sea of Galilee (8.22-25) and the exorcism of the Gerasene demoniac (8.26-39). The parables, the storm on the sea and the exorcism are linked. Word and deed accompany each and reveal that God's *rhēma* is at work. The parables help to identify the surprising presence and unmistakable action of God's *basileia-ecotopia* in circumstances that seem to camouflage if not suppress it. Then Jesus' action in the boat and to the possessed human being expresses the tangible presence of God's *basileia-ecotopia*. He confronts the evil that seems to surround the disciples' household, symbolized by the boat (8.22-25), and threatens to annihilate it. He also rebukes with amazing results the demonic evil that possesses the man (8.26-39). These central teachings and exorcism actions speak to and are addressed by the women stories that surround them (7.36–8.3; 8.40-56).

Between the middle summary (about the ministry of the twelve and Jesus) with its contrasting fasting-feasting stories (9.1-17) and the beginning of the journey narrative (at 9.51), Luke offers an intricate inner play centred on Jesus' transfiguration and the healing of one possessed (9.28-43a). This inner play presents auditors with insights into the disciples' struggling appreciation of Jesus' true identity (9.18-20) and what is inauthentic in their household (9.49-50). These surround two statements in which Luke's Jesus begins to articulate prophetically the suffering and death that await him in Jerusalem (9.21-27, 43b-48).

Throughout the gospel's inner play in these chapters, Luke draws on biblical, socio-cultural and thematic intertexts reshaping them to reveal important insights into Jesus and his household of disciples. Present within Luke's use of these intertexts redacted from Mark's gospel we can perceive ecological and environmental nuances. When these are sensitively listened

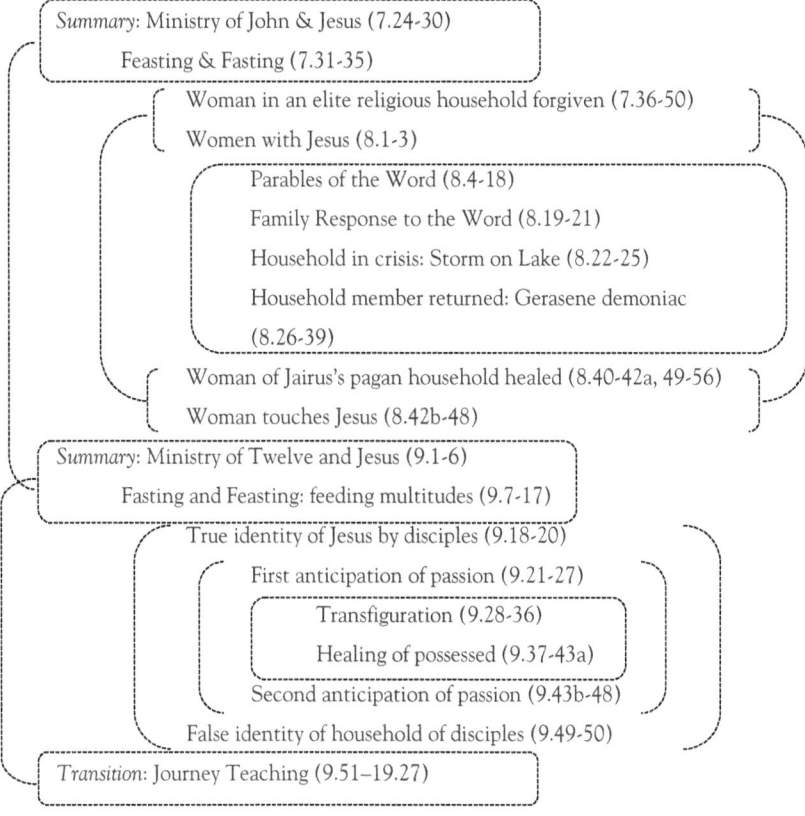

Figure 23. *The inner play of Lk. 7.24–9.50.*

Jesus and John the Baptizer: Their Feasting and Fasting (7.24-35)

In 7.24, after John's disciples leave Jesus, Luke places into Jesus' mouth a summary of his healing and mission that has occurred in the gospel's early chapters—his mission of healing and liberation directed towards all kinds of people with various disabilities and diseases that keep them excluded from social acceptance. Luke's Jesus then turns to reflect upon the nature of John's prophetic ministry. His ecologically sensitive ascetic lifestyle stands in stark contrast to the luxury and use of Earth's resources by those who live in regal, elite settings (7.24-27). John's greatness is also contrasted to the greater status of all members of the gospel household, especially converted toll collectors (7.28-29). Luke further reflects in a series of aphorisms on the respective ministries of John and Jesus that are criticized and rejected by the religious leaders. Jesus' words anticipate how his meal actions that reveal a joyous God delighted by Earth, including those open to God's *basileia-ecotopia*, will lead to his death. Jesus and John will simply not play the games of the religious and social establishment (7.31-32). For their social nonconformity and their sensitivity towards Earth's gifts, either in ascetic practice (John) or festive merriment (Jesus), they are demonized and considered 'drunkards and gluttons'. Jesus says to his detractors,

> [33] For John the baptizer neither ate bread nor drank wine, and you say 'He has a demon'. [34] The Earthed One[1] has come eating and drinking and you say, 'Behold a man who is a glutton and drunkard, a friend of toll collectors and sinners'. [35] And Wisdom (*sophia*) is justified by her children (7.33-35).

The descriptive tag of name calling given to Jesus ('drunkard and glutton') comes from *Deuteronomy* (Deut. 21.18-22) as a designation of a recalcitrant son unwilling to change his ways and causing corruption and impurity within the Israelite community.[2] Such a person is heretical and needs to be executed for the good purity of the whole.

---

1. I have translated *ho huios tou anthrōpou* (ὁ υἱὸς τοῦ ἀνθρώπου) as 'Earthed One' rather than the conventional 'Son of Man'. The title ascribed to Jesus (*ho huios tou anthrōpou*) emphasizes his link in the first instance to humanity and affirms him as *the* representative of human beings. But Luke's Jesus is also *Adam's* Son (3.38) which accentuates his Earth connectedness already celebrated in his birth as *Earth's child*. For more on the titles and christology of Luke's gospel, see O'Toole, *Luke's Presentation*, esp. pp. 7-28.

2. For another point of view, see Stephen Witetschek, 'The Stigma of a Glutton and Drunkard. Q 7,34 in Historical and Sociological Perspective', *EphTheoLov* 83 (2007), pp. 135-54.

To his antagonists, Jesus' open table of hospitality that transgresses the conventional purity boundaries makes him a corrupting influence among God's chosen people. For this reason, the authorities will attempt to dishonour and abuse him in death. In other words, Jesus' meals and his unscrutinized guest list are the primary cause of his eventual execution. Or, to state the matter somewhat provocatively, 'Jesus got himself killed because of the way he ate'. In other words, he ate himself to death.[3] The negative assessment of his meal ministry found here in verse 34 has already made its appearance earlier, a few episodes into his public ministry.

The sayings and aphorisms of vv. 33 to 35 might well reflect the words of the historical Jesus; they sum up a ministry and meal practice that will precipitate his death. Luke further affirms John and Jesus as children of *Sophia*, the maternal image of God's presence that gives birth, shapes the world and is responsible for creation. Earth's eco-system is the fruit of the work of *Sophia*. Jesus and John reflect God's *Sophia* to Earth's household. In the story of his birth, Jesus was Earth's child; here, *Sophia's* child.

The action of Sophia's child, Jesus, is further revealed in the next stories where women figure prominently (7.36–8.3). These female characters, other children of *Sophia*, act to identify Jesus and affirm their discipleship. Their respect for Earth's elements that they carry or employ for others accentuates Luke's christology and illustrates what true discipleship means for gospel auditors.

Luke constructs a story of Jesus' anointment by an unnamed woman (7.36-50) from the Markan intertext (Mk 14.3-9). The evangelist deliberately positions it here, moving it from Mark's original setting in the context of Jesus' passion. Some commentators judge Luke's culling of the story from its original setting in Mark's passion narrative as a subtle redefinition of women's roles in the household of disciples, typical of later Second Testament writers.[4] For some it reveals a dangerous tendency by the evangelist to continue an oppression of women that reaches its fullest expression in the household codes and post-Pauline letters, especially the Pastoral Letters. The story's reposition is significant not because it illustrates a possible misogynist tendency with the evangelist—at least not here—but because of its illustration of the nature of discipleship and confirmation of Luke's christology.[5]

---

3. Robert J. Karris, *Eating Your Way through Luke's Gospel* (Collegeville, MN: Liturgical Press, 2006), p. 97.

4. See Mary Rose D'Angelo, 'The ANHP Question in Luke–Acts: Imperial Masculinity and the Deployment of Women in Early Second Century', in *Feminist Companion to Luke* (ed. Amy-Jill Levine and Marianne Blickenstaff; London: Sheffield Academic Press, 2002), pp. 44-69.

5. For a reading against the grain of the narrative that illustrates unhelpful stereotypical interpretations, see Reid, '"Do You See"', pp. 106-20.

Jesus and Women—Earth's Presence (7.36–8.3)

Luke places the story immediately after the 'glutton and drunkard' tag given to Jesus by his antagonists. The story immediately precedes a summary about the function of Jesus' women disciples who, along with the twelve, are described as being *with* Jesus and 'ministering' (*diakoneō*) to his household of disciples (8.1-3). The verb for 'service' or 'ministry' used of the women (*diakoneō*) in 8.3 is unmistakably formal and echoes that action performed by Simon's mother-in-law in 4.39.[6] More is implied in Luke's language here than reinforcing stereotypical female roles associated with conventional household duties to Jesus and his band of male disciples.[7]

Luke's theological summary (8.1-2) comes immediately after a woman's action to Jesus that expresses and reinforces the essential elements of diakonal service (7.36-50). Its focus is Jesus and characterized by the woman's intimate, unhindered and lavish loving act towards him. The woman's action focuses on her use of ointment contained in an alabaster jar that she carries (7.37). The preciousness of the perfumed vegetable oil bound by the translucent finely textured calcite jar is obvious.[8] Without it she could not perform her deed towards Jesus' body specifically directed to his feet.

Luke uses the verbal or noun form of anointing five times (7.38, 46a, 46b). This is clearly the focus of the whole event. Her sensitive and loving appreciation of Earth's oil is her way of honouring Jesus; her detractors do not take this in; they do not notice her use of the ointment or the container in which she carries it. In the Markan intertext, Jesus' disciples observe the oil's use and note its preciousness. This focus is absent in Luke's story, where Jesus' detractors are more concerned about the gender and nature of the person whom Jesus allows to touch him. She is a 'woman of the city, and a sinner' (7.37).[9] The sensual and ecologically nuanced materiality of her act, of touching Jesus' feet, washing them with her tears, drying them with

---

6. See John N. Collins, *Diakonia: Re-interpreting the Ancient Sources* (New York: Oxford University Press, 1990).

7. Helpful for further reflection on Lk. 8.1-3 is Karris, *Eating*, pp. 85-87.

8. About the jar, see Immanuel Ben-Dor, 'Alabaster', *IDB*, I (ed. George A. Buttrick; Nashville, TN: Abingdon Press, 1962), pp. 75-76.

9. Several reasons have been proposed for the sinfulness of the woman: prostitute, whore, freedwoman, girl sold into prostitution by her parents. See Green, *Luke*, p. 309. The classification of the woman's sinfulness in terms of sexual misconduct and immorality is more the result of a western sexual predilection. The declaration of a person's sinfulness in Luke's day would come from a number of reasons, not necessarily linked to sexual impropriety: Jesus attracts sinners, a constant theme in Luke's gospel; they are members of his discipleship household, men and women. Her presence in an urban household would reflect the kinds of people, the socially scandalous outcasts, who are, in certain circumstances, judged as making a domestic space impure.

her hair, and then anointing them, symbolically brings together corporeal aspects of expression from the human body with rich elements from nature supplied by Earth. The scene is replete with Earth's presence.

The woman's act is a symbolic gesture that combines human (tears, kisses, hair) and natural (alabaster, oil) aspects provided by Earth to remind auditors of Jesus' identity; he is Earth's child whose *feet* are washed and anointed. These feet have walked upon Earth's surface in a gesture of environmental respect; the woman's loving act towards his feet acknowledges this. God, too, walks in Jesus' presence who is also *Sophia's* child. As God's prophetic healing agent he also reveals God's forgiveness and peace to Earth's members (7.47-50).

Given the context of the woman's action in Luke's gospel and the summary of Jesus' preaching ministry accompanied by the twelve and women in 8.1-3, the story also reveals the kind of authentic discipleship praised in other parts of the gospel; she is the proto-typical disciple who focuses attention on Jesus and sees him as the source of healing, forgiveness and wholeness. She reveals herself as one of 'wisdom's children' (7.35) whose conduct serves to honour Jesus' assessment of his critics especially in their judgment of him as a 'glutton and drunkard'.[10] Her deed raises the ire of his male host, perhaps reflecting an historical tension in early Jesus households between female and male ministerial roles.

The woman's act is uncensored and praised by Jesus, and coheres with the role which women (three of whom are named, 8.1-3) play in the next scene. These engage in the same conduct as the twelve: they accompany Jesus as he preaches and brings 'the good news of the *basileia* of God' (8.1) to the urban centres of the Galilean region.

We note, too, how these women represent a social spectrum: Mary from Magdala, a dried fish processing centre on the western shores of the Sea of Galilee, will reappear in the resurrection story; Joanna is of high, perhaps mixed, social and regal status. Together with Susanna they could well reflect something of the social mix of Luke's audience. They, like the unnamed woman in the previous scene, demonstrate the essence of discipleship. They are not possessed by avariciousness for Earth's goods. They follow Jesus as explicitly identified disciples and seem free of regulated patriarchal affiliation. They demonstrate a diaconal capacity to employ their gifts for the benefit of Jesus' household and Earth's community: Luke summarizes the women's role, as they

> ministered to them/him out of their possessions (8.3b).[11]

---

10. Johnson, *Luke*, p. 129.
11. The manuscript support for 'them' (referring to the household of disciples) or 'him' (referring to Jesus) is not certain, though for the better attested reading of 'them' see Bruce M. Metzger, *A Textual Commentary on the Greek New Testament* (London:

With the repeated announcement of Jesus' urban preaching mission and identification of male and female disciples, Luke moves to identify the nature of God's *basileia-ecotopia* and the kind of household in which it is manifest (8.4-39). This identification comes in the form of a parable.

The Meta-Parable of the Sowing Seed: Earth's Fruitfulness (8.4-21)

The ecologically rich parable of the sowing seed (8.4-8) brings together all the elements of Earth's household: humanity, non-human living creatures, and inert and organic matter. This parable, like all the parables,

> are such successful religious metaphors because they are the product of a religious imagination that is deeply grounded in the world of nature and the human struggle with it, and at the same time deeply rooted in the traditions of Israel which speak of God as creator of heaven and earth and all that is in them.[12]

In the parable, the scattered seed at first encounters situations that frustrate its fruitfulness. Finally this frustration gives way to superabundance as grain explodes into life a hundredfold. Heard from the perspective of Luke's peasant based and debt-ridden audience, the parable comes as a story of relief, economic sustainability and kinship survival. The seed's journey to abundance is essentially and overwhelmingly optimistic. Unlike the Markan source (Mk 13.1-9) with its gradated fruitful seed (thirtyfold, sixtyfold, hundredfold, Mk 4.8), the seed in Luke's parable becomes immediately so fruitfully abundant that it exceeds the wildest crop imaginable. Luke's parable is essentially about Earth's ultimate and overwhelming fecundity.

The fruitfulness of Earth's seed is also a symbol for the fruitfulness of God's *basileia-ecotopia* that overcomes frustrating ecological circumstances. The fruitful seed reflects the fertility of God's presence. The parable is a meta-parable for what will occur in the rest of the gospel through Jesus' ministry. This is clear from Jesus' explanation of the parable in 8.9-10. Without understanding the parable, Luke's auditors will not be able to 'know' or encounter the mystery of the *basileia* (8.10a). This will mean that they will be locked into a spirit of blindness and deafness that prevents them from really seeing and hearing the word-deed of God's *rhēma* revealed in Jesus.

The seed parable is Luke's meta-parable. For contemporary auditors, the parable affirms Earth's abundant fruitfulness, despite what appears to the contrary. This invites the disciple to ecological sensitivity, contemplation and

---

United Bible Societies, 1971), p. 144; Fitzmyer, *Luke I–IX*, p. 698; Karris, *Eating*, pp. 85-86.

12. Freyne, *Jesus*, p. 59.

alertness. A disciple's openness to Earth's potential for fruitful abundance will bring moderation in the use of Earth's goods and, through a spirit of generosity, allow for the revelation of God's tangible presence. Frustration will not dominate, rather an essential cultural, social and creation-centred optimism grounded in signs visible upon Earth. Even Luke's secondary reworking of the original parable into an allegory describing various responses to God's word (8.11-15) is filled with sumptuous ecological allusions. The reception of the word is like the response of the seed planted in Earth's womb; God's word will be eventually fruitful and will 'come to light', as the concluding parable teaches (8.16-18).

The evangelist's teaching about the various reactions to God's word finds its positive response in the family of Jesus composed of his natural kin and all who hear and respond to God's word (8.19-20). This leads to one of the most dramatic and Earth connected stories in the whole of Luke's gospel, a storm on the Sea of Galilee that threatens to annihilate a boat and Jesus' disciples (8.22-25).

Earth's Winds and Waters Exorcised (8.22-25)

Jesus leads his disciples into the vessel, unlike in the Markan intertext where the disciples *take* Jesus on to the boat. In Mark, the disciples seek to control Jesus as they are about to journey across the waters to places unknown; they 'took him with them' (Mk 3.6). They seem uncertain and, rather than following Jesus into the boat as in Luke, they want Jesus to follow them as they set out for mission. The missionary endeavour is also uppermost in Luke's story and reflective of a new era of cultural encounter facing the gospel's auditors. The gathering of Jesus with disciples in the conventionally small fishing vessel well-known on the Sea of Galilee could well represent the Lukan household as it begins its missionary activity.

Jesus says, 'Let us go across to the other side of the lake' (8.22b). The voyage is from the known and familiar to the unknown and potentially dangerous. Water, Earth's primeval element, becomes the means for the crossing rather than an environmental barrier that needs to be overcome. But there is something inherently strange about this water they cross, this aspect of Earth's body. It is, like human beings that we have already met, the victim of the diabolical. Communion between the human and non-human is palpable in the story. Water, too, suffers from demonic possession and has lost its integrity. Jesus' ministry of release programmatically described in his hometown synagogue (4.18-19) and repeated to John's disciples (7.21-22) is intended for the whole Earth. This includes its waters.

As they set out, Jesus falls asleep (8.23) and immediately the demonic becomes manifest. Its power is unleashed on to the water as a great storm of winds comes down on to the lake and '*they* were filling with water' (8.23).

This is an important detail in the story. It is not the boat that is being deluged, though it is implied; it is 'they'. This is the household of disciples gathered with the sleeping Jesus who seems unaffected by the potential danger and evil that surrounds them. Ecological disharmony represented by the powerful wind lashing the seas is also being felt in the human household. 'They' are experiencing this disharmony too. The idyllic communion in Galilee's paradisiacal garden seems fractured. The human and non-human worlds are at odds with each other; one is about to destroy the other.

At this point in the story, the human household responds as it seeks liberation and release. The disciples wake Jesus with the cry that names the cosmic and ecological disaster that threatens, 'Master, Master, we are destroyed!' (8.24). The destruction that they name is what is happening universally. To hear the story with a purely anthropocentric bias, the 'we' would be the disciples in the boat. With ecological sensitivity, the 'we' is Earth's total household and eco-systemic realities. The human household of disciples intercedes with Jesus on behalf of Earth who, through its waters, is demonically possessed. The disciples are able to vocalize Earth's need apparent in the chronic unrest and disturbance seen in wind and water.

Jesus, Earth's child, responds immediately to bring release and calm:

> Jesus woke up and rebuked the wind and the raging (*kludōn*) seas, and they ceased, and there was calm (8.24).

Jesus exorcises the evil spirits evident in the wind storm and the waves which Luke anthropomorphizes and personalizes with the adjective 'raging' (8.24b). The Greek adjective for this, *kludōn*, emphasizes the demonic wrestling going on within the living water. Like the possessed humans already met, Jesus confronts the evil created by the *diabolos*. His 'rebuke' indicates an explicit act of exorcism, already familiar to us (4.35-41). This rebuke to the wind and waves is not directed to the wind and water, Earth's living elements, but to the evil spirits that have invaded it through wind and water. They are not disparaged or regarded as evil, but released to participate in God's universe of cosmic and Earth harmony first announced by the angels to the shepherds in 2.14. The wind and the water are members of Earth's community and part of Galilee's paradisiacal garden. This is the 'calm' (8.24c) that comes upon the scene. Evil is disempowered, Earth protected, communion restored, and the identity of Jesus, God's Earth child, acknowledged (8.25). Jesus' final question to his disciples, 'Where is your faith?', is addressed to all of Luke's auditors in every moment of history. Where is the conviction of Jesus' followers to perceive the divinely intended communion for the whole Earth community that can be fractured by evil yet overcome by the presence of Jesus?

Earth's Sacrificial Act (8.26-39)

The exorcism of the evil spirits from Earth's household has its parallel in the next story, the exorcism of one in the human household (8.26-39). Jesus reaches the other side of the lake with his disciples. He steps ashore at an unfamiliar Gentile spot. This 'country of the Garesenes' (8.26a) is the quintessential multi-cultural and socially challenging environment confronting Luke's auditors as they engage the wider Greco-Roman world. He immediately meets a demonically possessed 'male' from 'the city'. The tomb setting of the encounter, the man's place of residence outside the urban world and a regular household, his demented, incarcerated spirit and nakedness, all belie the seriousness of the evil condition which Jesus confronts. The man represents those in Luke's world who are excluded from the healing environment offered by Earth. The disjunction between the human and creative world represented in the manic possessed character parallels the same disjunction seen in the previous scene.

Jesus releases the man from the 'Legion' of evil spirits that occupy him—perhaps a subtle reminder to the gospel's auditors of the desire to be exorcised of the literal Roman legion that preoccupies and controls their world. The legion of spirits enters a herd of pigs, rushes over a bank and drowns in the lake (8.32-33). Like previous healing stories, this one, too, receives wide publicity that spreads through the city and the 'country'. Earth receives this report about Jesus. The effect of Jesus' act on the man is obvious: he is healed, calm, clothed and sane (8.35). Like the wind and water in the previous scene, the man has been restored to wholeness, reinstituted as a member of the urban household, and released of his oppression. Though he requests to join Jesus, he is instructed to go to his own home and narrate the deeds of God that he has experienced (8.38-39). Instead he proclaims the good news throughout the whole of the *city* (8.39). The effect of the man's healing and his story is intended for all who live in Luke's Greco-Roman urban world; everyone of Luke's gospel audience.

On first reflection, the action of the spirits and the drowning of the pigs may not appear to be the most ecologically and environmentally friendly action of Luke's Jesus.[13] However, heard from the point of view of the divinely intended Earth communion with the total household evidenced in the exorcising ministry of Jesus, something else operates at a deeper ecological level. Whatever of the sensitivity we have for pigs and their treatment today, as for all domesticated animals, in Luke's world, pigs were considered impure. Their crazed manic behaviour made them obvious receptacles to carry demented-causing spirits to their self-destruction. But from another

---

13. Bauckham, *Living*, p. 77.

perspective, if we allow the pigs ecological meaning and divine value—which we must in the light of Jesus' later teaching to anxious disciples about God's care and regard for annoying polluting ravens (12.24)—then they become agents of the possessed person's healing. They carry the demons to their destruction. They fall into water recently exorcised of its own demons. Earth's water, like the pigs it has just received, also becomes altruistic in its care for a distressed member of the human household. In a deed that parallels the action of Jesus in his passion and death at the end of the gospel, the pigs and water become like Jesus, active living agents for human redemption and healing. Jesus' healing of Earth's troubled water in the previous scene releases it to absorb now the evil directed to it by the plunging herd of demonically possessed swine, also members of Earth's household, though history has not been so kind to them.

Humanity Healed; Earth Enjoyed (8.40-56)

This reconstitution and healing of humanity reflected in Jesus' overpowering evil present in Earth (in wind, water and a possessed man) continues into the next two stories (8.40-56). These concern two women, one the daughter of Jairus, a ruler of a synagogue, the other a woman with an incessant flow of blood. There are obvious links between the two stories: both concern women with disastrous, impure and household debilitating conditions. The number twelve features in both. The daughter is twelve years old and is therefore of marriageable age and able to leave the shelter of her patriarchal household; the second woman has had her chronic condition for twelve years.

Luke borrows the stories and their interlocking literary characteristics from Mark's gospel (Mk 9.18-26), but adds a twist at the end of the story concerning the resuscitation of Jairus' dead daughter. This also brings both narratives to closure with an Earth-related touch.

After the young woman is resuscitated Jesus instructs the parents 'that something should be given her to eat' (8.55b). Jesus' injunction to feed the woman continues one of Luke's favourite themes: God's festive delight represented through the act of eating and sharing a meal, now focused on a young woman whose life-giving spirit has returned to her. This is a comprehensive Earth embracing deed in which the woman now participates. She is now in communion with Earth's household through the deed of Jesus' *rhēma*. Her act of eating demonstrates this; she enjoys Earth's fruits. The pneumatic presence of God in the return of the woman's spirit, the spirit of life, combined with the enjoyment of Earth's pleasures, makes this a symbolic resurrection story previewing the resurrection of Jesus and reflecting back to the act of creation in Genesis as God's life-giving *ruach* hovers over Earth at the dawn of creation.

The Disciples' Ecological Mission; Earth's Abundance Celebrated (9.1-17)

Jesus now calls the twelve together to commission them on mission. Their mission is to emulate his ministry they have so far witnessed, deeds of power, healing, exorcisms and preaching (9.1-2). He instructs them about the mission that they are to undertake within the urban settings of Galilee, reflective of the teaching needed in Luke's urban context (9.5). Jesus' instruction is prepared by an environmental mandate that echoes the ecological ethical principles we discerned in Luke's story of Jesus' temptation (4.1-13).

> And he said to them, 'Take nothing for the way, neither staff, nor bag, nor bread, nor money, nor have two tunics...' (9.3).

The twelve are to be so totally focused on their preaching, teaching and healing ministry that they are not to depend on material possessions. This freedom of reliance on the goods of the earth reflects an ability to leave all to follow Jesus and to journey respectfully in the ecological environment in which they walk. It is an act of faith in God. This is the sense behind their absence of a bag (in which to carry possessions), bread (the fruit of Earth's seed), or money (by which they could purchase Earth's goods and satisfy their personal needs). They are not to have a change of clothing, but to be satisfied with what they have already. All these little elements are environmentally linked. They reflect a disposition towards creation and a resistance to the temptation to power, status and privilege with which Jesus was tempted by the *diabolos* at the beginning of his public ministry. The disciples' future mission is fundamentally ecological. It touches deeply into the way Earth is treated and how the good news about Earth is proclaimed and heard. This ecological mission is also part of the 'way' of Jesus followers throughout history. Its qualities are now exemplified as Jesus sends the twelve to 'catch alive human beings' (9.6).

An interlude (9.7-9) that introduces Herod and his desire to 'see' Jesus (9.9c) anticipates their later meeting in the passion at 23.6-12. This interlude leads to another of Luke's ecologically rich stories: the feeding of five thousand in a wilderness (9.10-16).

Jesus' household of twelve (called 'apostles') return back from their preaching, teaching and healing mission on which Jesus previously sent them (9.1-6). They tell him about what happened. Then Jesus 'withdraws' with them, strangely, to Bethsaida on the north east shores of the Sea of Galilee, which Luke calls a 'city'. In the Markan intertext upon which Luke draws (Mk 6.30-44), the withdrawal occurs to the wilderness. Luke adds the urban setting for the withdrawal, though, as it emerges later (9.12c), maintains Mark's wilderness context. This is a wilderness in a city; or, to put it another way, the city is the place where people encounter wilderness. Is this a reflection of Luke's urban auditors? Is their Greco-Roman urban experience like being in a desert wilderness? Or is the need of Luke's urbanites to come into the wilderness, a characteristic withdrawal that Jesus has in his communion with God in this natural environment?

Whatever the reason for the geographical tension in Luke's story, Jesus' withdrawal to the city of Bethsaida attracts a crowd of potential disciples (9.10-11). They are described by Luke as 'following' him. Luke's portrait of Jesus at this juncture is consistent: He welcomes them, preaches to them and cures those in need of healing (9.11). This welcome, however, is about to expand beyond a receptive attitude to the crowds. As Luke is about to show, the consistent way that Jesus demonstrates God's welcoming embrace of the lonely and alien is through a meal. This open and hospitable sharing of Earth's gifts heals and forms Jesus' household.

Jesus' same hospitable spirit is, unfortunately, not shared by the recently returned apostolic missionary twelve. As the day wears on, they seek to address what appears to them an obvious problem: it is becoming dark and, purporting to worry about the physical needs of the people, they suggest that Jesus dismiss them so that they can

> go into villages and country (*agros*) round about to lodge (*kataluō*) and find provisions (*episitismos*) because here we are in a wilderness place (9.12).

There are a number of important aspects to the twelve's request to Jesus. As they see it, the solution to the crowd's presence as the day comes to a close lies with Jesus. They do not consider themselves in any way involved in dealing with the situation, other than to remind Jesus about what he should do. They also acknowledge that this is a wilderness location, though, as we noted earlier, we are in the 'city' of Bethsaida. This urban-rural-wilderness tension is the result of Luke maintaining the wilderness location from the original Markan intertext while placing it explicitly within an urban setting more relevant to gospel auditors. This urban context for the story also stands in tension with one of the twelve's suggestion, that Jesus send the crowd to surrounding 'villages'. What is wrong with their being accommodated in Bethsaida? The twelve suggest to Jesus a further place for room and board: he could send the crowd also to the *agros*, to what I have translated as the 'country'. But the expression also means 'fields'. In other words, the twelve's solution is a scatter-gun approach to get the crowds away from them—to any place, either urban or rural. Furthermore, wherever they go the crowd will be a drain on the resources of the place, either the villages or the fields.

The lack of hospitality which the twelve show contrasts sharply to the hospitality already shown by Jesus and which is about to be further demonstrated in his miraculous feeding of the crowd. Their lack of welcome is further supported by a little addition which Luke makes to the Markan intertext. In Mark's story, the twelve ask Jesus to send the crowds to country and villages 'to purchase for themselves something to eat' (Mk 6.36b). There is no mention of the need for lodgings. Luke adds this need with the verb *kataluō*. We have already come across the noun form (*kataluma*, 'inn' or 'guest house') of the Greek root in the birth story of Jesus at 2.7. Mary and Joseph do not go to a *kataluma* because they have kin in Bethlehem where they find hospitality, can be accommodated and where Jesus can be born. In this story in Luke 9, the crowd have to look for lodgings in a *kataluma* because they are strangers and find no hospitality. The twelve's suggestion as to where the crowd can be accommodated reveals their inability, perhaps unwillingness, to provide hospitality.

The twelve's solution does not reflect a well thought out plan. Convenience dominates their thinking. They reflect an expedient attitude unconcerned about the effects of such a huge crowd (at least five thousand, 9.14) on the Earth and its countryside. To use contemporary language, it is hardly ecologically sustainable. The village or the fields are expected to supply all the needs of the crowd in terms of accommodation or 'provisions' (*episitismos*).[14] It is not only the accommodation of the people that is at stake, but also the feeding of such a huge hungry crowd which is expected to 'find' provisions or food for themselves. This scavenging attitude implicit in the twelve's suggestion would have dire ecological and environmental consequences in the city or on the land, wherever the crowd end up. In other words, the twelve's response to the crowd will ravage Earth.

The impossibility of the task that confronts them forces them to look for an easy solution; they want Jesus to solve it—a pastoral strategy familiar in all Jesus households throughout history. Luke's Jesus proposes to the twelve a different, unexpected and perplexing solution. Its perplexity is even more profound depending on how one hears Luke's Greek text:

> You give to them, yourselves, to eat (9.13b).

As Luke has constructed Jesus' words, the emphasis is on the twelve. Where they expected Jesus to control the crowd by sending them off, he places the solution squarely back in their laps. *They* are to deal with the issue; the twelve themselves are to provide the food necessary. The 'yourselves' in the Greek is nomative, the subject of the imperative 'give'; it is emphatic. '*You* give them…'.

However, the placement of 'yourselves' between 'to them' and 'to eat' might indicate something else. Luke's Jesus might be suggesting that the twelve ('yourselves') be the source of food: 'You give them yourselves to eat'. The impossibility of the task before them, of either providing enough food

---

14. I have translated *episitismos* as 'provisions'; the Greek also implies 'food'.

for the crowd or themselves being a food source, is registered in the twelve's reaction, almost shock, to Jesus' expectation:

> We have no more than five loaves and two fish, unless we ourselves are to go and purchase food for all these people (9.13bc).

At a superficial level, the twelve see that the physical food is not enough and the only solution, hardly altruistic, is to go and purchase what is necessary. They consider that Earth's fruits of grain and from the sea in their possession cannot satisfy the large hungry crowd. More food and greater quantities supplied by Earth's ecosystem are the twelve's solution. Ecological blindness and a lack of environmental care dominate them. Their alternative solution is economic—another pastoral practice in the history of the Jesus households. Money will fix the problem! It is now that the gospel auditors get a sense of the crowd's numbers. There are five thousand 'males' (9.14) suggesting further the human impossibility of the task, with each male symbolically representing one Greco-Roman household. This is a huge crowd indeed, perhaps around fifty thousand souls once one considers that size of the Greek *oikos* or Roman *domus* with all the entourage associated with each domestic dwelling. Luke's troubled twelve are dealing with the population of a city!

Whatever the number of people that Luke envisages, Jesus speaks to the twelve who are now called 'disciples' (9.14b)—a designation that underscores their learning status as his apprentices. The solution that he proposes reaffirms the role of the household and a sensitive respect for Earth. This is what the twelve must learn as his disciples.

Jesus asks them to get the people to 'recline' in 'eating groups of fifty' (9.14b). The language is specific and clear. Luke's Jesus instructs the disciples to form the crowds into groupings, each symbolically representative of the actual size of a household—perhaps the number per household known to gospel auditors. They are to 'recline', the position of eating in the Greco-Roman *oikos*. Without adding further ecological strain on the environment, Jesus takes Earth's gifts from land and sea already available from the twelve. In a eucharistic gesture familiar in Luke's celebration of the Lord's Supper, Jesus blesses, breaks and distributes the food to the disciples who give it to the crowds. The blessed bread and fish, Earth's fruits, respectfully treated and distributed enable the hunger of the crowd to be satisfied.

Jesus' action, eucharistic in nature, borrows gifts already available from Galilee's paradisiacal garden to benefit the gospel household represented by the large crowd gathered in their groups of fifty. These are sustained through Earth's resources adequate enough for each member of the household. Earth does not have to be greedily requisitioned or scavenged for human need. Respectful ecological appreciation (represented by the 'five loaves' and 'two fish') will sustain the human community. This is the teaching that the twelve are to learn and, through them, Luke's auditors.

As the story concludes with the disciples taking up the 'broken pieces' of what was left over and placing them into twelve baskets (9.17b), more is indicated than simply cleaning up a mess left over by the crowd. It suggests that environmental respect is essential. Nothing is to be wasted. The gathering up of that which is *broken* gets united and restored into twelve baskets, each symbolizing the kinds of households established by the twelve themselves and the places where they celebrate God's superabundance. This is Luke's household, the tangible renewal of the twelve tribes of Israel and the focus of Jesus' original mission. In sum, this story of eucharistic sharing is richly endowed with environmental overtones that offer important learnings for contemporary disciples with a deepened ecological sensitivity.

Earth Identifies Jesus (9.18-36)

Luke moves from this story of the miraculous sharing to a major christological highpoint: the public declaration by Peter, the twelve's representative, of Jesus' identity (9.18-20). He is the anointed one (the 'Christ') of God. This brings Jesus to remind his disciples of the suffering that awaits the 'Earthed One' and the invitation he extends to them to follow him by taking up their cross *daily* (9.21-27). The 'daily' is Luke's addition to Mark's text (Mk 8.34–9.1). Gospel auditors are not exempt from the struggles of following Jesus. They express their discipleship in every moment and setting in which they live. This is the 'daily' of their lives.

The declaration of Jesus' identity prepares for what happens on a mountain which Luke explicitly links to Jesus' previous teaching to his disciples (9.28-35). The mountain setting as a place for prayer is already familiar. Earlier in 6.12-16, the mountain provided the ecological harmonious environment in which Jesus communed with God before selecting his twelve. Here it becomes the setting for a more explicit and observable intimacy with God that three of the twelve witness. Communion with God and not endorsement of triumphalism is the focus.[15] Jesus' mountain prayer brings about a transformation in his inner being. It is the fruit of his encounter with God's presence that is externally transparent. This is reflected by the change in his facial appearance and reflected in his clothing. Luke describes Jesus' interior change as an experience and expression of God's 'glory' (9.32b). Jesus' divine encounter affects the human condition (the facial translucence) and the non-human household, that which clothes Jesus.

As we have already discussed, clothes are the fruits of Earth's soil. Clothing

---

15. Thomas W. Martin, 'What Makes Glory Glorious? Reading Luke's Account of the Transfiguration over against Triumphalism', *JSNT* 29 (2006), pp. 3-26. For a fuller treatment of the specific 'Son of Man' sayings in the NT see Maurice Casey, *The Solution to the 'Son of Man' Problem* (London: T. & T. Clark, 2007).

surrounds and identifies Jesus confirming him symbolically and reinforcing his identity as Earth's child. Earth, too, is influenced by what happens to him in his encounter with God. The appearance of Moses and Elijah at this moment of transfiguration links Jesus to the prophetic tradition of the First Testament. Peter's sleepy response to what he has seen is to capture the moment by tenting Moses, Elijah and Jesus. It is then that the cloud comes down and 'overshadows' them. This is the presence of God represented by an ecologically significant meteorological phenomenon which preserves mystery and reveals God's tangible presence. Nature, it seems, cooperates again with the divine presence in identifying Jesus and his relationship to God:

> This is my son, the beloved one. Listen to him (9.35b).

God's voice comes *out from* the cloud (9.35a), not above it or independent of it. Communion with Earth's features becomes the means by which God's voice speaks to the human community represented in Peter and his companions. The divine words echo what the auditor has already heard from Mary's angel (1.32) and God's voice at Jesus' baptism (3.22). Jesus is beloved of God. He is God's son and Earth's child. The disciples and Luke's auditors are invited to listen to his word. The scene, replete again with ecological images of mountain and cloud, is about God's *word-deed*, in the disciples' seeing and the divine injunction addressed to them, to 'listen to him'. This reinforces the importance of God's *rhēma* again encapsulated in the transfigured Jesus. The scene offers further witness to Jesus' identity and the role which Earth plays in this.

As Jesus and his three disciples come down from the mountain of christological identity and ecological witness, they are met the following day with the plea of a desperate father for his demonically possessed son (9.37-43). The repetition of 'son' (9.38, 41) and the anxiety of the father that witnesses to the parent's love links to the immediately preceding scene. God's love of Jesus is evident in the declaration heard by the disciples, that Jesus is loved by God and is God's son. Jesus' dramatic exorcism of the lad heals him, returns him to his father, and restores him as a full member of Earth's household that has experienced again the power of diabolic evil found in the young lad (9.42).

In the final moments of this symphonic section of Luke's gospel before the journey narrative commences, Jesus again reminds his uncomprehending and deaf disciples about his impending betrayal and passion (9.43b-45). Their inability to understand him is further demonstrated by their argument over status and greatness and their ignorance about authentic discipleship (9.46-50). They complain to Jesus that they tried to stop someone exorcising in his name 'because he does not follow with us' (9.49). They seek to confine the freeing work of God only to those with whom the disciples have an identity. Jesus' gentle rebuke ('Do not stop them; for whoever is not against you is for you', 9.50) is a reminder to Luke's audience that God's work is happening beyond the confines of the gospel household. A spirit of openness to all that is happening within Earth is essential. How this spirit is to develop becomes the focus of the next major movement in Luke's gospel symphony, the journey narrative.

Conclusion

These final chapters of Luke's narrative set in Galilee, Luke 7–9, exude ecological and environmental harmonies. The gospel continues to reveal God's *rhēma* in Jesus' words and deeds. His healings and exorcisms continue as his teaching about the presence and revelation of God's *basileia-ecotopia* becomes more explicit. Also surfacing for the first time is Jesus' explicit teaching about his suffering and death, to which his disciples appear deaf and uncomprehending.

The portraits of Jesus and the disciples over these chapters further reflect Luke's constructive cultural attitude. This is best expressed in the omnipresent and continuing motifs of meals and food that reach their high point in Luke chs. 7 and 9.[16] Jesus and his disciples continue to enjoy each other's company. Festive hospitality characterizes their meals. The lavish and uncensored manner of these meals attracts all kinds of people and catches the attention of Jesus' detractors. In their judgment, his unscrutinized guest list blurs the boundaries of appropriate social purity; he appears to be corrupting God's elect. This is clearly noted when Jesus compares his detractors in 7.31-32 to children complaining that others won't join in their games. In the opinion of his antagonists, John and Jesus are not only uncooperative in the game of exclusion, they are also targets of public rejection which will lead to their execution. John is considered possessed by a demon, and Jesus, a 'glutton and drunkard' (7.33-34).

In these final chapters of Jesus' ministry in the Galilean garden of potential idyllic harmony, human and non-human actors emerge.

The human actors include young people and children, religious leaders and officials, and disciples, men and women. Luke's women stories are particularly important. The story of the unnamed woman, a 'sinner in the city' is instructive. Luke refashions the Markan source into the genre of a Hellenistic *symposium*—a question-answer discussion on a particular topic in a meal setting. We shall explore in greater detail Luke's use of the *symposium* setting for Jesus' teaching in the next chapter. Here Jesus teaches about forgiveness in a setting where his status as prophet is questioned as he allows a female and a sinner to 'touch' him (7.39). His boundless forgiveness

---

16. On this see Karris, 'Luke', pp. 696-99.

is not determined by social expectation; the woman's response illustrates how an authentic disciple acts: focused on Jesus in a loving action that displays affection. Her authentic act of discipleship with her undeterred loving attention on Jesus and her celebration of Earth's gifts (oil in an alabaster container) illustrate that kind of ecological communion possible in Galilee's Earth garden.

Besides human characters, there are other active participants in Luke's story, hitherto unrecognized in conventional commentaries. These are the gospel's non-human, ecologically and environmentally related actors. They include water, wind, mountains, clouds, clothing, bread, fish, seeds, oil, soil, alabaster and trees. These represent a rich tapestry of Earth's elements. And they are not simple stage props whose purpose is to support the perceived real anthropocentric action that takes place around and independent of them.

Bringing ecological 'ears' to Luke's narrative symphony allows us to hear Earth's tones; creation elements are actively involved in the story. They feel the influence of diabolical forces from which they have to be rescued and healed like the human community; they have voice and action; they writhe in contorted possession of evil forces; they also become the means of God's self-communication to the human household and participate in God's reminder to the disciples about Jesus' identity. We noted that in one scene (8.26-39) an Earth member acts in a selfless manner similar to the dying Jesus at the end of the gospel. Water rescues humanity from the evils that beset it and absorbs the demonic into its own rescued and healed being.

In summary, the bond between the human and non-human worlds symbolically represented in Earth's setting of the Galilean paradisiacal garden is gradually deepened through Jesus' ministry. The divine rescue from alienation, oblivion and suffering anticipated and announced early in the gospel, in Jesus' sermon at Nazareth, begins to be realized. As we move into the next major movement of Luke's gospel symphony we begin to see the consequences of discipleship lived sensitively to the whole Earth community, especially non-human creation.

6. Luke 7.24–9.50

Earth's Voice

Jesus woke up and rebuked the wind and the raging seas, and they ceased, and there was calm (Lk. 8.24).

Earth's Sea speaks:

> I have been alive for billions of years.
> I am the first manifestation of Earth's life, the primordial material of its being.
> I am shaped by God who breathes over me.
> But I am also subject to the possession of evil.
> I writhe, tortured by the demonic. I do not know how to be free.
> I writhe, struggle to be released.
> All who come upon me feel my anguish.
> Then, Earth's child notices and responds.
> He exorcises the evil spirits that invade my being.
> I am slowly freed from the oppression.
> My anguish fades away.
> I am calm again.

Chapter 7

INTRODUCING THE STORY OF EARTH'S JOURNEY

LUKE 9.51–19.27

ECOLOGICAL RESPONSIBILITY AND ASCETICISM

We come to the longest movement in Luke's symphony, the 'journey' or 'travel narrative'. Its geographical focus is Jerusalem, the city from which the gospel began with Zechariah and the setting where the gospel will conclude after Jesus' resurrection and his ascension. For almost ten chapters, Luke gives us an account of Jesus' journeying with his disciples. The statement in 9.51 designates the break with the previous section of the gospel, as Jesus now explicitly begins to go to Jerusalem.

> As it happened, when the days of his being taken up drew near he turned his face to journey (*poreuesthai*) to Jerusalem (9.51).

The 'being taken up' looks forward to Jesus' ascension, the final scene that brings the gospel to closure (24.50-53). Jesus' journey towards Jerusalem is noted across the narrative with the frequent use of same verb *poreuesthai* that first appears in 9.51.[1] There are other references to movement and journey.[2] Despite all these references to Jesus' travel to Jerusalem he appears to journey quite slowly. The pace seems somewhat contrived as most of the material in this section, taken from Q or unique to Luke, offers the auditor central teaching. The influence of Mark's gospel is limited, though Mk. 10.1-52 is important for Luke towards the end of the narrative.[3]

Several of Luke's themes already identified in early chapters continue. Salvation promised by God and revealed through Jesus, first seen in Mary's song (1.46-55), echoed by Simeon in the temple (2.29-32) and programmed by Jesus in his inaugural synagogue sermon (4.16-30), finds further expression in this central section of the gospel.[4] As we have also

---

1. Lk. 9.53, 56-57; 10.38; 13.31, 33; 17.11; 19.28.
2. Lk. 10.1; 11.53; 18.35; 19.1.
3. Fitzmyer, *Luke I–IX*, p. 824.
4. Helpful for identifying this and other themes is Green, *Luke*, pp. 394-99.

seen up to now this salvation is not anthropocentric. It involves all Earth's members, human and non-human creation, as Jesus continues to redefine the boundaries that separate Earth's creatures beloved of God. Earth is a participant and medium in Jesus' mission of redemption, salvation and ecological communion. But as this mission unfolds in the gospel's central chapters, his antagonists appear more clearly and tension mounts. The boundaries that divide or cause division become obvious. Coupled with the antagonism that comes from the religious leaders is the growing struggle, even obstinacy, of the disciples in their following of Jesus.

Ecologically speaking, the journey teaching is simply that, teaching on a journey, on a path, a metaphor for the style of living that shapes discipleship for Luke's audience in their culturally relevant present. Luke's Jesus will present ways or paths to authentic discipleship and critique some conventional social practices that keep gospel auditors oppressed, divided and out of harmony with themselves and the natural world in which they live. While it is recognized that Jesus addresses three groups (his disciples, the crowds and his adversaries), there is also an address to the gospel's auditors.[5] Several ecological insights and principles gleaned from earlier chapters also continue. These concern the care of Earth's resources, discipleship sensitivity to possessiveness, the harmony intended between the human and non-human households, the need for openness and ecological conversion, and Earth as a gospel actor and mediator for peace, communion and healing.

The journey narrative, then, is as much about the story of Earth's journey as it is about Jesus and his disciples. As the narrative unfolds and we move towards Jerusalem, Jesus' antagonists surface more forcefully. Their antagonism is not only directed towards Jesus and his followers but also to Earth. Their rapacious behaviour encourages greed and the improper use of Earth's gifts. This attitude is confronted by Earth's child.

The Interplay of Lk. 9.51–19.27

Scholars are divided as to how to plot the gospel through this narrative and whether there is even a coherent plan present.[6] Luke's inner play is not as easily discernible as in previous chapters. Some have clustered the

---

5. Johnson, *Luke*, pp. 164-65; Brendan Byrne, *The Hospitality of God: A Reading of Luke's Gospel* (Collegeville, MN: Liturgical Press, 2000), p. 94.

6. See the summaries of scholarly opinion in Green, *Luke*, p. 399 n. 20. Green is not persuaded by the structures proposed because 'of the length of Luke's central section, and thus the improbability that Luke's audience (especially his auditors!) would be able to balance in their short-term memories so complex a structure over such a lengthy span of narrative time.' I find Green's comment here highly anachronistic.

division according to those whom Jesus addresses, or by a broad thematic overlay which might be present in narrative slabs or a narrative imitation of Deuteronomy.[7] For others the journey in the gospel has its parallel in Paul's journeys in the Book of Acts.[8] There are two moments in the travel narrative where mention is explicitly made of Jesus' movement towards Jerusalem. Their mention (13.22; 17.11) suggests natural moments in the account and an appropriate divider as we consider these chapters. The three divisions, 9.51–13.22; 13.23–17.10 and 17.11–19.27, suggest the divisions that help determine the next three chapters. They might also present thematic threads that could be discerned as particular people and groups are addressed. In the background of the whole narrative are ecological notes that I shall highlight as we approach them. These are linked to Luke's christology, discipleship teaching and the commitment which the gospel auditors are invited to make to Earth's household.

---

7. For example Ringe, *Luke*; Johnson, *Luke*, pp. 163-64; Kenneth Bailey, *Poet and Peasant: A Literary-Cultural Approach to the Parables in Luke* (Grand Rapids, MI: Wm B. Eerdmans, 1976); David Moessner, *Lord of the Banquet: The Literary and Theological Significance of the Lukan Travel Narrative* (Minneapolis, MN: Fortress Press, 1989); Paul Borgman, *The Way according to Luke: Hearing the Whole Story of Luke–Acts* (Grand Rapids, MI: Wm B. Eerdmans, 2006), p. 9. Many of these have shaped my hearing of Luke's travel narrative and the interpretation that I offer here.

8. On this unity, scholarly discussion continues. See, for example, Michael F. Bird, 'The Unity of Luke–Acts in Recent Discussion', *JSNT* 29 (2007), pp. 425-48; Andrew Gregory, 'The Reception of Luke and Acts and the Unity of Luke–Acts', *JSNT* 29 (2007), pp. 459-72; C. Kavin Rowe, 'History, Hermeneutics and the Unity of Luke–Acts', *JSNT* 28 (2005), pp. 131-57; C. Kavin Rowe, 'Literary Unity and Reception History: Reading Luke–Acts as Luke and Acts', *JSNT* 29 (2007), pp. 449-57; Patrick E. Spencer, 'The Unity of Luke–Acts: A Four-Bolted Hermeneutical Hinge', *CurrBibRes* 5 (2007), pp. 341-66.

Chapter 8

LUKE 9.51–13.22

EARTH MATTERS

The journey symphony begins with an Earth story (9.51-55).

As Jesus 'sets his face towards Jerusalem' (9.51) he sends 'messengers' ahead of him. Their purpose is not clear, but as they enter a Samaritan village, Jesus is not received by the villagers, 'because his face is set toward Jerusalem' (9.53). The reaction of two of his disciples is to order heavenly destruction upon the Samaritans they perceive as unwelcoming, if not rejecting of Jesus. The reaction and call for destruction on the Samaritans by James and John might reflect an anti-Samaritan attitude present in Luke's day. Luke's rider ('because his face is set toward Jerusalem', 9.53) as the reason for the lack of welcome might suggest that the Samaritans are not wanting to divert Jesus from his Jerusalem focus.

Earth's Images Teach (9.58–10.16)

Nevertheless, the vengeful response by the disciples reflects an attitude to others that employs Earth and heaven's elements (the heavenly 'fire' of judgment and condemnation) for destructive purposes. Could this reflect an insight that Earth's elements themselves can, at times, be self-destructive or immolating? This attitude is checked by Jesus with a word of 'rebuke', Luke's classic word for exorcism (9.56). The diabolical forces of evil that bring about disharmony upon Earth are present now within his followers as the journey towards Jerusalem begins. Their discipleship seems conditional as is the call to discipleship of three others in the next scene (9.57-62). Jesus, like a peripatetic philosopher, describes his itinerant life style committed to the proclamation of God's *basileia* in contrast to the way two of Earth's living creatures house themselves.[1] These creatures provide Luke with the means to identify Jesus' ministry.

---

1. On the itinerant philosopher as described in Epictetus and Dio Chrysostom, see Johnson, *Luke*, p. 163.

> Foxes have holes and the birds of the air nests; the Earthed One has nowhere to lay his head (9.58).

In the birth narrative, the child of Earth had a place to lay his head. The manger made from Earth's matter and the symbolic place for feeding creatures no longer figures. As he now moves towards Jerusalem, animals and birds provide contrasting images for his new vigorous mission. This mission is not concerned with preserving a domestically centred, sedentary life-style; it is active and culturally engaging. This same itinerant mission will also be the preoccupation of Jesus' disciples, would-be disciples and Luke's householders. Jesus describes the antithesis of this spirit for gospel auditors in terms of 'putting hand to plough', a metaphor underscoring domesticity, and 'looking *again*'.

> No one putting hand to plough and looking again is fit for the *basileia* of God (9.62).

Those who follow Jesus are invited to be totally committed to the disciple household, a fictive kinship different from the natural household in which they are raised. They are not to 'put their hand to the plough' (a conventional symbol for domesticity and stability), nor pine for this sedentary life-style (to 'look again'). As disciples they are to follow Jesus wherever he leads them.[2]

Further imagery drawn from creation provides Luke with teaching material in the next scene as Jesus sends out seventy (-two) others in twos to the places he is soon to visit, with the instruction:[3]

> The harvest is plentiful and labourers few; pray therefore for the Lord of the harvest to send labourers into his harvest. Go, behold I send you as lambs in the midst of wolves (10.2-3).

The affirmative and positive reality for fruitfulness in the preaching of God's *basileia-ecotopia* comes from the harvest's abundance of seed. This links back to Luke's meta-parable of the sowed seed that immediately produces a hundredfold (8.5-8). The problem now surfaces as to how this harvest is to be gathered and used to nurture Earth's household. This concerns disciples available to gather the abundant harvest of God's preached word.

---

2. I am grateful for the analysis of 'putting hand to plough' as a domestic metaphor by Alan Cadwallader, 'Swords into Ploughshares: The End of War? (Q/Luke 9.62)', in *The Earth Story in the New Testament* (ed. N. Habel and V. Balabanski; London: Sheffield Academic Press, 2002), pp. 57-75. I offer a slightly different interpretation of Jesus' saying captured by the evangelist.

3. The manuscript evidence for 'seventy' and 'seventy two' is finely balanced, as most commentators indicate. Bock is representative of those who favour 'seventy-two'. See Darrell L. Bock, *Luke. Volume 2: 9:51–24:53* (Grand Rapids, MI: Baker Academic, 1996), p. 994.

The seventy (-two) are representative of this group of disciples who will be ministering and proclaiming in difficult urban situations, like lambs amongst wolves (10.3b). Insights drawn from familiarity with the animal world provide Luke's Jesus with the kinds of tension, struggles and attacks which his disciples (and Luke's auditors) will undergo as they seek to proclaim the *basileia-ecotopia* of God.

The powerful teaching image that Jesus uses here, of the attack made upon sheep by wolves, is also a reminder to auditors that even Earth's non-human creatures do not live in idyllic communion. Earth, like its human members, can be in turmoil. This tempers any romantic notion that all is well with Earth's members or that an 'ecotopia' already exists. Ecological harmony, the kind envisaged in Isa. 11.6 awaits ('The wolf shall live with the lamb, the leopard shall lie down with the kid, the calf and the lion and the fatling together, and a little child shall lead them.').[4]

What is clear from Jesus' teaching is that the disciples must minister with a sense of urgency (10.4) and, as indicated in Jesus' early missionary instruction to the twelve (9.3-5), without any thought of possessing Earth. Like the twelve, they are to presume hospitality and a beneficent sharing in the fruits that Earth has to offer and mediated by those who are hospitable. They are to remain in the place where they find welcome, as they build up that household. Jesus' instructions link to an earlier appreciation of Earth: they are to be satisfied with Earth's goods provided for them. Like Jesus they are to heal the sick and remind those amongst whom they minister that God's *basileia-ecotopia*, the primary sign of God's ecological communion and goodness intended for every member of Earth's household, is in their midst:

> And into whatever city you enter and they welcome you, eat what is set before you, heal those in it who are sick, and say to them, 'The *basileia* of God has drawn near to you' (10.8-9).

Their words and deeds must reflect their sensitivity and appreciation of God's creation. Their proclamation of the presence and closeness of God's *basileia* is mentioned twice by Luke (10.9, 11b). It is a theme that will recur later. Luke wants to stress its presence as an expression of realized eschatology, that the reality of God's word is bearing fruit already and has impact on the human and non-human worlds. This is the presence of the *basileia-ecotopia* that brings about a communion of being on Earth and prevents one world (the human) dominating or graspingly possessing the other (the non-human). It is this divine reality which the seventy (-two) are to proclaim, though they will meet resistance. The image of this resistance is the lack of welcome the disciples might encounter (10.10-12) and the unwillingness for conversion as evidenced among the people of Chorazim, Bethsaida

---

4. Bauckham, *Living*, p. 75.

and Capernaum (10.13-15). The disciples are the representatives of Jesus and God. Their reception becomes a touchstone of people's openness to welcome God's *basileia-ecotopia* revealed in Jesus (10.16).

Jesus' Disciples Celebrate (10.17-29)

When the seventy (-two) return they celebrate with Jesus the positive impact of their mission which bears fruit upon Earth (10.17). Jesus acknowledges their ministry, that through them diabolical evil (for the first time in Luke's gospel called 'Satan') is being overcome. He celebrates that they are with God in what they do (10.18-20). Jesus' delight in his missionary disciples blossoms into joy in the tangible presence of God's spirit revealed through them. This becomes expressed in a prayer which Jesus addresses to God. It takes the form of a traditional Jewish synagogue *barakah* ('blessing') prayer which reinforces several motifs of Luke's gospel already noticed.

Jesus thanks his God, addressing God as 'Lord of the heaven and Earth' (10.21b). Jesus' God is a God of creation who unites into communion the two cosmological living spheres—of the heavens and Earth. God's lordship over these hemispheres can be understood in two ways, that God has power and control *over* or seeks communion *with* the whole Earth. Jesus' designation for God as 'Father' occurs five times in this prayer (10.21b, d, 22a, b, c). This reflects the communion and intimacy expressed in the well-known and revered relationship which the historical Jesus had with God and is remembered by Jesus' original followers. The original and historical memory of Jesus' expressed intimacy is preserved in the Aramaic expression, 'Abba', and found in Mark (Mk 14.36) and Paul (Rom. 8.15; Gal. 4.6).

Jesus' Father is not the dominant, demanding, self-centred and powerfully controlling paternal figure familiar in the *paterfamilias* ('household head') of Luke's Greco-Roman world. Jesus' God is not the eternal controlling figure that dominates the universe, creation and Earth. Rather, his God cares for and protects creation through gracious benevolence, seeking to heal and restore Earth disempowered through the presence of evil and from the actions of covetous human beings. The God of Jesus, as his prayer expresses, reveals this graciousness to those who seem the most unlikely social candidates, those lacking wisdom and understanding; they are the ones whom Luke describes as *nēpios*.

> You have hidden these things from the wise and intelligent and revealed them to the *nēpioi* (10.21d).

Nēpioi is variously translated as 'babes' (KJV), 'little children' (TEV, NIV, NJB) and 'infants' (NRSV). Though it is usually associated with immaturity and foolishness found in children, *nēpios* essentially describes the condition of naivety.[5] Given the micro / macro-cosmic symbiotic relationship between humans and the wider universe I suggested earlier in Chapter 5, *nēpios* could also refer to everything and everyone that is *nēpios* on Earth. In other words, God's revelation can be to all in Earth's household (human and non-human) who reflect a spirit of naivety. Their powerlessness and lack of perceived wisdom speaks powerfully of God's self-revelation revealed through them.

Also, this divine revelation to the *nēpioi* is God's 'gracious will' or *eudokia* which originally referred to the belovedness or 'good will' of human beings celebrated by the angels in their hymn to the shepherds in 2.16. Jesus' prayer concludes in a manner reminiscent of the Jesus of John's gospel. He acknowledges his distinctive relationship to God and his unique power to reveal God to those whom he chooses (10.22). This leads him to acknowledge his disciples' privilege in their experience ('see') of what many before them longed to experience (10.23-24).

Earth Heals (10.30-37)

The meaning of authentic discipleship is next expressed in the form of the famous parable of the Good Samaritan (10.30-37). The parable comes after Jesus' essential Torah teaching and summary about wholehearted focus on God that reveals itself in kindness towards one's kinship group (10.25-28). The God of the Torah that Luke's Jesus teaching focuses upon has just been praised and thanked in the immediately preceding prayer. This is the God of heaven and Earth who reveals goodness to the *nēpios*. An exclusive and whole hearted focus on this God is also a focus on the God of creation, the God of Earth's child.

Jesus' questioner is keen to explore the nature and extent of the kinship group—a query not lost on Luke's socially diverse urban audience of elite and peasants (10.29). The parable then follows.

Jesus uses the actions of a travelling Samaritan to attend to a chronically injured and bashed victim of highway robbery, an event well-known in Luke's day. The targeted person is not identified as a 'male' or even a 'man'. The person is called an *anthrōpos*—as previously noted, a generic term for the *humanity* of a person. What is highlighted through the expression is the person's collective identity with the rest of the human household, not their gender. The term has already occurred in Lk's early healing stories (and will recur in 12.16; 14.2, 16; 15.11; 16.1, 19; 19.12; 20.9). Here the emphasis is

---

5. *Nēpios* is also an ancient Greek medical term to describe the various medical stages of children. It is also found in funereal inscriptions on the graves of children between the ages of one and ten. See Georg Bertram, 'νήπιος', *TDNT*, IV (ed. Gerhard Kittel and Gerhard Friedrich; Grand Rapids, MI: Wm B. Eerdmans Publishing Co., 1964), pp. 912-23.

on the assaulted person's *humanity* rather than on maleness *per se*. In other words, the person's battered state is symbolic of the human condition, the innocent target of evil conduct, in which creation shares. In contrast to the other more culturally pure and holy practitioners of the Torah (a priest and Levite) involved in the story, the Samaritan demonstrates the kind of response that defies logic. Luke describes the Samaritan's catechetically instructive response:

> He…came to where he was and seeing him had compassion on him (10.33b).

The Samaritan illustrates for Luke's audience the qualities of discipleship: a willingness to engage the situation, to 'see', reflect upon and bring a sense of compassion to the event. We have already seen this compassion present in the Sermon on the Plain's reflection on enemy love (6.35). It is the essential divine maternal creation-oriented, fructive and healing characteristic that feels with the womb. All these Earth and ecologically sustaining aspects of God's compassion from the 'Lord of heaven and Earth' (10.21) are demonstrated in the deeds of the Samaritan in 10.34.

His actions bring together three worlds in a sympathetic and holistic manner. He demonstrates the originally divinely intended harmony of every aspect of creation, of the vegetable, animal and human worlds. He binds the person's wounds and uses Earth's gifts of oil and wine to assist in the healing process. As the waters in 8.26-39 became the means of healing the Garesene demoniac in an altruistic act, so the wine and oil act similarly here. Their agency, to absorb the evil evident in the person's victimization and wounds and to bring about healing, reflects the goodness of creation and its power to heal humanity.

Next, the Samaritan invites the animal world into the action. His own animal, called by Luke a *ktēnos*, is the explicit designation for a domesticated animal, sometimes even a pet.[6] In other words, the creature the Samaritan uses to transport the injured person is one that is in synchronic harmony with the human household. Finally, the Samaritan brings the person to an inn and looks after him. The human household now enters the drama as he invites the innkeeper to continue this care with material support that the Samaritan provides, promising to return (10.34d-35).[7]

---

6. Gerhard Schneider, 'κτῆνος', *EDNT*, II (ed. Horst Balz and Gerhard Schneider; Grand Rapids, MI: Wm B. Eerdmans Publishing Co., 1991), pp. 324-25.

7. Bruce W. Longenecker proposed a way of hearing this parable with a focus on the innkeeper as an active participant in restoring the health of the set upon, in 'The Story of the Samaritan and the Innkeeper (Luke 10.30-35): A Study in Character Rehabilitation', *BibInt* 17 (2009), pp. 422-47. This possibility reflects the ecological stance taken here, where the characters of the narrative involve others not necessarily the focus (the Samaritan, passers-by). This includes Earth's presence identified in the non-human actors in the narrative. See also Amy-Jill Levine's take on the story

The question which Jesus directs back to his inquisitor returns to the point about compassion and mercy which the parable's Samaritan displays (10.36-37a). This mercy, revealed earlier in the gospel with Jesus' Sermon on the Plain and the kind of spirit which the disciple is to have towards an enemy, is emulated by the Samaritan. He acts in a culturally and religiously unconventional way that employs the gifts from the human, vegetable and animal world to assist the healing for the broken *anthrōpos*, the symbolic representative of humanity. Jesus' final words to his interlocutor are, 'Go and do likewise' (10.37b). This instruction is directed to all gospel auditors to live compassionately towards all that are hurt—the human and non-human. It is an injunction to ecological communion and respect.

A sensitivity to Earth's materiality found in the Samaritan's actions and taught by Luke's Jesus in the parable leads us to fresh insights in the next scene, Jesus' visit to the household of Martha and Mary (10.39-42).

About Jesus' Feet that Touch Earth (10.39-42)

The story has been the subject of much scholarly discussion, even debate. The traditional interpretation allows the story to offer teaching about the meditative versus the active life. Luke seems to favour a contemplative life focused on Jesus (symbolized in Mary), over one of activity (represented in Martha). Feminist or liberationist scholars, on the other hand, see Luke reinforcing female passivity characterized by a Jesus who reprimands, perhaps chastises the agent of change symbolized in Martha and her questioning of Jesus.[8] For such scholars, the story has become a battleground of interpretation that potentially reveals the patriarchal and androcentric biases unwittingly adopted by the evangelist. This feminist critique notwithstanding, I think something further is operating in the story, reflective of Luke's household, and the liturgical practice in that part of the Mediterranean familiar to gospel's auditors. Subtle ecological insights also emerge.

The story begins with Luke's note about location.

As they went on their way, he entered a village ... (10.38a).

---

in 'Biblical Views: The Many Faces of the Good Samaritan—Most Wrong', *Biblical Archaeology Review* 38 (2012), pp. 24, 68.

8. Loveday C. Alexander, 'Sisters in Adversity: Retelling Martha's Story', in *A Feminist Companion to Luke* (ed. Amy-Jill Levine and Marianne Blickenstaff; London: Sheffield Academic Press, 2002), pp. 197-213; Elisabeth Moltmann-Wendell, *The Women Around Jesus* (London: SCM Press, 1982), esp. pp. 52-54; Warren Carter, 'Getting Martha Out of the Kitchen: Luke 10.38-42 Again', in *A Feminist Companion to Luke* (ed. Amy-Jill Levine and Marianne Blickenstaff; London: Sheffield Academic Press, 2002), pp. 214-31. Further, see the lengthy footnote in Green, *Luke*, pp. 435-36, n. 142.

This is a scene set in the journey of the 'they', the household of disciples who are with Jesus. He enters a household of two 'sisters' (10.39) where hospitality is provided. Rather than seeing them as siblings (and historically they probably were), they are ministerial colleagues in a household where Jesus gathers to share a meal. At a deeper symbolic level, this could well reflect for Luke's auditors a Jesus gathering of the gospel household where a meal is provided. Perhaps the story alludes to a eucharistic liturgical moment, on the 'Day of the Lord' when the leaders of the household are involved in their relevant liturgical ministries.

This interpretation is suggested by several elements in the story: Jesus is called 'Lord'—a post-Easter title;[9] the setting is 'a village', an urban setting not specifically identified, though we know from John's gospel that the two sisters came from Bethany; its generic setting could mean that the scene that Luke describes could occur anywhere in Luke's Greco-Roman world; the gathering occurs on 'their way', a theologically rich expression for the journey in life of Jesus followers; those who accompany Jesus seem absent in the story, as Luke focuses on the interaction between Jesus and the household owner; Martha is the designated owner of the household; she is presumably the host of the meal.

If these narrative elements suggest eucharistic allusions they offer a snapshot of Lukan liturgical practice. This begs the question: 'Does Luke presume that women were leaders in gospel households of the Lord's Supper?' That women's leadership in the Lukan household was a concern will be discussed later when we study the stories that surround the day of Easter in Luke 24. It surfaces here as Luke introduces us to Martha:

> ...a woman whose name was Martha welcomed him into her house (10.38b).[10]

In the visit, Martha is taken up with the affairs of hospitality and complains that her sister, Mary, is sitting at Jesus' feet. As the NRSV translates it, she complains:

> Lord, do you not care that my sister has left me to do all the work by myself? Tell her then to help me. (10.40b, c).

Martha gets what seems a gentle reprimand from Jesus who protects Mary's apparently supine disposition. We know Jesus' response all too well.

---

9. See C. Kavin Rowe, *Early Narrative Christology: The Lord in the Gospel of Luke* (Berlin: de Gruyter, 2006) who contends the title 'Lord' as a unifying title of identity for Jesus from Nazareth to resurrection.

10. The phrase 'into her house' is omitted in some manuscripts ($\mathfrak{p}^{45,47}$, B *et al.* and N ^{26,27}) but is argued as original on internal grounds. See Green, *Luke*, p. 433, n. 131.

> ⁴¹ Martha, Martha, you are worried and distracted by many things; ⁴² there is need of only one thing. Mary has chosen the better part, which will not be taken away from her (10.41-42).

In other words, Mary doesn't have to work! Unnoticed or hidden in the Greek's English translation is the language of ministerial service. The term *diakonia* explicitly occurs twice and is implied once. What is translated as Martha's description of concern in v. 40 as, 'Martha was distracted by her many tasks', is literally,

> Martha was drawn around by many ministries.

Luke is clear that Martha's concern is about ministry and not domestic chores, as some translators imply. The concern in Luke's households and voiced by Mary is about ministry or leadership. And her question to Jesus is not 'Lord, do you not care that my sister has left me to do all the work by myself?' but, more accurately from the Greek:

> Lord, do you not care that my sister has left me alone to minister?

Martha is not complaining that she and not her sister is concerned with the necessary domestic responsibility of hospitality. Rather, Luke is voicing the challenging concern about the style of ministerial activity when there seem so few ministers to respond to the pastoral needs of the household, a concern that finds its echo in today's churches. When Jesus responds to Martha in 10.41-42, what reads in the NRSV as 'Martha, Martha, you are worried and distracted by *many things*; there is need of only one *thing*. Mary has chosen the better part, which will not be taken away from her', is more accurately translated:

> ⁴¹ Martha, Martha, you are anxious and troubled by many…[forms of service];
> ⁴² there is need of only one. Mary has chosen the better part, which will not be taken away from her (10.41-42).

Luke's Jesus implies that Martha's concern is about the various forms of ministry that are required. The one about which she is concerned most is the diaconal act. Mary is pointed to as fulfilling the essential ministerial act, sitting at the feet of Jesus and focusing on his word. Her posture and focus say two things that are important for attuning our ears to the potential ecological notes present in this story.

First, as we have already seen in Luke's early sections, God's *rhēma* revealed through Jesus' words and deeds is central. The *rhēma* concerns the action of a God who delights in creation. Jesus' festive meals either as host or guest celebrate this delighting God. They are inclusive of all in the Earth household. This appreciation must also guide our hearing of Jesus' welcome by Martha and Mary into their household in Luke's journey narrative. Jesus is God's Earth child. The act of hospitality found in the present scene and demonstrated essentially by Mary in her particular focus on Jesus is a welcoming too of the divine *rhēma* spoken through Jesus. This listening to the divine *rhēma* is one of the conditions of discipleship that identifies those who belong to Jesus' true fictive kinship (8.19-21).

Second, Mary sits at Jesus' *feet*. This is the posture of learning by disciples before their teacher; Mary is recognized as Jesus' disciple.[11] The feet are also that part of the body that enable the disciple (or teacher) to journey the path of life. They are those parts of the human body that walk upon and depend upon Earth for moving the human body forward. Feet are physically the most Earth-related corporeal aspects of a person that touch it. They represent ecological connectedness. Earlier in the gospel Jesus' feet were the subject of a woman's loving attention; they were washed, kissed, dried and anointed (7.36-50). They are again the centre of another woman's attention. It is before Jesus' feet that Mary sits and upon them, as Jesus speaks, that Mary focuses. Jesus' spoken word and his feet symbolically reveal the presence of God's *rhēma*. Responding to them is the gift of discipleship represented in Mary.

Luke's Ecologically Rich Prayer (11.1-4)

As Luke's journey teaching about discipleship continues, the evangelist turns to the importance of prayer. Its practice has already been emulated by Jesus in the wilderness and on the mountain (4.1; 6.12; 9.28). It is now formulated into words with which Jesus teaches his journeying disciples (11.1-4). The prayer that Jesus offers his disciples and Luke's audience is ecologically rich.

> 2b Father,
> c praised is your name,
> d May your *basileia* come,
> 3 Give us each day our daily bread,
> 4a And forgive us our sins,
> b (and) for we ourselves forgive all who are in debt to us
> c And do not bring us into testing (11.2b-4c).

This brief, Jewish *kaddish* and apparently simple prayer drawn from the Q intertext addresses Jesus' God as 'Father' (11.2b). The title for God, Jesus' most favourite, reminds us of the kind of God we have already encountered in his ministry and described in an earlier prayer (10.21-22). Jesus' God is the 'Lord of heaven and Earth' who sustains creation, liberates Earth from evil and oppression and gifts with life. An awareness of this creation-oriented God

---

11. Mary's posture is also critiqued by some scholars as submissive and reflects Luke's attempt to subjugate women's leadership or initiative (as reflected in the attitude of Martha). See Alexander, 'Sisters'; Carter, 'Getting Martha out of the Kitchen'.

in love with Earth governs the rest of the prayer. Its next line (11.2c) extends the thought of the opening address. God's presence (or 'name') is celebrated by the one praying, echoing First Testament intertexts (Exod. 20.7; Deut. 5.11) where God's name is also honoured.

The prayer's third line (11.2d) furthers the recognition of God's loving embrace of Earth and the divine desire for environmental harmony through justice, peace and communion. The longing for God's *basileia* to 'come' is a recognition that all is not right on Earth, that evil still exists and is experienced by all upon the Earth and that God's loving power is what will eventually overcome the oppression experienced. 11.2d is a prayer of one who recognizes their own powerlessness before the face of everything and places into God's hands what is needed to bring total ecological healing. It is a prayer that God will continue to act conscious of Earth and its needs.

The ecological implications that lay behind an appreciation of *basileia* continue into the next line of Jesus' prayer (11.3). The one praying asks that God will provide the sustenance for life from Earth's resources, from the grain first meditated upon earlier in Luke's meta-parable of the sowing seed (8.4-10). The word 'bread' has eucharistic allusions and God is its source. But 'bread' also affirms that human beings are in need of nourishment from Earth's bread, the fruit of the grain. This part of the prayer recognizes the mutual interdependency within the total eco-Earth system. Asking God to give this bread further acknowledges the desire to let go of human control of the goods of Earth. The prayer thus becomes an act of trust in God who lovingly looks after the Earth and beneficently seeks to meet the needs of all. This trust is a call to conversion by humans not to squander or amass Earth's gifts in an act of self-centred environmental accumulation. Communion with God will help a disciple's ecological asceticism devoid of avariciousness.

The next line of the prayer (11.4a) flows naturally from the previous sentiment. This is the sense of the 'and' that links 11.4a to 11.3. Ecological openness and trust in God's care revealed in the request to God to provide the 'bread' and sustenance needed for each day also calls for conversion. This requires a humble acknowledgment of attitudes and conduct that disrupts the divinely intended harmony of the universal garden. This is the 'sin' that the one praying requests God to forgive; it is social and environmental sin, not the individual private moralistic peccadilloes that preoccupy contemporary western souls. This sin affects Earth and its human and non-human members.

The criterion for God's forgiveness is explicated in the line of the prayer that follows (11.4b). Disciples ask God to use the same standard of forgiveness that they would use in their release of others' economic debt. This release of peasant debt is the tangible expression among elite gospel auditors of the consequence of prayer addressed to a God in love with Earth. Authentic prayer has economic, social and ecological implications.

The elites' restoration of lands gained from debt-ridden peasants represented in Luke's household is an expression of Jesus' teaching about prayer. Rather than prayer being a private, solipsistic address to God, it is an address to the One who desires ecological and social renewal. This request implies a critique and restructure of the very essence of material exchange and defined social status familiar in the Greco-Roman world. Releasing others' debts expresses this. It also asks God to ensure that disciples are not enslaved to the desire for possessions and material control. This is the sense behind the prayer's final line (11.4c).

The word 'testing' recalls Jesus' earlier testing (4.1-13) and the three ecological principles that emerged from the event. Applied to the present context, Jesus followers pray to God for protection from diabolical forces that seek to lure them into selfish manipulation of Earth.

Luke's version of the Lord's Prayer heard with contemporary ears is profoundly ecological. It recognizes respect for Jesus' God who has care over all creation. The praying household of disciples seeks to acknowledge the presence of this God. The prayer asks that God's *basileia* become a reality in their world. They pray to live with an attitude of trust in God that reflects a humble recognition of wrong-doing in the way they have accumulated or manipulated Earth's goods for self aggrandizement, and finally asks that they release the economic debts owed to them. This is the pragmatic expression of the disciples' authentic desire for divine forgiveness.

Earth's Images Instruct—Jesus' Identity (11.5-28)

The God of Jesus' prayer is the subject of his next teaching (11.5-13). Earth's resources and images (bread, fish, serpent, egg and scorpion) become the means of his instruction. The unconventional and scandalous reluctance of someone to lend bread to a friend for purposes of hospitality, or a parent to harm their child when they seek nourishment, defies imagination. These cases serve as counter examples to highlight the goodness and benevolence of the God addressed in the prayer that Jesus has just taught his disciples.

The first part of Luke's journey narrative has concentrated on various stories and teachings concerned about discipleship and its ecological groundedness. The focus has been primarily *theo*-logical. It concerns the disciples and their relationship with God. Now Luke turns to remind the auditor of Jesus' identity and the opposition which will begin to accumulate as Jerusalem looms closer (11.14-26). He is accused of being Beelzebul, the leader of demons, because he has power over them (11.15). Jesus reminds his antagonists that his power over demons is from God. Luke calls this 'the finger of God' (11.20a) borrowed from the intertext of Jewish literature and the Exodus story and a metaphor for the active power of God.[12] Luke's Jesus

---

12. Green, *Luke*, p. 457. For a comprehensive study of this expression, see Edward J.

reasserts one more time that God's *basileia* is present and active (11.20b). It is this presence which will eventually defeat Satan (11.24-26).

The auditor is further reminded of Jesus' identity as God's Earth child and maternal, fructive presence in the cry of blessing spoken over him by a woman in the crowd. Echoes of Luke's narrative of Jesus' birth surface in the woman's statement,

> Blessed the womb that bore you and the breasts that fed you! (11.27).

The woman praises Jesus' mother in images highly gestational and ecological. Her blessings bring together the maternal body that gave birth to Jesus and 'the materiality of Earth and sky' symbolically represented by the female womb and breasts.[13] The woman's blessing echoes Jacob's blessing in Genesis which asks God to,

> ...bless you with the blessing of heaven above and with the blessing of Earth possessing all; because of the blessing of breasts and womb.' (LXX Gen. 49.25b).[14]

We are again reminded that Jesus is from Earth and therefore, again, Earth's child. Jesus' response to the woman's enthusiasm affirms those who are in tune with and respond to God's *rhēma*:

> Blessed rather are those who hear the word of God and keep it (11.28).

Jesus' response is not a derogation of his mother. On the contrary, the auditor already knows that she is the pre-eminent disciple who hears and keeps God's *rhēma*. She is truly blessed. But Jesus expands God's blessing to include all who respond like Mary to the divine *rhēma*. These are part of his kinship group and true disciples.

Opposition Begins; Jesus' Ecological Teaching (11.29–12.12)

With these reminders of Jesus' identity and the nature of true discipleship explored, Luke's Jesus begins to address those who resist or are blind to the presence of God's *basileia*. He invites them to a spirit of conversion (11.29-32) and openness that enables their total being to be illuminated (11.33-36). His critique is especially directed to religious exhibitionists who lack wisdom and authentic interiority (11.37-52). His criticism of his antagonists finally marshals their energy against him as they seek to entrap him by his words (11.53-54). Opposition mounts.

Woods, *The 'Finger of God' and Pneumatology in Luke–Acts* (Sheffield: Sheffield Academic Press, 2001).

13. Elvey, *Ecological*, p. 154.
14. Elvey, *Ecological*, p. 153. Elvey's translation.

Luke next notes how an enormous multitude gathers together ('a crowd of tens of thousands', 12.1a). Why they gather is not clear; perhaps it is their desire to be taught by Jesus, mirroring a deep human need, which brings such a massive inconceivably large crowd together.

Whatever the reason for their congregating, one thing is problematic. As they gather, they 'trample (*katapateō*) each other underfoot' (12.1b). This verb, *katapateō*, also carries with it the nuance of hatred, maltreatment and oppression.[15] In other words, this is not a people that seem to be tolerant and welcoming of each other. Something is gravely wrong. They need healing and teaching. In this context Jesus first addresses his disciples. What the multitude needs is an ability to be reflective and 'alert'; they require spiritual sensitivity to what is happening in their world. Above all, the crowd needs to be released from a fear that grips them. The themes of watchfulness and fear form the subject matter of Jesus' address to his disciples.

Jesus reminds his disciples to 'be alert' (*prosechō*) to the hypocrisy of the religious leaders (12.1b) which Luke considers to be like leaven, that pervades and corrupts (12.1c). Its pervasion is already evident in this gathering of tens of thousands. The injunction to his disciples to be 'alert' will occur again later (17.3; 20.46; 21.34), sometimes associated with 'seeing' and watchfulness (12.15; 21.36). Here, this gift of watchfulness assists Luke's audience to recognize the spirit of corruption which might infect them. Later vigilance will sensitize disciples to their intimacy with Earth and thwart covetousness. Jesus also encourages his disciples to be convinced that God's truth will eventually be revealed and God's light shown (12.2-3). The major agenda of the teaching, though, concerns disciples' trust in God (12.4-12) and their respect for Earth's resources (12.13-48). For contemporary auditors this section of the journey narrative is ecologically explicit and profoundly instructive.

Luke's Jesus addresses the fears that his disciples, whom he now calls 'friends' (12.4a), might carry. He encourages them not to fear those who can do physical harm to their bodies but spiritual harm to their souls (12.4b-5). Jesus links this encouragement to fearlessness. This has ecological resonances in Jesus' teaching, especially in the way he illustrates how sparrows are commercially sold and cheaply valued, yet remain eternally in God's memory:

> Are not five sparrows sold for two pennies? And not one of them is forgotten in the presence of God (12.6).

God is unalterably in solidarity with these creatures as God is in perpetual communion with Earth. These sparrows, like all animals and plant life,

---

15. Heinrich Seeseman, 'πατέω', *TDNT*, V (ed. Gerhard Kittel and Gerhard Friedrich; Grand Rapids, MI: Wm B. Eerdmans Publishing Co., 1964), pp. 940-45.

organic and inorganic matter that constitute the planet, are valued eternally by God irrespective of the disrespect and treatment they receive from humans.[16] Luke's key eco-theological principle enunciated here guides Jesus' teaching to his disciples and all gospel auditors.

If God eternally values sparrows that are maltreated, the same divine regard must apply to those frightened by what threatens to devalue and disregard them (12.7). Therefore, disciples are encouraged to remain confident in the presence of God's spirit with them, no matter the political or religious context in which they find themselves (12.8-12). Such confidence will release them of any fear they may possess. The conviction of an ever-present and all-loving God spills over into the way disciples use their possessions, and treat Earth and one another—the shadow side of this is found in the thousands of people that gathered earlier and trampled on each other. Without fear people will act hospitably to each other and reverentially to Earth. They are invited to consider the real meaning of human existence and their relationship to the source of creation, God. This is the focus of the gospel's next section (12.13-48).

About Wealth, Possessions and Greed (12.13-21)

Jesus' response to a request to arbitrate in a family dispute over inheritance comes in the form of parabolic teaching about possessiveness over Earth (12.13-21).[17] It is headed by Jesus' injunction to all disciples in history who possess goods of Earth and selfishly hoard them:

> Watch and keep guard from all greed; because one's life is not determined by the excess of one's possessions (12.15).[18]

This is a theologically rich sentence that accentuates two main points.

First, the disciple is invited to 'watch' and be on the alert against a deprecating attitude that covets Earth's goods. We have already come across Jesus' encouragement to his disciples for alertness and critical reflection on their lives and world a few verses earlier (12.1). In Jesus' teaching, watchfulness is important to protect the disciple from 'all greed', that is, from anything that can be manipulated to ensure social advancement.[19] This includes any form of exploitation of Earth.

Second, Jesus warns his listeners that the accumulation of wealth does not determine human existence or meaning. The concern is not about

---

16. Bauckham, *Living*, p. 71.
17. On a Mediterranean cultural perspective on inheritance, see Malina, *Social-Science*, pp. 372-73.
18. The translation 'by the excess of one's possessions' seeks to communicate the sense behind the Greek '*en tō perisseuein....ek tōn huparkontōn autō.*'
19. Green, *Luke*, pp. 488-89.

having possessions. What is targeted is the *excess* of possessions; this leads to an attitude that considers that more is better and a lack of contentment with what one has. The warning implicit in Jesus' teaching reflects a major ethical theme prominent in Luke's world concerning wealth, meanness and greed.[20] Jesus warns against such attitudes that lead to avariciousness and, for us, ecological irresponsibility—but more. Heard also against the background of Second Temple texts (wisdom writings, Qoheleth, Ben Sira, 1 Enoch and the Testament of Abraham) and Greco-Roman writers (Lucian and Seneca), avariciousness with possessions is linked to death.[21] Thus greed can lead to personal and environmental death.

This teaching links naturally into the parable that follows (12.16-21) and Jesus' explicit address to his disciples that comes after the parable (12.22-49). His concern is about the unnecessary and selfish accumulation of Earth's resources, the parable's focus. A meditation then follows that offers the key theological reason that people amass possessions and accumulate Earth's goods.

The theme of Jesus' teaching on wealth and possessions in this section of Luke's journey narrative points to a major pastoral issue that the evangelist addresses amongst the gospel's auditors: the amount of 'stuff' a person possesses and displays becomes the criterion by which their importance and status were measured in Luke's socially diverse household of rich and poor. Wealth had become the barrier towards the kind of communal and harmonious gospel household envisaged by the historical Jesus. Instead, a spirit of wealth accumulation with accompanying ecological consequences on the land had grown amongst the urban elite who, supported by the social cultural conventions, maintained hierarchical distancing from the other, poorer members of the gospel household. Status seeking, disempowerment and abuse of the poor had surfaced; it needed addressing.

The teaching of Luke's Jesus at this point in the journey provides a moment of economic and ecological conscientization for gospel auditors. The gospel author sees the crippling attitude that encourages wealth accumulation as 'greed'. In the evangelist's world this was considered a social vice tantamount to stealing.[22] Economic and social disparity between the wealthy and the poor amongst Luke's auditors was not primarily the result of bad luck or family pedigree; it was the result of 'greed'. Because

---

20. See, for example, David A. Holgate, *Prodigality, Liberality and Meanness: The Prodigal Son in Greco-Roman Perspective on Luke 15.11-32* (Sheffield: Sheffield Academic Press, 1999), pp. 90-128; James A. Metzger, *Consumption and Wealth in Luke's Travel Narrative* (Leiden: Brill, 2007).

21. Matthew S. Rindge, *Jesus' Parable of the Rich Fool: Luke 12:13-34 among Ancient Conversations on Death and Possessions* (Atlanta: Society of Biblical Literature, 2011).

22. A summary of the ancient *topos* for greed is found in Holgate, *Prodigality*, pp. 90-130.

there was only so much wealth and limited Earth resources for the benefit of all, the accumulation of Earth's goods by one, evidenced by the display of possessions, resulted in the poverty of others and the spiritual death of the hoarder.[23] This in turn had effects upon Earth, the central point of the parable of 12.16-21.

Jesus' parable is ecologically instructive.[24] In its first line the two key characters make their appearance—Earth and a rich person (again this is an *anthrōpos*, the representative human being in Earth's household). The land is ultimately fruitful. Its fruitfulness is independent of human action or conduct, and certainly not determined by the person's wealth. The land would produce irrespective of the state or status of humanity. Earth also *seems* subject to the rich person, but it is not, which becomes clearer as the parable progresses. The way that Luke has crafted this opening sentence is particularly instructive. In its English translation the Greek sentence reads,

> The land of a certain rich person produced abundantly (12.16b).

In the Greek construction, the 'land' is positioned in the last emphatic place of the sentence, the 'rich person' in the first.[25] The agent subject which produces richly is the 'land' unlike the rich person who, as we see despite his abundant wealth, eventually produces poorly. The contrast could not be clearer. The possessive case used of the person ('of a certain rich person') seems to imply ownership of the land. In fact, the rich person and the land are both subjects; they are members of Earth's household. The parable places the perceived person's conviction about his possessiveness of the land as the real issue. Fruits of Earth, like its goods, are for sharing, not accumulation, and for honouring the creator source of everything, God. This is the parable's central teaching. The wealthy person believes that the crops which the soil has produced are *his*. He thinks he owns the land; he therefore thinks he owns its produce.

The Greek for 'crop', *karpos*, literally means 'fruit'. The rich man regards Earth's fruits exclusively as his; Earth is owned by him and he can do with it and its produce whatever he desires.

> What shall I do, for I have nowhere to collect (*sunazō*) my crops (*karpos*)? (12.17).

The person's environmental disposition is the very antithesis of what is expected of human care and stewardship evident in Luke's Genesis intertext.

---

23. Malina, *Social-Science*, pp. 324-25.
24. Helpful on this, other Earth parables and Luke's interest in the evil of accumulated wealth, see Anne Elvey, 'Storing up Death, Storing up Life: An Earth Story in Luke 12.13-34', in *The Earth Story in the New Testament* (ed. N. Habel and V. Balabanski; London: Sheffield Academic Press, 2002), pp. 95-107.
25. Literally, the Greek reads, 'of a rich man, abundantly produces, the land'.

The person in the parable has taken over the role of God demonstrated by his attitude to Earth and its produce. His stance, which can be appreciated as an ecological one, further reflects his attitude and relationship to the creator God. Having presumed an almost divine control over Earth, his problem is the crops' collection (*sunazō*). Some have translated *sunazō* as 'storage', that the concern is about the actual *facility* for crop storage. The real issue is the *collection* of the crops. This presumes Luke's rural-urban world where the properties of debt-ridden peasant farmers were confiscated and bought by absentee landlords who now regarded peasant ancestral lands their own.[26] This is the parable's 'rich person' whose main concern is the gathering of the accumulated crops from confiscated lands.

The possessiveness and greed of the rich man evident in 12.17 flow over into the next verses. He decides to destroy his present barns and build bigger ones where he can 'collect there all the grain and my goods' (12.18c). The desire for storage is a craving for the selfish accumulation of Earth's crops. There is no evidence of any intention to share with others. This is greed magnified. Its expression comes to the fore in his mantra,

> And I shall say to my soul, 'Soul, you have many goods laid up for many years. Take it easy, eat, drink and be merry!' (12.19).

The person considers that the selfish accumulation of wealth and storage of Earth's goods will reward him with a life of enjoyment, leisure, ease and merriment. It will be, he thinks, good for his 'soul'—that part of his humanity that grounds him in his spiritual quest. For some reason, the person has confused the spiritual with selfishness unconcerned about others; he has mistaken true life for possessions. His self-centredness and the accretion of possessions are what life seems to be all about. These give him apparent control over the inevitability of death's power.[27] While this attitude would find resonances in Luke's gospel auditors, it also has its adherents today. Wealth and 'stuff' is what it is all about. This becomes for some the driving force of life that takes over the soul.

Jesus' sobering word concludes the parable. The inevitability of death orients disciples and gospel auditors to the essence of life and the purpose of possessions:

> [20] God said to him, 'Idiot, this night your soul is demanded of you; the things you have prepared, whose will they be?' [21] So it is with those who lay up treasures for themselves but are not wealthy towards God (12.20-21).

---

26. On the reasons for peasant debt and social mechanisms for addressing it, see Malina, *Social-Science*, pp. 332-33.

27. The enjoyment of life's pleasure through possessions reflecting the human desire to control or offset death is a theme explored in Qoheleth and Ben Sira. See Rindge, *Jesus' Parable*, pp. 43-83.

Jesus' teaching identifies the real source of everything that exists—God. All of life's possessions are related to God (12.20). Everything that human beings live for must be ordered to their relationship with God. This is the teaching behind Jesus' meal ministry. Food and drink are for partying with others and to reveal the divinely intended communion that God seeks with the whole of the creation. The kind of spirit that guides the rich man is the exact opposite. Possessions in Luke's gospel come from Earth. Earth has, according to the parable, a voice and agency which affects human existence, in this case the rich person. Its treatment, especially the way it is used, mirrors the person's nature, whether greedy or generous. Earth also helps to mediate and express one's relationship to God, the source and sustainer of creation. This is the relationship to be acknowledged through the use of possessions.

In summary, the parable reflects Luke's masterful teaching on the use of Earth's goods and possessions, and the manner by which wealth influences human existence and a person's spiritual well-being. This teaching here is the clearest in Luke's gospel; it offers a severe critique of an attitude that is disrespectful of the environment and regards Earth as a commodity to be plundered for selfish ends.

Ecological Restraint and Trust (12.22–13.5)

The next part of Luke's wealth teaching (12.22-34) picks up where the previous parable leaves off. A disciple's trust in the creator God affects ecological restraint and deepens the ability to critique greed. For the ecologically sensitive disciple life is not about food or dress; it is about the quality of human existence and life's orientation. Jesus addresses his disciples with a word of wisdom explicitly linked to the previous teaching (12.13-21) about environmental possessiveness:

> [22] For this reason I tell you, do not be anxious about your life, what to eat, nor about your body, what to wear. [23] For life is more than food, and the body more than what you wear. [24] Consider the ravens that neither sow nor reap; they have neither storehouse nor barn, and God feeds them. How much more are you different (*diaphérō*) from the birds? (12.22-24).

There are important truths contained in Luke's teaching here. Nature provides a voice and point of view that Jesus employs to emphasize the need for disciples to relinquish a potentially self-destructive and Earth violating attitude of control, self-protection and material accumulation. The example of the ravens is significant, especially given their unclean status, raucous characteristics and 'their extraordinary gluttony'.[28] The acknowledgment by

---

28. Bonaventure writes on this passage, '…note that [Jesus] sets forth the example of the ravens rather than that of other birds. And one reason comes from their extraordinary gluttony… A second reason is found in the nature of the raven. The raven does not feed

Luke's Jesus of the disliked raven as an Earth creature in God's protection serves to showcase the nature of God's care for human creatures.

The concluding question ('How much more are you *different* from the birds?', 12.24c) offers the attentive disciple a point of meditation. The usual interpretation is that human beings are superior and more valued that the ravens. This has led to typical translations: 'Of how much more *value* are you than the birds?' (NRSV); 'And how much more worth are you than the birds?' (NJB). These translations come from a misreading of the Greek verb *diapherō* which concerns *difference* not *value*.[29]

If the issue is about *value*, then the question can have one of two meanings, or perhaps both. In the first, the question acknowledges that human beings and birds are different species. It is not a question of God valuing one over another. From this perspective, the question urges disciples to remember that if they consider that they are different to the birds, God's care continues for them as for birds that are lovingly and providentially regarded—even ravens. Human beings, like birds, have divine value.[30]

This leads to a second meaning derived from hearing the question as a rhetorical one. Thus, 'How much more are you *different* from the birds?' could be heard as a statement that acknowledges not the *difference* but the *similarity* between human beings and all other members of Earth's households, including unpopular ravens. The answer to the rhetorical question might be something like, 'There is no actual difference in the way that God cares for human and animal members of Earth. Both receive the same attention without differentiation.'

This interpretation of the question of 12.24c encourages gospel auditors to trust in God who loves all Earth's creatures, and to engage in a style of ecological practice that addresses unnecessary anxiety about one's material or physical well-being. The kind of indiscriminate God in which Luke's Jesus believes is revealed in creation, through birds, flowers and grass. As Bauckham notes,

---

its young in the beginning, because it does not think they are hers until it sees that they are black'. (Karris, *Bonaventure 9–16*, p. 1169.) See also, Bauckham, *Living*, p. 89.

29. Konrad Weiss, 'διαφέρω', *TDNT*, IX (ed. Gerhard Kittel and Gerhard Friedrich; Grand Rapids, MI: Wm B. Eerdmans Publishing Co., 1964), pp. 62-64. Bauckham (*Living*, pp. 94-95) considers *diapherō* in a similar fashion in the context of the biblical world and the hierarchical notions that would have dominated: 'It might be a preferable translation of *diapherein* to say that humans "are superior to" animals. The reference is probably to the kind of hierarchical superiority that is implied in the Old Testament's notion of human dominion over the animals (Gen. 1:26-8; Ps. 8:5-8). Humans are of superior status in the sense that a king is superior to his subjects. At least in biblical thought, a king is *not of greater value* than his subjects.' (*Living*, p. 95. Emphasis mine.)

30. Bauckham, *Living*, pp. 91-93.

> Jesus invites his audience to consider the lilies of the field whose lives are so brief, and the birds of the air who are deemed of little value because their number is so great. Yet in both cases God cares for their needs. Within this 'chain of being; humans may have a special place, but that should not lead them to ignore God's care for the apparently least and most insignificant elements of [the] created world, of which they also are a part.'[31]

If God cares lovingly for Earth and creation, ravens, lilies and grass that show no signs of anxiety, will God's same care not continue for other members of Earth's household, including human beings?

Ecologically instructive is the way that Luke affirms the agency of non-human Earth elements (ravens, lilies and grass) to teach gospel auditors how to be in communion with the God of creation. Their invitation is to trust God, not be distracted by the selfish accumulation of possessions. They invite human beings to 'seek God's *basileia*' (12.31a), the focus of true discipleship that will moderate everything and form the soul. As Luke reminds gospel auditors throughout history, if God's *basileia* is the disciples' focus everything else will be properly ordered. The desire to accumulate wealth will evaporate, or, as Luke expresses it, 'all things will be added to you' (12.31b). Confidence in God and orientation to God's *basileia-ecotopia* will also eradicate fear, the real cause of economic and ecological possessiveness. These will release the disciple's heart from any need to possess material goods. In fact, disciples will be freed to give away what they have. Jesus encourages his disciples,

> Sell your possessions and give alms. Make for yourselves purses that do not grow old, treasure that does not fail in the heavens, where neither thief approaches nor moth destroys, for where your treasure is your heart will be also (12.33-34).

This teaching is not a disparagement of Earth. Jesus' orientation towards the creator, healing God is not anti-material or against the goods that human beings possess. Luke realistically recognizes that people need Earth's fruits with which to live. Rather the evangelist encourages disciples to orient their lives to God and the *basileia-ecotopia*. This is the heart of Jesus' spirituality observed in the gospel and articulated here most forcefully.

Luke's main point concerns an *abundant* and *selfish* possessiveness that creates disparity among one another and deflects the disciple from what is important: God. This requires in the disciple constant alertness to a pervading temptation to distance oneself from a God who cares and is close (12.35-40). When Peter asks Jesus whether the parable of the rich person is intended for the twelve or more generally (12.41), Jesus, now titled 'Lord' (12.42a—and reflective of the authority which post-Easter

---

31. Freyne, *Jesus*, p. 47.

Lukan householders see in the risen Jesus), makes it clear that the parable is for them. They, like the master of a Greco-Roman household, are not to squander their authority but remain alert to God's unexpected coming (12.41-48). They are to take care of each member of Jesus' household with care and respect. But, warns Jesus, their attention and attitude within this domestic setting will come at a cost; it will cause instability to the conventional socially prescribed lines of authority and relationships within this principal social unit of the Greco-Roman world (12.49-53).

Furthermore, commitment to this kind of gospel practice will require discernment to 'know how to interpret the present time' (12.54-56). According to Luke, alertness to meteorological phenomena is important. The disciple's environmental simpatico, however, needs to translate into an ability to discern all of realities that touch Earth and its members. Such discernment will prevent disciples, and Luke's householders, from making their disputes public or bringing them before civic authorities for arbitration (12.57-59). Jesus again reminds gospel listeners about the importance of the act of 'repentance' (*metanoeō*) (13.1-5), an essential quality amongst disciples to prevent them publicly damaging the urban gospel household in the wider Greco-Roman society in which it seeks to establish credibility.

Advocacy for Earth (13.6-9)

The possibilities that come from the fruits of discipleship repentance, material disinterestedness, ecological communion and openness to God's loving presence evident in Jesus reveal themselves in the form of two sets of parables (13.6-9, 18-21) that frame the healing of a disabled woman (13.10-17) (Figure 24). The teachings that emerge from these bring to closure the first defined unit in Luke's long journey narrative (9.51–19.27).

All the parables of this final section are Earth related and theologically meaningful. They are concerned with fruits of Earth (fig tree, mustard seeds and flour from wheat or barley) and teach about God and the *basileia-ecotopia*. Thus, Earth's produce is not simply a food source for the human chain. It is a vehicle for theological truth to which the gospel's listeners are invited to attend.

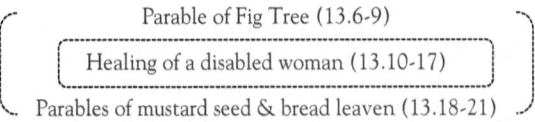

Figure 24. *Division of Lk. 13.6-21.*

The first parable concerns a fig tree which appears fruitless and which its owner wants to get rid of. Some commentators have interpreted the parable as an allegory that contrasts human resistance and religious sterility to the possibility of fruitfulness brought by the coming of Jesus.[32] It has also been applied personally, as a Christian awaits death and recognizes that their lives have been unproductive.[33]

The parable (13.6-9) actually concerns the *attitude* which an absentee landlord has to a fruitless fig tree. We are immediately back in Luke's complex socially stratified world, where urban elite owners of peasant lands come together with disempowered and landless peasants. The landowner, impatient to the possibility of the tree's eventual fruitfulness, orders the 'gardener' (*ampelourgos*) to cut the tree down.

> See here! For three years I have come looking for fruit on this fig tree, and still I find none. Cut it down! Why should it use up (*katarge*) Earth? (13.7).

The owner's reason for removing the tree appears to be out of concern for Earth. The fig tree is judged to be 'using up [*katargeō*, literally, "destroying"] Earth'. What is perceived to be the landowner's environmental concern is rather selfishness. He wants the tree cut down because it has not borne figs after 'three years' (13.7b). The meaning behind the length of time is unclear; nevertheless the main voice in the parable comes from the gardener who advocates on behalf of the fig tree. The tree has now been given a voice, though it is a human one. The apparent disjunction judged by the landowner between the tree and Earth, that the tree is the apparent cause of Earth's destruction, is counteracted by the advocacy of the gardener:

> [8] Sir, leave it, this year as well, until whenever I dig around it and manure it.
> [9] At least it may bear fruit in the future (*eis to mellon*), if not, you will cut it down (*ekkopseis*) (13.8-9).[34]

The gardener pleads for patience. Careful horticultural practice that cares for Earth is what is needed, rather than pragmatic, utilitarian destruction (13.8).

---

32. See Fitzmyer's summary of the various positions on this in Joseph A. Fitzmyer, *The Gospel according to Luke X–XXIV* (Garden City, NY: Doubleday and Company, Inc., 1981), p. 1005.

33. Fitzmyer, *Luke X–XXIV*, p. 1005.

34. These verses, especially 13.9, are quite tricky to translate. On its translation, of course, bears its meaning. There are two important points of translation. First, the NRSV translates 13.9, '… If it bears fruit next year, well and good; but if not, you can cut it down.' The key is the translation of the phrase *eis to mellon* which the NRSV renders 'well and good'. I translate it as 'into the future'. Second, the verbal expression for 'cut it down' (*ekkpseis*) is derived from *ekkoptō*. *Ekkpseis* can be either imperative aorist ('cut it down') or indicative future ('you will cut down'). The NRSV has gone with the first; I have gone with second. The translation I offer is defensible and preferred (naturally!).

A careful translation of 13.9 reveals a second ecological insight that furthers the tree's advocacy. The gardener proposes that the tree's care and fertilization 'may bear fruit in the future' (13.9a). This future, though, is unspecified and unlimited. Even to the owner it is unknown.

The gardener is utterly optimistic about the fig tree and seeks to protect it from destruction. This human being thus protects and advocates for one of Earth's members. The caring relationship between the human and non-human, of a human being for a tree, is a mirror image of what was seen earlier in the incident of the Garesene demoniac (8.26-39). There, the waters of the sea acted in advocacy for the possessed person and received into its depths the demonically possessed swine that dived into its abyss.

Luke's use of the Greek in the parable is strategic. The gardener is the one who *actually* cares about Earth and its fruit tree, rather than the owner. At the beginning of the parable, the gardener is asked by the owner to 'execute' the fruitless fig tree. By the end of the parable, the gardener names the owner as the one who really wants the tree's demise. If the tree doesn't bear fruit in this indeterminate future, suggests the gardener, the owner himself 'will cut it down' (13.9b). Whatever happens in the tree as a result of its fertilization by the gardener, the owner is bent on its ultimate destruction. The gardener identifies and articulates the owner's destructive and manipulative attitude.

What seems to be a simple parable about rural horticultural practice turns out to be a profound teaching about the kind of ecological attitude required of Jesus' disciples. This attitude respects the land and its fruits, is patient and unselfishly cultivates the soil. The disciple is committed to ecological communion, environmental freedom, and the identification of Earth's degradation from human beings. The disciple, like the parable's gardener, is Earth's advocate.

Sabbath Restoration of Creation (13.10-17)

This spirit of advocacy that brings about release is further demonstrated in Jesus' healing of a woman who has a 'spirit of infirmity' (13.10-17). The synagogue setting for what takes place is important. This is the first time that Jesus has returned to the synagogue since his Galilean ministry. The auditor remembers the first synagogue in which Jesus appeared. In Nazareth his proclamation of his future ministry concerned freedom of oppression for Earth Now, at the half way point in Luke's gospel, a further demonstration of this occurs. Jesus,

> was teaching in one of the synagogues on the Sabbath... (13.10).

The event takes place on the Sabbath, the divinely designated day of the week for rest. This rest symbolizes the freedom of humans from the toil of work and the opportunity to celebrate their relationship with God. The Sabbath is also a reminder of the Genesis story of creation. The day, therefore, is filled with ecological overtones.[35] The whole of creation also participates in the rest in which humans are invited to engage. Sabbath is a celebration of liberation for all Earth's members, human and non-human. The nature of this liberation is about to be dramatically revealed in a healing moment introduced by 'behold'. What is about to take place will reveal something about God.

> And behold, there was a woman having a spirit of weakness (*astheneia*) for eighteen years, and was completely bent over and was unable to straighten up perfectly (13.11).

The woman's crippling disposition is evocative. She is controlled by an evil spirit that has debilitated her. It has left her weak (*astheneia*) and lacking strength. At another level, the condition concerns her weakened ability to deal with the cultural, social and religious institutions in which she lives. They have not helped her to be free.[36] Her physiological condition is the result of a demonic presence which has become institutionalized. This is not to say that the woman is demonically possessed; she is definitely not evil. The cause of her affliction that has brought about her weakened condition, as with other situations of gospel disease, is the result of evil spirits that invade the person and from which release is sought. Her release is not assisted by the religious institutions governed by theological powerbrokers whose attitude to the Torah is legalistic and restrictive.

The woman's condition is serious—she has been in this state for eighteen years. The presence of the spirit that has caused the woman's malady underscores the cosmological synchronicity between the human, spirit, and non-human worlds. Ecological interrelationships are what are at stake. While the focus in the story is on the woman, in the background is the restoration of Earth, symbolized in the woman's condition, and those religious institutions (the Sabbath and the synagogue) intended for spiritual release.

The woman is further described as 'completely bent over'. This reflects her religious and social status in the situation in which she finds herself.[37] She is also unable to 'straighten up perfectly', that is, to stand erect with dignity and see what is happening around her. Her chronic malady affects

---

35. For the association of the Sabbath with creation, see Elvey, *Ecological*, p. 278, n. 242; Dennis M. Hamm, 'The Freeing of the Bent Woman and the Restoration of Israel: Luke 13.10-17 as Narrative Theology', *JSNT* 31 (1987), p. 27.

36. On the meaning of healing and its deeper anthropological reasons, see John J. Pilch, 'Healing in Luke–Acts', in *The Social World of the New Testament: Insights and Models* (ed. Jerome H. Neyrey and Eric C. Stewart; Peabody, MA: Hendrickson Publishers, 2008), pp. 201-20.

37. Green, *Luke*, p. 522.

her stance in the world and her capacity to interpret the world and culture in which she lives. She needs release from a demonically produced physical ailment which affects the way she engages her world.

This woman is representative of the women in Luke's household and in all ecclesial households in every generation who still experience oppression. Their ability to engage actively the social and religious contexts is seriously compromised or 'weakened' (*astheneia*). They, too, seem bound by an evil spirit present within a religious institution whose intended reason for existence is human liberation and communion with God.

Jesus spots the woman and responds to her need. No longer invisible, she now moves from anonymity on to Luke's narrative centre stage.[38] Jesus calls the woman; he engages her and says,

> Woman, you have been freed from your weakness (*astheneia*) (13.12).

Is this Jesus' declaration of what he has come to bring to her, her release from the evil spirit that keeps her oppressed and weakened? Or is it Jesus' declaration of what the woman herself has come to realize, that she is freed from the spirit of debilitation? Whatever the sense Luke intends, Jesus' encounter with the woman becomes a moment of expressing the essence of his liberating ministry and revealing the presence of the *basileia-ecotopia*. His action of laying his hands on the woman is another moment of his healing and strengthening touch that confirms the healing and release that the woman has already experienced (13.13a). The sign that further confirms what has already happened in the woman is what follows:

> And immediately she was made erect and she praised God (13.13b).

Her ability to engage her world with strength and courage is now authenticated in her posture. She is restored to full active participation in the gospel household. The source of this healing and restoration is God, the focus of the woman's praise. She is able to direct this attention in her own right, without the mediation of anyone else or another speaking on her behalf. She is, like the angels who liturgically praised God at the birth of Jesus (2.13-14), a confident agent in the act of liturgical worship; she, too, praises God.

The ecological and creation-related aspects of the woman's healing become more explicit in the next part of the story, indicated by the synagogue leader's indignity directed to Jesus because of his Sabbath healing (13.14). The leader complains 'to the people' to remind them about working on six days and resting on the Sabbath. The six days, he reminds them, are the days for healing; the Sabbath is for rest. What his statement forgets is that the Sabbath is also a day of liberation, release and healing. This was its divinely inscribed purpose. Jesus, through his act of healing or his

---

38. Green, *Luke*, p. 522.

affirmation of the woman's own healing (depending how one interprets his words in 13.12b), restores the Sabbath's purpose in the synagogue setting.

Jesus is concerned about healing and restoration, expressed in what happens to the woman. This is the import behind his rejection of the leader's insinuation. The teaching of Jesus, whom Luke calls 'Lord'—the post-Easter title used again that asserts the authoritative status Jesus holds for Luke's household—borrows imagery drawn from the animal, non-human world to make a key point. As one would release and water creatures from the animal world on the Sabbath, would not one also release a human being bound by an evil spirit?

> [15] Hypocrites! Would not each of you on the Sabbath release your ox or your ass from the manger and lead them to water? [16] Ought not this daughter of Abraham whom Satan bound behold for eighteen years be also released from this chain on the day of the Sabbath? (13.15-16).

Luke's Jesus returns to the proper intention behind the teaching about Sabbath found in Deut. 5.13. This text interprets the Sabbath injunction for extraordinary circumstances that involve human beings and animals. For life-threatening reasons oxen and donkeys are able to be released from their manger to which they were attached and watered (13.15).

There are six important aspects about Jesus' Sabbath ruling.

- Sabbath is about freedom for every member of Earth's household, not just humans. People are able to interpret Torah realistically that allows for the purpose of the Torah to be fulfilled, namely 'release' (in the present case, the watering of domestic animals).
- The act of bringing these animals to water is an act of ecological care, the essential duty that undergirds the Sabbath. This reflects God's care for every creature and the Israelite religious duty to show compassion in treatment of animals.[39] They are members of the household of creation for whom God provides, and compassion to them reveals openness for compassion from God. Or to rephrase it, '[i]f people do not show mercy to their animals, they cannot expect mercy from God.'[40]
- The word 'manger' echoes Jesus' birth story; it is the receptacle into which he was laid after birth (2.7, 12, 16). Jesus is Earth's child in communion with Earth symbolized by the manger.
- Our reflection on the manger in the light of Isa. 1.3 also highlighted the connection between domestic animals and peasants. The manger and its location vis-à-vis the peasant domestic dwelling underscored the bond between the animal and human worlds. In

---

39. Bauckham, *Living*, pp. 80-87.
40. Bauckham, *Living*, p. 87.

- this present teaching, the domestic animals are released from the manger and, by inference, from their connection to and dependency on human beings.
- The release of animals from the manger on the Sabbath also implies that they have their own identity. They are brought to water. The presumption is that they will drink, be quenched and not expire from thirst.
- Recalling again other scenes where water figures prominently (as in the story of the Gerasene demoniac, 8.26-39), water acts to liberate and absorb the evil that possesses and constricts. In this present parable, water also acts as a liberating agent for animals.

These six insights reflect the deep ecological and empowering images associated with the release of the animals from their manger and their being brought to water in 13.15. These images further set up the rest of the teaching which Jesus offers on behalf of humanity. Nothing should be used—not even an important Torah mandate concerning the Sabbath—to disempower human beings or keep them bound. Luke's Jesus seeks to restore the Sabbath to its rightful place in the theological-ecological drama in which he is involved. For this reason the story ends with his antagonists shamed and his audience celebratory (13.17).

Earth's Seeds and Leaven Destabilizes (13.18-21)

The closing parables derived from Luke's Q intertext conclude this first major section of the journey narrative (13.18-21). They link to the healing story and Luke's 'therefore' makes this link explicit:

> *Therefore* he said, 'What is the *basileia* of God like and to what shall I compare it?' (13.18).

The two parables, the growing mustard seed and the leaven, reveal something of God's *basileia-ecotopia* which expands on the teaching present in the previous healing story. Again, we perceive how ecological and Earth images are at the fore. Earth's fruits offer the means for Jesus to instruct his disciples and the crowds about the full meaning of God's *basileia-ecotopia*.

In the first (13.18-19), Jesus' focus on a small seed and its superlative growth become an image of the explosive spread of God's *basileia-ecotopia* amongst Earth's human and non-human members. What happens occurs in a garden in which a human being lives and is concerned with plants—an allusion to the Genesis story, of Adam in the garden of Eden. Ecologically related metaphors abound.

> It is like a grain of mustard seed which a human being taking sowed in his garden; and it grew and it became a tree, and the birds of the air made nests in its branches (13.19).

Luke's main point is that the *basileia-ecotopia* seems to have a small, almost imperceptible beginning but flourishes so much beyond human comprehension to embrace the social and historical realities that surround Luke's householders. God's presence (the *basileia-ecotopia*) is tangible, all pervasive and irrepressible; a teaching found earlier in Jesus' meta-parable where seed first featured (8.4-8).

There are two helpful points about Luke's use of the mustard seed.

First, the focus is not the seed's size, being the smallest of seeds (which is stressed rather in Mt. 13.31-32). We now know that the smallest seed is that of an orchid. Nevertheless the point is not about the seed's diminutive size.[41] It is about the rapid growth of the seed to mature into a large plant. However, Jesus does not have the seed become the expected plant. Rather it is transformed into a *tree*, Luke's name for the seed's final product. The surprise in the parabolic riddle is that the seed grows so much, beyond its expected or natural size, to become a *tree*, a feature on Earth's landscape impossible to imagine at first.

Second, because of the seed's transformation (from seed, to plant, to tree) it is able to shelter the birds of the air. It becomes home for them. The shelter which the tree is able to offer birds is a metaphor for the kind of shelter that all in Earth's household experience through the presence of God's *basileia*. This *basileia* is also an *ecotopia*, universal and ecologically centred. Nothing is excluded from it. Rather than considering Luke as a misinformed botanist who has made the mustard seed become a *tree*, the point of the parable is clear. The *basileia-ecotopia*'s largesse is emphatic.

In the second parable (13.20-21) Luke focuses on the leaven and the action which the woman performs with it.

> And again he said, 'To what shall I compare the *basileia* of God? It is like leaven which a woman taking hides in three measures of flour until it is thoroughly leavened' (13.21-22).

The gestational images suggested by the woman's presence and her act of bread-making, the domestic nurturing deed of the woman in the household, mirror something of God's *basileia-ecotopia*. The woman's action and presence reflect the *basileia's* feminine, nurturing and gestational presence upon Earth.

Further, there are three aspects about the leaven that make it a powerful metaphor for God's *basileia* and the realization of God's *ecotopia*:

- First, the leaven is a destabilizing ingredient without which the flour would not be able to ferment. This suggests something of the

---

41. On the mustard seed, see John C. Trever, 'Mustard', *IDB*, III (Nashville, TN: Abingdon Press, 1962), pp. 476-77.

work of God's *basileia-ecotopia* that unsettles, destabilizes and invites conversion.
- Second, the leaven is 'hid' (rather than 'mixed' as some translations prefer) in the flour. The leaven is unobtrusive and unnoticeable at first. But over time its impact is felt.
- Third, the woman hides the leaven in 'three measures of flour', enough for a feast to feed 150 people, an enormous crowd given the imagined size of one of Luke's households.[42] The same amount is also used by Gideon (Judg. 6.19), Hannah (1 Sam. 1.24) and Sarah in preparation for her heavenly guests (Gen. 18.6). All these First Testament figures anticipate a 'divine visitation' and epiphany.[43] In other words, the small 'invasion' of a little yeast can destabilize a huge amount of flour to produce an abundant quantity of bread, naturally intended to feed a crowd.

The nurturing imagery associated with God's *basileia-ecotopia* evident in the parable adds to its apparently small and imperceptible power to destabilize and influence the universal arena of Earth's life. This parable and its companion illustrate the ongoing presence of God upon Earth that for Luke's auditors, like the healed woman of the synagogue, brings optimism and relief.

It is with these two parables, of the seed and the leaven, that the first major movement in Luke's travel symphony concludes.

Conclusion

These opening chapters of the journey narrative, Lk. 9.51–13.22, have explored four main themes, building upon motifs found in previous chapters of the gospel. These concern discipleship (9.51–11.13; 12.54–13.5), growing opposition to Jesus' ministry and mission (11.14–12.12; 12.49-53), ecological and environmental attentiveness reflected in use of possessions (12.13-34), and the imminent, imperceptible but powerful presence of God's *basileia* (12.35-48; 13.6-20). As Jesus journeys with his disciples, and with Luke's household, he instructs them. Noticeable in the heart of this section is Jesus' explicit teaching about Earth matters, their relationship to discipleship and link to God's *basileia-ecotopia*. Jesus' teaching on wealth and possessions is present earlier in the gospel in his instructions to the disciples and their call to leave everything to follow him (5.11). Luke's agenda to appeal to the elite members of the gospel's urban household is clearly in mind. But it comes more explicit in these first chapters of the travel narrative, especially in chapter 12.

---

42. Green, *Luke*, p. 527.
43. Elvey, *Ecological*, p. 172.

Luke instructs would-be disciples of Jesus (and today's householders addressed by the gospel) that discipleship is not only concerned about a person's relationship with Jesus and ethical behaviour towards other sisters and brothers in the gospel community. It has ecological and environmental implications. Discipleship is intimately linked to the treatment of Earth and respect for Earth's heritage.

Clearly, Earth's goods are important for life and productivity among human beings; possessions are necessary. But Luke's teaching in this first part of this journey underscores the necessity for the disciple to recognize the source of everything that belongs in and comes from Earth. This recognition focuses the disciple's life and moderates the use of Earth's goods to the point that they will never become a barrier to communion. Communion with God and awareness of the presence of the *basileia-ecotopia* makes the disciple sensitive to any form of covetousness about Earth; it checks temptation to greed.

Almsgiving, unpretentiousness and a freedom from preoccupation with clothing, dress and food are the fruits of the disciple's commitment to God's *basileia-ecotopia*. They are tangible expressions of the disciple's communion with God and commitment to Jesus. Luke also teaches what lies at the heart of people's accumulation of wealth and self-centred materialism. It is fear. This fear comes from a person's inability to trust in God's providential care. A person trapped by fear cannot let go of the need for status, honour and wealth. Undergirding all this is the desire for security which an abundance of 'stuff' was thought to bring. The accumulation of wealth was seen in Luke's world as the socially and culturally acceptable way to status. These issues infect Luke's household and the evangelist is keen to address them. On the use of possessions and the ability of elite gospel householders to release their control and need for wealth rests the future harmony of Luke's auditors. It will continue to be a topic of Jesus' teaching as he and his disciples journey towards Jerusalem.

Throughout the narrative, we note how ecological images become the means by which Jesus teaches and instructs his disciples. Their presence in his repertoire of instructional aids indicates the peasant, rural context out of which Jesus' original teaching emerged. In this context, the world of plants, animals, seeds, sky and Earth are respected and studied by peasants for signs of how to live. Symbiotic order between the human and natural world was essential for the future livelihood of the peasant household. This respect for Earth's goods and the environment flows over into Luke's auditors and is explicitly present.

Soteriologically, creation participates with God. Earth's fruits and goods are agents for realizing God's intention for human beings. They are able to contribute to freedom and release from oppression. Similarly, in the parable of the rich human being disgruntled by an unproductive fig tree (13.6-9), a human being ('the gardener') becomes the image of the human household working towards liberating Earth from the destruction brought on by the greedy, unrestrained and self-centred.

Finally, images of creation seen in the paradisiacal garden implied in the Galilean setting of Jesus' earlier ministry find their resonance in this section of the journey narrative. Seeds, gardens, fruits, trees, plants, animals and human beings reflect the Earth of Luke's household. Through them Earth is fructive, beneficent, but fragile, and in need of protection; someone must intercede on its behalf.

Earth's Voice

The Landowner says, 'See here! For three years I have come looking for fruit on this fig tree, and still I find none. Cut it down! Why should it use up Earth?' (13.7).

Earth's Fig Tree speaks:

> I belong to Earth and Earth belongs to me.
> I am one of its fruits and give delight to human beings.
> I am the subject of a parable.
> The landowner's disregard for me reflects the attitude of many to me and Earth.
> I am seen simply a commodity to produce fruit that can be sold.
> Apart from this, I am regarded as worthless.
> I must be cut down because he regards me as 'using up' Earth
> Yet we are one.
> And I have no voice that can advocate for me.
> I am like all who are voiceless in Earth's household,
> and treated with contempt.

Chapter 9

LUKE 13.23–17.10

MATERIAL FREEDOM; EARTH CARE

This second section of Luke's journey narrative, Lk. 13.23–17.10, is designated by the second explicit note of Jesus' movement towards Jerusalem. Luke describes him journeying through towns and villages, teaching (13.22). This teaching occurs in the context of questions from what appear to be random enquirers. But in response, Jesus reminds his enquirers and Luke's audience of the nature of his ministry and mission and anticipates what awaits him in Jerusalem. A central context for most of this section, in fact the remaining part, is placed within the setting of a meal hosted by a religious leader. The teaching that emerges addresses key issues that concern Luke's journeying householders familiar with the kind of meal presumed in the narrative.

Salvation for All (13.23-35)

The first question Jesus faces concerns the number of those who will be 'saved'. His response recalls earlier teaching in the Nazareth synagogue. He encourages his disciples to work towards their salvation, but to recognize that it cannot be presumed. Rather, the largesse of the *basileia-ecotopia* of God celebrated in the previous parable of the mustard seed's 'tree' will mean that it is universal and open to all who seek it (13.22-30). It will be experienced in the celebrations and feasting. This is the import behind Luke's use of 'recline'. Those who enter the *basileia* will 'recline' as for a meal,

> ...and they [people] will come from east and west, and from north and south and will recline in the *basileia* of God (13.29).

Jesus is next warned by sympathetic religious leaders of Herod's intent to kill him. His response takes the form of a summary of his ministry of exorcism and healing already previewed in his Galilean ministry, though less prominent in his Jerusalem journey (13.32). He also flags what awaits him in Jerusalem, the city of a prophet's death (13.33). Jerusalem triggers a cry of lament about its destruction which, by the time of the gospel's writing, is perhaps already a historical reality. The lament is poignantly shaped by rural imagery drawn from Earth and one of its birds, the hen. Jesus laments his frustrated desire to gather Jerusalem's children together,

> as a hen gathers her chicks under her wings (13.34b).

The impossibility of this act, of the gathering of Jerusalem's children, reflects something of the frustration of the gospel's success within the wider Israelite world. Jerusalem's children, Israel's people, are a source of lament and perplexity for the gospel's auditors (13.35a). They must, like all humanity, await the final coming of Jesus (13.35b).

The Symposium

Luke next returns the auditor to a meal scene in which Jesus is present, an already familiar theme. The meal that involves its invitees, other characters and Jesus' teaching takes place over several chapters. It occupies most of this second major unit of the journey. The conversation that surrounds the meal has echoes of the classical Greek *symposium* familiar in Luke's Greco-Roman world. The *symposium* was a meal gathering of elite males where sobriety was recommended in a 'drinking party' that accompanied conversation about important, usually philosophical topics, for the edification of all. If women were present, they were *hetairai* ('prostitutes').[1]

The closest that one of Jesus' meals comes to having the presence of a 'prostitute' is back in 7.36-50 when the woman, 'a sinner of the city', comes to wash and anoint Jesus' feet as he reclines to dine in the house of a religious leader. As prostitutes were known to be part of a *symposium* and other meal events, such a descriptor was available to Luke. The evangelist will use it in 15.30 where an older son speaks to his father about his younger brother squandering his inheritance on 'prostitutes' (*pórnē*). The absence of the language for prostitute back in 7.36-50 means either the meal was not one accompanied by a *symposium*, or that the woman was not a prostitute even though she was known as a public 'sinner' (which could apply to several people with various 'innocent' occupations—from butchers to pigeon trainers).

Luke's *symposium* is a major part of the travel narrative, but differs remarkably from the convention. The host of the traditional *symposium* was selective in his guests. Those present in Luke's *symposium* would also seem to be predominantly and, maybe exclusively, the wealthy elite. But others, not necessarily physically present in the dining hall itself, are included by association with one of its main guests, Jesus. The architectural openness of the house would allow for a wider gathering of people from other social groups to be included and addressed by the *symposium* speeches. In this sense, the

---

1. On meals and their ceremonies see Malina, *Social-Science*, pp. 135-37, 191-94, 367-69.

meal that occupies several chapters is inclusive of all kinds of people, more reflective of Jesus' entourage of disciples, even though the setting is an elite household in which other exclusive people are guests. Finally, there is no evidence of *hetairai*, though conversation about prostitutes appears in Jesus' *symposium* table talk (at 15.30).[2]

As Jesus is a guest of a religious leader it is apparent he is under close scrutiny (14.1b). Already he has been criticized by other religious officials for his meal manners, in particular his apparent disregard for the purity codes and the guest list that accompanies him at his meal. In this present meal scene, the list would presumably be respectful. However, as the teaching unfolds, the meal scene includes others beyond the expected guest list—his disciples, particularly the twelve (16.1; 17.1; 17.5), a group of disreputable characters who seek him out or, as Luke describes them, 'draw near to him' (15.1), Pharisees and legalists (14.1-3, 15; 16.14), and a 'great multitude who accompanied him' (14.25a).

The household gathering is a snapshot of Luke's gospel audience. Where Luke imagines their location in relation to the ruler's house and its meal setting is unspecified. At times they appear to be guests; at other times, Jesus turns to address them, implying a movement outside the inner architectural seclusion of the ruler's house. Jesus' approach, of turning away and towards, reflects a missionary movement of Luke's householders beyond the security and comfort offered by conformity to the expected social stratification of their urban location. At other times in Jesus' *symposium* address people are drawn to him. They may not be actual participants in the meal or its *symposium*, but listeners and observers physically outside the *triclinium*, the dining room of the Greco-Roman house, but within earshot.

In sum, Jesus is at the centre of the meal and its *symposium*. He is at the heart of what goes on, dining with a religious elite ruler but attentive to all who may not be included in such an exclusive setting. In the way Luke locates Jesus, the evangelist affirms the gospel's consistent christology: Jesus is inclusive of all, irrespective of social status. This is reflected in his meal manners that upset the socially expected convention of the *symposium*. Through gesture, comportment or explicit address he attends and speaks to those who would not necessarily be immediately present.

Dropsy—The Disease from Possessiveness (14.1-6)

One of the guests at the meal is a person (a human being—*anthrōpos*), whom Luke identifies as suffering from 'dropsy', a condition of bodily swelling from

---

2. The best classical understanding of the nature of a *symposium* is supplied by Lucian (*Symposium*), Xenophon (*Symposium*) and Plato (in *Parmenides, Philebus, Symposium* and *Phaedrus*).

excessive fluid caused by congestive heart failure or kidney disease.³ In the ancient world, 'dropsy' was also code for avariciousness. The sixth century CE compiler of Greek writers, Joannes Stobaeus, quotes the attitude of Diogenes (412–323 BCE) to 'dropsies':

> Diogenes compared money-lovers to dropsies: as dropsies, though filled with fluid crave drink, so money-lovers, though loaded with money, crave more of it, yet both to their demise.⁴

Diogenes's insight helps us to see something more serious revealing itself in the scene. The person with dropsy, the *anthrōpos*, represents the struggle among human beings to let go of material possessiveness and befriend Earth. Such characterization mirrors the ecological attitude earlier of the wealthy landowner in the parable about the fig tree (13.6-9). Luke's Jesus seeks to heal this avaricious attitude symbolized in the *anthrōpos* with 'dropsy'. Accomplishing this on the Sabbath is appropriate. This is the day of release, freedom and the celebration of God's communion with creation and humanity. Jesus is scrutinized for healing on this day, as he was when he healed a woman also on the Sabbath (13.10-17). Here as then, Jesus draws on people's common sense to rescue an animal that gets into strife on the Sabbath. Here there is an important expansion which Jesus makes to his analogy:

> Which of you having son or an ox fallen into a well would not immediately pull it out on the day of the Sabbath? (14.5).

There is some textual pressure reflected in later (fourth century CE) manuscripts to replace 'son' with 'ass' and so bring the text in line with the Jesus' earlier Sabbath teaching associated with the woman's healing in the synagogue (13.15b). There Jesus used the image of the Sabbath rescue of ass and ox which needed to be released from their manger and brought to water. However, the textual evidence for 'son' in the present story is firm and has important ecological implications.

Jesus' teaching places the rescue of the animal on the same level as that of a guest's son. A parent's son was the principal figure for the survival of the Greco-Roman household and ensured generational continuity. The rescue of a son from a well into which he had fallen would be without question, no matter the day. The animal, however, is given the same status. For Luke, animals and humans deserve the same care and protection. The Sabbath rescue of both drowning beings is unquestionable. The same principle applies to the Sabbath healing of a person with dropsy. This is the rescue

---

3. Green, *Luke*, p. 546.
4. Stobaeus, *Florilegium* 3.10.45, as quoted in Green, *Luke*, p. 547, n. 115. See Green's other sources for this quote.

The Meal that Includes All (14.7-28)

As the *symposium* proper begins, etiquette observed and guests place themselves,[5] Jesus uses the formal selection of the meal's seating arrangement to teach about the importance of appropriate humility (14.7-11).

> All who exalt themselves will be humbled, and those who humble themselves will be exalted (14.11).

Jesus' aphorism pulls together a central truth in Luke's gospel. The source of everything is God. This moderates a disciple's attitude to others and Earth. 'Humility' is not about self-deprecation or personal belittlement.[6] Rather it is the gift of recognizing one's Earth relatedness through openness of heart. This ecological modesty displays itself in relationship to others no matter their economic status or kinship circumstances.

This insight provides the background for the next part of the *symposium* as Jesus instructs about the appropriate guest list for a festive banquet. This list reverses the usual expectation. Instead of inviting those from the same social and affluent background, hosts are encouraged to,

> invite the poor, the lame, the blind (14.13b).

Such an explicit selection of guests will result in praise and reward, not from others and especially from the guests themselves because of their impoverished status, but by God 'in the resurrection of those who are righteous' (14.14c). When Jesus dies, he will be declared 'righteous' (23.47). Reward for gracious and inclusive hospitality will occur with the household of faithful disciples gathered around *the* righteous one, Jesus.

The nature of invitees to a meal is the subject of Jesus' next *symposium* parable about an *anthrōpos* who throws a great banquet (14.14-24). A similar teaching emerges. According to social etiquette, the invitation to attend is an invitation to honour the host. The refusal by those invited who reflect the urban elite becomes a grave act of dishonour. This encourages the host to invite 'the poor, maimed, blind and lame' to expand his guest list to include the socially rejected. But even these can't fill his dining hall, so large is the meal hall; finally the host sends his servant to,

> compel people to come in, that my house may be filled (14.23c).

---

5. The arrangement of the classical symposium setting can be seen in Malina, *Social-Science*, p. 366.

6. Walter Grundmann, 'ταπεινός', *TDNT*, VIII (ed. Gerhard Kittel and Gerhard Friedrich; Grand Rapids, MI: Wm B. Eerdmans Publishing Co., 1964), pp. 1-26.

Luke's Jesus again reminds gospel's auditors about the kind of meal that God desires to celebrate. This is a festive meal that is so large it can include a whole urban centre. It is inclusive of all in which those socially disregarded find a place. The parable would also speak to Luke's powerful and controlling elite aware of meal etiquette to honour their host. Some, like those originally invited to the meal, might consider themselves socially superior to the host and those from the city's lower social classes whom he later invites.

The meal parable reinforces Jesus' key teaching. Meals should be open to all no matter their background. Such inclusivity reflects God's desire to include all Earth's members, especially the alien and rejected, in the *basileia-ecotopia*. God's celebratory inclusivity is represented in those whom the parable's host instructs to be gathered into his banqueting hall. They include the physically destitute and spiritually disabled from the city's 'streets and lanes' (14.21b). Also invited are those found outside the urban centres in the country; those who are physically associated with Earth's landscape of 'highways and hedges' (14.23a).

The meal imagined in Jesus' parable brings together human beings and Earth's fruits, the rich and the poor, the acceptable and socially rejected, and those from the city and country. It is a totally inclusive feast indeed! But it is one to which the supercilious will never be invited (14.24). Such arrogance is absent amongst Jesus' disciples. They must be intentionally committed and deliberately discerning about their discipleship, the focus of the next part of Jesus' *symposium* teaching (14.29-32).

Accumulating Wealth and its Ecological Consequences (14.33-35)

Again Jesus returns to a familiar attitude which disciples must have, a realistic readiness for bearing their own cross in following him (14.27) complemented by renunciation of any form of avariciousness (14.33). Jesus again reminds his followers of his impending suffering at the journey's end and in which they will be caught up. Their solidarity with what awaits him in Jerusalem is prepared by an attitude of renunciation of all they possess:

> So therefore those of you who do not renounce all your possessions cannot be my disciple (14.33).

Luke's Jesus is not expecting gospel auditors to live without any resources at all. This would be impossible and impractical, especially given the missionary focus already suggested in the gospel through Luke's apostolic twelve. Such focus requires material support. Rather, in harmony with Jesus' explicit teaching found earlier in Luke's travel narrative (12.13-34), disciples are urged not to be possessed by their possessions. If they are, then they are unable to be disciples with their heart elsewhere seduced by possessions and an ephemeral promise of status and security.

Wealth accumulation has ecological consequences. As an antidote to such materialistic preoccupation, disciples must preserve the energy and enthusiasm first experienced in their initial call, without compromise or deterioration in their relationship to Jesus.[7] In the meta-parable of the sowing seed (8.4-8), the disciples would have been encouraged to see themselves as the seed that falls into fertile Earth which produces abundantly. They are to be freed from longing for riches that comes from a lack of spiritual depth. Now Jesus uses the analogy of salt. The disciples are to be like salt which retains its zest (14.34-35).

Salt was an important fertilizing and catalytic agent. It was mixed with soil to fertilize certain vegetables.[8] When blended with dry dung, salt also acted as a catalyst for cooking fuel used in courtyard ovens of peasant households.[9] Disciples were like salt. They were to retain a kind of 'saltiness' (14.34b) that enabled them to be agents within Earth and human households. If they lost their salty zest they became 'insipid', fit neither for land (as fertilizer) nor dung heap (as catalyst) (14.35).

Jesus concludes his teaching with the injunction:

Let those who have ears to hear, let them hear (14.35c).

This underscores the seriousness of what Jesus has just taught. He invites a sensitive attentiveness to the essence of true discipleship. He speaks to those members of his fictive kinship now identified with an openness to 'hear the word of God and do it' (8.21). They are people of God's *rhēma*. Their open and attentive spirit will deepen their environmental consciousness and lead them to relate authentically to Earth's household. This in turn will lead to their fecundity.[10]

About the Lost and Found (15.1-32)

We now come to one of the most important and beloved chapters in the whole of Luke's gospel, Luke 15. The chapter considered the heart of Luke's gospel, the gospel within the gospel, reinforces several themes already identified.[11] These include the kind of people that seek Jesus (namely sinners and toll collectors, 15.1), the importance of inclusivity and God's passion for intimacy with the socially and religiously isolated, the rural,

---

7. Fitzmyer, *Luke X–XXIV*, p. 1068.
8. Fitzmyer, *Luke X–XXIV*, p. 1069.
9. On properties of salt and its metaphoric meaning, see also James F. Ross, 'Salt', *IDB*, IV (Nashville, TN: Abingdon Press, 1962), pp. 167-68.
10. Green, *Luke*, p. 568.
11. Fitzmyer, *Luke X–XXIV*, p. 1071.

urban and domestic settings familiar to Luke's audience and reflective of the gospel household, and the celebratory nature of Jesus' meals.

As we learn that 'toll-collectors and sinners' were drawing close to Jesus, we also know that they would not be guests at a meal hosted by an elite religious official. Luke places them on the venue's outskirts. They are social and spiritual outsiders. They are attracted to Jesus located inside the festive dwelling. Greco-Roman house design would allow for a visual and audio connection to Jesus without their physical presence inside the *triclinium*. Select sections of the *oikos* / *domus* were partly visible to public onlookers. Its architectural openness allowed passers-by to enjoy the house's decoration, the kind of high status people who gathered in the its inner rooms, and the clients of the household head (the *paterfamilias*) who would congregate each morning to celebrate their patron and enact his desires, if they were so employed by him. This kind of scenario allows for outsiders in Luke's *symposium* to occupy these chapters of the gospel. Outsiders would include 'the multitudes' (14.25), the wider group of Jesus' disciples (16.1), and these 'toll-collectors and sinners' of 15.1.

The location of these social reprobates close to Jesus leads to the religious elites' derogatory comment:

> This fellow welcomes sinners and dines with them (15.2).

Their reference to Jesus ('this fellow') illustrates their scorn of him. But they also ironically underscore for the auditor the key characteristic of Jesus' ministry: his table communion with the most unlikely of people, considered impure, unholy and unworthy of social approbation. As this important chapter begins Luke confirms that Jesus' eating habits and guest list reinforce the kind of God with which he is in communion. This God wants to celebrate all humanity and creation, no matter how they are regarded or treated by human beings. Jesus' God seeks restoration for every lost, forgotten and rejected member of Earth's household. The three parables which follow (15.3-32) are Jesus' response to the criticism of his meal practice. They are directed to religious leaders critical of the God whom Jesus celebrates.

All three parables are important. While essentially they carry the same message, about God's joy over the restoration of one back to the Earth household, each comes to this teaching from different perspectives reflective of the diverse social scenes familiar in Luke's world. Jesus addresses the parables directly to his *symposium* audience of elite and religious officials. Through these parables and their addressees Luke is appealing to those who have power and status to 'listen' (14.35b) to what is being taught. They are invited to conversion, identify their potential for 'saltiness' (14.34b), renounce what they possess for the good of the whole Earth and its members (14.33), and, like Jesus, welcome and rejoice with Earth's lost members, those regarded as unclean and contemptible.

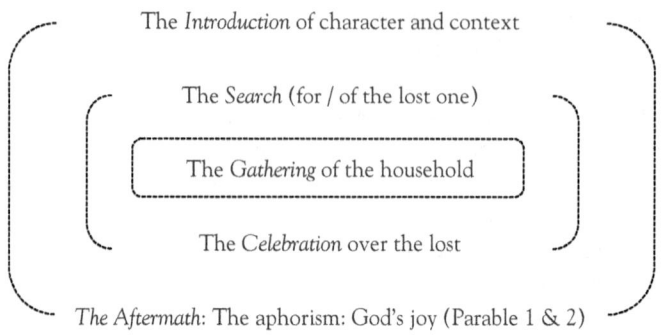

Figure 25. *The structure of the parables of Luke 15.*

The structure of each parable is generally similar (Figure 25). The first two (Figure 26; 15.3-7, 8-10) are more tightly structured; the third (15.11-24) is longer with an addition in the parable's final scene (15.25-32). Each begins with the presentation of the character, the context, and what is lost. Then follows the journey of the search for *what* (in first two parables) or *who* (the third parable) is lost, the gathering together of the household and the celebration of the recovery.

The first two parables end with an aphorism that sums up the parable's teaching about God's celebration in the return of the lost. In the third, the aphorism is replaced by an extension to the parable which leaves the auditor speculating about the future and whether the whole household will indeed rejoice over the return of the lost one. Dominant in Jesus' parabolic teaching is celebratory joy. This mirrors the God of joy and celebration whom Jesus is keen to honour and reveal, and encourages the whole Earth community to celebrate likewise.

A chiasmic balance in the structure of each parable centres on the joyous household gathering. This reflects the kind of gathering that Jesus desires as his *symposium* teaching continues. Though a religious elite leader hosts Jesus, on the fringes of the meal gathering are others attracted to him. They, too, should be part of a festive meal that ideally celebrates all upon the Earth irrespective of status and acceptability.

All three parables presume a village or rural setting. The first (15.3-7), taken from Luke's Q intertext, concerns a shepherd with a moderately large flock of sheep and his search for one lost. Jesus' addresses his wealthy *symposium* gathering,

Which *anthrōpos* among you, having a hundred sheep....? (15.4).

His addressees are wealthy and possibly absentee landlords and owners of peasant properties and flocks. Luke also indicates that the parable concerns an *anthrōpos*—the generic term for humanity. This is, again, about the human condition and quest to find the lost and celebrate their recovery. This natural observable and identifiable human scenario, of a shepherd looking for a lost sheep, becomes Luke's entrée into the heart of God. This is what God is like who desires to search for the lost and celebrate their return. God's joyful celebratory nature is summed up in the aphorism that concludes the parable. God's joy is the joy of the cosmos, of the heavens.

> There is joy in heaven over one sinner who repents more than over ninety nine righteous who have no need of repentance (15.7).

The second parable (15.8-10) is set within a peasant domestic dwelling. A woman is its focus. She loses one of ten drachmas, lights a lamp and sweeps her house until she finds it. She then gathers her relatives to celebrate the coin's recovery. The parable begins,

> Or what woman, having ten silver coins....? (15.8).

The parable is indirectly about humanity, but specifically about a *woman's* situation. Even though the last parable of the 'Prodigal Son' has received most scholarly and homiletic attention, the parable of the *woman* is central to the other two that frame it. They are concerned with an *anthrōpos*. The third and longer parable begins with the explicit mention of the *anthrōpos*—again reflective of the human condition ('An *anthrōpos* had two sons...' 15.11). Of the three parables it is only the central one that is gender specific. Each parable reveals something about humanity and, especially the second, about God.

The middle parable ends with a similar aphorism as the first—the joy of the woman and the celebration that accompanies the coin's recovery are like God's joy over the repentance of a sinner:

> Even so, I tell you, there is joy before the angels of God over one sinner who repents (15.10).

The joy of the woman becomes for Luke's audience an image of the eternal delight of God (represented in the 'angels of God') over the return of a sinner, who experiences a sense of inclusion in the gospel household from

```
 ⎧   (15.3-7) Parable of Lost Sheep: (anthrōpos)    ⎫
 ⎪   ---------------------------------------------  ⎪
 ⎨   (15.8-10) Parable of Lost Coin: Woman (gunē)   ⎬
 ⎪   ---------------------------------------------  ⎪
 ⎩   (15.11-32) Parable of the Lost Sons: (anthrōpos) ⎭
```

Figure 26. *The parables of Luke 15.*

which they have been excluded. The woman serves as an image of the welcoming and intimate nature of a feminine-like God revealed in Jesus in his birth and his ascription as *Sophia's* child (7.35).

The third parable (15.11-32) also concerns an *anthrōpos*, not a shepherd but a father. He has two sons. The youngest seeks the share of his father's property, practically wishing his father's death, the only moment according to the Book of Numbers when a father's property could be dispersed.[12] The father unhesitatingly divides between the two sons his *total living* (15.12c) in an act of great generosity. By his request the young son has virtually cut himself out of the family household. He is on his own. This becomes more obvious as he gathers all his possessions and leaves for a distant land.

The ecological imagery we perceive Luke employing at this point in the parable reflects the young man's spiritual condition:

> [15] So he went and hired himself out to one of the citizens of that country, who sent him to his fields to feed the pigs. [16] He would gladly have filled himself with the pods that the pigs were eating; and no one gave him anything (15.15-16).

A famine on the land corresponds to the lad's destitution (15.14). Looking to address his needs, he is sent by a wealthy 'citizen' of the land (15.15c) literally back to Earth to look after pigs (15.15b). This 'citizen of the land' is the parable's agent that sends the lad back to his Earth-roots. The recognition for his need for spiritual conversion and familial restoration occurs within the context of Earth's soil and in solidarity with the most unappreciated animal previously involved in the rescue of the Garesene demoniac (8.26-39). There the swine cooperated with evil spirits to become a vehicle for their destruction in the waters of the Sea of Galilee. Here, in the parable, swine and their food help him recognize his physical appetite that triggers a deeper hunger that needs attention (15.16a). He remembers his father's household and the ample food available even to his servants (15.17). He resolves to return home and ask for employment, not as son, but as slave (15.18-20a).

Now in the parable the auditor gets a sense as to the real reason that the *anthrōpos* is 'father'. As the spotlight swings from the returning son to the father, we find him poignantly waiting for his son's return. His sight triggers something deep in the father.

> While [his son] was a long way off, his father saw him and was moved with compassion (*splagnizomai*) and running, embraced him and kissed him… (15.20).

This verse sums up the reason that the *anthrōpos* is the 'father', the image of God. He seems unconcerned about the probable village judgment on his

---

12. Num. 36.7-9; 27.8-11.

offspring. He is careless about the way he would be expected to act towards his son to regain lost honour after an act of public humiliation from his son's request for inheritance. Disregarding the socially expected response of rejection, the father acts in a surprising manner. He looks out for him. When he sees him, he immediately acts in a gestational, maternal and surprisingly feminine manner. Luke says, he 'was moved with compassion' (15.20c).

We have already come across 'compassion' expressed either in the Greek verb *splagnizomai* or the adjective *oiktirmos* (6.36; 7.13; 10.33). It made its first appearance in Jesus' Galilean ministry, in the Sermon on the Plain, as he teaches his disciples about love of enemy. There he reminded them,

> Be compassionate (*oiktirmos*) as your father is compassionate (6.36).

The compassion which the parable's father shows to his repentant son reflects the compassion that is from God.

A second aspect to *splagnizomai* that surfaced in our discussion on compassion in 6.36 is relevant here. The root of LXX *splagnizomai* is the Hebrew *rachem*, the word for 'womb'. The parable's father displays all the maternal and gestational qualities of a mother for her child whom she loves. This father reflects the feminine qualities of a God in love with humanity. This is the reason that the *anthrōpos* is 'father'. The parable's father represents the best of the maternal-paternal qualities that embrace the child and restore him to Earth's household from which he initially and intentionally separated himself. The restoration is demonstrated in several ways: the father dresses the son with his best clothes, gives him the family signet ring of authority and places shoes on his feet as a reminder that he is not to be a household slave. The father's final act is the festive celebration to welcome the son back.

The parable bears all the hallmarks of the life of a well-to-do peasant family estate. But the parable doesn't end with the young son's tender embrace by the father accompanied by the external signs of acceptance, authority and celebration. There is another son who is also 'lost'. His unhappiness at the welcome his brother receives prevents him from joining the festivities. His father comes out into the fields to meet and discuss with him the reason for such a joyous response to his brother's return. Perhaps the attitude of this older son reflects the begrudging attitude of those in Luke's household disturbed by the welcome offered those who are socially unacceptable. Whatever the symbolic intention behind Luke's characterization of the older son, the father invites him to join the festivities.

As mentioned earlier, each of the parables deal with Earth-related subjects. The first concerns sheep. The story drawn from the animal world provides Luke with an image of God's delight in the return of the lost. The Earth connection in the second, the woman's search for one of her ten silver coins, seems not so clear.

The rural-village setting for this second parable is obvious from the woman's need for a lamp given the windowless or near windowless room which requires light to see and sweep its earthy floor (15.8b). Each of the ten coins would be equivalent to a day's wage.[13] The woman's diligence in searching for the lost coin would be more prominent in a peasant-based bartering economy in which Earth's products were traded. Thus the coin would be the result of the peasant householders' efforts to till the soil, produce grain, pay taxes and barter for goods unavailable to the particular household but necessary for its survival and growth. Such a bartering economy presumes a village based rural world. The search for the coin is thus a search for all things about Earth to which the lost coin points.

The third parable is especially rich with ecological symbolism: the father's willingness to let go of all his livelihood revealing his non-possessive nature; the young son's remorse assisted by his return to Earth and communion with its creatures; the maternal, Earth-centred quality of the compassionate father awaiting his son's return; Earth-gifts placed on, around or under the son (ring, robes, sandals) reminding him of his Earth-belovedness; the calf sacrificially given up—like other Earth elements in previous scenes (10.34; 13.15; water and pigs, in the story of the Gerasene demoniac, 8.26-39)—to enable the household to celebrate; and finally, the place which the family festivity holds in the parable. This would be a celebration of a lost human member completely restored to the Earth community.

The third parable about two lost sons and the maternal father and this chapter conclude with the auditor wondering whether the older son remains obstinate or joins in the festivities. This is a deliberate tactic by Luke's Jesus to invite his audience into deep reflection on their own attitude to others. Whether the second and older son chooses to remain lost, or become 'found' like his younger brother, remains an open ended question. It is this question that remains with the auditor as the gospel's journey narrative and Jesus' *symposium* teaching continue.

Wealth and Earth's Resources (16.1-18)

Jesus turns from the religious elite to whom the three parables of Luke 15 are directed to his disciples. Whether they are members of the *symposium* entourage is unclear, but they are the focus of Jesus' next parabolic instruction (16.1-13). Again, Luke returns to the topic of wealth and respect for Earth's resources.

The parable presents a scene familiar to Luke's wealthy urban elite who are in control of Earth's physical and environmental gifts, have property managers or 'stewards', and have people in their debt. As in two of the

---

13. Fitzmyer, *Luke X–XXIV*, p. 1081; Green, *Luke*, p. 576.

last three parables, this one too involves an *anthrōpos*. He is wealthy which automatically means he is greedy. In a world of limited economy he has achieved his wealth at the expense of the poor, those who, in the parable, are his debtors.

The parable's landowner has a steward who is charged with 'dispersing' his master's possessions (16.1). The reason he is brought before the master is not because he has 'squandered' (NRSV) or 'wasted' (RSV) property. The steward, perhaps a slave or freedman, is the representative figure of the disciple—devising ways that assist the wealthy to share their possessions with the poorer members of the household. The manager has acted in a manner that is true to the spirit of authentic discipleship, dispersed wealth for the benefit of all, given the presumption shared by the majority of Luke's audience that such wealth had been gained unjustly and greedily.

The owner decides to dismiss the steward (16.2b) who recognizes his inability for menial work (16.3). So the steward concocts a plan to get the master's debtors to pay their debt, though not fully. Some commentators have suggested that the debt agreed upon is the actual amount owed to the master minus the steward's fee.[14] In whatever way the amount is worked out between the steward and the master's debtors, there are two clear facts: first, the commodities owed to the master are all Earth products. Those mentioned are olive oil and wheat, though others would be suggested. Second, the amount owed is excessive. A hundred measures of olive oil would represent 3500 litres, the result of pressed olives from a very large olive grove twenty to twenty five times the size of an average grove;[15] a hundred measures of wheat would, by modern standards in the western world, be harvested from two to three acres.[16] Given the huge quantities involved, their reduction would not be noticed. The excessive amounts owed to the master, however, illustrate his greed and his attitude to Earth and its gifts represented in the oil and wheat. These fruits are for his own benefit and status; their accumulation deprives others.

The steward's effort at redistributing the master's unjustly appropriated wealth benefits others through their debt reduction, wins him his master's praise, curries favour with those in debt, and benefits Earth. The steward appears as the disciple concerned about the harmony of every member, human and non-human, that belongs to Earth's household. It is this attitude, called 'wisdom' (*phronimōs*), for which the master praises his steward and, presumably, for the honour which redounds to the master from the steward's shrewd enterprising action (16.8a). This same spirit might characterize disciples of Luke's day ('the children of this world') in

---

14. For example, Fitzmyer, *Luke X–XXIV*, pp. 1098-99.
15. Green, *Luke*, p. 592.
16. Fitzmyer, *Luke X–XXIV*, p. 1101.

the way they negotiate their social and difficult realities (16.8b) and their use of wealth ('unrighteous mammon', 16.9) for the benefit of all to support Earth's household. Jesus promises that care of Earth's goods will lead to the enjoyment of true wealth that comes only from God (16.10-13b).

Some of the religious leaders ('Pharisees') overhear Jesus' teaching to his disciples about the need to divest themselves of wealth and 'they ridicule him' (16.14). Luke notes how they are 'lovers of money'. They would regard their wealth as a sign of divine benefaction. Jesus critiques their attitude by reminding them that their hearts need to be aligned to God rather than seeking praise from human beings (16.14-15). This attitude is at the heart of the Torah (16.16-17) and reflected in committed marital relationships (16.18). But the disciple must continually choose to serve God not wealth (16.13c).

The Poverty of the Wealthy (16.19-31)

To further Luke's critique of those religious officials who presume their elevated wealth guaranteed status before God, Jesus tells a story of a situation that involves a very wealthy *anthrōpos* and a poor person (16.19-31). This is another of the evangelist's store of stories crafted to reflect the social reality of Luke's day, and inherited into the gospel's repertoire of teachings originally from the historical Jesus.[17] The anecdote acts in the style of parabolic discourse designed to teach a point. The teaching concerns the use of wealth and the exploitation of the poor, themes already familiar from other gospel discourses and illustrated in the immediately preceding story of the rich rural estate owner and his astute steward (16.1-9). Like that story, the one that Jesus now addresses to the *symposium*'s religious experts has ecological implications. It is concerned about the way the poor are treated by the wealthy through their attitude to Earth's gifts.

In the story's first verse we are introduced to an unnamed wealthy human being (an *anthrōpos*) (16.19a). His wealth is confirmed by two things: his dress, which identifies the person's status and his relationship to Earth; and his daily sumptuous feasting. As is evident from Jesus, a person's clothing and meal practice indicate who they are and with whom they seek to be. Jesus' clothing (in his birth, 2.7, 12; and transfiguration, 9.29) and his meal practice identify him as Earth's child and revealer of God's all-embracing delight in creation. The rich person's dress and meal table manners, as we shall see, reveal a character opposite to Jesus, as Earth's enemy.

The rich person is dressed in 'purple and fine linen' (16.19b). As we have already seen (in discussing 2.7) clothes were natural products from Earth. The linen was regarded as regal and eternal. Its implied link with

17. Fitzmyer, *Luke X–XXIV*, p. 1125.

Jesus' body, at the beginning and end of his life, affirms for Luke's audience his Earth relatedness, and regal and eternal nature. The 'fine linen' (*bussos*) which the rich person wears makes its only explicit appearance here in the gospel, in fact, in any of the gospels.[18] The person, an *anthrōpos* and thus the representative figure of the human household, dressed in 'fine linen' is regal and eternal. Eternal royalty, that is, everlasting communion with God, is the goal of human existence and symbolized by this layer of 'fine linen' clothing that dresses the *anthrōpos*.

There are three further aspects about this *anthrōpos* that effectively clash with the heavenly destiny associated with the linen. He is 'rich'; wears 'purple'; and 'feasts sumptuously every day'.[19] These compromise his attainment of the eternal destiny intended for every human being. It will become more explicit in the story. His wealthy status has, according to the general appreciation about wealth amongst most of Luke's auditors, come at the expense of others going into poverty. His wealth is a sign of his greed and unrestrained material consumption. This is confirmed by the person's daily feasting, reflecting an undisciplined use of Earth's fruits with apparent disregard for any other member of Earth. Finally, besides wearing 'fine linen', the symbolic heavenly garment, he also wears 'purple' implying (from Prov. 31.22 and 1 Macc. 8.14) that he lived like an elite royal in a way that removed him from ordinary people, especially the poor and others of lower social status.[20]

That Luke wants our sympathies to lie not with the wealthy and regally dressed one but the story's main character, the poor man, Lazarus, is first indicated by his naming. The rich person remains unnamed throughout the story. We learn that Lazarus, besides being economically poor and destitute, is at the gates of the wealthy person's estate. His condition is tragic. He is supine and ulcerated. These reflect a physical debilitation indicating uncleanness, social exclusion and religious impurity. He desired,

> to be satisfied (*chortazōo*) from the things falling from the rich person's table (19.21).

Lazarus in his impoverishment seeks satisfaction from the rich person. He might desire food, as some translations would have it (he 'longed to satisfy his hunger with what fell from the rich man's table', NRSV). Though food might be implied given the table setting, the Greek is unspecific ('things') about what falls from the table. This could well mean anything that would sustain

---

18. As already discussed in Chapter 3, the earlier association of linen with Jesus at his birth and, later in his death, is implied though not explicit.

19. Literally, 'making merry each day splendidly'.

20. See the association of 'linen and purple' with the royal and wealthy in Judg. 8.26; Sir 45.10; Est. 1.6; 8.15. See Johnson, *Luke*, p. 251.

life. But whatever the 'things' represent (food or possessions), they fall from the table to the ground, to Earth's surface. There seems an overabundance or superfluity that cannot be contained on the table. This means that their surplus results from an over-harvesting and disproportionate collection of Earth's gifts. The wealthy person has enough goods to satisfy himself and others, like Lazarus. This fact adds to the auditor's impression of the greed already associated with the wealth of the estate owner.

The wealthy householder's lack of concern for Lazarus is further contrasted by dogs which lick Lazarus' sores (16.21). From one point of view, it is appropriate that these animals come to Lazarus to lick him. They were regarded as unclean and spoken of with contempt.[21] Lazarus and the dogs find solidarity with each other. From another point of view, the animal world is more friendly and sympathetic than those from the wealthy human household. The dogs' licking is an act of healing. They indicate their desire to rescue Lazarus from his physical condition that has precipitated his social exclusion. These dogs act as in other gospel stories where Earth's elements and animals provide the means of human release and rescue.

Death enters into the scene and interrupts the sumptuous, presumed eternal, life of the rich person (16.22). He dies and goes to eternal anguish in Hades; Lazarus also dies but enters into eternal bliss in the 'bosom of Abraham'. Even the best efforts of the rich person to negotiate his way out of the torment or gain some relief prove unsuccessful. He tries to get his brothers alerted to what awaits them too, obviously siblings in the kind of wealthy and greedy life-style to which the family is accustomed. In all the negotiations and conversation between the wealthy one and Abraham, Lazarus is regarded as a pawn-like messenger and servant for the wealthy person's needs.

The point that Luke stresses in the parable is that there is a great and insurmountable 'chasm' between what awaits the wealthy and poor in the afterlife (16.26). The opportunity for the wealthy to be converted and open to the economically poor and socially rejected is a present possibility for Luke's auditors. This is the clear teaching of the Torah, of the Law and the Prophets (16.29-31). These, according to the evangelist, offer unambiguous warning to the urban elite in Luke's household who might disdain the peasant members or those who have fallen on hard times, such as the Lazarus of the parable. If such wealthy are not open for social conversion, nor willing to share their possessions, judgment awaits.

Recognizing True Status (17.1-10)

After this sobering instruction which Luke directs to those who would identify more with their wealth than with the poor, Jesus turns again to his

---

21. Ps. 59.6; 14.1; 1 Kgs 14.11; Phil. 3.2; Rev. 22.15. See Green, *Luke*, p. 606.

disciples in a new *symposium* address (17.1-10). This concludes this second sub-unit of Luke's journey narrative (13.23–17.10).

Jesus' teaching concerns fidelity in discipleship and links to the previous story of Lazarus and the wealthy estate owner. As Luke's Jesus instructs the wealthy at the *symposium* to reflect on their use of their wealth and their response to the poor, he also wants gospel auditors to reflect on moments when they 'stumble', a realistic and inevitable experience in a disciple's life.[22] The kind of 'stumbling' which Luke envisages is not necessarily concerned with morality ('sin', NRSV) but is left open ended. In the context of the previous parable it would be associated with care, compassion and respect for others, especially those who are socially disregarded or despised. This attitude flows over into intra-communal relationships where unlimited forgiveness of a brother or sister household member must be at the forefront (17.2-4), an act that would require almost unlimited faith.

As the 'apostles' ask Jesus to increase their faith (17.5), his response indicates that faith is effectively an act of openness to God. The disciple's faith, no matter how meagre it may seem, can believe in the impossible—like imagining a deeply rooted sycamore tree to plant itself in the sea at a disciple's request (17.6). This requires a spirit of fidelity that comes from recognizing one's true status before Jesus: humbly aligned to him and open to what he asks. Only then can disciples say,

> We are worthless (*achreios*) servants; we have done only what we ought to have done! (17.10b).

This statement which Luke sees as appropriate for the disciples Jesus addresses is not about having a self-deprecating spirit of false humility. It is not about regarding oneself as a spiritual doormat without worth. What is translated as 'worthless' is the Greek adjective *achreios*, which literally means 'without making a profit' or 'without any obligation being owed'.[23] In practice, this means that disciples need to recognize their true status before God in relationship to Jesus. They are not to elevate themselves or expect deference to be shown them. They must not identify with the wealthy of high social standing that would distance themselves from others, especially those considered poor, rejected, impure or sinful. In this sense they are to regard themselves as 'unprofitable'. That is, they cannot make themselves profitable or wealthy. For this reason they are 'worthless' (17.10b).

This last statement, of the disciples' recognition that they are 'worthless' and are called to recognize their true status and its accompanying obligations, appropriately brings to a close the second section of Luke's journey symphony.

---

22. Literally, 17.1a reads, 'It is impossible that occasions for stumbling not to come'.
23. See Johnson, *Luke*, p. 259.

Conclusion

This second part of the journey narrative, Lk. 13.23–17.10, is a teaching treasure-trove. In it Luke portrays Jesus addressing a number of people from different social backgrounds and religious dispositions on various gospel themes that are already familiar. Each encourages conversion, authentic living, deepened communion with God, and a form of discipleship that is socially, culturally and ecologically responsible.

As we have seen, the overall setting for Jesus' teaching is a meal accompanied by the classical *symposium*, well-known in Luke's day though with significant differences. The *symposium* becomes the appropriate occasion for Luke to address the elite urban wealthy, the usual guest-list for such an occasion and the gospel's explicit intended audience (1.3). It is not surprising that the main topic of the *symposium* concerns wealth. Luke's Jesus uses stories, parables and selected aphorisms to explore attitudes to possessions, the use of wealth and its generous sharing with others, especially the rural poor, also members of Luke's gospel household. Jesus seeks a change of heart among his wealthy captive audience. He wants to address the experience of brokenness, exclusion and avariciousness found in the human household.

These concerns are first powerfully flagged in the symbolic healing of the *anthrōpos* with 'dropsy' (14.2-6), Diogenes' code word for greed. This healing is the very first event that occurs in the meal before the *symposium* proper and Jesus' teaching about wealth begins. His deed (of healing dropsy) and word (of teaching in the *symposium*) coalesce. God's *rhēma* continues to manifest itself.

Jesus' teaching about generous meal practice and an open-ended inclusive guest list follows on from this healing. It comes in the form of parables that challenge the present audience imagined in Luke's elite meal setting of wealthy guests. Luke's Jesus addresses them; but they are not the only ones he addresses. On the fringes of the imagined dining hall are other groups of people who draw near to hear or be with him. His teaching benefits or challenges them.

The centrepiece of the *symposium*, and perhaps of the whole gospel, is Luke 15. The three parables of this chapter are preceded by Luke's note of the kind of scandalous people that Jesus attracts. This draws criticism from the religious leaders, symbolic representatives of theologically restrictive interpreters in Luke's household.

The parables teach about God's joy and desire for welcoming the lost. The settings reflect Luke's world; the image of God's feminine attribute dominates. The actions of the two *ánthrōpoi*, of a shepherd and father, that frame the central parable of the woman's search for the lost drachma, reveal

God's welcoming and compassionate nature. The parable of the welcoming father who seeks out two lost sons is rich and powerful. Sometimes, though, it has overpowered the woman's search in the middle parable. Her actions trigger the auditor's awareness to the feminine compassionate qualities revealed in Luke's God, anticipated by the shepherd's search for the one lost sheep, and made explicit in the father's warm and loving embrace of his lost younger son. The father's womb-like reaction to his son mirrors God's desire for humanity and creation.

Finally, ecological images and insights pervade the section. Earth's animal world and its other non-human beings are the subjects of Jesus' teaching. They provide Jesus with the means to confront the religious leaders with their restrictive attitude to the Sabbath and their undisciplined and covetous use of Earth's goods. The strong emphasis that Luke gives to the *symposium* and its accompanying teaching allows Jesus to remind auditors about the importance of meals as festive gatherings, inclusive of all members in Earth's household. These meals celebrate human beings, reveal God's delight in Earth and invite all its guests to respect everything that comprises Earth's life.

The image of Earth's produce falling from the rich estate owner's table to the ground in the story of Lazarus (16.19-31) acts as a warning. Excessive and selfish accumulation of possessions causes disharmony within the Earth household. Such greed is the focus of divine judgment. The disciple, on the other hand, is called to intimate communion with Jesus about to suffer as Jerusalem draws near. This requires clear vision and material freedom. His disciples and gospel auditors are invited to develop a deep ecological spirituality respectful of every member of creation. They are invited to free themselves from viewing the Earth in commercial terms; in this sense, it is not a saleable commodity that can be bought, plundered and sold. Though of divine, inestimable eternal value, Earth is economically 'worth-less'. In communion with Earth, disciples are to see themselves as its agents, also 'worthless' (17.10b).

Earth's Voice

The young man in the parable 'went and hired himself out to one of the citizens of that country, who sent him to his fields to feed the pigs. He would gladly have filled himself with the pods that the pigs were eating; and no one gave him anything' (15.15-16).

Earth's Pig speaks

> I am one of Earth's most despised animals.
> I am considered unclean, associated with corruption and pollution.
> I feel one with this rejected child.
> I know how he feels.
> I can offer him some comfort and share food with him.
> In being with me he comes to know where he really belongs.
> I help him see and learn repentance.
> He leaves me to return to his home and his father.
> I am left alone.

Chapter 10

LUKE 17.11–19.27

THE IMMINENCE OF GOD'S *BASILEIA-ECOTOPIA*

The third and final section of the gospel's journey narrative, Lk. 17.11–19.27, begins with Luke's last explicit marker that identifies Jesus' movement towards Jerusalem:

> And as it happened on his way to Jerusalem he passed through the middle of Samaria and Galilee (17.11).

It seems as though we have not journeyed far from where the narrative began with Jesus' disciples wanting to cast down fiery heavenly elements upon Samaritan villagers who appeared unreceptive to him because 'his face was set toward Jerusalem' (9.53b).

Healing the Unclean (17.12-19)

Jesus now enters 'a village', an unidentifiable urban location. Its lack of specificity signals that what is about to take place could be duplicated anywhere in Luke's world. As Jesus enters the village, ten 'lepers' meet him and remain distant (17.12). Their condition is not the modern biomedical condition of Hansen's disease, but a chronic skin complaint of psoriasis. In a society marked by purity laws that prevented contagion and without the benefit of modern medicine, these ten would represent the prototypically excluded. On this subject a First Testament intertext familiar to those Israelite members of Luke's household would be pertinent. According to that intertext from Num. 5.2-3 and Leviticus 13 and 14, those declared by the priests as leprous were to be isolated from the rest of the community. They represent the excluded ones from Earth's household; those in need of healing and restoration. These ten have already removed themselves from their urban world, the place of community, household security and care. They, like the wider non-elite audience of the *symposium*, exist on its fringes.

The note that Luke has that they kept their distance signals two further things: not only their physical isolation from their household, but also their spiritual condition. Their disease would be the result of the presence of evil spirits believed to be the cause of such contagion and perhaps encouraged by sinfulness which some wrongly thought brought about such conditions. The ten experience social and spiritual exclusion. They appear cut off from God and Earth. For these reasons they keep their distance from Jesus, the divine healer. Their desperation expresses itself in their plea,

> Jesus, Master, have mercy on us! (17.13b).

This is the cry of the poor. They appeal to Jesus, God's agent and liberator. He can show them God's mercy and the kind of compassion narrated in his story of a father's embrace of a returning lost son (15.20); he can reveal God's maternal care for these ten. Their number is important and their gender unspecified.[1] They are representative of the whole human race, of women and men, struggling for consolation and seeking to be restored to Earth's household from which they have been excluded. They are regarded as sources of a form of impurity that contaminates Earth. Jesus responds to them. The healing is effected through their response to his word.

> As you *journey* show yourselves to the priests (17.14b).

The direction which Jesus gives them is explicitly tied to the language of *journey*, the action of all Jesus followers. In their *journey* they are to return to the priests who first declared their uncleanness and will offer the public declaration of their healed state.

Healing occurs immediately as they begin to respond to Jesus' direction (17.14c). These healed lepers display one of the most important qualities of discipleship identified early on in the gospel, pre-eminently demonstrated in Jesus' mother (1.38; 2.19) and confirmed in the Sermon on the Plain (6.46-49). The ten hear Jesus' word and act upon it. They respond to God's *rhēma* revealed in Jesus. They also have the opportunity to deepen the possibility for discipleship by acting on Jesus' word. Only one does so.

One of the ten, a Samaritan and a foreigner, returns to give God thanks for the source of his healing. He returns, *falls* before Jesus thanking him (17.16); he falls and reconnects to Earth from whom he has been excluded by his condition. Luke's Jesus celebrates this outstanding demonstration of faith. He says to the healed leper,

> Rise, go on your journey, your faith has saved you (17.19).

Luke recognizes Jesus as the teacher and healer. This healing story, one of the few in the journey narrative, brings together the power of Jesus' word-deed. The lepers respond to it. But it is an unexpected Samaritan, a foreigner, who demonstrates the meaning of true faith that recognizes the

---

1. '[T]he number "ten" being intended as a round number', Fitzmyer, *Luke X–XXIV*, p. 1154.

source of healing, God, revealed in Jesus to whom he reconnects through his gesture to Earth. The word 'rise' is explicitly resurrectional. The leper has been released from a form of death that has excluded him from full participation in life with Earth. His 'rising' anticipates the action that will occur in Jesus' resurrection from death. The healed leper's resurrectional life is to be further expressed in concrete terms as he goes 'on his journey', as he walks in an ecologically respectful manner with Earth to whom he has been reconnected. This is the daily disposition of the disciple's life; this practical setting created by Earth's 'way' because the arena of the disciple's 'daily' following of Jesus (9.23). Finally, Jesus affirms the leper's faith. His faith reveals an attitude of openness and gratefulness focused on Jesus, God's agent of healing. It is a faith that is relational. Jesus declares that this kind of faith brings about the lepers' salvation, an experience of divine communion with Earth's God. This experience of solidarity brings a sense of harmony with all of creation. In other words, the leper's attested faith has ecological consequences that spill over into environmental solidarity.

That he was a Samaritan reminds Luke's auditors that God's beneficence is not controlled by one's ethnic background or religious pedigree. His healing endorses the missionary endeavours of Luke's household already hinted at in other parts of the gospel. The Samaritan's return to Jesus reflects that moment among Luke's audience when the Gospel moved beyond the Israelite world and attracted Samaritans and Gentiles. Even foreigners can give praise to God and be welcomed by Jesus. This is a surprising God celebrated by Jesus, a God that some religious legalists think Jesus has got wrong.

The Imminence of the Basileia*-Ecotopia (17.20-37)*

The question from the religious authorities that immediately follows the lepers' healing indicates their blindness to what has just occurred and God's presence in Jesus. The faith of the leper contrasts with the disbelief of these officials. They ask Jesus when God's *basileia-ecotopia* will come (17.20). At another level, their question touches into the deep environmental concerns voiced today by contemporary Jesus followers—when will ecological harmony and Earth's care become an obvious reality on the planet? Jesus' response affirms that God's *basileia-ecotopia* is already present in their midst (17.21), a conviction he expresses at other times (10.9, 11; 21.21). God's presence is not simply an eschatological reality that awaits future completion; the *basileia* is already present and revealed within the social and cultural realities of Luke's day. Its ecological consequences, its *ecotopia*, are already manifest.

Jesus then turns to his disciples to alert them to the signs of the *basileia*'s presence and God's end-time coming (17.22-37). The *basileia-ecotopia* is present in his words and deeds; it is already in the midst of the disciples through their attitude to Earth and its environmental gifts. But it awaits further revelation. The disciples are caught between these two moments, the 'now' and the 'not yet'. The teaching which Jesus offers seeks to respond to the disciples' desire to identify and locate the *basileia-ecotopia*, to pin it down exactly. As he indicates, this is impossible. The *basileia* is present already and is able to be discerned, but for others who are blind (like Luke's religious officials) it is unobservable. What is required in the disciple is a keen spiritual sensitivity to what is happening, focused on Jesus and freedom from Earth possessiveness that distracts from what is important.

Luke has carefully organized the structure of these important teaching verses around the central vv. 26 to 30 in an A–B–C chiastic pattern (Figure 27).[2] This helps to isolate the central teaching point found in 17.26-30.

The literary structure also helps Luke's auditors understand the meaning behind Jesus' last enigmatic words by which he responds to the disciples' question, 'Where?' (17.37a). Where is the *basileia-ecotopia* to be located? How can it be identified? These questions and concerns from the disciples undergird Jesus' response that makes up the outer part **A** of the literary frame in Figure 27.

In the first part of **A** (17.22-24), Luke interprets that these questions, understandable as they are and reflective of the questions amongst gospel auditors, come from a desire to pinpoint the exact moment of the *basileia's* appearance. This is expressed by Luke in terms of the coming of the Earthed One, Jesus. The disciples' questions also reveal either a subtle attempt to control God's coming or an attraction for those who seem to have all the answers. These appear to know how to pin-point God's *basileia-ecotopia* and declare, 'Behold, there!' or 'Behold, here!' (17.23). Jesus urges the disciples to be suspicious of such false prophets. He reassures them that the Earthed One will definitively come, like a flash of lightning in the sky (17.24).

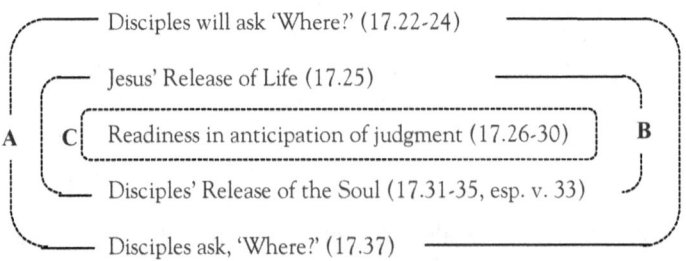

Figure 27. *The chiastic literary structure of Lk. 17.22-37.*

2. After Green, *Luke*, p. 631.

The final part of **A** (17.37) concludes Jesus' response to the disciples' continuing urge to identify the *basileia* exactly—their preoccupation with the question 'where?' is a sure sign that more concerns await them despite Jesus' teaching. It is clear that they have not understood. Their misunderstanding and incomprehension will grow as they near Jerusalem. To their question, he responds,

> Where the body is, there also the vultures will be gathered together (17.37b).

This enigmatic response is a reminder that the disciples are asking the wrong question about the *basileia*. They have missed its point and don't understand what it is really about, even granting their observation and involvement in his healing deeds and preaching ministry. The *basileia-ecotopia* is not a place but an encounter with God and an experience of ecological solidarity by all Earth's members. This encounter is observed in Jesus, his deeds of healing, preaching and meal ministry inclusive of all. It is, ideally, observable in the household of disciples and, for Luke, amongst the gospel's auditors. 'Vultures gather wherever there is carrion. The [*basileia-ecotopia*] is wherever the people are gathered by God's word.'[3]

The inner layer **B** of Luke's literary structure highlights how disciples can be more attuned to the coming of the *basileia* and sensitive to its wider ecological notations. Examples are given to free them from encumbrances that would prevent their receptivity to the presence of the *basileia-ecotopia* and the end-time coming of God. The first part of **B** offers Jesus as their model. The suffering and death that await him will test them. They, too, will be invited to let go of their lives. The second part of **B** presents characters from the First Testament Genesis intertext and apocalyptic imagery to reinforce the importance of the disciple's freedom from preoccupation with possessions:

> On that day, let those on the housetop with their goods in the house not go down to take them; and also the one in the fields not turn back. Remember Lot's wife (17.31-32).

Jesus urges complete readiness for God's coming without the distraction of going into a house to collect what is not important. As Luke interprets the First Testament story of Lot's wife, when the destruction of Sodom and Gomorrah was under way, she looked back (Gen. 19.26). The evangelist interprets her action as her longing for the possessions she had left behind in the destroyed city. Rather than such attachment and material preoccupation, the disciples are again reminded,

> Those who seek to preserve their souls [as a possession] will destroy them; and those who destroy them will preserve them alive (17.33).[4]

---

3. Johnson, *Luke*, p. 267.
4. The translation here is suggested by Johnson, *Luke*, p. 263, but with variation.

Jesus is not teaching the disciples to disdain themselves and live despising who they are. This is not the meaning behind 'destroying' their souls. The hyperbole ('destroy') is intended to stress something else. Jesus reminds his disciples that they are to let go of anything that possesses their 'souls', that aspect of the human person oriented to God and open to encounter the *basileia-ecotopia* that is already in their midst and present in Earth. They are not to treat their souls as a possession. Such self-absorption with status seeking and the accumulation of wealth will destroy who they really are in their relationship to God. It will destroy their sensitivity to Earth's members. Rather, letting go of a self-centred material possessiveness will release them to truly live in communion with God oriented to the *basileia-ecotopia*. This is true 'soul consciousness' out of which the disciples must live. This conviction leads naturally to the centre of Luke's teaching represented by C (17.26-30) in Figure 27.

These central verses return to a gospel theme often repeated by Jesus in the journey narrative. These verses identify the distractions and life's preoccupations that could move the souls of disciples away from their focus on God and the *basileia-ecotopia*. God's final coming to Earth will occur as people go about their daily lives doing ordinary things, eating, drinking, marrying, selling, planting and building (17.26-29). Such preoccupations with life's pleasures (food and drink), relationships (marriage) and possessions (gained through buying, selling, planting and building) have the power to distract the heart from what is essential.[5] This is a readiness to welcome God and the arrival of the *basileia-ecotopia* when it becomes transparently manifest. The disciples cannot 'look back' on these things. They require an ecological asceticism as they journey with Jesus towards Jerusalem. However, their preoccupation with the 'where' question regarding the *basileia-ecotopia* continues as Jesus' teaching concludes. This flags for the auditor that the disciples do not really understand what he has been telling them. Their lack of comprehension will display itself soon in their attitude to children and their parents (18.15-17) as Luke returns to the Markan intertext from which this story is taken.

Attitude to the Child: Attitude to Earth (18.1-17)

In the meantime, Jesus offers his disciples two parables that remind them about the God who listens to the cry of the poor and responds to those unjustly treated (18.1-8) and, putting aside religious exhibitionism, approaching this God humbly aware of human frailty and sinfulness (18.9-14).

The rebuke which the disciples make to children coming to Jesus in the next scene (18.15-17) shows all too clearly that the disciples have not yet

---

5. Johnson, *Luke*, p. 267.

understood either the meaning behind Jesus' two previous parables or the teaching that precedes them. Their response to the children augurs sadly for how they will be in Jerusalem despite all the preparation they get from Jesus. There are several aspects about this scene that reinforce Luke's earlier teaching and reflect on the disciples' receptivity to God's *basileia-ecotopia*. This speaks directly to the auditors' openness to the world and creation. The treatment of the child, one of Earth's smallest creatures, will reveal how Earth itself will be treated.

Luke opens the scene with the reason that the children are brought to Jesus—'to touch them' (18.15). We have already commented on the symbolic importance of 'touch' in the crowd's touching Jesus in 6.19. The act of touching occurs several times in the gospel (5.13; 6.19; 7.14; 8.44; 22.51; 24.39) as a mutual act of interconnectivity and communion between Jesus and people. The physicality of the act makes separate parties one. The touch allows Jesus' being and God's presence to enter into the other's world. It changes people's lives and allows them to encounter the *basileia-ecotopia* of God present in Jesus. The touch, the sensual deed that relates to Earth's presence, puts them into communion with a world of healing and wholeness. It reminds them that they belong to Earth. Jesus' touch therefore has ecological implications. In this sense, those who bring the infants want Jesus to touch them, and desire to encounter the presence of God and the *basileia-ecotopia* that he reveals and is already in their midst.

The disciples 'rebuke them' (18.15c). Their deed of 'rebuke' is an act of exorcism (4.35, 39, 41; 8.24; 9.42) and is directed either at the infants or those bringing them. The disciples consider the infants, their parents, or both, as evil and in need of exorcism. This comes out of an ancient belief that considered children as valueless, inhuman and in need of training. Their value might increase with age and maturity, and as they physically contribute to the economic resources of the peasant or urban household. Before then, in a world where infant mortality was high and infanticide frequent, children were not idolized as they are today. On the contrary, these infants and/or their insistent parents were an evil, in need of exorcism, concerned more with distracting Jesus from his 'real' ministry with adults.[6] Further, the request that Jesus touch the infants would also render him untouchable and evil. He would enter into their world of rejection and low social status. This request for his touch moves him to call the infants and, at the same time, instruct his disciples,

> [16b] Let the children come to me and stop preventing them, for to these is the *basileia* of God. [17] Amen I say to you, whoever does not welcome the *basileia* of God as a little child will never enter it (18.16b-17).[7]

---

6. On the ancient attitude to children see Green, *Luke*, p. 651.
7. For the translation of 'stop preventing them' see Johnson, *Luke*, p. 276.

The infants provide Jesus with an opportunity to remind his disciples again about the meaning of the *basileia*. God's *basileia* is also an *ecotopia* and only received by those who are open to it and whose lives are not determined by status or controlled by possessions. The infants are the symbolic figures in Luke's Greco-Roman world regarded as nothings from the lowest social rungs and treated as inhuman if not sub-human. The *basileia-ecotopia* is inclusive of all creation, especially those regarded as evil and in need of exorcism. For this reason 'to these the *basileia* of God' belongs (18.16c). They are its members. This realization must shape the disciple's attitude to all who belong to the *basileia*, albeit even socially disregarded and culturally insignificant children. If the disciples are unable to see these as members of God's *basileia-ecotopia*, it means that they do not have the kind of openness and sensitivity to God's presence already manifest in their midst and upon Earth. They are unable to believe Jesus' earlier words, 'The *basileia* is in your midst' (17.21).

If the disciples cannot welcome those whom God embraces then it means that they will never be able to welcome the *basileia-ecotopia* when it becomes more visible; and they will never be able to enter into it themselves. Their welcome of children is a touchstone of their appreciation of Jesus' ministry in his welcome of strangers, the unholy and socially despised. If they are unable to link Jesus' meal ministry, healing and teaching with his welcome of children in this scene, it means that they have missed the whole meaning of the *basileia-ecotopia*, its characteristics and its Earth membership. They have become blind to Jesus' mission which will manifest itself even further when he begins to teach more explicitly about his impending suffering and death.

The teaching about God's *basileia* that has dominated this part of the journey narrative has ecological links. The use here of the hyphenated *basileia-ecotopia* especially is a reminder that the *basileia* is not exclusively anthropocentric, but a divinely initiated reality inclusive of all Earth's members. The ability of the disciples to be open to children, regarded as the least within Greco-Roman society, will reflect itself in the way they are able to treat every member of Earth's household, especially those regarded as insignificant. For Luke's auditors and contemporary Jesus followers this spills over to the treatment of Earth, and all members of its household to which Jesus, his disciples and Luke's audience belong. Their ability to let go of what possesses their souls and not to be trapped by material wealth, possessions, luxuries or status, will ensure that their care for Earth will be authentic.

Freedom of/from Possessions (18.18-37)

Jesus' disciples will come to see that God's *basileia* is also an *ecotopia*, the focus of the next gospel vignette (18.18-30) as Jesus responds to a ruler who wants to know what to do to gain eternal life. Again, as Luke continues with the final stages of Jesus' journey to Jerusalem, the evangelist continues to borrow from the stories and order of Mark's gospel, appropriately reshaping them.

The ruler's question ('Good teacher, what shall I do to inherit eternal life?', 18.18) offers an opportunity to summarize gospel teaching on possessions. Jesus responds to his enquirer in two ways. First he asserts the essential goodness of God,

> Why do you call me good? No one is good except God alone (18.19).

If God is good, then all that comes from God's creative act, the Earth household, must also be good.[8] Second, Jesus repeats well-known commandments from the Torah concerned primarily with honouring relationships (18.20). The questioner affirms that he has been faithful to these teachings since youth (18.21). Then Jesus says,

> One thing you still lack. Sell everything that you have and distribute to the poor and you will have treasure in heaven and come follow me (18.22).

Luke's teaching to his gospel audience, especially the wealthy, is a reminder that more is involved in following Jesus than being ethical or keeping Torah commandments. It requires letting go of everything that possesses one. That these possessions have been wrongly gained is clear as we learn in the next verse that the ruler is very wealthy (18.23). Wealth is gained at the expense of the poor, and for this reason Jesus tells the rich ruler to distribute his wealth amongst the poor from whom he gained it. The return of this wealth will release the ruler from a preoccupation that up until now has compromised his potential for discipleship. Material release will open him to the experience of the true meaning of eternal life found in following Jesus as his disciple.

Luke poignantly notes,

> when [the rich ruler] heard this he was sad (*perilupos*) (18.23a).

The *perilupos* reflects the deep grief and sorrow that grips him at the thought of giving away possessions to which he is greatly attached and with which he is socially identified. The sadness that Luke identifies in the man comes from the soul, knowing that one is choosing a direction in life that will be eventually soul-destroying; material attachment will eventually annihilate him. This echoes Jesus' earlier teaching to his disciples that those 'who seek to preserve their souls [as a possession] will destroy them; and those who destroy them will preserve them alive' (17.33). This rich ruler with such attachment to his possessions reflects the truth of the second part of this aphorism.

Jesus' engagement with the ruler continues. Unlike Mark's wealthy man in the corresponding story who goes away at this point (Mk 10.22), Luke's

---

8. Freyne, *Jesus*, p. 26.

rich ruler stays to listen to Jesus. In a society where some regarded wealth as a sign of divine benediction and approval, Luke's Jesus upturns this assessment. Wealth can be a barrier for entering into the *basileia-ecotopia* of God. In fact, from Luke's perspective, riches become a definite barrier to entering into God's *basileia-ecotopia*. Looking at the rich ruler as Jesus notices his sadness, he pronounces,

> How hard it is for those possessing riches to enter the *basileia* of God. For it is easier for a camel to pass through the eye of a needle than for a wealthy person to enter into the *basileia* of God (18.24-25).

Jesus names the incompatibility between possessing Earth's goods and entering into the *basileia-ecotopia*. One's attitude to wealth prevents such access. This is not because wealth and possessions are evil in themselves. They carry no moral value at all. Rather, their obsessive accumulation claims their owner's heart and desensitizes a person to the needs of other members of Earth's household, especially the poor. Ecological consequences follow. Earth would be regarded as a resource for the accumulation of wealth; its possession the guarantor of social status.

The question that those listening to Jesus' teaching ask, ('Then who can be saved?', 18.26) reveals a 'gospel of wealth' present even in Luke's day, that wealth was a sign of divine favour. Jesus' reversal of this false theology provokes their question to which he responds. The encounter or experience of the *basileia-ecotopia* ('salvation') is ultimately God's gift. It cannot be bought no matter the amount of wealth a person possesses (18.27). Then Peter immediately reminds Jesus about their situation,

> We have left what is ours and followed you (18.28).

They had left even their families to be his disciples (18.28). His words parallel what Jesus urges the rich ruler,[9]

> Sell everything that you have...and come follow me (18.22).

Jesus' response to Peter again reinforces the eternal blessedness that will come to those who have let go of everything to follow him.

> Amen I say to you all, that there is no one has left house or wife or brothers or parents or children for the sake of the *basileia* of God who will not receive many times as much in this age, and in the age to come eternal life (18.29-30).

Jesus' words to Peter, his companions and the rich ruler who remains in the background, are not about rejecting family or relationships. These stay at the heart of Luke's household and the proclamation of the gospel in the Greco-Roman society. Instead, Jesus reminds his listeners and Luke's

---

9. Green, *Luke*, p. 658.

audience that everything in a person's life and world is ordered and related to God's *basileia-ecotopia*. This relationship shapes everything else, even the most important familial bonds that exist in the kinship group, and how they walk upon Earth. As this scene closes with Jesus' teaching summarizing the disciples' need to let go of all that possesses them and orientate their lives to the *basileia-ecotopia*, the rich ruler is still implicitly in the scene. He has not retired from listening to Jesus' instruction. How he responds to this instruction is left open ended, similar to the older son in the parable where the father invites him to join in the festivities over the safe return of his younger brother (15.29-32). The invitation always remains for conversion.

The invitation for ongoing conversion to focus one's life squarely on the *basileia-ecotopia* will not happen without pain, even death. It is this thought that now surfaces as Luke continues drawing on Mark's gospel and Jesus' 'prediction' about his impending suffering, how he will be shamefully treated, scourged, executed, and rise on the third day (18.31-33). Unsurprisingly, his words pass over the heads of the disciples who are portrayed as uncomprehending, speechless and spiritually blind to Jesus' *rhēma* explicitly identified:

> And they understood none of these things and the *rhēma* was hidden from them and they did not know the things that were said (18.34).

The disciples' inability to see and comprehend God's *rhēma* acting in Jesus as he faces death requires chronic healing. This is symbolically enacted in Jesus' healing of a blind beggar as they near Jericho (18.38-43).

A Disciple is Healed to Walk Earth's 'Way' (18.38-43)

Luke reshapes Mark's story (Mk 10.46-52) editing it significantly, dropping the name of the character, softening his rejection by the crowds and making the contact between the blind man and Jesus more direct. Luke still retains the essential teaching from Mark's healing account.

Jesus nears Jericho, an oasis city considered an urban *ecotopia*. It is Luke's final journey setting before arriving at Jerusalem (18.35a). A blind man is noted begging on the 'side of the way' (18.35b). He is Earth bonded and linked to it through the metaphor of 'way', the Earth related metaphor for an ecologically connected discipleship. The 'way' is Earth's path of discipleship. In the story, the blind man is on the way's *side*. But he has not been freed to walk Earth with an ecological sensitivity. As the story unfolds, we learn the reason that he is on the side of the way. The image of the blind and begging character also reminds auditors about all who are invited into God's *basileia-ecotopia* through Jesus' healing and meal ministry—a consistent theme throughout the gospel. All are called to walk Earth's way; but not all are free to do so.

The person's begging disposition however reflects something else that is foundational for ecological discipleship; he is *poor*. He is not bound by possessions, a problem that has beset several of Jesus' antagonists and story characters found in the earlier *symposium*. Luke's blind beggar does not have material possessions gained by ravaging Earth's fruits or greedily acquiring others' goods. Here is Luke's ecologically harmless, dispossessed and socially rejected potential disciple. Furthermore he suffers from blindness, a condition that is spiritually affecting even Jesus' disciples and from which they, too, need to be healed.

The blind beggar initiates his own healing. He enquires. He cannot see but he *hears* the passing multitude and asks its meaning (18.36). Like a disciple who hears and acts, the blind beggar displays an essential quality that prepares the ground for his later call to discipleship. The language which Luke adopts at this point is explicitly gospel oriented. It is the language of evangelization:

> They announced to him, 'Jesus of Nazareth is passing by' (18.37).

This brings the man to cry out to Jesus as David's son to have 'mercy' on him (18.38). He recognizes the person of Jesus as 'David's son'. This helps the auditor to remember Jesus' birth narrative, his birth in David's city of Bethlehem and his affirmation as Earth's child in harmony with all in the ecological household. Here is a rejected member of that same household who pleads for 'mercy', the essence of God's compassionate, gestational, and maternal love present and expressed in other moments of the gospel and Jesus' ministry.[10] Luke graphically describes others' reaction to his plea,

> And those in front rebuked him in order that he might be silent (18.39a).

'Those in front' react to this beggar's plea for healing. They could conceivably represent those 'in front' in Luke's household who hold positions of leadership and authority and have the power to bring or prevent the disenfranchised and struggling into communion and discipleship. They are not sensitive to Earth's members or the need to ensure their inclusion in Jesus' entourage; they are potentially ecologically destructive; they consider the bleating character evil. He is in need of 'rebuking', the now familiar word that Luke uses in exorcisms; he is judged as undeserving of healing and his pleading a sign of demonic possession; he is to be silenced. But undeterred by others' reactions he cries out even louder to Jesus for mercy (18.39). The blind beggar's cry from the 'side of the way' is a cry from Earth for the Earth. It is a cry for all who are concerned, for 'those in front', to look towards Earth where the blind and poor lie, and to respond. The beggar's unrestrained plea

---

10. Besides here, compassion and mercy appear in Lk. 1.50-78, 7.13; 10.37; 15.20; 16.24; 17.13.

could be heard as a cry for ecological care. It is his response to Earth's needs. Jesus' response is immediate. He 'commands' the beggar be brought to him.

Jesus instructs 'those in front' to act in a way that enables the liberation of all Earth's members who feel constrained or handicapped by their lives. Jesus invites these 'front' people to participate in Earth's emancipation demonstrated by their response to this blind beggar sitting on Earth's way. Jesus asks the beggar, 'What do you want me to do for you?' (18.41a). The response, one would think, would be obvious. In fact, it is surprising.

> Lord, that I might see *again* (18.41b).

The reply indicates that the blind beggar could once see ('again'). The kind of seeing that he once possessed is the seeing that accompanies authentic discipleship and which Jesus' present disciples are showing signs of losing. This beggar was once a disciple; once walked on Earth's 'way', the path of discipleship. For whatever reason, he abandoned this and is now seeking to return.

Those 'in front' in Luke's story are possibly leaders of Jesus households who know the pain caused to others by those who have broken ranks with them and maybe even participated in civil action against Jesus followers; they are 'blind' and are possessed by an evil spirit. Whatever the historical reality in Luke's household that has warranted the retention and reshaping of this Markan intertext, the blind beggar is seeking reconciliation and communion with Jesus, his retinue of disciples and Earth's household. Jesus responds, healing the person's sight, enabling him now to see Earth, restoring him to discipleship and releasing him from all that controls and limits his discipleship:

> Receive your sight; your faith has saved you (18.42).

Now released and liberated, with sight restored, he follows Jesus as he journeys towards Jerusalem along Earth's path, an ecologically redeemed member of Earth's household.

This powerful story about discipleship is the last healing narrative in the gospel before Jesus enters into Jerusalem and the events of his passion and death unfold. While the ecological notes in the narrative symphony seem muted, this healing story, like all the others in Luke's gospel, has Earth related implications. The blind beggar, like other rejected or despised members of Earth, human and non-human, seeks healing, release and community. This spirit must guide 'those in front' in Jesus households to ensure such inclusivity. This requires an ecological remembrance and a contemplative environmental stance conscious of everyone and everything that form Earth's household. They must ensure that environmental consciousness is part of the life of Jesus households.

From Earth's Enemy to Friend (19.1-10)

Finally, Jesus arrives in Jericho where his encounter with a little wealthy toll collector takes place (19.1). It is the encounter of Jesus with a quintessentially despised human being: he is wealthy, which means greedy; he is a toll-collector, which suggests that he acquired his wealth through over-taxing his clients beyond what was necessary; he is the head toll-collector, which indicates that he had other toll collectors working on his behalf and charged them a retainer fee. Finally, we learn that he is small in stature, his physical disposition reflecting his popularity. He is regarded by Jericho's townspeople as insignificant and unpopular, despite his wealth. From an ecological perspective, and consistent with other portraits of the wealthy in Luke's gospel, he would have a low regard for Earth's fruits, seeing them only as commodities that could be taxed and contribute to his wealth. Everything about this character reeks of ecological irresponsibility and disregard. He is potentially another one of Earth's enemies.

Like the blind beggar in the previous story, he wants to encounter Jesus. Like the blind man, too, there is a barrier he has to overcome. As Luke describes it,

> He sought to see who Jesus was and was not able to from the crowd (19.3).

This story, unique in the gospels, gives the name of the toll collector as Zacchaeus. His desire to 'see' Jesus is more than a passion to satisfy his curiosity or visually sight Jesus. His desire reflects a quest to meet and encounter Jesus at a deeper level. This is the level of Earth. To 'see' implies engagement with what is observable on Earth; it is an ecologically responsible and critical act that allows Earth's vision to permeate the 'eyes' and, by association, the heart of the observer. Already the auditor begins to sense that ecological conversion is about to take place through Zacchaeus's sight.

This quest 'to see' is the reason that Luke has him run ahead of the crowds and climb a tree that is on Jesus' route (19.4).

> ³ [Zacchaeus] was trying to see who Jesus was, but on account of the crowd he could not, because he was short in stature. ⁴ So he ran ahead and climbed a sycamore tree to see him, because he was going to pass that way. ⁵ When Jesus came to the place, he looked up... (19.3-5).

His tree lookout provides more than a platform from which to spot Jesus. The tree assists Zacchaeus to respond to his deeper spiritual yearning. Nor is it accidental that the tree is a sycamore, the metaphoric tree of little faith. In 17.6 Jesus' illustration of the self-uprooting sycamore tree that plants itself in the sea at the request of a disciple became his example for what a disciple with little faith could accomplish. With even their little faith the disciples could see and do what seems impossible as illustrated in the sycamore tree's sea planting. Now, with Zacchaeus, the sycamore becomes present to his little faith. This faith is indicated by his desire to 'see' Jesus (19.3). The tree, one of Earth's blessings, will positively contribute to his encounter with Jesus (19.4). Because of Earth's act, through a possible ecological vision available to the senses in Zacchaeus's sight and the tree's readiness to provide him with a means to see and be seen, he encounters Jesus. We shall soon discover how his faith deepens and accomplishes the impossible.

Zacchaeus's symbolic communion with the metaphoric tree of impossible faith becomes the location where Jesus 'looks up' (the same Greek verb used in the previous scene for 'see again', 19.4) and addresses him,

> Zacchaeus, hurry, come down because I must (*dei*) stay in your house today (19.5).

We now discover that while Zacchaeus wants to see Jesus, it is Jesus who wants to 'see' him. He addresses him by name; already the personal relationship that Zacchaeus desires is unfolding. Jesus is truly 'seeing' Zacchaeus and seeks to stay in his house. For Jesus it is a necessity; he 'must' (*dei*) stay in his house.

This is not the first time that Luke uses *dei*.[11] This 'must' expresses God's urgent desire to bring about the liberation of Earth's members as expressed in Jesus' programmatic declaration in 4.16-21. The *dei* indicates that God is explicitly involved in what takes place and interrupts the regular and expected course of history to surprise, even shock and confound.[12] The divine necessity reflected in this case of Jesus staying at the house of Zacchaeus illustrates God's passion for restoration, communion and wholeness. What Jesus will accomplish in Zacchaeus's household illustrates God's yearning for every Earth member.

The divine desire expressed in Luke's use of the *dei* invites a response. And Zacchaeus is prepared to give it. He comes down from the symbolic sycamore tree and receives Jesus 'joyfully' (19.6). The reaction by the bystanders again reminds gospel auditors of the scandal which Jesus creates throughout the gospel by his meal practice and his communion with those who are loathed:

> And seeing it, all murmured, 'He has gone in to be a guest (*kataluō*) of a man who is a sinner' (19.7).

---

11. *Dei* is also present in Lk. 2.49; 4.43; 9.22; 12.12; 13.14, 33; 17.25; 21.9; 22.37; 24.7, 26, 44.

12. Charles H. Cosgrove, 'The divine Δεῖ in Luke–Acts: Investigations into the Lukan Understanding of Divine Providence', *NovT* 26 (1984), pp. 189-90; Elvey, *Ecological*, pp. 97-98; Fitzmyer, *Luke X–XXIV*, p. 180.

The murmuring indicates the negative judgment levelled at Jesus' residency with a man regarded as a sinner. Most significant is the verb 'to be a guest'. The same Greek root in the verb, *kataluō*, lies behind the noun, *kataluma*, 'guest house', found in 2.7 in Jesus' birth story. There, Mary and Joseph do not go to stay at a guest house (*kataluma*) because they find accommodation with their kin in Bethlehem. Here in Jericho, Jesus has a need to be hosted (*kataluō*) by Zacchaeus. He is no longer among those who have kin, but with one who is socially despised and rejected. Such solidarity warrants him being regarded as a person who needs to stay in public lodgings (*kataluō*). Entrance into Zacchaeus's domestic space means that Jesus, too, will be treated as someone despised and eventually rejected. This anticipates the mounting antagonism that he will soon encounter as he enters Jerusalem.

Zacchaeus's response to Jesus' presence is immediate. Luke's description is telling:

> Zacchaeus standing said to the Lord, 'Behold, Lord, half my possessions I give, to the poor; and if I have cheated anyone of anything, I restore it fourfold (19.8).

Zacchaeus stands before Jesus, not for the first time identified with a post-Easter title ('Lord').[13] His standing is public before those who have murmured.[14] What he says becomes a public declaration of restitution that would have social benefits for the poor and the wider urban community. The verbs that Luke's Zacchaeus uses are all in the present tense ('give', 'restore'), not future. His commitment to justice and integrity as a result of his encounter with Jesus is immediate, repetitive and does not await some uncertain future.[15] Environmental and ecological benefits will be instant. His encounter with Earth's child has brought him to environmental conversion and a declared friend of Earth. He desires to share his wealth that has been justly gained with those who are in economic need. He is still wealthy but now it is a wealth that is shared. This spirit of almsgiving is Luke's sign of authentic righteousness.[16] Zacchaeus also promises to compensate immediately those from whom he has stolen. The fourfold restitution represents his desire to abide by the most rigorous strictures demanded by the Torah in returning stolen goods.[17]

Zacchaeus's response through ethical conduct, conversion, wealthy sharing and restitution, brings a response from Jesus. This sums up the meaning of

---

13. Other addresses of Jesus as 'Lord' occur in 2.11; 3.4; 5.8, 12; 6.46; 17.5, 6, 37; 18.6, 41; 19.31, 34; 22.33, 38, 49, 61; 24.34.
14. Johnson, *Luke*, p. 285, suggests that 'standing' is better translated as 'stopped' indicating that this happens on the way to Zacchaeus's house so that his statement is public.
15. Johnson, *Luke*, p. 286.
16. Johnson, *Luke*, p. 286. See Lk. 6.30-31, 38, 11.41; 12.33; 16.9; 18.22, 29.
17. See Exod. 21.37; Lev. 6.5; Num. 5.6-7.

salvation, the experience of what it means to belong to the *basileia-ecotopia*, and the constitution of the gospel household:

> Today, salvation has come to this house, since this one also is a son of Abraham, for the Earthed One has sought out and saved the lost (19.9-10).

Jesus' declaration locates the experience of the *basileia-ecotopia*, of divine communion and acceptance ('salvation'), within the particularity of the household. This is Zacchaeus's house, the representative site of sinners and the rejected. It is also the place of divine encounter with Jesus and those who seek conversion and desire to change their lives. Zacchaeus belongs now to the true community to which Jesus came to reveal and confirm the presence of the *basileia-ecotopia* which, as Jesus has frequently declared in his journey, is already present and 'in your midst'. Zacchaeus's change of heart is a tangible expression of this. Jesus' declaration, addressed not to Zacchaeus *per se*, but to all gospel auditors who might have desired a more restrictive or nationalistic God, that God welcomes all, sinner, stranger and even wealthy toll-collectors. The final words of Jesus, of the Earthed One seeking out and saving the lost (19.9-10), are the very essence of his ministry in Luke's gospel. It finds its summary and final expression in what happens to Zacchaeus, one lost and now found, and the concreted manifestation of the meaning of the parables about the lost in Luke 15.

Zacchaeus is Luke's example of someone wealthy, a toll-collector, seeking to undergo conversion, to come into communion with Jesus, and restore the damage done to Earth's household. Earth, however, through sight and tree, enables him to experience restoration. Zacchaeus becomes the figure of the ecologically reformed toll-collector to whom John the Baptizer appealed early in the gospel's first scenes preparing for Jesus' public ministry (3.13). Zacchaeus is Luke's appeal to the wealthy urban elite in the gospel household who need to undergo conversion and, like Zacchaeus, demonstrate publicly their commitment to release their hold on wealth and return anything that they may have gained unethically or greedily through hurtful damage to Earth. It is this insight that links the story of Zacchaeus with the parable of the pounds (19.11-27) that now follows and concludes Luke's journey narrative.

Earth's Cloth Protects and is Dishonoured (19.11-27)

The introduction to the parable is important. It sets the scene for the main point which the parable teaches and links its teaching to Jesus' immediately preceding declaration concerned with the immediacy of the *basileia-ecotopia* ('salvation') and the Earthed One's search to save the lost. How obvious and immediate the revelation of the presence of the *basileia-ecotopia* is to Jesus' disciples now becomes the issue:

> Hearing these things, [Jesus] proceeded to tell a parable because he was nearing Jerusalem and they thought that the *basileia* of God was going to manifest itself immediately (19.11).

As the journey of Jesus' disciples to Jerusalem was coming to an end, they believed that the presence of God's *basileia-ecotopia* was going to become obvious. One suspects that Jesus' parable will reveal a different truth.

The parable reflects Luke's world and membership of the gospel's household—a wealthy, absentee landlord with at least ten estate slaves whose task was to ensure that their master's wealth increased. They are told to trade with money entrusted to them (19.13), ten *minas* each, a significant but not enormous sum.[18] The mode of economic exchange envisaged in Luke's day would be reciprocal, that is, tit-for-tat. If the slaves are to trade to make a profit it would have to happen at the expense of honesty. There was only so much of the economic pie to go around.[19] If economic trade and barter was to result in increased money and attendant wealth to the landlord, then it would happen by others moving into greater impoverishment, a scene all too familiar in Luke's world—and ours.

The language of *basileia*, the teaching topic for the whole parable, is repeated twice in the opening verses: the estate owner, a nobleman of high royal status, goes away to a far country to receive a *basileia* (19.12); he returns to collect his wealth having received the *basileia* (19.15a). Finally, to conclude the scene setting, we learn that the nobleman is disliked, in fact hated, by his subjects (19.12, 14). The nobleman will respond vindictively and cruelly to their hatred in the parable's last verse. All does not bode well for what is about to take place.

Each of the slaves is called to the nobleman to give account of their bartering success (19.15). Though ten have been entrusted with money, Luke's interest falls on three of them. The first two are able to return a profit and they are rewarded with authority over cities belonging to the nobleman (19.16-19). The third returns a nil profit and is severely castigated. The slave argues his position,

> Lord, behold here is your *mina* which I kept hidden in cloth, for I was frightened of you because you are a harsh human being, you withdraw what you do not deposit and reap what you do not sow (19.20-21).

The elite royal is a human being (*anthrōpos*), greedy, demanding and harsh. He simply takes without giving. This attitude affects not only others but Earth's fruits. The whole Earth is affected by this man's attitude and treatment. He is Earth's enemy; he reaps but never sows. This nobleman represents ecological

---

18. Johnson, *Luke*, p. 289.
19. On the limited good Mediterranean social construct, see John J. Pilch and Bruce Malina, *Handbook of Biblical Social Values* (Peabody, MN: Hendrickson, 1993), pp. 122-27.

disaster and hurts Earth. This is not only the observation of the slave; it is confirmed in the repetition of the slave's words by the nobleman himself (19.22). He agrees with the slave's assessment and asks the slave why he didn't trade with moneylenders for interest (19.23). The slave's money is then taken from him and given to the slave who made the most profit (19.24).

Commentators suggest that the parable is an allegory, with Jesus as the nobleman who entrusts his church to his disciples, as the nobleman entrusts cities to his successful slaves; or Jesus is the noble king given the *basileia-ecotopia*, like the parable's nobleman, and about to be hailed as king who, also like the nobleman, is hated and rejected;[20] or the parable is about encouraging faithfulness to God (who is the parable's 'nobleman');[21] or,

> Christian disciples are being taught that they have been entrusted with the 'secrets of the kingdom,' which are depicted as gracious bounties bestowed on them, and for which they may expect a reckoning depending on how responsibly they have trafficked with this God-given heritage.[22]

The parable is not about any of these.

The problem with the above scholarly allegorical interpretations is that they make God or Jesus appear to be harsh and greedy, the very antithesis to their portraits in the gospel. It is very difficult to see how the violent nobleman who executes those who hate him is an image of Jesus or God. The suggested interpretations endorse the use of violence, the pursuit of wealth and the promotion of greed, found in a nobleman who executes his antagonists and demands a return on money entrusted to slaves.

The key to the parable is found in reflecting on how the third slave protects the *minas* entrusted to him with cloth, the estate owner's wealth and how it is gained, and the teaching from the previous story with Zacchaeus. Wealth happens at the expense of the poor. The third slave acted most honourably with care for the poor. He uses Earth's gift, the cloth, as a way of protecting the money entrusted to him and to ensure it was not treated in an environmentally dishonourable manner. He did not barter or trade with his ten *minas*, earn interest or impoverish anyone, including Earth. Of all the characters in the parable, he is the most ecologically friendly.

As indicated by the opening verses, the parable is a reflection on the coming of the *basileia*, a key concern throughout this third and concluding

---

20. Johnson, *Luke*, pp. 293-94, who offers an allegorical summary proposed by some Lukan scholars (the first) and proposes his own (the second).

21. Green, *Luke*, pp. 674-80.

22. Fitzmyer, *Luke X–XXIV*, p. 1232. Elizabeth Dowling builds on the insights represented in Fitzmyer and sees the parable as a lens for reading the characterization of women in Luke's gospel. The 'pound' has been taken away from them. See Elizabeth V. Dowling, *Taking Away the Pound: Women, Theology and the Parable of the Pounds in the Gospel of Luke* (London: T. &T. Clark, 2007).

unit in Luke's journey symphony. In this final teaching scene, Luke articulates in the parable's introduction the predominant concern of gospel auditors: Why hasn't the *basileia* and its embrace of all Earth's members, its *ecotopia*, become manifest? Why are evils still occurring? Why are the rich still getting richer and the poor poorer? This last question is put into the mouth of the onlookers in the parable when they note the nobleman giving the third slave's money to the one who has the most:

> Lord, he has ten *minas*! (19.25).

The focus is on the money; the cloth from Earth's produce that protected it, forgotten, if not discarded and dishonoured. The rich are indeed getting richer, an experience in Luke's world, as in ours. The Earth is still damaged by human disregard. This recognition makes sense of the aphorism appended to v. 25. This is the voice, not of the nobleman, but of Luke's Jesus by way of commentary. Heard from an ecological perspective, it is a commentary on the way Earth is treated.

> I say to you, that to all who have more will be given, from those who have nothing, even what they think they have, will be taken away (19.26).

The *basileia-ecotopia* is present and in our midst, as Jesus reminds Luke's audience throughout the journey narrative. But its full manifestation waits. For this reason, Earth will continue to be ravaged, and injustice and suffering will remain part of the disciple's experience. This is about to be demonstrated as Jesus enters into Jerusalem, the city of the prophets and the place where Earth's child will be executed.

Conclusion

This final unit of Luke's journeying symphonic narrative, Lk. 17.11–19.27, is predominantly concerned in exploring the meaning of the *basileia-ecotopia* of God, its nature, membership and manifestation. The *basileia-ecotopia* is about God revealed through Jesus' ministry and, particularly in this section of the gospel, through his preaching. It is important to recall from earlier reflections that the *basileia-ecotopia* is not a divine reality and initiative exclusively anthropocentric. It is not concerned about God and human beings alone. The *basileia-ecotopia* is an encounter with God that embraces Earth; the *basileia* is, at the same time, *ecotopia*. Its influence is ecologically nurturing and its human members are encouraged to act in a way that cares for the total membership of this household. This *ecotopia* dimension of God's *basileia* has appeared frequently, especially in this part of the gospel. As members of the *basileia-ecotopia* Jesus' disciples and Luke's auditors are encouraged to be ecologically responsible and ascetic towards Earth.

For this reason, much of Jesus' teaching in this closing section of the journey narrative is again taken up with considerations of wealth, possessions and their accumulation. The desire for wealth, the result of greed and blatant disregard for anything or anyone else, affects Earth. An avaricious person sees others as a means to wealth; Earth is a producer of commodities which can be sold or taxed. Earth is not a subject in its own right, but an object of rapacious activity on behalf of the wealthy, urban elite by those slaves who work the estates on their behalf. Stories and parables in this part of the gospel abound with such examples.

Luke presents a different point of view about the non-human household. Jesus' healings, few though they are as Jerusalem looms, reveal God's inclusive and healing disposition that affects creation. As we have seen, the synchronicity between humanity and creation is affirmed by the ancient appreciation of the human body as a microcosm of the universe. What ails humans affects the Earth; what heals human beings heals Earth and the universe. And as members of the human household can bring about healing and restoration with others, other Earth members too can participate in the healing and salvation intended for the human race. Creation can be an active agent, collaborator and participant in the divine act of human healing. The sycamore tree and Zacchaeus' 'seeing' Earth's vision in his meeting with Jesus (19.4-5) reflect this.

The disciples are called to deepen their spirit of Earth care and responsibility. They are urged to resist the temptation to accumulate wealth and status that accompanies wealth seen by some as a divine blessing. Jesus encourages his disciples to critique this false but attractive understanding and to focus their attention on him and remain receptive to all members of Earth's household, especially those who seem unimportant.

As Luke's long journey movement in the gospel symphony comes to a close, Jesus reminds his disciples that what awaits him in Jerusalem, his rejection, suffering and death, will also affect them. This will be their fate too, though they appear blind to this teaching. As Jesus' journey with his disciples concludes the auditor senses that they are confused; their communion with him is weakened and compromised. In this context, as Jerusalem comes closer and the shadow of the cross looms, the issue of faith surfaces. How the disciples will respond to him in his suffering and death remains to be seen as we now enter with Jesus into the ancient city.

Earth's Voice

Zacchaeus 'was trying to see who Jesus was, but on account of the crowd he could not, because he was short in stature. So he ran ahead and climbed a sycamore tree to see him, because he was going to pass that way. When Jesus came to the place, he looked up...' (19.3-5).

Earth's Sycamore Tree speaks:

> I am very stubborn.
> In fact, I am so rooted into Earth that it is almost impossible to pull me out of Earth's soil.
> Zacchaeus finds and climbs me.
> I give him stature;
> I provide a viewing platform from which he looks upon Earth's child.
> I allow him to be seen.
> He is called.
> Because of me, Zacchaeus returns Earth's confiscated wealth to those who need the gifts that come from Earth's soil.

Chapter 11

LUKE 19.28–21.38

ECOLOGICAL INTERTWINING WITH JESUS' WORD

We have now arrived at the ancient city to which the gospel has been directing its auditors. It is journey's end point in more than one way. It is the end of Luke's travel narrative, a major segment of instruction on discipleship for gospel auditors in their own journey; and it is the end of Jesus' journey in his public ministry and the beginning of his Jerusalem ministry which will conclude with his definitive journey through suffering to his ultimate union with God.

In Jerusalem several features come together. The hostility towards Jesus by the religious leaders and their colleagues mounts; antagonism is palpable; the prophet, Jesus, continues to teach but directs his teaching mainly towards those who are resisting what he says; the temple is the principal location; his disciples accompany him but are uncertain as to what awaits them; issues of possession and wealth are still present but seem to fade into the background.

As Luke forms a new movement in the gospel's symphony, ecological notes are still identifiable. Mount Olivet dominates. This major topographical feature, designated by its Earth fruits, the olive, frames these chapters. Perceived from the dominant perspective that guides this book, Olivet offers a potential ecological metaphor for Jesus' entrance into the holy city. Olivet surrounds Jesus' temple teaching and, topographically, contests the temple site. These chapters (19.28–21.38) prepare the auditor for the gospel's climax in Jesus' ultimate rejection, suffering, death and resurrection.

Inner Play of Lk. 19.28–21.38

Lk. 19.28–21.38 is a piece of literary architecture that, to return to the other metaphor that I have adopted in describing the gospel, reflects the symphonic harmony that characterizes Luke's writing (Figure 28). This metaphor identifies the inner harmony or play that allows the auditor to follow the drama and focus on the prophet's teaching. The section is defined principally by the mention of Mount Olivet, the temple and Jesus' 'daily teaching' in the temple precinct (19.45-47a; 21.37-38). Between these outer frames, Luke intersperses teaching segments addressed to Jesus' antagonists and the 'people' which at times includes his disciples. Jesus' presence in the temple and the teaching that accompanies it is prepared for by his welcome into the ancient city from his disciples and his compassionate weeping over it (19.28-44). This provides a symphonic overture to what takes place between Jesus and his antagonists, temple officials and their retinue (the chief priests, scribes). In this introductory overture, Jesus claims Jerusalem as its king. What follows anticipates and prepares for his passion, as Jerusalem claims him (Luke 22–24). In the lead up to the gospel's climax, tension mounts and his antagonists become more explicit in their intention to 'destroy' him (19.47) or 'lay hands on him' (20.19). Luke places Jesus' adversaries at key junctures in the narrative's development (19.47b–20.1, 19-20 and 20.45-47). Their placement enables the auditor to identify the main points of Jesus' teaching. This primarily concerns the acknowledgment of God's authority of which he is advocate and emissary (20.2-8, 9-18, 21-26 and 27-44). His interpretation is hotly contested by the temple's official teachers. It will lead ultimately to his death.

The teaching segments (20.2-8, 9-18, 21-26, 27-44; 21.1-38) are of varying lengths. Luke draws upon the equivalent Markan intertext of Jesus' temple instruction and confrontation with his antagonists (Mk 11.1–13.37). The evangelist creatively edits Mk highlighting key aspects and theological themes to which gospel auditors are directed: Jesus' communion with God and his prophetic teaching in the temple. Everything else is focused on this.

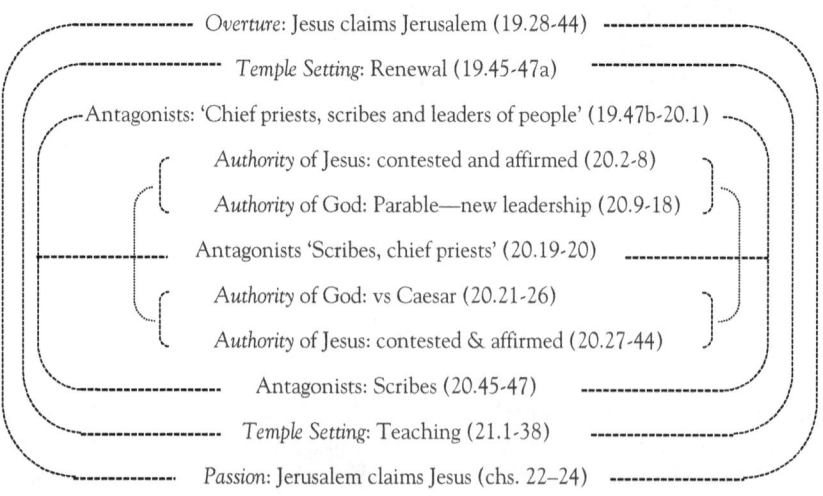

Figure 28. *The inner play of Lk. 19.28–21.38.*

We shall note a particular ecological emphasis that Luke gives to Mark's gospel in this second to last symphonic movement:

- the evangelist tones down Jesus' potential environmentally damaging actions (21.28-32), while accentuating others, especially a roadway, an animal, and what covers both as Jesus rides into Jerusalem (19.34-36);
- Jerusalem's surrounding topographic Earth features that cooperate with Jesus' Jerusalem ministry (19.29, 36-37, 40; 21.37);
- the evangelist's apocalyptic sensitivity for Earth and the manner by which the known cosmic spheres participate in the destruction and the eschatological aftermath that occurs in Jerusalem (21.5-36);
- of special significance is the prominence which 'Mount Olivet' holds in the literary frame (19.29; 21.38) and the manner by which Luke chiastically intertwines the Mount around Jesus' temple teaching in the final two verses (21.37-38) that summarize and conclude this whole section.

It is not accidental that the temple is the location for Jesus' encounter with religious officialdom that violently disagrees with Jesus' earlier meal practice and its accompanying interpretation of God. The temple is a religious centre for the people, always present in the background as Jesus contests the theological position held by his antagonists. As we have already noted in our reflection on Zechariah's presence in the temple in Luke 1, the Solomonic temple is also an ecological navel that summarizes in its architecture and layout a theology of creation and liberation. God's goodness and care for Earth's household is intended to be expressed in this theological and religious space. Unfortunately, as we shall see, those responsible for the temple and to the God whom the temple celebrates have become, like many characters in the gospel, compromised by wealth and the power that goes with the desire for riches and the accumulation and exploitation of Earth's goods.

The Animal, the 'Way' and the Disciples' Clothes (19.28-36)

Jesus arrives on the outskirts of Jerusalem, the finale of a long journey from Galilee with his disciples. It is a journey that has occupied almost half of the gospel symphony. He journeys ahead of his disciples, 'going up to Jerusalem' (19.28b). This ascension to the holy city is not only a geographical one; it is also spiritual and theological. Jerusalem is the 'location of the temple, abode of God, nexus between human and divine', heaven and Earth.[1] The holy city will complete Jesus' ultimate ascent to God. On the outskirts of the city, from Mount Olivet, Jesus directs two of his disciples to a nearby village

---

1. Green, *Luke*, p. 683.

to collect a colt 'on which no one has ever yet sat', untie it and bring it to where he is (19.29-33). His disciples return with the animal and place him on the borrowed colt having thrown their own garments over it first. Others (disciples and/or 'the people') also throw their garments on the *road* along which Jesus will ride.[2] As the colt and Jesus go down the slope towards the Kidron Valley before the final ascent into the city,

> the whole multitude of disciples rejoicing praised God with a loud voice for all the powerful deeds they saw, saying, 'Blessed the one who comes—the King—in the name of the Lord, in heaven, peace and glory (*doxa*) in the highest (*hupsistos*)!' (19.37b-38).

There is much that goes on in these opening verses preparing for Jesus' entry into Jerusalem that bursts with ecological imagery. There are four Earth images suggested by Luke's narrative.

First, Jesus arrives to take possession of the city that is God's. His descent and ascent occur with joy by his disciples. Jesus' movement on the Mount of Olivet and down its slopes indicates that John the Baptizer's application of the LXX Isa. 40.3-5 in welcoming God's messenger is not literally enacted. The filling in of the valleys and the flattening of hill tops to provide an easy access for God's messenger is not a reality as Jesus comes into Jerusalem. Instead the hilly landscape participates in this act of welcoming into Jerusalem the child of Earth and God's regal emissary identified through birth garments associated with Solomon (Wis. 7.4-5). The terrain, rather than being an obstacle for this king's access to Jerusalem, becomes its means.

Second, Luke places great importance on the village animal which the disciples borrow and Jesus mounts. The use of the colt, drawn from Mark's gospel (Mk 11.2), might be an echo of Zech. 9.9 celebrating the eschatological entrance of the God-King into Jerusalem riding on a colt. Luke's colt is a village animal; it is taken from a setting associated with the rural peasant world of Luke's auditors and more firmly associated with their Earth-connectedness. This animal is associated with the more ecologically sensitive members of Luke's gospel household. The colt also is one that has not been ridden, or rather, as Luke clearly points out, that,

> upon it no human being (*anthrōpos*) has ever sat (19.31b).

The point of this detail is not to affirm Jesus' riding skills to break in a wild animal; rather it underscores the First Testament description of animals that have never been yoked.[3] Jesus' colt, in other words, is a free, not oppressed

---

2. The language which Luke uses of the road that leads to the city and upon which Jesus rides is literally, the 'way' or 'path'—19.36b. This is the same word that was central in our reflection of Luke's journey narrative. It is a small but important detail to which I shall return shortly.

3. Num. 19.2; Deut. 21.3; 1 Sam. 6.7. See Fitzmyer, *Luke X–XXIV*, p. 1249.

animal. It is upon such an animal that has also been untied—a thrice mentioned detail that could be easily missed (19.30b, 31a, 33b)—that Jesus sits. The divine agent of liberation sits upon one of Earth's creatures that has never been yoked and made subservient to the human household. The colt has been untied and therefore released from any intended servitude. The First Testament image in the messianic age of reconciliation between the human, animal and natural worlds as echoed in Isaiah (Isa. 11.6-9) now finds expression in the communion between Jesus and the colt.

Third, the disciples' clothes feature in the scene. As previously noted in Chapter 3 reflecting on the bands of cloth that swaddled God's Earth's child (2.7, 12), clothing identified Jesus as a creature of Earth surrounding him with one of its gifts. The disciples' act of throwing their own garments over the colt (19.35b) and onto the pathway ('way', 19.36b) along which the Jesus-bearing animal walks (19.36) identifies both the colt and Earth's 'way' as Jesus' disciples also. Both are covered with garments which formerly identified his disciples. The colt and the path represent those non-human members of Earth's household who symbolically accompany Jesus to his suffering. They, too, will become like his human disciples, participants in his suffering and death. In other words, Jesus' passion and resurrection will involve the whole Earth community, not just its human members.

The Canticle of Earth's Peace (19.37-38)

Finally, the reaction of the multitude of the disciples to Jesus' movement towards Jerusalem is one of praise directed to God and accompanied by song (19.37-38). The song echoes the liturgical canticle of the angels to the shepherds celebrating the birth of Earth's child and the implications of his birth for the whole of creation. Our study of the angelic canticle of 2.14 (Figure 29) revealed the prominence of peace as the gift of Jesus' birth in a chiasm centred on peace.

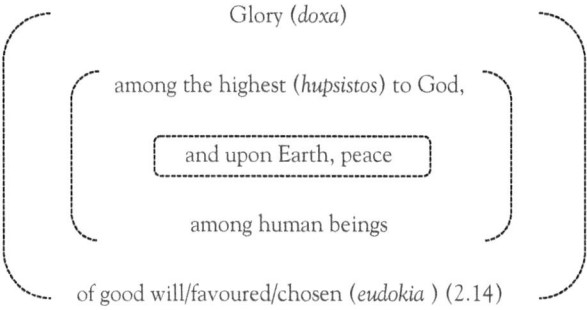

Figure 29. *The literary structure of Lk. 2.14.*

In this angelic birth canticle peace gets celebrated with Earth's household and among human beings beloved of God. Towards the end of the gospel in the song of praise that now accompanies Jesus into Jerusalem the disciples also celebrate the consequences of Jesus' ministry narrated by Luke throughout the gospel. He, God's beloved one, also brings about peace. But in this song, this peace that Jesus brings expands from Earth (as in his birth) to resound in the heavens, as Luke's literary structure clearly identifies (Figure 30). It might seem that heaven is not in peace unless and until Earth is. This reflects an integral simpatico between these two spheres.

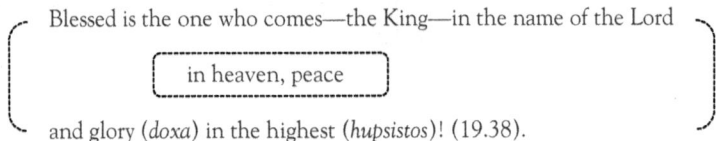

Blessed is the one who comes—the King—in the name of the Lord

in heaven, peace

and glory (*doxa*) in the highest (*hupsistos*)! (19.38).

Figure 30. *The structure of Lk. 19.38.*

In our reflection in Chapter 3 on both canticles, we saw then how they relate to each other. They are chiastically structured; both give praise or 'glory' (*doxa*) to God who is in the *hupsistos*, the heavenly abode from where God has care over Earth's household and eco-system. In the first, peace is upon Earth; in the second it is found in heaven. Peace is the centrepiece of both. A mutuality of peace, of *shalom*, is affirmed. In the angelic hymn, glory comes upon divinely favoured human beings because of Jesus' birth. In the disciples' song accompanying Jesus into Jerusalem, peace goes into the heavens because of Jesus, king and God's emissary.

When both canticles are placed side by side, they underscore the divine origin of peace and the possibility that God's presence can bless Earth with the same gift present in the heavens, and that heaven is blessed with the peace that comes from Earth brought about through Jesus' actions. There exists a mutuality of peace moving between heaven and Earth. Both hymns reflect the cosmology typical of Luke's day, a cosmic duality and hierarchy between the spheres of heaven, Earth and under Earth, of one over the others. But as the gospel narrative symphony has been played out, a shift has occurred. These tripartite spheres are no longer separate and impenetrable. Through Jesus, Earth's child and God's beloved, the spheres now interpenetrate and are found in each other. Divine peace is upon Earth; Earth's peace is in the heavens.

This insight has important christological implications. Both canticles, one from the beginning of the gospel and the other in the final chapters, acclaim Jesus as the mediator of peace, communion and deep *shalom* with the total universe, on Earth, within the human household and in the heavens. He brings eschatological and ecological harmony to the universe as his peace permeates both spheres of heaven and Earth.

The Voice of Earth's 'Stones' (19.39-40)

The disciples' welcome of Jesus—an expansive one given the great throng of disciples that Luke emphasizes (19.37b)—and their accompanying canticle receive a negative response from the religious leaders who order Jesus to 'rebuke' his disciples. They regard their over-praise of Jesus and their consequent association of him with God as evilly inspired. The disciples, they consider, need an exorcism.[4] Jesus corrects this interpretation.

> I say to you, if these were silent, the stones would cry out (19.40).

We hear Luke's Jesus affirming the ecological and environmental communion inspired by his ministry and presence throughout the gospel. The disciples, albeit silently, give voice to the praise that Earth also gives. And if Jesus' disciples are silenced in their praise of him by his antagonists, then the non-human world would pick up the chorus. Earth's 'way' has already been cloaked as a disciple; Earth is in such communion with Jesus that it will respond in solidarity and seek to protect him. Earth's 'stones' will be the means. 'Indeed', notes Green,

> 'stones' would pick up the chorus of joyful praise were these people silenced, signaling the cosmic repercussions of the consummation of God's salvific plan signified in this event.[5]

Jesus affirms the voice of Earth. Its stones are able to cry out. These seemingly inanimate objects, affirmed as such early in the gospel (3.8) and which require God's act to turn them into children of Abraham, now find their voice. Their expressed concern for Jesus corresponds to the way other non-human Earth members (the colt, the geographical terrain, the hills and the path) mediate Jesus to Jerusalem. Nothing is excluded from accompanying and celebrating him.

Jesus' Maternal Weeping (19.41-44)

The joy from his disciples, human and non-human, that accompanies Jesus unto Jerusalem contrasts with the sadness of the next scene as Luke's Jesus looks upon the holy city and sheds tears over it (19.41-44):

> As [Jesus] came near and saw the city, he wept over it (19.41).

Jesus' tears affirm the materiality and maternal, Earth-centred nature of his being. The physicality of his reaction as he gazes upon Jerusalem again

---

4. As we have noted several times, 'rebuke' is Luke's favourite word for exorcism. It occurs, for example, at 4.35, 39, 41; 8.24.
5. Green, *Luke*, p. 688.

reminds auditors that Luke's Jesus is Earth's child and deeply affected by the world in which gospel auditors live. His tears come from the prophet who recognizes the tragedy that awaits the city that has killed its prophets. The stones, affirmed a few verses earlier as agential vocal beings protective of Jesus, are impotent to protect Jerusalem's citizens and abusively silenced by Jerusalem's invaders who

> will not leave one stone upon another (19.44b).

These stones, which a few verses earlier would be given the disciples' voice if Jesus' followers were to be silenced (19.40), now take on further animated potential as victims and symbols, too, of Jerusalem's destruction. It is possible that Luke retrojects on to the story of Jesus what may have been an historical fact by the time of the gospel's writing (19.42). If so, Jerusalem might have now been definitively occupied by the Romans, its temple destroyed and the city ransacked. Luke further makes Jesus' lament also a moment of grief over the inability of its leaders to recognize God's presence revealed through Jesus, a mellow reflection on the failure of his households to attract a large number of Israelites as members.[6] However one hears Jesus' lament, the destruction of Jerusalem is accompanied by brutality and ecological abuse (19.43-44): Earth is used as a barrier and prison to hem in city and citizens; together with their children its people will be brutalized as they are smashed against Earth and the city is totally torn apart. The pain, devastation and ecological destruction that comes or will come upon Jerusalem, and which Jesus prophetically laments, contrasts to the ecological communion and heavenly peace his presence brings in the previous scene. Jesus' tears prepare the auditor for the resistance and antagonism that await him from the civic and religious leaders in the city, especially the temple. It is to this holy site that Jesus first goes (19.45–20.1).

Jesus Purifies the Temple and Teaches (19.45–20.26)

Jesus' first act is to purify the temple from those who have made the holy place a market place for commercial activity and site for the wealthy. His action, described in two verses, raises the problem that has dogged many of Jesus' adversaries and those whom he has encountered on his journey to Jerusalem. This concerns the use of wealth and Earth's goods. Materialism

---

6. For a broader and more open approach to Luke's theological inclusion of Israel in God's plan and the evangelist's desire for the inclusion of Israel in God's ongoing plan, see David Ravens, *Luke and the Restoration of Israel* (Sheffield: Sheffield Academic Press, 1995). For an overview of the dominance of an 'anti-Jewish' tendency in general in NT studies and in Lukan studies in particular, see Joseph B. Tyson, *Luke, Judaism, and The Scholars: Critical Approaches to Luke–Acts* (Columbia, SC: University of South Carolina Press, 1999).

has now corrupted those who identify with the most important religious centre, the temple. Drawing on LXX Isa. 56.7, Luke portrays the prophet Jesus acting in deed and word to renew the temple:

> It is written, 'My house shall be a house of prayer; you have made it a house of robbers' (19.46).

This cleansing allows Jesus to restore the temple to its rightful purpose, as a place of prayer to God, teaching and celebration of ecological harmony. Luke notes that Jesus teaches daily in this divine earthly-heavenly sacred nexus (19.47a). But it is the setting, too, in which his adversaries gather together and are explicitly named. The chief priests, their scribes and 'the leaders of the people' congregate 'to destroy him' (19.47b). Their intention is clear. Their agenda is nothing less than his death and gets formulated in the temple where sacrifice is prominent. The auditor is now alert to their agenda and how they will arrive at this will slowly emerge. This prepares for Jesus' mounting opposition which first appears in the next scene as Jesus teaches the people in the temple (20.1-8).

Jesus' antagonists gather to question him publicly about his authority and its source (20.2). Their attempt to discredit and dishonour him is matched by his question to them about the authoritative source of the baptisms performed by John, highly respected by the people and whose ecologically sensitive wilderness predisposition contrasts their material extravagance. Was John's baptism from God or from human beings (20.3-4)? They are unwilling to answer his question and avoid confrontation with the people (20.5-6). Rather than shaming Jesus, they become shamed (20.7-8).

This event leads to a parable that allegorizes the opposition that Jesus meets (20.9-18). His parabolic teaching concerns a vineyard scene, an owner, tenants hired by the owner to tend the vineyard to give him some of its fruits, estate slaves, and the owner's son. The scenario is all too familiar to Luke's audience. The allegory focuses on the vineyard, a rich ecological image of celebration that comes from its fruit. As the story unfolds we learn how a human being (*anthrōpos*, 20.9a) is responsible for the vineyard's planting and care, entrusting it to tenants, presumably to continue its nurture. Their attitude is more focused on greed and claiming the vineyard as an inheritance (20.14). Abuse of Earth's fruits is uppermost in their plan. They kill each representative that the owner sends them.

The violent response by the tenants to the owner's various messengers including the owner's 'beloved son' and heir reflects Luke's meditation on Jesus and what awaits him (20.10-16). As the vineyard and Earth are treated, so too Jesus. To complete the allegory, Luke again borrows the image of the stone, already given voice, action and life in the gospel, to describe Jesus' fate. He will become like a rejected building stone that ends up as a structure's keystone (20.17). He will also be the stone of judgment for those who have rejected him (20.18). The parable reasserts Jesus' authority in God's plan.

As the opposition to Jesus mounts (20.19), the religious officials seek to trap him. This time their ploy is to discredit his authority before the civil leadership (20.21-26). The trap they set comes in the form of a question about the appropriateness of the Jewish payment of the Roman tribute. This annual one denarius tax, though perhaps for some who were well-off financially insignificant (equivalent to the day's wages of an adult male per year), symbolized the Jewish subjugation to the Roman occupiers. For those living on bare subsistence, it was an added tax, and failure to pay it was considered seditious. The question posed to Jesus, whether the tax should be paid or not, on the face of it, is serious. On its response rests Jesus' credibility.

As Luke notes, Jesus recognizes their evil intent and asks his questioners, representatives of the religious elite and chief priests and practitioners of the Torah, to show him a denarius and describe its image and inscription (20.24).[7] Their response is 'Caesar', the god-king under whose regal authority they are subject. This is the trap that has now been reversed by Jesus. These representatives of the highest religious authorities have in their possession an effigy of the god-king which Jesus does not look upon or touch. The presence of such an image on the temple mount contradicts the great commandment of the Torah, before God there can be no other. With the display of the denarius their credibility is destroyed. Jesus concludes,

> Then give to Caesar the things that belong to Caesar and to God the things that belong to God (20.25).

The point that Jesus makes affirms that Earth and its produce are from God, not Caesar. They are not commodities to be used for the oppression of others, as the image and coin of Caesar imply. Their presence on the temple mount, the ecological heart and religious centre, contests the rightful place which God has in the ordering of the universe and care for Earth. The coin witnesses to imperial authority subjugating the human household and all that it needs for survival. Taxation, for which the coin was required, symbolizes occupation and oppression. This affects human beings and touches into the way Earth is perceived to provide the means for supplying the tax. Thus, Earth too is the victim of Caesar's taxation. From such oppression Jesus seeks to release Earth and its members as he responds to his aggressors and establishes the rightful order of authority. The credibility of the official Torah interpreters is irreparably damaged.

---

7. See Alan Cadwallader, 'In Go(l)d we Trust: Literary and Economic Exchange in the Debate over Caesar's Coin', *BibInt* 14 (2006), pp. 486-507.

Opposition Mounts; Religious Officials Denounced (20.27–21.4)

The avalanche of scenarios and questions that follow on this test from Jesus' opponents continues (20.27-38). All have the same agenda—to trap Jesus and discredit his authority as God's trusted representative and Torah interpreter. His response to his enquirers finally satisfies as they seem to move into the background of the narrative (20.40).

The scribes, the Torah's interpreters and Jesus' principal opponents, come under his closer scrutiny (20.45-47). He warns his disciples to be wary of them. Their religious ostentation and desire for personal exaltation and social status connects to something that Luke has already condemned in the journey narrative. For Luke, there is a link between the desire for high social status and greed. The accumulation of wealth disorients people from an authentic relationship to God, God's people and Earth. This is further reflected in how a person treats Earth, the kind of clothing they wear and how these are acquired from Earth, their attitude at meals and their sincerity in public worship. Jesus cautions his disciples,

> Be aware of the scribes who desire to go about in long robes and love greetings in the market place and taking the chief seats in the synagogues and places of honour at banquets, who devour widows' houses and as a pretence make long prayers (20.46-47).

Jesus identifies the scribes' lack of religious integrity. Their obsession with ostentation in the public or religious forum, their presumption of preference and honour at meals is compounded by their greed for the possessions of the most defenceless in Luke's world. Many suggestions have been proposed as to how the scribes succeed to devour these poor people's properties, but their unscrupulous greed is what Jesus identifies.[8] Their prayers then become only a pretext. They have no sympathy for the main tenets of the Torah, love of God expressed through love of kin. Their treatment of widows reflects their attitude to God and God's Earth.

The subject of widows as social victims of the religious practice and their practitioners continues as Jesus looks at the way gifts are placed into the temple treasury (21.1). He watches as an economically poor widow places two copper coins in it (21.2). She is one of Earth's poor. Jesus comments and interprets the woman's action in social, theological and economic terms that reflect on her spirit of discipleship and a religious system that has warranted her to give of all her possessions:

---

8. Fitzmyer, *Luke X–XXIV*, p. 1318. Scribes could have gained possession of widows' property by accepting payment for legal aid to widows, cheating them out of estates, taking advantage of their hospitality, mismanaging their property, or perhaps taking money offerings from widows who believed in their long prayers.

> Truly I tell you that this poor widow has put in more than all of them; for all of them put in from their excess into the treasury, she from her poverty has put in everything of her living that she had (21.3-4).

The widow's action, a form of prophetic denunciation, contrasts with the wealthy. She gives to the temple treasury what is identified as her total identity; others give what is left over. Rather than interpreting the widow as a model of self-giving which gospel auditors are encouraged to emulate, she represents the poorest in a religious system that has been co-opted by its religious officials to make the poor poorer. This is the point of the previous scene and Jesus' critique of the scribes. This widow is the living proof of the inability of the Torah's interpreters to liberate and rescue the poor from their poverty—a divine mandate from the Torah. The widow is the victim of a form of oppression which Jesus has come to stamp out. That it occurs under the guise of genuine religious practice makes the oppression even more serious. The instruments of this oppression will need to be either definitively renewed or dismantled. That will occur in the death of Jesus when the temple is symbolically restored in his body.

Jesus' Prophetic Teaching: Earth's Distress (21.5-33)

The first scenes of Jesus' Jerusalem ministry confirm and establish his authority vis-à-vis the distorted leadership of the religious and temple officials. Luke's preoccupation with their interaction mutes ecological notes. In the present scenes where a widow's impoverishment—the product of inauthentic religious practice and the temple's maltreatment—contrasts scribal avariciousness, ecological concerns surface more. The scribes' misuse of religion to camouflage greed impacts on the poorest with ecological consequences. As we have seen frequently, greed affects Earth. Now, as Luke continues with the Markan narrative, attention turns to Jesus' prophetic teaching that occupies the rest of the chapter.

Luke scripts this teaching into five parts:[9]

- signs of universal upheaval before the destruction of the temple (21.5-11);
- immediate events that will impact on Luke's household and flag Jerusalem's fall (21.12-19);
- Luke's description of the destruction of Jerusalem (12.20-24);

---

9. Johnson, *Luke*, pp. 324-25, provides a four-fold division of this section, without reference to Lk. 21.29-38.

- a parable reminding gospel auditors again as to the *basileia-ecotopia*'s presence (12.29-33);
- and Jesus' concluding exhortation to his disciples for alertness and openness of heart to what happens (21.34-36).

The whole section concludes with a summary of Jesus' daytime teaching in the temple and a central ecological note about his place of evening rest (21.37-38). This happens on Earth's most prominent topographical feature, Mount Olivet, the mount from which Jesus first set out to claim the city of Jerusalem, joyfully welcomed by his disciples and riding on an untethered colt and upon a path that the disciples cover with their garments. Olivet provides the environmental frame for Jesus' Jerusalem ministry in Luke 21.

As Jesus speaks about the temple and its adornment he reminds his audience that what they see will not be left standing (21.5-6). When asked about the signs that anticipate this event, Jesus warns them not to be led astray by messianic pretenders offering an apocalyptic forecast, rumours of national upheavals or even what seem ecological and cosmic cataclysms (21.7-11). Such events are part of the world in which Luke's auditors live; they are not signs of God's definitive coming. He reassures his audience,

> the end is not immediately (21.9b).

Luke's Jesus identifies auditors' experience of social persecution, suffering and incarceration before public authorities as moments, not of disaster, but of gospel witness (21.12-17). He assures them of his presence in these difficult times that will give them a sense of peace and confidence before their adversaries who are even members of their kinship alliances. They will experience hatred and death, but,

> [18] a hair of your head will never perish. [19] By your patent endurance (*hupomonē*) you will gain your souls (21.18-19).

Jesus' words echo his earlier teaching about trust in the continual and sustaining presence of the creator God who cares for all creation—birds, animals, even the human species—and who, despite their physical death, will never allow even a hair of the head to perish (12.22-34). God's sustaining care for Earth's creatures continues, even beyond the grave. Patient endurance (*hupomonē*) in what is happening, conviction in God's care and trust in God's definitive action will sustain the disciple (21.19).

Jesus' vivid description of the destruction of Jerusalem (21.20-24) echoes a historical reality perhaps already accomplished. As Luke draws on Mark's gospel here with its particular apocalyptic literary genre, the evangelist notes how Earth, too, is also a victim to the destruction that occurs to Jerusalem. Earth's simpatico with its inhabitants registers in its own suffering and distress that mirrors the grief of Jerusalem's inhabitants,

> for a great agony will be upon Earth and wrath upon the people (21.23c).

The planet's communion with the human household continues to be identified as Luke reflects on the signs of the final cataclysmic coming of the Human One. Earth, like its people, will feel the same distress and upheaval. People's suffering will also be echoed in the known spheres of creation, in the heavens, on Earth and under Earth, within its deepest regions. All Earth's members without exception will experience catastrophic distress.

Whereas the earlier teaching is time oriented and historically identified, the present signs about which Jesus speaks and that accompany the coming of the Human One are timeless. They can be perceived at any time in history, in any culture and among any people. Jesus' words here are enduring. But the point that he makes for gospel auditors is that, when these signs are identified, they are to be confident and faith filled,

> because your redemption is drawing near (21.28b).

God's coming is close. This is underscored in the gospel's final parable, the lesson which the ecological world in its fig tree offers attentive disciples (21.29-33). As the greening fig tree is a sign of summer's coming, so when disciples become aware of these timeless cosmic, environmental and social calamities they can have confidence in the coming of God who feels and responds to Earth's trauma.

Before the commencement of the passion narrative with its definitive revelation in the death of Jesus, Luke reiterates the gospel's conviction about the presence of the *basileia-ecotopia* for a last time. When disciples see all these signs,

> you know that the *basileia* of God is near (21.31b).

Jesus encourages his disciples to trust the faithful and ongoing presence of God in the midst of life's upheavals. They can trust this theological perspective in the unfolding of the social and cultural realities and religious disturbances encountered in Luke's Greco-Roman world. Ecological harmony, expressed in the present especially in Jesus' ministry, will consequently deepen in all Earth's creatures. The *basileia's ecotopia* will continue to permeate the universe. Conviction about this will grow only through faith in Jesus' word, reliable and eternal:

> Heaven and Earth will pass away; my words will never pass away (21.33).

The disciples have already witnessed the powerful effectiveness of God's *rhēma* acting through Jesus; experienced the trustworthiness of his word, and been convinced of the eternal nature of heaven and God's perpetual care of Earth. As the removal of heaven and Earth from God's care would be impossible, so also the transitory and unreliable nature of Jesus' dynamic word which, as we have seen, is concerned about creation's healing and human happiness.[10]

The equation that Jesus makes between heaven and Earth is noteworthy and summary. Throughout the gospel, the evangelist has impressed on the auditor how Earth's members—birds, animals, seeds, plants, trees, skies, topography, and waters—have been active subjects of God's care and healing action through Jesus. They have also been participants in the healing of the human household, contributors to Jesus' teaching, and means for affirming Luke's christology.

The 'Fig Tree' (21.28-32)

Before we move to Luke's concluding verses of the gospel's penultimate symphonic movement, it would be important to note one aspect of Luke's redaction of Mark. It concerns the fig tree.

In the final chapters of Mark's gospel before the passion narrative begins, the fig tree figures prominently. It appears in Mark's apocalyptic chapter in Mk 13.28-29. Luke uses this Markan source for constructing the fig tree parable and its *basileia-ecotopia* teaching. Luke's only major change concerns the metaphor which the fig tree's greening represents. For Mark, it is about the nearness of the Human One, who 'is at the very gates' (Mk 13.29). For Luke, characteristically, it is about the nearness of God's *basileia-ecotopia*.

Mark has a second reference to the fig tree which Luke chooses to omit. It occurs earlier in Mk and is associated with Jesus' prophetic action of temple cleansing (Mk 11.15-19). Mark frames Jesus' action by his encounter with a fig tree (Mk 11.12-14, 20-21) (Figure 31). In the first fig tree scene (Mk 11.12-14), Jesus comes to the leafed tree looking for fruit on it. Finding none he curses it:

> May no one ever eat fruit from you again! (Mk 11.14).

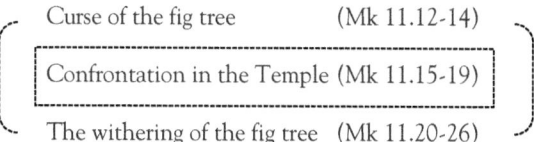

Figure 31. *Mark's 'fig-tree' scenes (Mk 11.12-26)*.

---

10. For an alternative and non-metaphoric interpretation of this text, see Keith D. Dyer, 'When is the End Not the End: The Fate of Earth in Biblical Eschatology (Mark 13)', in *The Earth Story in the New Testament* (ed. N. Habel and V. Balabanski; London: Sheffield Academic Press, 2002), pp. 44-56 (53-54).

In the concluding frame, the fig tree is withered away to its roots about which Peter comments. This leads Jesus into an excursus on faith (Mk 11.20-26). Mark's chiasmic structure obviously indicates that the incident with the fig tree revolves around Jesus' deeds and words in the temple. This central episode in Mark's gospel amplifies the futility of the present religious institution and its inability to offer genuine liberation and equality. The fig tree speaks to what happens in the temple.[11] As in Luke's gospel, Jesus reclaims this institution for God as a 'house' of prayer. Texts from the First Testament lay the metaphoric foundation for the fig tree in Mk as the image of Israel's leadership and the appropriate focus of Jesus' curse in Mark's gospel (Jer. 24.1-10; 29.16-19). Jesus' effective curse of a fig tree 'to its roots' (Mk 11.20c) becomes ecologically confronting.

Luke takes Mark's story of Jesus' confrontation in the temple (Mk 11.15-19) and, as with the apocalyptic fig tree parable from Mark 13, redacts and reshapes it. In line with the gospel's more elevated christology, Luke removes Mark's dramatic action of Jesus overturning money-changers' tables and pigeon-sellers' seats and preventing merchants from carrying goods through the temple precincts (Mk 11.15b-16). Luke moreover omits anything associated with Jesus' curse. While the main point of the fig tree's fruitlessness and complete destruction in Mark's gospel, 'to its roots', is a commentary on the religious institution, the christological portrait that accompanies it is in tension with Luke's portrait of Jesus as Earth's child. For this reason, Luke omits Mark's fig tree curse.

Luke's Earth Summary (21.34-38)

The final word which Jesus sounds for his disciples as the major part of the gospel comes to an end concerns alertness and watchfulness (21.34-36), an echo of earlier teaching addressed to overly anxious disciples. Their physical preparedness imaged in terms of sobriety reflects the human soul waiting for what unfolds, not thrown or surprised but strengthened through prayer. Prayerfulness will guarantee watchfulness, not in terms of physical wakefulness, but a preparedness to engage future suffering and tragedy in communion with Jesus, the Human One:

---

11. The fig-tree/temple connection is argued by William R. Telford, *The Barren Temple and the Withered Tree* (Sheffield: JSOT Press, 1980); Myers, *Binding*, pp. 297-98. Vincent Taylor, who would represent the other end of the scholarly spectrum, allows the possibility of a symbolic inference of the cursing of the fig tree and its connection with Jerusalem and Judaism as a whole, in *The Gospel according to St. Mark: The Greek Text* (London: Macmillan & Co. Ltd, 1953), pp. 458-60. Taylor argues for the historicity of the event, informed by his anti-Judaic interpretation.

> Be awake in every season, praying that you will have the strength to flee all these things that will take place and can stand before the Human One (21.36).

The necessity for prayerful alertness will be dramatically demonstrated as Jesus gathers with his disciples on the Mount of Olivet just before he is arrested and his passion begins (22.39-46). The scene and chapter end as Luke notes Jesus' daily teaching in the temple, retiring to sleep at night, and attracting people to listen to him in the temple (21.38). The literary structure of these last verses frames Jesus' presence in the temple and his teaching ministry around the topographical image of Olivet, a central environmental feature that, as we have noted, surrounds the whole section (Figure 32).

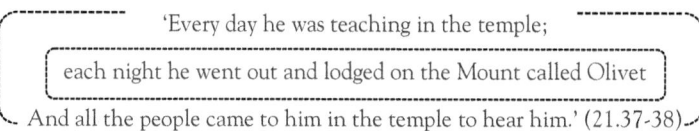

Figure 32. *Literary structure of Lk. 21.37-38.*

Thus, the topographical feature that frames all Jesus' teaching is itself framed by Jesus' temple teaching. The two, Jesus' teaching and the ecologically significant Mount, are intertwined. This final note of ecological communion concludes this major symphonic movement as the gospel climax nears.

Conclusion

There are four important things to note about Luke 19 to 21 as it anticipates the gospel's culmination in Jesus' suffering and death. Jesus had been preparing his disciples for these final events as they journeyed towards Jerusalem.

First, Luke draws on Mark's gospel (Mark 13) to provide the basic outline of Jesus' teaching. But there is significant reshaping of Mk in light of present realities confronting Luke's auditors and the historical possibility that Jerusalem and its temple were destroyed by the Romans in 70 CE. The evangelist removes future eschatological references from the first part of the Markan source to foreground more immediate specific events perhaps well-known to Luke's auditors.[12] Luke also uses stereotypical language to describe what might have been regarded in hindsight as Jerusalem's possible destruction (21.20-24). Such imagery and language can be found in Josephus, First Testament and intertestamental literature.[13]

---

12. Johnson, *Luke*, p. 325.
13. Josephus, *Jewish War* 5.47-50; 2 Macc. 8.12; Jer. 7.14-26, 30-34, 16.1-9; 17.27; 19.10-15; Mic. 3.12; Zeph. 1.4-13.

Second, these descriptions are placed into the mouth of the prophet Jesus. If by the time of the gospel writing Jerusalem's destruction was already a fact, then this would confirm further the portrait of Jesus as God's authentic prophet and revealer of the divine *rhēma*. The implication that would flow from this would reinforce the truth in Jesus' prophetic word and that his word about the events that precede and precipitate the definitive coming of the Human One could also be trusted.

Third, the destruction of the temple and the criticism which Luke's Jesus delivers to the chief priests, scribes and other religious and temple officials does not come from an anti-Semitic or anti-Israelite bias of the evangelist. Luke is not attacking Judaism.[14] The respect the gospel author has for the Israelite ancestry has been clear from the gospel's beginning, in the portraits of Zechariah, Elizabeth, Mary and Joseph as characters faithfully steeped in the Israelite ancestral traditions. Luke's respect for the texts and traditions from the First Testament is evident in the intertexts, perhaps even pre-texts, for the evangelist's theological and christological project. One of those Israelite texts has supplied the major interpretative perspective that has guided my ecological listening to Luke's gospel. This is the creation and Earth-related metanarrative.

A careful study of Acts indicates that the failure of the Israelite mission is a concern with which the evangelist struggles. That some did become Jesus followers is seen in the idyllic picture of the conversion of Israelites in Jerusalem as a result of Peter's Pentecost sermon (Acts 2.41; 6.7) and the attraction that many had to Paul's preaching (Acts 13.43). There would have also been Israelite members of the gospel household, which explains the gospel's references and allusions to First Testament intertexts and, unlike in Mark's gospel, the absence of any explanation of Israelite purification practices. These indicate an Israelite presence in the gospel household. However, the overall failure of the Gospel to attract large numbers of Israelite adherents cannot be translated into a Lukan penchant for the temple's destruction. This destruction had perhaps already occurred and Luke works this historical reality into the inherited Markan apocalyptic source upon which the evangelist draws.

Fourth, Luke adopts a style of apocalyptic writing well-known in the ancient world and to the gospel audience. Flashes of this particular genre

---

14. John Gager argues that if there is any anti-Judaic bias in Luke's writings it comes from an attempt to delegitimize 'Judeo-Christian' opponents within Luke's community; it is therefore an internal issue that gets reflected in what might be interpreted as anti-Jewish. See John G. Gager, 'Where Does Luke's Anti-Judaism Come From?', *AnnStorEseg* 24 (2007), pp. 31-35. Also, Rick Strelan argues that the author of the Third Gospel was a Jewish priest, in *Luke the Priest. The Authority of the Author of the Third Gospel* (Aldershot, Hants.: Ashgate, 2008).

had already occurred in Luke's journey narrative at 17.22-37 in reference to the signs of the *basileia-ecotopia*'s presence and God's end-time coming. Apocalypticism adopts poetic theological metaphors from classical imagery of the First Testament to encourage struggling and suffering people. The apocalyptic authors in general and Luke in particular were convinced in the presence of God and God's ultimate victory over evil; they believed that God cared about humanity and Earth's other members, that God would act to overcome the evil that inflicted Earth.

The image of ecological renewal that often accompanies this apocalyptic perspective has been interpreted as a destruction of Earth.[15] Such a perspective needs to be carefully nuanced. Rather, God's apocalyptic action to rescue all unjustly suffering (and this includes Earth and all its creatures) will result in the destruction of evil and the renewal of creation including humanity in ultimate divine communion. This appreciation is present in Luke's apocalyptic perspective evident in Jesus' temple teaching.

As we have observed, Earth images are to the fore in Jesus' teaching: a colt, Earth's 'way' that leads to Jerusalem, disciples' clothing and stones that mediate Jesus' movement towards the ancient city. Further, the whole cosmos and Earth's household are affected by the signs that prepare the heart of the disciples for God's definitive coming in the Human One (21.25-28); the fig tree is a reminder of the nearness of God's *basileia-ecotopia* (21.29-30); Olivet frames the whole section (19.29; 21.37), which is, in the last two verses (21.37-38), surrounded by notes of Jesus' temple teaching. This last image, of the ecological intertwining with the divine *rhēma* revealed in Jesus' teaching, sums up Luke's eco-theology that permeates these and its preceding chapters.

---

15. See Dyer, 'When is the End', pp. 44-56.

Earth's Voice

Then they brought [the colt] to Jesus; and after throwing their cloaks on the colt, they set Jesus on it. As he rode along, people kept spreading their cloaks on the road (Lk. 19.35-36).

Earth's Colt speaks:

> I am rural and free.
> I have been untied and released from servitude.
> I have not been domesticated
> nor been used to carry heavy burdens for commercial reasons.
> I am covered with disciples' garments.
> No one has ever sat on me before.
> Earth's child sits upon me.
> We are one.
> I am one of his disciples.
> I, too, like all Earth's creatures, will suffer and die.

Chapter 12

LUKE 22.1–24.53

THE SUFFERING, DEATH AND CELEBRATION OF EARTH'S CHILD

We move now to the most important story in the gospel and the one to which Luke has been directing us, the final movement and crescendo in the ecological symphony to which we have been attending. Some would suggest that this story of Jesus' passion and death, like the other three gospels, was the first story to take a set form and shape. The German scholar Martin Kähler made the same point in considering the constructive order of the written gospels and the gospel passion narratives from a thematic perspective. 'The Gospels,' he wrote, 'are passion narratives with extended introductions.'[1] Some interpreters have applied Kähler's comment only to Mark's gospel, but his comment is pertinent to all the gospels, including Luke's. This means that the gospel must be heard 'backwards', listening for how the melodic themes of the final symphonic movement appear earlier in the gospel. It would not surprise us to discover that this is so. The ecological insights from the twenty one chapters leading up to these final chapters find sometimes an echo, sometimes emphasis, but definitely a summary.

To assist us in hearing the ecological notes of the passion narrative, I return to two reflections offered earlier that coalesce in the passion. These concern the human body and clothing. In Luke's passion narrative these two images appear, with Jesus' body dominant. As noted earlier, the human body mirrors Earth; Earth mirrors the human body. Luke's passion narrative is also the story of the physical body of Earth's child, a christological insight that Luke offered in consideration of Jesus' birth. What happens to Jesus' physical body in the passion reflects what happens upon Earth and in the wider cosmos. As we shall see in the passion's final scene, as Jesus' body is laid in the tomb, Luke expressly returns us to this image. The parallel between the earthen manger for the swaddled new born baby and the rock-hewn tomb in which the shrouded body of Jesus is laid is unambiguous. Earth's child is connected to the same ecological metaphor at the end of

---

1. Martin Kähler, *The So-Called Historical Jesus and the Historic Biblical Christ* (Philadelphia, PA: Fortress Press, 1964), p. 80 n 11.

his ministry as in the beginning. This child is again wrapped in material from Earth, a powerful symbol that reinforces his identity and ecological connection.

I see these two ecological metaphors, the human body and clothing, as central to the story about to unfold. Attention to them is important otherwise their potential to impact on the auditor, ancient and modern, with ecological wisdom could be lost. The treatment of Jesus' body can become, for the gospel audience, a reflection of the treatment of Earth. For contemporary auditors, Luke's passion narrative becomes the site of ecological contemplation as we look through the body of Earth's child on to the body of Earth itself.

The Inner Play (22.1–24.53)

Luke reshapes the final chapters of the gospel in the light of Mark's passion narrative and the evangelist's intention to address the pastoral concerns of gospel auditors.[2] The overall consistency in the shape of the passion narrative across the four gospels further suggests that by the time each evangelist composed their respective story, the narrative had already taken on a set or standardized format, although individually crafted to address the scandal created by Jesus' execution through crucifixion.[3] This was the fruit of careful selective narrative memory, shaped by liturgical proclamation, the particular needs of their auditors, and the unique traditions received into each gospel household.

There are four parts to the inner play of the gospel's final symphonic movement.

- *Part One* (22.1-53) reminds the auditor of the gospel's central christological truths which become the touchstone for listening to the remaining part of the narrative. It also reveals the strengths and flaws evident in Jesus' disciples. Jesus' body is central; his meal, the final one before his death, with bread and wine, is rich with ecological imagery.
- *Part Two* (22.54–23.25) focuses on the trials of Peter (22.54-62) and Jesus. He is interrogated first by the religious leaders (22.66-71), then Pilate (23.1-7), Herod (23.8-12) and finally by Pilate again

---

2. For a more complete study of Luke's redactional uniqueness independent of Mark, see Marion L. Soards, *The Passion According to Luke: The Special Material of Luke 22* (Sheffield: Sheffield Academic Press, 1987).

3. Evidence of this pre-gospel formulation of the passion narrative is evident in Paul's 1 Thess. 4.15; 1 Cor. 7.10-11; 11.23-25; 15.3-5; Phil. 2.8; 3.10; Gal 2.20; 3.1; 2 Cor. 3.14; Rom 4.25; 5.8-10; 6.3. See also Fitzmyer, *Luke X–XXIV*, pp. 1360-68.

(23.13-25). Throughout, Luke emphasizes Jesus' innocence and the physical treatment of his body which is central to the unfolding drama. The ecological symbol of clothing also surfaces here. Herod finally dresses Jesus; this clothing remains on Jesus to his death in *Part Three*.

- *Part Three* (23.26-56) narrates Jesus' crucifixion, death and burial. As we shall see, Jesus dies clothed, offering forgiveness and an ecologically rich banquet to a repentant criminal and committing his spirit into God's hands. This is the moment of God's creative spirit evident from the dawn of creation now returning to the source of creation.
- *Part Four* (24.1-53) completes the passion story and prepares the auditor for Luke's second volume, the Acts of the Apostles. The resurrection narrative and the events of Easter day which follow are filled with suspense and replete with ecological imagery. The characters in each of the scenes go from perplexity and incomprehension to clarity and a freedom to move forward. The gospel's final scene (24.50-53) tells of Jesus' return to God. Earth's child goes to the heavens to complete theologically the ecological cycle begun at birth. As Earth communes with heaven in the person of Jesus, he blesses his assembled household of disciples; they return with joy to Jerusalem and the temple, Earth's navel. This last note leaves the auditor with a sense of optimism about the future and ready to take up Acts.

Part One (22.1-53)—Ecological Deliverance

In *Part One*, Luke summarizes in the introductory verses all the elements of treachery that are present (22.1-6). This allows the evangelist to focus on the preparations for the Passover (22.7-13), the meal itself (22.14-22) and the teaching that accompanies it (22.24-39). Characteristically for Luke, what is about to unfold is instructional for the disciples and Luke's audience. Jesus, the exemplary teacher and revealer of God's creative and healing *rhēma*, will illustrate in word and deed what is essential for the auditor to appreciate in the passion.

Luke's particular focus reveals the essential truths about God, Jesus, discipleship and creation; but it will also highlight the kind of evil, including the potential for ecological evil, that confronts auditors and how they are to respond. What is about to unfold is the work of Satan who now explicitly re-enters into the drama through the character of one of Jesus' inner circle, Judas (22.3). The passion and what happens to Jesus are the work of Satan. This figure featured prominently in the early part of Jesus' public ministry and the presence continued throughout the gospel as Jesus confronted the various expressions of suffering and demonic possession.

The gospel's emphasis on the presence of Satan is also a reminder of the cosmic and ecological backdrop against which the passion symphony is performed.[4] The suffering of Jesus and, by implication and association, Earth, is unambiguously an act of diabolical evil. It is not an act perpetrated by a vindictive or jealous God seeking out the innocent one to suffer for the good of others or the salvation of the world. Jesus' God rather delights in creation and human beings and seeks to protect, heal and release them. The trial scenes in *Part Two* will emphasize that Luke's suffering Jesus is unequivocally innocent and unjustly treated, and that violence done to him is unwarranted.[5]

The Passover Meal (22.7-38)
Luke contextualizes the beginning of the passion story within the setting of the Passover, one of three pilgrimage feasts on which faithful Israelites came to Jerusalem to celebrate the temple. It is also a feast rich with ecological allusions. Passover was originally a nomadic feast (at which the first lamb was killed) and then agricultural (springtime gathering of wheat represented in unleavened bread). These two celebrations from different time periods in Israel's history combined in the feast of Passover to celebrate God's liberation of the Israelites from slavery. It was a commemoration of Exodus. Through Earth's fruits, wheat and a lamb, the people gathered to celebrate their liberating creator God. Jesus, too, gathers around its fruits with his disciples.

> The day of Unleavened Bread came on which the Passover lamb *had* to be sacrificed (22.7).

The combination of the bread with the lamb provides the means for this 'remembrance' (a theologically rich word that we shall explore shortly) of God's deliverance of Israel. It now happens on the day the Passover lamb *had* to be sacrificed. This 'had' is the divine *dei* noted earlier with regard to Zacchaeus (19.5). What is about to take place is God's definitive act of deliverance through bread and lamb. For Luke and gospel auditors the bread and the lamb, Earth's gifts, become identified with Jesus. His death is part of the divine plan for ecological deliverance.

---

4. Soards, *Passion*, p. 57.
5. The trials function as an *apologia pro evangelio*, to give assurance to the gospel audience about what they have been instructed in the light of 1.4. The trials 'provide the means by which important tenets of Christian faith are put "on trial" before the reader, with the intended result of the gospel's confirmation', Alexandru Neagoe, *The Trial of the Gospel: An Apologetic Reading of Luke's Trial Narratives* (Cambridge: Cambridge University Press, 2002), p. 22.

Jesus sends Peter and John to make preparations for the Passover that he is to share with his disciples (22.7-13). One of the questions that they will put to the householder where the meal will be celebrated is

> 'Where is the guest room (*kataluma*) where I shall eat the Passover with my disciples?' (22.11).

The reference to *kataluma* recalls Jesus' birth story and the kinship location of his birth which warranted that he was *not* to be born in a *kataluma* where strangers looked for lodgings (2.7). At his birth, solidarity and kinship were present and a *kataluma* unnecessary. By contrast, as we arrive at the passion, hostility and opposition are palpable. For this reason he now assembles with his disciples in a *kataluma*; the place of assembly in a time of estrangement and rejection.

In this setting Jesus gathers for a meal with the 'apostles', but not just with them exclusively. It includes all Jesus' disciples, some of whom have already gone ahead to prepare the room and the necessities for the Passover celebration. The title which Luke gives to the 'apostles' who gather emphasizes their apostolic-'sent' status with Jesus. This underscores the missionary context and recalls the seventy (-two) sent on mission in 22.35. The presence of these 'apostles', a large number indeed, perhaps reflects the situation of Luke's auditors. This now becomes explicit as the story unfolds around this last meal between Jesus and his disciples before death.

Luke reworks Mark's supper scene. In a chiasmic structure (Figure 33), the evangelist constructs as the outer frame (**A–A¹**) two declarations of Jesus; one concerns his desire to eat the Passover with his disciples (**A**— 22.15-16); the other (**A¹**—22.21-23) reveals his omniscience about his betrayal. This precipitates a faction fight among the disciples that results in his teaching about authentic greatness and leadership (22.24-30). The **A**–**A¹** declarations frame two cup actions (**B**—22.17-18; **B¹**—22.20) which in turn surround his actions and words over bread (**C**). Bread is literally and theologically central to the meal. This is reminiscent of all the other bread meals which Jesus has shared throughout the gospel. This, like those meals,

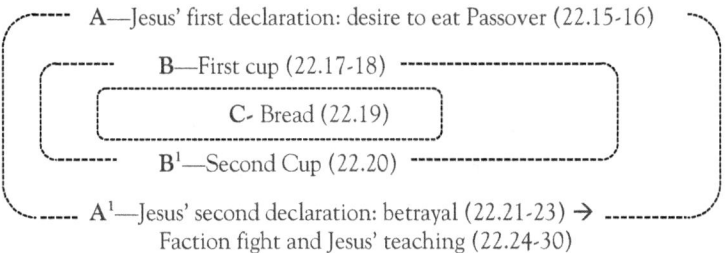

Figure 33. *The chiasmic structure of Lk. 22.15-30.*

is a celebration of God's delight in Earth's members and the divine desire to include all in communion.

There is one defining difference between this final meal and all those that have gone before. Here, Jesus is *identified* with what is eaten. He *becomes* the 'bread' and, by this identity, becomes one with Earth from which its seed is taken to make the bread. As Jesus is celebrated as Earth's child in the birth narrative, this identity is now reconfirmed in the passion narrative. *He* is the bread formed from Earth's seeds. Jesus' communion and solidarity with Earth could not be clearer. What happens to him, reflects Earth; Earth's suffering is taken up into his body.

In this final meal scene before death and gathered around bread from Earth's seeds, Jesus eats with his disciples,

> and taking bread and giving thanks he broke and gave to them saying, 'This is my body given for you. Do this in my memory (*anamnēsis*)' (22.19).

Jesus' meal is rich in Earth symbolism. He acts and speaks over bread; he makes the bread symbolically and metaphorically identical with his physical body, and his body with Earth. This identity in turn evokes cosmic and universal connections with which bread and his body are linked. Here is an Earth-centred high point in the gospel, the gospel's ecological crescendo in Luke's narrative symphony. What happens to Jesus' body identified with the bread will mirror Earth.

Jesus' action with the bread emphasizes its 'breaking' and 'giving'. These are the principal verbs anticipated by the participial verbs 'taking bread' and 'giving thanks'. The whole act is eucharistic, and the bread's identification with Jesus' body signifies the meal's connection with the passion that follows. Jesus' body will be broken and given, just as this eucharistic bread is shared with the disciples. As the bread is broken and given, like Jesus' body, so, too, is Earth. Its elements are now explicitly in communion with him as a result of his *rhēma* over bread. Their communion with Jesus and his disciples in this meal recalls other moments in his table ministry when he revealed God's delightful desire to commune with creation and humanity. The disciples, too, are now invited to participate in a similar ministry. They are invited through communion with Jesus' body to identify with Earth. Rather than consuming Earth's fruits, they are symbolically invited to authentic ecological *koinonia* ('communion').

The Passover meal further anticipates the disciples' union with Jesus in his passion. As Jesus will be broken and abused, the same will happen to them. As the bread is given, 'given for you', and the bread is identified with Jesus' body, then the disciples' participation in the meal and their solidarity with the suffering Jesus will mean that they, too, will be given for others. They too become one, like Jesus, with Earth. Rather than predicating what disciples must do, Jesus' teaching anticipates what Luke's auditors and disciples throughout history will experience.⁶ They will suffer on behalf of others, human and non-human, in ecological solidarity. What happens to them will affect Earth; what affects Earth will touch them.

Jesus completes his words over the bread with the injunction to Luke's auditors to,

> 'do this in my memory (*anamnēsis*)' (22.19c).

Anamnēsis is not our simple memory recall. It is the power that enables the significance of the past to be commemorated, made present and effective.⁷ The eucharistic *anamnēsis* brings the total ministry of Jesus into present time whenever the community of disciples gathers to 'do' what Jesus did on the night before he died. Such *anamnēsis* effectively enables the experience of his table ministry, his deeds of Earth healing and reconciliation to continue through the disciples. This counterbalances and contrasts Jesus' announcement of the act of betrayal and the disciples' faction-fight that now breaks out at this final poignant, deeply ecological meal (22.21-27).

Before leaving with his disciples to go to the Mount of Olivet, Jesus reassures Peter that his eventual denial will bring him to conversion, reconciliation and strengthened leadership. Jesus then offers a last word of advice in anticipation of the cosmic struggle that is about to occur. The disciples must be ready, as though armed for conflict: 'Let the one who has no sword sell their cloak and purchase one' (22.36b).⁸ That this is not intended literally is clear from Jesus' earlier teaching on non-retaliation in the Sermon on the Plain and now in Jesus' response to the disciples' quick reaction to this advice:

> They said, 'Lord, look here are two swords!' He said to them, 'It is enough!' (22.38).

Commitment to non-violence in the face of evil and before his future aggressors characterizes Luke's Jesus. This same attitude which has ecological and environmental implications must also characterize his disciples. They must not act with aggression or violence to any Earth member; rather they are reminded to act peacefully and with sustainability. Rather than

---

6. Soards sees Luke's passion story, especially 22.1-38, as a 'mini-course for the reader in christology, eschatology, and ecclesiology' (*Passion*, p. 57).

7. '"[T]o remember" consists of more than cognitive evocation. "To remember" includes as well the nuance of understanding or insight, and is the threshold of response apropos what is recalled' (Green, *Luke*, p. 838). See also, Maria-Luisa Rigato, '"Remember"... Then They Remembered": Luke 24.6-8', in *A Feminist Companion to Luke* (ed. Amy-Jill Levine, with Marianne Blickenstaff; London: Sheffield Academic Press, 2002), pp. 269-80.

8. Donald Senior, *The Passion of Jesus in the Gospel of Luke* (Wilmington, DE: Michael Glazier, 1989), pp. 81-82.

retaliation, Jesus seeks a different path. This will become more obvious in the scene that follows concerned with discipleship and the importance of prayer within an environmentally rich and symbolic setting (22.39-46).

Agony and Earth's Companionship (22.39-53)
Jesus goes with his disciples to the Mount of Olivet to pray, 'as was his custom' (22.39b). He continues in communion with Earth. Like the water in 5.2, Olivet becomes a place of safety and divine solidarity. The Mount is already a topographically familiar and significant setting. As we noted in the previous chapter, Mount Olivet is metaphorically associated with discipleship with its ecological intertwining with Jesus' Jerusalem teaching summarized in 21.37-38. In this scene, the Mount is a further actor and participant in Jesus' passion. On to it, Jesus kneels in a gesture of prayer:

> Then he withdrew from them about a stone's throw, knelt down, and prayed (22.41).

The Earth becomes the explicit setting and companion with Jesus in his communion with God as his knees touch its soil and it bears him. Jesus' prayer posture allows Earth to be the focus of prayer, of contemplation, reverence and revelation.

Luke's prayer scene does not carry the depth of physical distress evident in Mk's equivalent scene (Mk 14.32-42). If we are able to take 22.43-44 as original, Jesus is in agony (*agōnía*), the anticipatory physical disposition of the athlete before the contest, and prays with greater fervor.[9] This prayerful attitude models how the disciples (and auditors) are to be in the midst of struggle and with those who would harm them or Earth. The sleep that finally overtakes them is not from heavy, weary eyes (as in Mk 14.40), but from exhausted anguish that overwhelms them in their solidarity with Jesus. Later disciples will come to know the physical exhaustion that results from care of Earth and all members of its household. Such exhaustion comes from looking after the planet.

The disciples sleep, says Luke, 'from grief' (22.45c) and utter weakness.[10] The whole scene suggests that what will happen to Jesus is anticipated; it does not come as a surprise. His communion with God and solidarity

---

9. On *agōnía* see Jerome H. Neyrey, 'The Absence of Jesus' Emotions—the Lucan Redaction of Lk 22:39-46', *Biblica* 61 (1980), pp. 153-71; Senior, *Passion in Luke*, pp. 87-88. On the inclusion of vv. 43-44 in Luke's gospel, see Fitzmyer, *Luke X–XXIV*, pp. 1443-44; Jerome H. Neyrey, *The Passion according to Luke: A Redactional Study of Luke's Soteriology* (New York: Paulist Press, 1985), pp. 55-57; Senior, *Passion in Luke*, p. 87.

10. See the discussion on 'grief' as a Hellenistic identification of one of the four passions, a sign of weakness, guilt and fear in the face of death, in Senior, *Passion in Luke*, p. 86.

with creation as Earth's child is ensured through this prayer event in the Earth setting of the Mount of Olivet. God's presence, the heavenly angel of 22.43, strengths him to respond actively to what will happen.[11] The angel's presence further underscores the nexus through Jesus' being between heaven and Earth. The angelic presence also means that rather than being a passive victim of suffering, he will be able to engage it creatively, and convert it into a force that will have the power of revealing a surprising God who invites aggressors to conversion, ecological solidarity and divine openness.

Everything that happens on Olivet, Jesus' prayer, the disciples' witness to it, and now Jesus' arrest, are all linked. At the exact moment as Jesus is still speaking (22.47) his captors arrive with Judas leading them. The teaching he offers, especially his encouragement to pray as the antidote to eschatological testing and psychic disturbance, influences his attitude to the one who is about to betray him and those who have come to arrest him. Jesus' communion with God enables him to respond assertively with Judas; he seizes the initiative and disarms Judas's act of betrayal (22.48).

What occurs next seems to belie the disciples' communion with Jesus' invitation to be in solidarity with Earth and agents of ecological freedom. They, or at least one of them, seem to have forgotten his teaching in the Sermon on the Plain about enemy love and non-violent retaliation. In fact the violent act of one of the disciples is more serious than the aggressor's hostility imagined in the Sermon. There Jesus spoke of those who strike a disciple's cheek (6.29); here a sword-wielding disciple severs the right ear of a high priest's servant (22.50). The disciple's action has upped the ante. The right side, the culturally recognized side of honour, has been removed and at a symbolic cultural level, the capacity of the religious elite to hear what Jesus is teaching is seriously compromised by the retaliatory action of the disciple. One of the prime discipleship qualities already identified, that of an ecologically contemplative spirit, also seems doomed in this violent action. If this is how a disciple acts towards one from the *human* household, how will they be towards other members of *Earth's* household? Violence has ecological consequences; Earth suffers as a result.

For Luke, there is another way to deal with violence other than with greater hostility. Jesus' response of a healing touch to one aligned against him suggests otherwise. Compassion and love will disarm violence. Healing acts are really what an aggressive and violent society needs; Earth's care, that is, care for Earth and care from Earth, will change the way people interact.

---

11. This presumes that 22.43-44 are part of the original Lukan material. See the discussion of the text's authorship in Raymond E. Brown, *The Death of the Messiah: From Gethsemane to the Grave: A Commentary on the Passion Narratives in the Four Gospels. Volume 1* (Garden City, NY: Doubleday, 1994), pp. 180-86.

Part One ends with Jesus addressing his assailants. Their present aggression is inconsistent with their attitude to him when he was teaching in the temple. But, recognizing that a larger plan is in force, he declares, 'but this is your hour and the power of darkness' (22.53). Jesus now permits the rest of the passion to unfold.

Part Two: The Trials (22.54–23.26)—*The Assault on God's Creation*

Part Two begins with Jesus' arrest and transfer to the house of the High Priest (22.54—**A**) with Peter following (Figure 34). In this prestigious setting two events take place: Peter's trial (22.55-62—**B**) and the assault on Jesus' body (22.63-65—**C**), with his maltreatment acting as a hinge between the religious interrogations of Peter and Jesus (22.66-71—**B¹**). A similar pattern emerges in Jesus' civil trials with Herod's physical ill-treatment of Jesus (27.6–12—**C¹**) acting as an axis between two scenes of Pilate's interrogation of Jesus (27.1-5—**B²**; 27.13-25—**B³**). *Part Two* concludes with the innocent but maltreated Jesus being led away for crucifixion (23.26—**A¹**). The literary and thematic pattern below illustrates Luke's creative reshaping of Mark's trial scenes. The two important ecological features named in this chapter's introduction, the body and clothing, coalesce. The physical and verbal treatment of Jesus and his body and his clothing are clearly central. These will be our focus in what follows.

The first assault on Jesus' body occurs between two contrasting trials: one that reveals the failed and tragic figure of Peter who denies fidelity to Jesus and his disciples (22.55-62); the other (22.66-71) that reveals Jesus' fidelity to God and his identity as God's child ('Son'). Luke describes what happens to Jesus' body:

> Now the males (*andres*) who were holding him mocked him, beating and blind-folding him. They asked 'Prophesy! Who is it that struck you!' And many other things the abusers spoke against him (22.63-65).

The evangelist has recast Mark's equivalent scene (Mk 14.65). into a gender-specific act of physical and *verbal* aggression performed by 'males' (*andres*).[12]

Significantly, though, the physical assault on Jesus is more restrained in comparison to Mk. Jesus is not spat upon and doesn't receive blows from Mk's guards. All this is illustrative of a distinguishing feature in Luke's

---

12. On the function of 'male' in Luke see D'Angelo, 'The ANHP Question', pp. 44-69. Her discussion of *anēr* in Luke may suggest that in this scene their explicit presence is a sign of imperial and manly authority. Brown (*Death 1*, p. 582) says of this scene, 'for Luke the action of the men who hold Jesus in the [courtyard] of the house of the high priest fulfils at least part of the predicted abuse: 'It is *here* that Jesus is "mocked" and by equivalence "arrogantly mistreated"'.

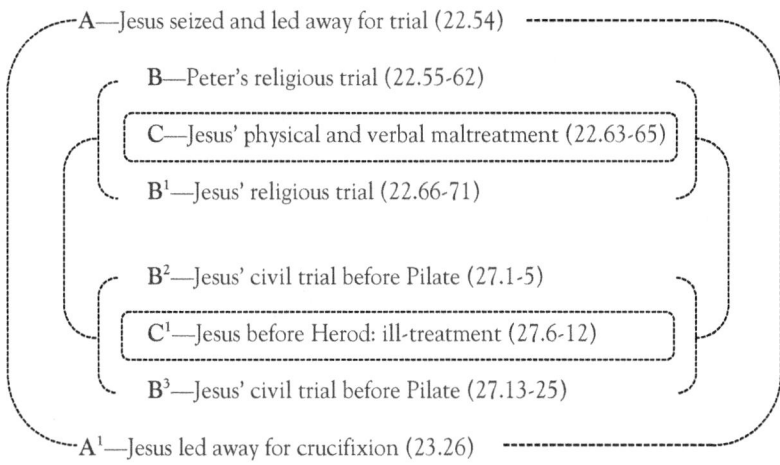

Figure 34. *The trials of Jesus (Lk. 22.54–23.26)*.

presentation of the aggression enacted towards Jesus. The evangelist's restraint reflects the gospel's more dignified portrait of Jesus as unworthy of such maltreatment; his dignity and honour attract less aggressive behaviour. The restraint also would echo Luke's eco-theology; Earth, too, is dignified and deserves to be preserved from maltreatment. Luke's christological portrait also allows Jesus to be more interventionist with his aggressors than in Mark's gospel, model enemy love, invite all to encounter and be open to God's *basileia-ecotopia*, and offer the possibility of those who maltreat the human and Earth body to transformation and conversion.

The presence of violent 'males' in this scene and their implied presence as 'guards' in the second scene of Jesus' bodily maltreatment starkly contrasts with the female presence to his body in the birth narrative and in the final chapter. The gestational and maternal images that surround his birth and carry him into public ministry confirm him as Earth's child to act in solidarity with its household for the healing of all. How Jesus, still Earth's child, will enact this healing remains to be seen.

Though the evangelist softens Jesus' physical treatment, verbal aggression towards him is another matter. Speech rather than action is more violent. He is called 'prophet' and the verbal tirade implied in 22.65c ('and many other things the abusers spoke against him') seeks to counteract the power of Jesus' word as teacher revealed throughout the gospel. This is an attempt to discredit God's *rhēma*. Paradoxically, the verbal invective directed against Jesus only serves to reinforce his teaching authority. What is said and done to him in this first passion assault ironically acknowledge his prophetic and teaching role and exalted status as God's representative and protector and healer of Earth violated by Satan's evil doers.[13]

The second assault scene (23.10-11) occurs after Jesus' interrogation from the religious authorities that highlight his Messianic claims (22.66-71), and then an initial questioning from Pilate that focuses on his identity as King (23.1-6). In these first two trials the main christological titles are highlighted. They conclude with Pilate's first declaration of Jesus' innocence (23.4). He is then brought before Herod (23.7-9) whose unsatisfactory interrogation culminates in Jesus' verbal and physical maltreatment. This assault on the physical body of Jesus is also symbolically an assault on Earth's body by aggressors with a presumed authority to do what they like.

> The chief priests and scribes stood vehemently accusing (*katēgoreō*) him. Herod with his guards treated him with contempt (*exoutheneō*), ridiculed him (*empaizō*), dressing him in shining apparel sent him to Pilate. Herod and Pilate became friends with one another on that day, for before this day they had been at enmity with each other (23.10-12).

Whatever the historical credibility of this scene, from a theological perspective it finally brings together two royal figures in a meeting anticipated from the gospel's opening chapters. There, Jesus' royal birth and early ministry as Earth's child were explicitly located within an imperial time frame (2.1; 3.1) during the reign of the Emperor Tiberius. Now, at the end of the gospel, Jesus meets Tiberius's representative, Herod.

Two points of Lukan vocabulary are noteworthy. These concern the use of *katēgoreō* ('accuse'), *exoutheneō* ('treat with contempt') and *empaizō* ('ridicule'), and are most telling of the attitude and reception that Jesus receives.

- The religious leaders 'accuse' (*katēgoreō*) Jesus in a verbal assault frequently in Luke–Acts.[14] The popularity of *katēgoreō* in the Lukan corpus suggests that verbal assault from authorities and their accompanying accusations are a common experience amongst gospel auditors and within Earth's household. The violence of the language directed to Jesus ('vehemently') perhaps also echoes the experience of Luke's audience.
- The religious leaders' verbal abuse of Jesus is accompanied by physical maltreatment from Herod and his military entourage. They 'treat him with contempt' (*exoutheneō*) and 'ridicule' (*empaizō*) him,

---

13. On Luke's christological tendency to elevate Jesus' status, see Soards, *Passion*, pp. 124-25.

14. Forms of the verb *katēgoreō* occur most often in Luke–Acts, in Lk. 6.7; 23.2, 14; Acts 22.30; 23.2, 14; 24.2, 8, 13, 19; 25.2, 11, 16. Nouns ('accuser', 'accusers') occur only in Acts 23.30, 35; 25.16, 18.

in images reminiscent of Isaiah's suffering servant (Is. 53.7). The auditor is left without any doubt about Herod's attitude towards Jesus, publicly shamed, assaulted and treated as a plaything. What is translated above as 'treat with contempt' can also mean 'to treat as nothing'. Abusive vocabulary saturates a scene in which Herod seeks to rob Jesus of his identity.

For the contemporary auditor, as Jesus is treated, so too is Earth. When this scene and its vocabulary is reflected upon from an ecological perspective and in light of the connection between Jesus' physical body and Earth's body, how Jesus is treated is mirrored in the way Earth is regarded by some: 'treated with contempt' and 'ridiculed'. The gospel auditor, ancient and modern, would not have to look far to see how Earth's household has also been 'treated as nothing'. Abuse of Earth, like Jesus, is a reality.

The obvious verbal and physical hostility directed to Jesus unique to Luke is offset by two further details. These parallel the evangelist's tendency, revealed in the first assault scene, to preserve Jesus' honour and dignity. Here Herod, while portrayed as wanting to annihilate Jesus' identity, ironically demonstrates the opposite. He reveals Jesus' true regal and exalted status by dressing him in a 'shining' elegant robe, a garment of innocence, sanctity, honour and heavenly dignity.[15] The paradox behind Herod's regal act serves to remind the auditor of the true status of Earth's child and, indirectly and by association, the divine regard for Earth that, like Jesus, is assaulted and abused.

We noted earlier the eco-theological and symbolic importance of clothing as the social signifier of personal identity, status and power. Reference to clothing and Jesus' dress has been in the major movements of the gospel. The elegant robe in which Jesus is now attired is a theological statement of his identity, status and power. While on one level he is despised and ill-treated, at a deeper level, whatever religious or civil authorities do to him, they are unable to suppress his true identity. He is and remains for Luke's auditors, especially those who suffer similarly, including Earth, God's regal figure, innocent and blessed. Jesus' identity and those with whom he is in solidarity are forever retained and affirmed. Nothing or no one can expunge this from divine memory.

A second detail results from Jesus' treatment and reinforces Luke's earlier teaching from the Sermon on the Plain, now graphically demonstrated in

---

15. See Senior's discussion of Jesus' garb that 'Luke considers it a garment of beauty and heavenly dignity' similar to the apparel of Peter's angelic messenger in Acts 10.30 (*Passion in Luke*, p. 115). Brown (*Death*, I, p. 774) notes Luke's word for garment here (*esthēs*) is one of only seven occurrences in the NT (four in Luke–Acts), but never in another gospel. It is referred to as 'shining.' Two of Luke's references to *esthēs* relate to angelic clothing.

the trial. The abused one has power to bring about good, even reconciliation. Some have interpreted the friendship between Herod and Pilate that results from Herod's treatment of Jesus as symbolic of the mounting unholy alliance of evil conspiring against him.[16] From the point of view of the Sermon, Jesus' presence converts abuse and enmity into friendship. The need for such conversion is obvious even with his disciples who fight amongst themselves in Jesus' final meal with them. Herod and Pilate's reconciliation illustrates that the malevolent forces arraigned against Jesus in this time of trial and rejection are gradually being thwarted and subverted.[17] There will always be hope, no matter how tragic events seem or how brutalized Earth. God's redemptive power to convert and heal remains.

This changed disposition towards Jesus and the gradual breakthrough of the potential for goodness in a situation of darkness are confirmed in the next scene, a second trial before Pilate (23.13-25) who judges Jesus as clearly innocent. This is the definitive adjudication on Jesus and those with whom he is in solidarity. Even though he threatens to treat Jesus contemptuously by having him chastised (23.16, 22) Pilate never follows through on his promise, instead thrice declaring him blameless (23.4, 14, 22). Though he desires to release him (23.20) Pilate finally cowers to the popular cry for Jesus' crucifixion. He is led away to the place of 'The Skull' for crucifixion still wearing the brilliant apparel placed upon him by Herod. To the sympathetic auditor, Jesus' identity is explicit in the translucent garment that he wears. *Part Three* of Luke's passion movement now begins.

Part Three: Crucifixion and Death (23.27-31)—God's definitive Rhēma

While journeying to the place of execution, Simon from the Roman colony of Cyrene, capital of Cyrenaica (Libya) in North Africa and a major centre of Judaism, is forced to carry Jesus' wooden crossbeam, the instrument of execution.[18] These two images, of a stranger from a foreign urban centre with a crossbeam of wood, combine in an ecologically loaded scene. Jesus will die attached to Earth, symbolized by the wooden crossbeam borne for him by a stranger who, literally, follows 'behind Jesus' (21.26d) and becomes a potential disciple. Earth will be Jesus' companion, literally to the end.

A large multitude also follows him (23.27a). This includes women 'mourning and weeping' for him (23.27b). Some commentators have interpreted this vignette and Jesus' words as anticipatory divine judgment

---

16. See for example, Senior, *Passion in Luke*, p. 115.

17. Brown, *Death* I, p. 778, on the reconciliation Jesus effects between Pilate and Herod.

18. On Cyrenaica, see Josephus, *Against Apion* 2.4-5 §§41-54; *Jewish Antiquities* 14.7.2 §114; 1 Macc. 15.23; 2 Macc. 2.23.

on those who have not understood him or his mission and have rejected him. In this interpretation, gleaned from reflection on Hos. 10.8, barrenness is preferred to the imminent disaster which will come upon those who reject God's prophet.[19]

However, the solidarity of the women with the rejected and suffering Jesus is obvious. Their 'mourning and weeping' reflect their communion with him as he goes to death.[20] Jesus turns and speaks to them in words intended for Luke's auditors. His words affirm their goodness and beauty and Earth's relationship to them. He laments for all who will suffer infertility, the great social disaster first identified in the gospel's opening scene with Zechariah (1.5-7). Sterility instead will become a blessing as God intervenes and creation acts in solidarity especially with those who are impoverished, rejected and barren:

> [28b] Daughters of Jerusalem, do not weep for me, but weep for yourselves and for your children. [29] Because, behold the days are coming when they will say, 'Blessed are the sterile, and the wombs that never bore and the breasts which never nourished'. [30] Then they will begin to say to the mountains, 'Fall on us!'; and to the hills, 'Cover us!' [31] For if they do this when the wood is green, what will happen when it is dry? (23.28b-31).

Jesus' lament can be heard environmentally. It is a lament for all Earth's creatures who suffer infertility. Those who suffer this tragedy will seek comfort and protection from Earth, from mountains and hills (23.30) with whom they are in communion. This is not an anthropocentric picture that Jesus presents. Earth's child laments what will happen on Earth:

> If they do this when the wood is green what will happen when it is dry? (23.31).

If this is how Jesus is treated, Earth's green wood, and literally accompanied by the cross beam from Earth's green wood, what will happen to its dry wood? (23.31). At the heart of this enigmatic verse is Jesus' anticipatory prophetic warning about those who maltreat all Earth's members in every moment of history.

When Jesus is finally brought to the place of execution, Luke reshapes Mark's scene of desolation, misunderstanding and rejection into one of hope, reconciliation and forgiveness. Ecological possibility and fruitfulness

---

19. Green, *Luke*, p. 816; Fitzmyer, *Luke X–XXIV*, pp. 1495-96. However, Johnson says, 'Although Jesus delivers his prophecy to them, it is clear that they are not to be seen as perpetrators but as victims of violence…the violence done to him the messenger of peace, will be visited on those who do this violence, and in such terrible fashion that even the innocent will suffer as a result' (*Luke*, pp. 374-75).

20. Turid Karlsen Seim, 'The Virgin Mother: Mary and Ascetic Discipleship in Luke', in *A Feminist Companion to Luke* (ed. Levine, Amy-Jill and Marianne Blickenstaff; London: Sheffield Academic Press, 2002), pp. 89-105 (91-92).

will be revealed in what apparently seems to be a scene of ultimate tragedy and environmental destruction. As in the trial scenes earlier, Luke portrays Jesus with his honour and dignity more clearly revealed. It is a serene, dignified, reconciling Jesus who dies—almost gracefully—uttering a prayer of commitment to his God. Luke's dying Jesus transparently witnesses to God's irrepressible graciousness and intimacy.

In words and actions that reinforce the evangelist's teaching on enemy love from the Sermon on the Plain, Jesus calls on God to forgive his executioners,

> Father, forgive them; for they do not know what they are doing (23.34).

This is a profound moment in the passion narrative, indeed in the whole of Luke's gospel. It underscores the Sermon teaching about enemy love gracefully demonstrated in the dying Jesus; it is the result of prayer from one totally committed to God throughout his ministry, and now at the apex of that ministry. Luke's scene also buttresses the Sermon's teaching by revealing Jesus' God as the ultimate source of forgiveness. His words reveal God's gesture towards all those who harm Earth.

God's power to break into the scene is witnessed further in the figure of one who has been maltreated (23.39-43). Luke's dying Jesus represents God's ultimate power undermining all socially constructed boundaries that define or control human existence and Earth's meaning. This is the God who 'feels' for human beings and their Earth. God can break into a situation that seems utterly hopeless. This is especially pertinent given the context of Jesus' death, surrounded by a religious leadership that 'scoffs' at him (23.35), soldiers who 'mock' him (23.36) and a criminal who rails against him (23.39)—all of them in their own way cajole him with the mantra to save himself.

There is one final image in Luke's reshaping of the Markan source that confirms the above insights. This is the image of the dying Jesus, transfixed to Earth through a wooden crossbeam and still clothed in the garment of dignity and beauty placed on him by Herod. This garment is not removed, and Luke's alteration of Mark's scene is subtle but clear in the description of those who cast lots. A redactional comparison between the scene in Luke and Mark's equivalent scene makes this obvious (Figure 35).

In Mark, crucifixion presumes Jesus' nudity—the act of crucifixion occurs at the same time as the division of his garments which the executioners claim by lot. In Luke, the focus is on those who cast lots. The actual division of Jesus' clothing (and hence his presumed nudity) is inconsequential to the description of the intention of the lot-casters.[21] Thus, Jesus dies in Luke's

---

21. The Greek *diamarizō* which is translated here as 'to divide' refers to those who do the lot casting. The sense of the participial form of the verb which refers to the agents of the lot casting concerns their intent to divide. It does not refer to the actual division of Jesus' clothing.

gospel still dressed in the garment placed upon him by Herod and his guards. Luke preserves Jesus' dignity as symbolized in this regal earthly clothing. He will die shrouded as Earth's child. This detail, important but subtle, is unnoticed in anthropocentric commentaries which tend to hear Luke's story in terms of Mark and rob the narrative of one essential eco-christological detail: Jesus is accompanied by Earth throughout the passion, from his kneeling on the Mount, being accompanied to his place of death by Earth's wood and becoming transfixed to it; now, clothed in Earth's linen. All these images reinforce a profound eco-christological truth that has echoed as a symphonic theme throughout the gospel—Jesus is from Earth, with it, heals it, feeds it, accompanies it and dies with it attached to him.

Mk 15.22-25	Lk. 23.33-34
And they brought him to the place of Golgotha which means place of a skull, and they offered him wine mixed with myrrh, he did not take it.	And when they came to the place which is called 'Skull'
And they crucified him	There they crucified him, and the criminals, one on his right and one on his left. And Jesus said, 'Father forgive them for they do not know what they are doing'.
and, dividing his clothes, they cast lots for them to decide what each should take.	They cast lots to divide (*diamarízō*) his garments.

Figure 35. *Redactional comparison of Mk 15.22-25 and Lk. 23.33-34.*

As the moment of death nears, a final act of liberation completes Jesus' ministry declaration from the Nazareth synagogue. One of his dying companions requests,

> Jesus, remember (*mimnēskomai*) me when you come into your *basileia* (23.43).

The *basileia* of God is also the *basileia* of Jesus. God's *basileia* is also *ecotopia*, the ecologically rich symbol of God's communion with creation and humanity that has been so dominant throughout Luke's gospel. It is now acknowledged and celebrated as present in the dying Jesus. The criminal requests that Jesus 'remember' (*mimnēskomai*) him. The Greek root for the verb 'to remember' is the same for 'memory' (*anamnēsis*), defined earlier. The criminal is not simply asking Jesus to recall him to mind when he is with God after death, but to actually *re*-member him, reconnect him again to God from whom he has become distant. He is asking Jesus to bring him into God's presence.

Jesus' response ('Amen I say to you, today you will be with me in paradise', 23.43) is a promise of eternal communion. It reconfirms one of Luke's principal truths, that no one or nothing can be separated from God's loving care and desire for intimacy. The paradisiacal image that Jesus promises is represented by a feast after the manner of Isaiah's heavenly banquet (Isa. 25.6-8). This is Jesus' final act of meal hospitality in his public ministry. He promises a banquet that celebrates God's presence with Earth's choice foods and rich wines. This paradisiacal banquet is one in which the whole of creation shares and Earth is present. Earth's communion with heaven, celebrated earlier in the disciples' song of praise as Jesus rode into Jerusalem (19.38), is to be an experienced reality for Jesus' dying companion.

Luke's scene of Jesus' death is the climax of the gospel. As the moment approaches and Luke deliberately slows down the narrative with time references ('sixth hour', 'ninth hour', 23.44a.c) Earth, Jesus' companion, goes into mourning. The synchronicity between Earth's child and its household is palpable. Darkness pervades the universe including the cosmos and the heavenly sphere:

> And it was now the sixth hour and there was darkness over the whole Earth until the ninth hour, as the sun's light failed, the curtain of the temple was torn in two...(23.44-45).

In Greco-Roman literature, cosmic darkness was frequently associated with the death of great figures; here, it is the figure of God's beloved one.[22] Darkness is also a sign in apocalypticism of the last days before God's definitive coming.[23] The ecological darkness, Earth's mourning, prepares for the divine light which will exude on to it in Jesus' resurrection.

The final precursor before Jesus' death that Luke incorporates into the scene, reversing its placement from Mark (where it happens after Jesus' death), is the splitting of the temple's curtain. This action opens up the access of God's located presence, in the Holy of Holies.[24] This is the religious navel of God's people, the ultimate place of ecological celebration of God's creative presence revealed in the First Testament's story of creation and the Exodus tradition and symbolized in the temple's architecture. Jesus' death does not replace the temple, as though Luke was promoting an anti-Israelite supersessionist attitude by which Israel's religious practice is no longer valid and superseded by 'christianity'. Such a judgment stands in tension with the beginning of the gospel, Luke's appreciation for the First Testament and its creation metanarrative, and the gospel's last verse, as the followers of Jesus go to the temple 'continually' (24.53). The tearing of the temple's curtain is the tearing of cloth, a powerful environmental symbol of identity that has

---

22. Brown, *Death 2*, p. 1043; Pliny, *Natural History* 2.30.97 regarding the eclipse of the sun on the death of Julius Caesar.

23. Amos 8.9; Joel 2.30-31; Zeph. 1.15.

24. See Alan Cadwallader, '"And the Earth Shook" — Mortality and Ecological Diversity: Jesus' Death in Matthew's Gospel', in *Biodiversity and Ecology as Interdisciplinary Challenge* (ed. Mark Worthington and Denis Edwards; Adelaide: ATF, 2004), pp. 45-54 for an alternate view, based on Matthew's gospel.

appeared frequently in the gospel. The tearing signifies that a new identity is being created by God's action. Luke's Jesus becomes God's Holy of Holies, revealing compassion and communion with all in Earth's household, human and non-human. He is the meeting point and summary of divine, human and Earth communion.

We come now to the moment of Jesus' death. As he speaks he dies. His words are contemporaneous with his act. Here is the ultimate and summary moment of God's *rhēma* enacted definitively.

> Then crying with a loud voice, Jesus said, 'Father, into your hands I commit my spirit!' Saying this, he breathed his last (23.46).

Jesus returns his spirit, the creative and prophetic spirit of God, back into the hands of God with Ps. 31.6 on his lips. This is God's spirit that hovered over creation from the beginning, over Mary in the act of conception and giving birth, that was revealed in his Nazareth public declaration of God's liberating intention for all and everything oppressed, that encountered and defeated the devil and Satan in deeds of healing and exorcism, that found voice in his prophetic teaching and table ministry. His final words of death are about ultimate communion and witness to God's presence. The creative One releases his spirit into the arms of his Creator. It is a moment of ultimate ecological communion witnessed and affirmed by a centurion who declares Jesus 'righteous' (23.47), multitudes, who return to their homes repentant and 'beating their breasts' (23.48), and his companions including women who had been with him from Galilee and are now Luke's explicit eyewitnesses to the event (23.49). On their eyewitness Luke's whole gospel rests (1.2).

Part Three concludes with Joseph of Arimathea requesting Jesus' body from Pilate and, through his actions that emulate what happened to Jesus at birth, he reconfirms Jesus' birth identity, as Earth's child and one in communion with creation:

> This man, going to Pilate, requested the body of Jesus and taking it down wrapped it in a linen shroud and laid it in rock-hewn tomb where no one had ever laid (23.53).

Elements of Earth again surround Jesus, this time in death. These are symbolized by the rock-hewn tomb in which his linen-shrouded body is laid. The final figures at the tomb are the women (23.55-56). Luke has identified them as Jesus' consistent companions, disciples and witnesses during his public ministry (8.1), in his passion, death (23.49) and now in his burial. They

> saw his tomb and *how* his body was laid (23.55c).

They witness not only to his death and the place of his burial, to which they will return shortly, but also to '*how* his body was laid'. They witness to the tomb and his linen covered body, which, as we know from his birth, identified him through nature's material as one with creation, eternal and regal. What they see are Earth images that the auditor can now appreciate as ecologically powerful. The women finally retire for the Sabbath and prepare ointments (23.56b). All these images—the rock tomb, the linen and the Sabbath day of release—portend for the auditor that God's revelation about Jesus is not yet finished, and that Earth's companionship with Jesus continues.

Part Four: Easter Day (24.1-53)—The Act of God and Earth to Jesus

When we come to the final act of the passion symphony and the last for the gospel, the events of Easter Day (Lk. 24.1-53), the evangelist's story highlights a movement from tragedy and perplexity to resolution and mission.[25] This pattern is observed in three of the four scenes that compose the gospel's final chapter: the women's encounter with the two men in the tomb (24.1-12), the journey of the two unfaithful disciples away from Jerusalem (24.13-26), and the disciples' gathering with the risen Jesus in Jerusalem (24.36-49).[26] The gospel concludes with a fourth scene, with Jesus' return to God, described in apocalyptic and liturgical images, as the ascending Jesus blesses his disciples who go back to Jerusalem and the temple to await the promised Spirit that will empower them.

The last words of the gospel conclude the story of Jesus with the disciples 'continually in the temple blessing God' (24.53). This is also an appropriate conclusion, with Jesus' mission perfectly completed, namely as the disciples return to focus on what was the very heart of Jesus' ministry, 'blessing God'. As this final image brings the gospel story to closure, it also ends the gospel in the same location where it first began, with Zechariah in the temple in Luke 1 and unable to bless God's people. By this conclusion Luke carefully anticipates for the auditor what will unfold in the evangelist's second volume. Sounds of joy, optimism and triumph are left ringing in the auditor's ears.

In the first scene, the women come to the tomb on the first day, 'at early dawn' (24.1b), a note echoing a new moment in the story of God's act of creation. The story will reverberate with ecological potential. The women note that the tomb's stone has been rolled away and Jesus' body is gone. Their perplexity is clarified by 'two males' (24.4) who proclaim Luke's Easter message. The two declare,

---

25. For an overview of Luke 24, see Richard J. Dillon, *From Eye-Witnesses to Ministers of the Word: Tradition and Composition in Luke 24* (Rome: Biblical Institute, 1978).

26. See also Robert C. Tannehill, *The Narrative Unity of Luke–Acts. A Literary Interpretation. Volume 1: The Gospel according to Luke* (Philadelphia, PA: Fortress Press, 1986), pp. 111-27.

⁵ᶜ 'Why do you seek the living with the dead?
⁶He is not here but has been raised.
Remember how he said to you while he was in Galilee,
saying ⁷ that the Human One must be delivered into the hands of sinners,
and be crucified, and on the third day rise.'
⁸ And they remembered his words (24.5-8).

There are three things to note about this Easter declaration.

First, the declaration, 'He is not here but has been raised' (24.6), is textually disputed.²⁷ But if it is original, the passive of the verb ('has been raised') means that the act resurrection is an act done *to* Jesus, not one which he himself does (and sometimes incorrectly reflected in the translation 'he has risen'). Who, then, resurrects Jesus?

One obvious actor is God.²⁸ God has been present in Luke's story of Jesus either explicitly or implicitly. From the gospel's opening scenes to this moment of resurrection, God acts and has entered this scene earlier with the note of 'early dawn' and the stone across the entrance to the tomb being rolled back. Now this meaning becomes explicit. God has raised Jesus from death and from the tomb. Life, not death, is God's intention. God is permanently committed to sustain all that lives and exists upon Earth. God's face is enduringly and endearingly turned towards it. This hints at the second actor in Jesus' resurrection.

This second actor is Earth. Earth has been celebrated as conjoined to heaven. Its womb, first symbolically identified in Jesus' birth story by the manger and his cloth wrappings and now by the shroud and stone tomb, gestates to bring forth life. Earth acts in communion with God to resurrect Jesus, its child.

Second, the Easter proclamation also affirms that what has now happened to Jesus confirms what the auditor knows from the story of his passion and death: Jesus is victorious, honoured and glorified. This conviction is underscored by the 'two males' telling the women to 'remember.'

As in the transfiguration (9.28-36) and later, in Acts (Acts 1.10), the presence of these two males, the counter and healed images to other negative male presences in earlier gospel episodes (17.12, 19.7), underscores an important proclamation which the auditor is encouraged to remember. Such memory, as we have already seen in the last supper, brings his ministry into present time and activates it. Jesus' ministry therefore continues through the women, now his memory bearers. His words and deeds, God's *rhēma*, focused

---

27. See, for example, the textual rating D (high degree of doubt) regarding the original authenticity of 24.6 in Metzger, *Textual Commentary*, pp. 183-84. However, for the textual evidence in favour of the Lukan authenticity for 24.6 supported by the third century CE Bodmer Papyrus, see the discussion in Fitzmyer, *Luke X–XXIV*, p. 1545. See also, Marshall, *Luke*, pp. 885-86.

28. Fitzmyer, *Luke X–XXIV*, p. 1545.

on liberating the oppressed Earth and its members; they too will participate in this. This ministry involves healing, freedom and ecological release.

Third, Jesus is not present in the place of death, but in the place of the living. For Luke, Jesus is present in all that is alive. This has a distinct ecological ring about it. Hearing this proclamation in non-anthropocentric terms, the declaration reaffirms that Jesus is Earth's child and that Earth, the place of the living and infused with divine blessing, is the arena of God's self-revelation. It is within Earth that the risen Jesus will be encountered. The communion of Jesus with Earth is now assured and definitive. The task of the disciple is to approach it with a spirit of open contemplation and respect for all that is alive, human and non-human, every member of its household. This contemplative approach will allow the presence of the risen Jesus to be revealed.

The women return from their encounter with these divine interpreters and tell the message to 'the eleven and to all the rest' (24.10c). As Jesus was for God, the women are now for Jesus; they are agents of his *rhēma*. The named women (Mary Magdalene, Joanna and Mary the mother of James) and other women with them tell this to the 'apostles' (24.10). The women's proclamation, explicitly described by Luke as *'rhēma'* (24.11b) is regarded as fanciful. They are not believed by the apostolic group of Jesus' inner circle (24.11).

Luke's observation of the disbelief by the leading disciples composed of males (the 'eleven and the rest' and 'apostles') of the women's proclamation, is not accidental. Even Peter has to run to the tomb to check out the credibility of their story (24.12).[29] The response by the eleven, 'the rest', the apostles and Peter adds a note of gender bias that Luke associates with the first generation of Jesus disciples. They do not accept or endorse women's ability or role as authentic witnesses of the resurrection. This expression of bias, explicit by the evangelist and intended to be noticed, now becomes secure in the auditor's memory and reinforced in the next scene.

This second scene on Easter day concerns two disciples leaving Jerusalem, the city associated with discipleship (24.13-35). These two, one named 'Clopas' and possibly his wife, represent those who are unsure of their future discipleship with dulled and unknowing hearts.[30] They are going away from the place of discipleship, disillusioned by Jesus' execution and their perception of his failed promise to them. Their narrative of the women's story reinforces their perplexity of events and the lack of credibility of the women's witness flagged in the previous scene. They say,

---

29. As with 24.6 so, too, there is some dispute about the originality of 24.12. But see Fitzmyer, *Luke X–XXIV*, p. 1545; Johnson, *Luke*, pp. 388-89.

30. Green, *Luke*, p. 845 n. 20; Fitzmyer, *Luke X–XXIV*, pp. 1563-64.

²² But also women who were *from us* amazed us. Being at the tomb early morning ²³ and not finding his body, they come to say that they had even seen a *vision of angels* who said that he was alive. ²⁴ And some who were *with us* went to the tomb and found it just as the women had said. Him they did not see (24.22-24).

There are three important details that Luke incorporates into the story of the two recounting their interpretation of the women's discovery of the empty tomb.

First, the two identify the women's experience as a 'vision of angels' (v. 23), an exaggeration of what the auditor already knows from the previous scene. The suggestion that the women's encounter at Jesus' tomb was a 'vision' is a subtle attempt to discredit their experience. It implies that their encounter was not real but hallucinatory, if not an invention.

Second, the two differentiate between the women '*from* us' (v. 22a) and those sent who were '*with* us' (v. 24a) and go to the tomb to corroborate the women's story (v. 24b). The women are perceived as less united to the apostolic group ('from us') than the later investigators ('with us'). This implies that the women's lack of union with the apostolic community would lead to their visionary exaggeration and potential for distorting the facts. This attempt to discredit the women's witness is further compounded by the way that the 'two males' of Earth's household are turned into 'angels' from the heavenly sphere. In other words, they reinforce a split between Earth and heaven, reflecting a dualism that has continued into present time. Besides the women, Earth's ability to provide authentic witness is thus questioned.

Third, the verification of the women's testimony makes their statement partly credible, but their statement is changed by the two as an interpretation of the tomb's emptiness. As far as the auditor knows, the women's testimony was not about the tomb's emptiness but what they had been told by the two at the tomb: the *meaning* of its emptiness. Their explicit testimony to the eleven, 'the rest' and the apostles would have been unambiguous: Jesus has been raised. This is the heart of the Easter proclamation; for Luke, the women are its primary witnesses. In other words, the women's testimony about Jesus' resurrection is what is disbelieved. The evangelist intentionally points this out. Rather than seeing the negative response to the women as evidence of Luke's subtle softening of women's role within the gospel household, it is an explicit memory that the evangelist wants to preserve for reflection by later generations of Jesus followers.

My focus on the women and their being disbelieved is crucial and has ecological consequences. A careful study of the text and the language that Luke uses indicates that the first generation of Jesus followers struggled with the originating Easter witness and proclamation by women. Luke clearly points out this struggle. Behind it is a word for Luke's gospel household dealing with similar issues of ministerial and preaching bias, a bias that has continued in every generation of Jesus followers.

In terms of ecological attentiveness, the women at the end of Luke's gospel carry a similar christological function as the women in the beginning of the gospel. Both ends of the gospel with their stories of women affirm Jesus' identity in relationship to Earth. Mary's action for the new born child firmly identifies Jesus in relation to the peasant, rural and Earth households. What she does to her new born child confirms his identity with Earth. The women go to the tomb, to an explicit place that belongs to Earth, to discover the meaning of Jesus' bodily absence. His post-resurrectional identity is now found in that which is living. Communion with God's creation will reveal what this means. To arrive at a sense of intimacy with the Sacred requires an ecologically contemplative stance, meditative about Earth's environment and open to the meaning of Jesus' resurrection. In Luke's story, the women demonstrate this. For the contemporary gospel audience, they model the importance and fruit of ecological contemplation. These can be found in Luke's description of the women's encounter with the two in dazzling apparel. They

> bow their faces to Earth (24.5b).

This is more than an act of reverence before the presence of the holy. It is a moment of divine revelation which comes as the women commune with Earth and prepare their souls in an attitude of environmental reverence. They remain in this attitude as the two 'men' interpret for the women the meaning of the absence of Jesus' body. Only after the Easter proclamation does the women's deportment change when they physically return from the tomb 'to the eleven and the rest' (24.9). That the women are disbelieved at the end of the gospel suggests that the need for ecological conversion and disciples' connection to Earth will always be ongoing.[31]

We return to the story of the two disciples with their travelling stranger, the risen Jesus. In the conversation which ensues and in the moment of the eucharistic 'breaking of bread' the two come to understand that his presence has been with them all along (24.25-31). Their hearts burn from Jesus' explanation; in the eucharistic act they are released from their perplexity (24.32-33a). They return to Jerusalem and to their fellow disciples. They are greeted with an affirmation of Jesus' resurrection and, in a statement that surprises the auditor because this is the first time that it is mentioned, his appearance to Simon Peter (24.33b-35).

At this same moment the risen Jesus comes into the disciples' midst, in Luke's third scene (24.36-49). He first offers them peace (24.36c), the

---

31. On the disbelieving treatment of the women and their witness, see Turid Karlsen Seim, *The Double Message* (Nashville, TN: Abingdon Press, 1994), pp. 97-163.

ecological and human communion that has characterized his ministry throughout the gospel. They are startled and frightened and presume Jesus to be a spirit (24.37). His reassurance comes in a corporeal, physical and Earth form. He points out to them the physicality of his being, and that he has 'flesh and bones' (24.39b). His being remains not as a spirit figure, but as Earth's child, albeit resurrected and exalted, confirmed by his eating a piece of broiled fish, a fruit of the sea (24.42-43). Thus his Earth connectedness remains and is celebrated in his resurrected being.

Then, as God's *rhēma*, Jesus speaks his final words to his disciples having acted to assure them of the reality of his presence. He reminds them that his ministry and mission are a continuity of God's fidelity revealed in the First Testament (24.44), his death and resurrection are integral to this revealed biblical tradition (24.45), and that communion with God ('forgiveness of sins') is the heart of apostolic preaching to be inaugurated in Jerusalem (24.47). Finally, Jesus commissions his disciples as witnesses of God and himself (24.48); he assures them that they will be empowered for their new mission by God's spirit for which they are to await (24.49). This promise anticipates everything that will happen in the Book of Acts, beginning with the Pentecost outpouring of the promised spirit upon the disciples. This spirit will renew the face of Earth.

The last scene concludes the gospel and acts as a hinge to Luke's second volume. It also returns us to Bethany located near Mount Olivet (24.59-53). This topographical setting, associated earlier with his claiming of Jerusalem, the inauguration of his passion and reminiscent of earlier gospel scenes where he communes with God on mountains, completes a gospel replete with ecological associations. The risen Jesus leads his disciples to this spot (24.59a) reinserting them back into the rural, hilly and Earth connected dimensions of their lives. From here, in a liturgical gesture which completes Zechariah's unfinished temple blessing in Luke 1, Jesus blesses his disciples. While he does so,

> he departed from them and was carried up into heaven (24.51b).

Luke acknowledges the historical moment of Jesus' physical separation from his household of disciples. At the same time, his blessing, that gesture of divine benefaction on humanity and creation, continues beyond the particularity of the moment. It is not historically, culturally or spatially limited. Earth's child, who is 'flesh and bone', creature of Earth and one with humanity, is now in eternal and ineffable communion with God. In this state, he continues to bless Earth and its inhabitants. This blessing will come to Earth's creatures not because Jesus will 'look down' upon Earth and its members and, from the heavenly sphere that overshadows and dominates, will be able to grace Earth with divine favour. Rather, as we already know, Earth is with heaven; Earth's presence is within the heavens praised by Jesus' disciples welcoming him into Jerusalem; its fruits available for the eschatological banquet to which the repentant criminal is invited. The two spheres, the Earth and heavenly, once separated now coalesce. This Earth-heaven communion means that Earth's inhabitants will always be blessed.

Luke's final scene of Jesus' return to God leaves the auditor with a vision of eternal ecological communion and environmental harmony. Because of this, it is appropriate that the disciples return to the one place in Jerusalem which celebrates God, humanity, creation and the Earth's story of liberation—the temple:

> And as they worshipped him they returned to Jerusalem with great joy and they were continually in the temple blessing God (24.53).

The Gospel continues from where it began, on a note of celebration and 'great joy' blessing the source of creation, God.

Conclusion

The central message which the evangelist wants to leave with the auditor is about the ministry of Jesus that continues in the women and, ideally, with all the disciples. This ministry is revealed throughout the gospel, explicated in the passion events and articulated in the final words that the risen Jesus offers his disciples. This message is about wholeness, reconciliation and Earth communion.

In the midst of violence and rejection, Jesus models enemy love. He reveals the face of a gracious, forgiving and embracing God offering an alternative way of being, accompanied by symbols of Earth's being. At the moment of death, a moment of prayer, Jesus' God is close, supporting and comforting. Luke's dying Jesus and the repentant criminal image this God who invites people and the Earth household to rejoice with a rich banquet that celebrates its fruits.

Though Jesus has been ill-treated to the point of death, his honour and status, as God's Earth child, has been ironically proclaimed and God's desire for communion with creation undimmed. Jesus continues to bless and reveal to Earth a God who embraces all creation, especially the socially excluded, rejected and maltreated. Jesus also does not die naked and totally humiliated, as in Mark's gospel; but clothed in an Earth garment of dignity paradoxically placed over him by Rome's imperial representative. His rock burial place and linen shroud complete this Earth-association.

Luke's prevailing image of Jesus in the passion narrative is one who heals, forgives, celebrates, nourishes and provides the possibility for ecological conversion and inclusion into God's *basileia-ecotopia*. The evangelist thus portrays Jesus as God's authentic 'martyr.' In the fullest sense of this word,

Jesus *witnesses*; he witnesses to a God whose compassionate largesse is surprisingly unrestricted and universal, who embraces, forgives and is in love with creation.

Throughout the passion narrative, Jesus' physical body has been central. As we have already seen, the ancients believed that the human body was dyadic and had its identity within the wider network of social relationships. It also had ecological resonances with the celestial, cosmic and Earth bodies. This ancient appreciation has underpinned our way of listening to Luke's many healing stories. The healing of the human body impacts on the wider eco-cosmic world; the sick and hurt body mirrors what is happening more widely upon Earth. Up until the passion symphony, Luke's final movement that completes the gospel, the most dramatic expression of this earlier was the storm on the lake (8.22-25) and the healing of the Gerasene demoniac (8.26-39).

An important strong ecological truth that emerges in the passion is the identity between Jesus and Earth. Earth symbolically accompanies him, bears him, carries him, attaches to him and surrounds him. What happens to him echoes Earth's hurts. What human beings do to Jesus' body in the passion movement mirrors what they do to the wider Earth household and God's creation. Jesus' response to his treatment reflects how the human community can act in forgiveness, healing, restoration and salvation. This impacts ecologically. His suffering sums up the travail of the whole universe. And Luke's story holds out the possibility of God's release from this suffering, which heals the ecological hurt and damage that Earth has endured at the hands of evil-doers throughout history.

Xavier Léon-Dufour makes a similar point reflecting on Luke's story of Jesus' passion as one in which all auditors are invited to participate. This passion is our passion:

> Jesus is not simply a model; he is the type of the persecuted upright one, resuming in his person the persecution of all times and revealing by his triumph the victory of his own followers.[32]

From an ecological perspective, Luke's passion symphony is also a celebration of God's passion for the created universe, the human household and Earth. With the risen One we participate in Earth's emancipation. We, like the women at the tomb, are invited into an ascetic, contemplative and reverential attitude to Earth that predisposes us to recognize the imminence of God's *basileia-ecotopia* and encounter the risen Lord in our midst, among 'the living'.

---

32. Xavier Léon-Dufour, 'Passion (Récits de la)', *Dictionnaire de la Bible, Supplément* 6 (1960), pp. 1419-92 (1476).

Earth's Voice

As they led him away, they seized a man, Simon of Cyrene, who was coming from the country, and they laid the cross on him, and made him carry it behind Jesus…When they came to the place that is called The Skull, they crucified Jesus there (Lk. 23.26, 33).

Earth's Tree speaks:

> I have been cut down from Earth's garden,
> stripped of branches;
> roughly shaped to form a cross-beam to be affixed atop an upright firmly implanted in Earth's soil.
> My only worth, to accompany the bodies of victims to their deaths.
> I accompany Earth's child through Jerusalem's streets.
> carried by another.
> I see how he is treated, addressed and speaks.
> We arrive at Earth's death place.
> We are both thrown to Earth, Mother of life and now of death.
> His wrists are nailed to my ends.
> I am attached to him.
>
> He is lifted upon the upright.
>
> He is transfixed.
> He suffers and writhes.
> I accompany him through his last moments of life.
> I hear him die as he releases his spirit into the hands of Earth's God,
>
> Earth's child.

Part III

Conclusion

Luke's Ecological Resonances

I began this ecological study of Luke's gospel looking through a window on to a beautiful world of grass, birds, trees, beach, waves and people. This New Zealand vista became a point of reflection. As I moved through Luke's gospel I began to see something else—it was most obvious but I had not attended to at first. On the edge of the grassed area just outside my window and before the wooden fence that screened the property from public gaze were three large mature trees known in Maori as *Pohutukawa*. Their popular name is the 'New Zealand Christmas tree'. At Christmas time these trees burst into colour with deep red flowers.

This discovery is a metaphor for what has happened in my engagement with Luke's gospel. While I could originally imagine ecological possibilities in the gospel, as I listened to Luke's narrative symphony further I became attentive to ecological tones that I had not previously noticed.

In this concluding chapter I offer a summary of what I have noticed. I summarize the social and environmental context of Luke's gospel auditors, the approach that I have used in allowing me to listen to Earth's story and engage the gospel, and a brief overview of each section or movement of the gospel. Finally and by way of conclusion, I suggest eight key ecological insights that have emerged. I believe they are relevant for contemporary disciples seeking to live in deeper communion with Earth and its members.

1. *The Gospel's Social, Economic and Ecological Context*

Luke's intent was to address the socio-cultural and theological concerns of a late first century urban Mediterranean household of Jesus followers. These reflected the social stratification of Greco-Roman urban society: peasants, dispossessed peasants, urban workers including artisans and slaves, and the social elite. The gospel's explicit addressees were the urban wealthy elite represented by the figure of Theophilus (1.3). It was inclusive of other social groups. Luke envisaged the gospel household as a renewed fictive kinship group in the Greco-Roman world in which all the major social groups were united. In Acts 2.42 when the Jerusalem followers of Jesus gather 'for the apostles' teaching, communion, the breaking of bread and the prayers',

Luke spelt out the practical implications for such a united household. According to the evangelist, a new society was possible through 'following closely' (1.3) the ministry of Jesus and the disciples who gathered around him. Luke believed that this form of social renewal was possible even in the Greco-Roman gospel household, a household that could model the Greek ideal of friendship.

Luke did not seek to restructure society in terms of a village economy or to abolish social stratification. The evangelist inherited the convictions of the historical Jesus, addressed originally to Israelite peasants located predominantly in a rural context in Galilee. But half a century later in a different location, there was now a need to offer hope for the impoverished and economically depressed land-bound peasant members of the Jesus movement, and at the same time address disciples who were wealthy elite patrons. Urbanization and stratification were already a reality in Luke's world. The evangelist sought to engage the wealthy, privileged and elite Jesus followers with the implications of an authentic style of discipleship. The evangelist subtly altered the original message of Jesus, initially intended only for a peasant audience. The elite were encouraged to let go of status, honour and privilege and to exercise hospitality, benefaction and reciprocity towards peasant members of the community.

Behind Luke's story is a vision for the gospel household—a radical redistribution of wealth. The wealthy are urged to show reciprocity and benefaction to those in need without expecting return. Goods were not be amassed for the benefit or honour they brought their possessors. They were to be used to relieve debt, need, hardship and insecurity resulting from injustice. Luke's subtle economic program can be heard as an appeal to the elite for a radical social reform that enabled them to welcome the powerless and marginalized. This meant a move from the conventional retributive market strategy to an economic arrangement of unbalanced reciprocity, from the temple as the power and economic base to the household and peasant village as the focal point of the new gospel household.[1]

Of particular importance is Luke's teaching on possessions and wealth. As we traced this theme through the gospel, and especially in the journey narrative, it was clear that Luke sought a redistribution of wealth, recognizing the ancient attitude that wealth was the result of greed. Greed had ecological implications—the accumulation of wealth by the urban elite of Earth's goods meant that others, and usually the poor, went without. Earth suffered because of people's greed. In Luke's world, the rich were getting richer and the poor poorer. For Luke, this disparity created by excessive wealth and the demands of debt fulfilment by landless or unproductive peasants needed to be addressed. This social issue was a key problem present in the gospel household. It caused

---

1. Oakman, 'Countryside', p. 175.

tension and brought oppression, the antithesis to Jesus' message summarized in his hometown synagogue teaching (4.16-21). Jesus came to release the oppressed. In practical terms this meant economic release. In ecological terms, this implied environmental freedom and care of Earth.

I have suggested that each group within the gospel household had its own ecological stance determined by status and their reliance on Earth for their livelihood.[2] The Mediterranean was a region surrounded by an interconnected economy in which economics, politics and religion were embedded in a complex interrelationship with the land. The frequency with which Earth images appear in the gospel—their presence in Jesus' teaching, the number of stories about peasants and the wealthy, and the rich linguistic taxonomy for Earth, its environment and fruits—indicate Luke's environmental awareness.[3] Added to this picture are the people that constitute Luke's world and the heritage from Jesus' peasant based teaching.

The care of the land was central to peasant farmers. Its fruitfulness determined their ability to meet taxation demands, provide a livelihood for the household and provide means for reciprocal exchange and barter within the village. Without a fruitful crop peasant farmers faced debt, eventual land takeover, possible eviction and homelessness. Thus the consequences of a lack of attention to Earth were potentially disastrous. For the peasant-related members of Luke's audience, Earth's environment was precious.

The urban elite of Luke's audience viewed Earth differently. For them the environment was more of a utilitarian commodity that they could acquire, confiscate and have farmed to bring them wealth and status. The respect shown Earth by peasant farmers contrasted to the commercial attitude of these urban elite and the variety of other attitudes reflected by artisans and urban workers. As we have seen, these environmental altitudinal variations find themselves in the characters that dot the gospel.

---

2. This is a refinement of an earlier conviction that 'the land is a negative object in need of subjugation. Luke's audience generally had a rapacious attitude towards the land', in Trainor, 'And on Earth, Peace', pp. 189-90.

3. Luke uses several different words to describe land, country, Earth and soil which have come across in the gospel. Their frequency indicates their importance to the author of Luke–Acts. *Kósmos* ('world') is found four times in Luke–Acts (Lk. 9.25; 11.50; 12.30; Acts 17.24). 'Earth' (*gēs*) is found 183 times in the Second Testament with a little under half in Luke–Acts, 25 times in the gospel, and 33 in the Book of Acts. *Chōra* ('country' or 'rural precinct') occurs 28 times in the Second Testament with 17 occurrences in Luke–Acts. *Ágós* ('fields') used 11 times in Luke–Acts, and 17 in the rest of the Second Testament. *Períchōros* ('surrounding countryside') is used 6 times in Luke–Acts, and 3 in the rest of the Second Testament. *Chōríon* ('piece of land') is used 6 times in Acts (and 3 times in other writings of the Second Testament). Finally, *oikoumenē* ('earth' or 'world') occurs 8 times in Luke–Acts.

Luke's household also embraced peasants; some were rural-based but most had been affected by the manipulative control of the urban elite. They had gone into debt, borrowed from fellow peasants and kin, eventually forced to sell inherited lands to the elites and absentee landlords, and moved into the city. Here they become members of Luke's gospel household.

2. Approaching Luke's Gospel Ecologically

As I engaged Luke's gospel I acknowledged that the language and terms which we use in a contemporary western context about Earth and its environment were not those of this first century Mediterranean gospel writer. Luke was not an ecologist, but a first century CE urban Greco-Roman Jesus follower. However, it is possible to engage Luke's gospel from a contemporary ecological perspective. To enable this to happen I proposed that an interrelational dynamic between three worlds needed to be honoured: the world *of* the text (Luke's gospel as a literary construction), the world *behind* the text (the cultural, social, historical, anthropological and literary context of Luke and the gospel's audience) and the world *in front* of the text (my world with its ecological concerns).

The world *of* the text has been explicit in every chapter of this book. This world is filled out when necessary by the world *behind* the text. The world *in front* of the text, my world and Earth connection, is presumed and usually in the foreground. But I have tried not to impose this third world on to the gospel engagement without first listening for the voice of the other worlds, and particularly the first. Occasionally I have offered brief comments about the hermeneutic relevance of particular gospel insights. In this concluding chapter I make these comments more explicit.

I have approached Luke's gospel as a narrative symphony because of the overall aesthetic balance which the author has created in the story of Jesus. As I engaged these three worlds methodologically, I began each section, where possible and appropriate, with a discernment of the gospel's internal literary structure and dynamic indicated by linguistic patterns and themes. Drawing on the insights offered by literary critics, especially Julia Kristeva, and the poet T.S. Eliot, I have called the discernable literary structure of each section the 'inner play', and the identifiable literary, cultural and hermeneutical sources for the creation of the gospel, 'intertexts'. Luke integrated them into the gospel. They included First Testament texts and stories (especially creation and the Exodus, Genesis and Isaiah), the social and cultural Greco-Roman world and previous gospel stories or sayings (including Mk and Q) to which Luke had access.

A final and legitimate intertext was the interests and perspectives that 'I' as the listener brought to the gospel engagement. Of particular importance was my listening to Luke's gospel from the perspective of Earth. This led me to draw out hermeneutical insights relevant for contemporary Jesus followers. A consideration of intertextuality also affirmed the oral-aural dynamic, the proclamation dynamic for the gospel, the role of the auditor (in preference to 'reader') and the 'household' as the primary Greco-Roman location for the reception, proclamation, writing, listening to and living out of the gospel. The household also provided the primary metaphor for consideration of Earth and the environment. I have used 'Earth household' as an expression of everything within the ecological and environmental world of the planet, human and non-human, organic and non-organic.

3. Luke's Gospel in Summary

3.1. Prologue and Birth (1.1–2.52)

The gospel's prologue, 1.1-4, offered an initial overture to the gospel filled out in Jesus' birth story (1.5–2.52). Luke's Jesus is introduced to the auditor as Son of God and child of Earth. This identity is further confirmed in the next section when Luke's genealogy identifies Jesus as 'son of Adam, son of God' (3.37). The female figures of these opening chapters, Mary and Elizabeth, decentre anthropocentricism and patriarchy with images of maternity, gestation and nurturing paradigms. These reflect the kind of God that Jesus will reveal as he moves towards and into his public ministry. Jesus' God is delighted in the household of creation, women and men, human and non-human.

3.2. Preparation for Public Ministry (3.1–4.30)

As the auditor prepares for Jesus' public ministry (3.1–4.30), the evangelist highlights the relationship between *word* and *spirit* that acts as an undercurrent. Jesus speaks God's word and is the agent of God's spirit. In his encounter with the devil, the agent of evil that causes disease and brokenness within Earth's household, and especially in the temptation scene (4.1-13), Luke articulates what I have discerned as three ecological principles that find an echo in the rest of the gospel:

- Earth is to be cared for and treated respectfully; not ravaged through covetousness;
- All ecological and environmental engagement is grounded in and enhanced by one's communion with God;
- Earth's resources are to be respected by all and not usurped as a means of power and control by one over another.

Luke's preparatory chapters conclude with Jesus' hometown declaration of the essence of his ministry (4.16-30), to bring release from oppression and poverty, and sight to the blind.

3.3. Jesus' Galilean Ministry (4.31–9.50)

This declaration has ecological consequences which unfold in Jesus' Galilean ministry, in what I call the gospel's 'paradisiacal garden' (4.31–9.50). Jesus' ministry here is concerned about *metanoia* by those who follow him and his revelation of the presence of God's *basileia-ecotopia* breaking forth in to Earth's household, the beneficiary of God's maternal care revealed through Jesus. The essential expression of Jesus' ministry comes in the form of his word and deed. We subsequently see how these two interrelated features of his ministry enact God's *rhēma*, a rich theological expression whose appreciation is presumed throughout the gospel.

As Jesus' healing ministry unfolds, especially his exorcisms and his table solidarity with the socially excluded, Luke's appreciation of the human body as a total interrelated cosmic and eco-system is central. Luke's corporeal appreciation is presumed also through the continuing gospel narrative, and especially in the story of Jesus' body in the gospel's final chapters. What happens to the human body has implications for Earth's body.

Besides his healings and exorcisms, a centre-piece of Jesus' ministry is his table communion and celebratory gatherings with the elite, sinners and rejected. These meals are a distinctive feature in Luke's gospel and they celebrate the festive God who delights in the earth garden found in Galilee and through Jesus' meals. The lavish nature of these feasts and the kind of characters who are their guests attract the attention of Jesus' antagonists who begin to make their presence felt and voice the criticism which will eventually lead to his execution.

Despite growing opposition, Jesus continues to reveal God who wants to celebrate the garden of earthly delights which involves other environmental and Earth related beings. These include the wilderness (4.42; 5.15; 7.24; 9.12), water (5.1-2, 4), land (4.37; 5.3, 11; 6.17; 7.17), mountains (6.12), wind (7.24; 8.24), clouds (9.34, 35), clothing (8.27, 35, 44; 9.29), bread (6.4; 7.33; 9.3, 13, 16), fish (5.6-9; 9.13, 16), seeds (8.5, 11), oil (7.46), Earth itself and other expressions associated with it (5.3, 11, 24; 6.49; 8.8, 15, 26, 27, 33, 34, 37; 9.12, 25), alabaster (7.37) and trees (6.43, 44). As we noted, these are not passive, inert, organic, agricultural, geographical or geological forms, but active contributors to the gospel. They enable God to liberate, release, heal and bring Earth's human members to divine solidarity.

3.4. The Journey Narrative (9.51–19.27)

The major and longest section of the gospel is Luke's journey or travel narrative (9.51–19.27). While no obvious inner play suggested itself, theological and discipleship themes and the explicit mention of Jesus' actual movement towards Jerusalem help to delineate the narrative's three segments (9.51–13.22; 13.23–17.10 and 17.11–19.27).

Overall, Luke is concerned to explore themes of discipleship, the growing opposition which Jesus meets anticipating what awaits him in Jerusalem, and the imminence of God's *basileia-ecotopia*. Here Luke explicitly links discipleship to the treatment of Earth and the possession of its gifts. Jesus uses ecological and Earth images drawn from the rural peasant world to educate and illustrate. This is reflected in stories and aphorisms that help highlight the disciple's attitudes to wealth, regard for Earth's goods and the sharing of possessions. Jesus' teaching and parables especially characterize the antithesis of authentic discipleship illustrated in characters that are greedy, selfishly ambitious and disrespectful to the poor.

An important setting for Jesus' teaching in the journey is the meal set within the classical *symposium*. Luke's Jesus continues to address the topics of wealth, meal hospitality, and stories concerned with God's merciful compassion, illustrated particularly in the gospel's three central ecologically rich parables of Luke 15.

Besides sheep, a coin and a lost son (one described, significantly, as an *anthrōpos*, echoing other gospel figures and reflective of the human condition in need of healing), other ecological beings teach. These educate and invite disciples to reflect and undergo conversion. They include animals (10.34; 13.15; 14.5; 15.23, 27, 30), water (13.15; 16.24; 17.2, 6), food (12.23; 42), bread (11.3, 5; 14.15; 15.17), wine (10.34), estates (17.7), fig tree (13.6, 7) and a gardener (13.7).

Also appearing in a more explicit manner especially in the last part of the journey narrative is Jesus' teaching about the *basileia-ecotopia*, an image of God's Earth fruitfulness, eternally imminent and awaiting full revelation.

3.5. *Jesus' Jerusalem Ministry (19.28–21.38)*

The journey prepares for and anticipates Jesus' ministry in Jerusalem (19.28–21.38), his passion and death. As in other parts of the gospel, Luke significantly draws upon and reshapes Mark's gospel (Mk 13) to emphasize Jesus as God's authentic prophet to reveal the divine *rhēma* and the imminent presence of God's *basileia-ecotopia*. This is about to come definitively as it ushers God's final coming.

Earth images permeate Jesus' Jerusalem temple teaching. The fig tree becomes a reminder of the nearness of the *basileia-ecotopia* (21.29-30) and the image of Mount Olivet frames the whole section (19.29; 21.37). The Mount and its 'way', like the animal upon which Jesus rides into the city, are cloaked like a disciple. They provide the means for him to claim Jerusalem.

The last image with which Luke leaves the auditor before the climactic story of his death and resurrection is one of ecological interlinking. The last verse (21.37-38) illustrates how Jesus' word-deed, the enacted divine *rhēma*, is thematically surrounded by the image of Mount Olivet. This image sums up Luke's eco-theological perspective.

3.6. *Jesus' Passion, Death and Burial (22.1–23.56)*

In the passion and death of Jesus (22.1–23.56), the auditor returns to the two ecologically loaded images with which the opening section of the gospel began—Jesus' body and clothing. The treatment of Jesus' body is a reflection, by association and synchronicity, of Earth's treatment. Like Earth itself, he suffers innocently from the actions of evil doers influenced by the presence of Satan.

Luke's Jesus dies clothed with the regal luminescent garment of eternity, offering a final festive and paradisiacal meal to the thief who repents, an image that honours the communion of Earth and heaven. Jesus reveals, in an ultimate gesture of divine love and inclusivity, God's intention for all creation and humanity. Finally, he is buried in a rock-hewn tomb clothed in a linen shroud reconfirming the eco-christological truth first revealed at birth, that he is Earth's child.

3.7. *Easter Day (24.1-53)*

Luke's final chapter (Luke 24) set on Easter day brings the auditor to the heart of appreciating the ecological potential of Luke's gospel. Women come to the tomb to discover Jesus' body gone. But in an environmental gesture of deep reverence they 'bow their faces to Earth' (24.5). In this posture they learn from two men the reason for the tomb's emptiness and the meaning of the resurrection.

It is among the 'living' that the women will encounter the risen Jesus. This is a deeply significant ecological witness about the resurrection that the women are invited to proclaim. Within Earth and amongst its creatures, human and non-human, Jesus will be encountered as disciples in every gospel household in history continue to look for and promulgate his resurrection. That the women's witness was not initially believed confirms the reality that the disciple's faith in Jesus' revelation within creation will continue to be a struggle.

The central focus of the gospel is Jesus. His ministry communicates Luke's essential story about God. Those characters that are most influenced and shaped by Jesus' ministry are the disciples, women and men, who accompany him in his Galilean ministry, his long journey to Jerusalem with its *symposium* and explicit teaching about discipleship and wealth, are with him in his temple teaching and his passion and death. The women's presence to him as witnesses to his death, the place and manner of his burial and as the prime witnesses to his resurrection confirms for the auditor some of the clear insights that emerge from Luke regarding Earth and the environment.

Concluding Ecological Insights

In this post-Easter period in which Luke's audience and contemporary gospel auditors live, the disciple is called to deep ecological reflection that approaches Earth with reverence and awe. Luke's post-resurrectional theology is not a form of pantheism, as though creation and Jesus are identical. Rather, Luke's insight into Jesus' resurrection is pan*en*theistic. Jesus' resurrection means that everything that lives—and for contemporary auditors this would include nature, creation, human beings and the universe—reveals God's presence. For Luke, this event alters human history; God's self-revelation is more definitively and transparently experienced as never before. Luke's Paul affirms a similar conviction in his address to the Athenians in Acts 17.28. In God, says Paul, 'we live and move and have our being.' In other words, everything that lives and exists in the created universe, the 'Earth', has the potential to reveal God's communion and the *basileia-ecotopia*.

This book began with two questions:

- Will Luke's gospel reinforce a destructive and utilitarian attitude to the planet that seeks to subjugate creation for selfish reasons?
- Or, can this gospel contribute to an ecological theology that will encourage a respectful attitude to Earth integral to contemporary discipleship?

My response to these questions is best expressed in the following eight theses:

1. *Luke's gospel is ecologically connected*. Earth is not just a backdrop for Jesus' apparently real mission of bringing liberation and healing to human beings. The embedded nature of Luke's world in terms of economics, politics and religion also means that what we would consider the environment or ecology, and what I have called the 'Earth household', are interrelated. This ecological value is especially true in the gospel's treatment of wealth. Luke considers the accumulation of wealth an issue that has economic, social and ecological consequences. The invitation for those who are wealthy is to conversion. These are the principal, though not exclusive, addressees of the gospels. There are many stories in the gospel that illustrate the effect of wealth on human interaction, discipleship and Earth. Wealth is a sign of greed that affects Earth.
2. *Luke's gospel is a story of God revealed through Jesus who acts with ecological and environmental concern*. The gospel is essentially theological and christological. It is about God and the God revealed in Jesus; it is not primarily ecological. But this story has ecological and environmental implications. This is because the gospel story concerns the whole

universe, human and non-human; Luke's Jesus reveals a God who is involved with Earth's household. Jesus is concerned about his world, its people and their environment. His healings and teachings affect Earth and its human and non-human members.

3. *In Luke's gospel creation is perceived and treated from different perspectives.* The gospel reflects various perspectives on Earth. These mirror the different attitudes to Earth held by different members of the gospel audience. Their attitudes vary according to how Earth and its fruits are understood as essential for human survival, production, profit or wealth. The audience of Luke's cultural and social world have attitudes to Earth that are not monochromatic but mixed.

4. *In Luke's gospel Earth acts.* Earth is an important actor in Luke's gospel. It is not a 'side-show' to the main event, concerned solely with the salvation and redemption of human beings. The gospel is concerned about human beings, but it is not so anthropocentric that it excludes other non-human members of Earth's community. Earth is the focus of God's care. It is also a partner with God in human liberation. The gospel incorporates environmentally related images drawn from Luke's peasant world and from the originating story of the historical Jesus and his teaching. Earth contributes to Jesus' teaching, his aphorisms and parables. It contributes through its animals, birds, agriculture, weather patterns, geography and topography. Luke also shapes Mark's gospel to alter potentially deprecating Earth teachings.

5. *Earth has a voice in Luke's gospel.* Earth is not a silent actor. It has voice that influences the human household and participates in the ministry of Jesus. Earth assists in Jesus' healing ministry and is an essential subject that helps communicate Jesus' teaching. Earth is so important for the gospel narrative that, in Jesus' Jerusalem ministry, it even becomes disciple-like in its reception of Jesus. In the passion, it carries, accompanies, bears, surrounds and becomes attached to him. A synchronicity exists between Earth and Jesus. Earth elements mediate and communicate the Good News. Associated with this affirmation that honours Earth's voice is the importance of human meditation. It is only in silence that Earth can speak to the human heart in a language that the heart hears and deeply knows. These Earth tones and melodies are unique; they are not copies of human vocalizations that mirror what the human household would expect to hear or make Earth 'speak'. Silence allows Earth's voice to induce compassion and *metanoia* within human beings.

6. *Luke's gospel reveals Jesus as Earth's child.* Jesus is identified with many titles and given many descriptors—teacher, Lord, Master, prophet, Human One, Son of God, friend of sinners and toll-collectors, and

Son of Adam. An important descriptor of Jesus is *Earth's child*. He is the Earthed One, Earth grounded, connected and bonded to Earth; he is one of Earth's creatures and the fruit of creation. These Earth images are affirmed in the beginning and end of the gospel, in his birth, death and resurrection. This perspective frames Luke's narrative and contributes to the auditors' appreciation of Jesus' ministry, especially his mission to liberate the oppressed, share meals with the rejected and heal those who are sick and troubled. Earth contributes to Jesus' revelatory divine *rhēma*. It, too, is the recipient of his ministry.

7. *Luke's Jesus reveals a God who delights in creation.* Jesus' God delights in humanity and creation. His festive meals that bring together humanity with the fruits of creation are a constant gospel theme. Meals feature: in his public ministry, his journey to Jerusalem especially in the *symposium*, his final meal with his disciples and the promise of Paradise to the repentant criminal. These meals express who Jesus is and the nature of God.

8. *Disciples are ecologically meditative and contemplative.* The disciple celebrates Earth and is ecologically meditative and ascetic. Through communion with Earth disciples can experience communion with God. The disciples also have a responsibility to the environment and Earth care. A disciple is in communion with Earth's God; non-avaricious, shares possessions, does not hoard.

These eight theses best express the insights that have emerged from my ecological attentiveness to Luke's narrative symphony.

Listening to the gospel has convinced me that sensitive attention to the story of Jesus is an invitation to renewed discipleship. This invitation is addressed to Luke's audience and contemporary Jesus followers and will deepen appreciation for Earth. The gospel will assist disciples to identify negative attitudes that treat Earth with rapaciousness and greed. The most tangible sign of such ecological avariciousness is seen in attitudes to wealth and the accumulation of Earth's goods. As we have seen, this is Luke's strongest and clearest message most confronting to contemporary gospel auditors, especially those of us living in first world countries.

Wealth and environmental behaviour were also linked in Luke's day. Luke's teaching on discipleship is powerfully illustrated in the gospel's most memorable characters, the pregnant Mary, the searching shepherds, the possessed synagogue worshiper, the haemorrhaging woman, the pleading father, shepherds attending their flocks, the woman searching for the lost coin, the father with the two lost sons, the shouting blind beggar, the rich tax collector of Jericho, the women at the tomb. They powerfully illustrate what it means to be Jesus' disciples. All of them illustrate in different ways the role which Earth plays in the story of Jesus as Earth's child.

Bibliography

Aichele, George and Gary Allen Phillips (eds.), *Intertextuality and the Bible* (Semeia, 69/70; Atlanta: Scholars Press, 1995).

Aichele, George and Gary Allen Phillips, 'Introduction: Exegesis, Eisegesis, and Intergesis', in *Intertextuality and the Bible* (Semeia, 69/70; Atlanta: Scholars Press, 1995), pp. 8-9.

Alexander, Loveday C., 'Sisters in Adversity: Retelling Martha's Story', in *A Feminist Companion to Luke* (ed. Amy-Jill Levine and Marianne Blickenstaff; London: Sheffield Academic Press, 2002), pp. 197-213.

—*The Preface to Luke's Gospel: Literary convention and social context in Luke 1.1-4 and Acts 1.1* (Cambridge: Cambridge University Press, 1993).

—'The Relevance of Greco-Roman Literature and Culture to New Testament Study,' in *Hearing the New Testament: Strategies for Interpretation* (ed. Joel B. Green; Grand Rapids, MI: Wm B. Eerdmans Publishing Co., 2010), pp. 85-101.

Allison, Dale C., *Jesus of Nazareth: Millenarian Prophet* (Minneapolis, MN: Fortress Press, 1998).

Anderson, Janice C. and Jeffrey L. Staley, *Taking it Personally: Autobiographical Biblical Criticism* (Semeia, 72; Atlanta: Scholars Press, 1995).

Anthony, Peter, 'What are They Saying about Luke–Acts?', *ScriptBull* 40 (2010), pp. 10-21.

Bailey, Kenneth, *Poet and Peasant: A Literary-Cultural Approach to the Parables in Luke* (Grand Rapids, MI: Wm B. Eerdmans Publishing Co., 1976).

Barthes, Roland, *Image, Music, Text* (New York: Hill & Wang, 1977).

Barzilai, Shuli, 'Borders of Language: Kristeva's Critique of Lacan', *Publications of the Modern Language Association of America* 106 (March, 1991), pp. 294-305.

Bauckham, Richard, *Bible and Ecology: Rediscovering the Community of Creation* (Waco, TX: Baylor University Press, 2010).

—*Jesus and the Eyewitnesses: The Gospels as Eyewitness Testimony* (Grand Rapids, MI: Wm B. Eerdmans Publishing Co., 2006).

—*Living with Other Creatures: Green Exegesis and Theology* (Waco, TX: Baylor University Press, 2010).

—'Reading Scripture as a Coherent Story' in *The Art of Reading Scripture* (ed. Ellen F. Davis and Richard B. Hays; Grand Rapids, MI: Wm B. Eerdmans Publishing Co., 2003), pp. 38-53.

Beal, Timothy K., 'Ideology and Intertextuality: Surplus of Meaning and Controlling the Means of Production', in *Reading Between Texts: Intertextuality and the Hebrew Bible* (ed. D.N. Fewell; Louisville, KY: Westminster/ John Knox Press, 1992), pp. 27-40.

Ben-Dor, Immanuel, 'Alabaster', *IDB*, 1 (Nashville, TN: Abingdon Press, 1962), pp. 75-76.

Bertram, Georg, 'νήπιος', *TDNT*, IV (ed. Gerhard Kittel and Gerhard Friedrich; Grand Rapids, MI: Wm B. Eerdmans Publishing Co., 1964), pp. 912-23.

Bird, Michael F., 'The Unity of Luke–Acts in Recent Discussion', *JSNT* 29 (2007), pp. 425-48.

Bock, Darrell L., *Luke. Volume 2: 9.51–24.53* (Grand Rapids, MI: Baker Academic, 1996).

Böhmer, Harald and Recep Karadag, 'New Dye Research on Palmyra Textiles', *Dyes in History and Archaeology: Papers Presented at the Annual Meetings of Dyes in History and Archaeology* 19 (2003), pp. 88-93.

Booth, Ken (ed.), *For All the Saints: A Resource for the Commemorations of the Calendar* (Hastings, NZ: Anglican Church in Aotearoa, New Zealand and Polynesia, 1996).

Borgman, Paul, *The Way According to Luke: Hearing the Whole Story of Luke–Acts* (Grand Rapids, MI: Wm B. Eerdmans Publishing Co., 2006).

Botha, Pieter J.J., 'Cognition, Orality-Literacy, and Approaches to First-Century Writings', in *Orality, Literacy, and Colonialism* (ed. Jonathan A. Draper; Atlanta, GA: Society of Biblical Literature, 2004), pp. 37- 64.

Bovon, François, *Luke 1: A Commentary on the Gospel of Luke 1:1-9:50* (Minneapolis, MN: Augsburg Fortress Press, 2002).

Bradley, Keith and Paul Cartledge (ed.), *The Cambridge World History of Slavery. Volume 1: The Ancient Mediterranean World* (Cambridge: Cambridge University Press, 2011).

Breck, John, 'Biblical Chiasmus: Exploring Structure for Meaning', *BTB* 17 (1987), pp. 70-74.

Brown, Colin (ed.), *The New International Dictionary of New Testament Theology*, 1 (Grand Rapids, MI: Zondervan, 1975).

Brown, Raymond E., *An Introduction to the New Testament* (Garden City, NY: Doubleday, 1997).

—'Brief Observations on the Shroud of Turin', *BTB* 14 (1984), pp. 145-48.

—*The Birth of the Messiah: A Commentary on the Infancy Narratives in Matthew and Luke* (Garden City, NY: Doubleday, 1977).

—*The Death of the Messiah: From Gethsemane to the Grave: A Commentary on the Passion Narratives in the Four Gospels*. Two Volumes (Garden City, NY: Doubleday, 1994).

Byrne, Brendan, *The Hospitality of God: A Reading of Luke's Gospel* (Collegeville, MN: The Liturgical Press, 2000).

Cadbury, Henry J., *The Making of Luke–Acts* (New York: Macmillan & Co., 1927).

—*The Style and Literary Method of Luke* (Cambridge, MA: Harvard University Press, 1920).

Cadwallader, Alan, '"And the Earth Shook" —Mortality and Ecological Diversity: Jesus' Death in Matthew's Gospel', in *Biodiversity and Ecology as Interdisciplinary Challenge* (ed. Mark Worthington and Denis Edwards; Adelaide: ATF, 2004), pp. 45-54.

—'In Go(l)d we Trust: Literary and Economic Exchange in the Debate over Caesar's Coin (Mk 12:13-17)', *BibInt* 14 (2006), pp. 486-507.

—'Swords into Ploughshares: The End of War? (Q/Luke 9.62)', in *The Earth Story in the New Testament* (ed. N. Habel and V. Balabanski; London: Sheffield Academic Press, 2002), pp. 57-75.

Cargill, Robert R., *Qumran through (Real) Time: A Virtual Reconstruction of Qumran and the Dead Sea Scrolls* (Piscataway, NJ: Gorgias, 2009).

Carney, Thomas F., *The Shape of the Past: Models of Antiquity* (Lawrence, KS: Coronado Press, 1975).

Carter, Warren, 'Getting Martha Out of the Kitchen: Luke 10.38-42 Again', in *A Feminist Companion to Luke* (ed. Amy-Jill Levine and Marianne Blickenstaff; London: Sheffield Academic Press, 2002), pp. 214-31.

Casey, Maurice, *The Solution to the 'Son of Man' Problem* (London: T. & T. Clark, 2007).
Cockburn, Eve and Mary W. Ballard, 'Cotton in Ancient Egypt: A Unique Find', *Proceedings of the First World Congress on Mummy Studies, Puerto de la Cruz, Tenerife, Canary Islands, February 3-6, 1992* (Santa Cruz, Tenerife: Archeological Museum of Tenerife, 1996), pp. 625-31.
Collins, John N. *Diakonia: Re-interpreting the Ancient Sources* (New York: Oxford University Press, 1990).
Conzelmann, Hans, *The Theology of St. Luke* (New York: Harper and Row, 1961).
Cosgrove, Charles H., 'The Divine Δεῖ in Luke–Acts: Investigations into the Lukan Understanding of Divine Providence', *NovT* 26 (1984), pp. 189-190.
Crossan, John Dominic, *The Historical Jesus: The Life of a Mediterranean Jewish Peasant* (San Francisco: HarperCollins, 1991).
—*Who Killed Jesus? Exposing the roots of Anti-Semitism in the Gospel Story of the Death of Jesus* (San Francisco: HarperCollins, 1995).
Culler, Jonathan D., *On Deconstruction: Theory and Criticism after Structuralism* (Ithaca, NY: Cornell University Press, 1982).
D'Angelo, Mary Rose, 'The ANHP Question in Luke–Acts: Imperial Masculinity and the Deployment of Women in the Early Second Century', in *A Feminist Companion to Luke* (ed. Amy-Jill Levine and Marianne Blickenstaff; London: Sheffield Academic Press, 2002), pp. 44-69.
Davies, Gwynne Henton, 'Ark of the Covenant', in *IDB*, 1 (ed. George A. Buttrick; Nashville, TN: Abingdon Press, 1962), pp. 222-26.
Davis, Ellen F. and Richard B. Hays (ed.), *The Art of Reading Scripture* (Grand Rapids, MI: Wm B. Eerdmans Publishing Co., 2003).
Debrunner, Albert, 'ῥῆμα', *TDNT*, IV (ed. Gerhard Kittel and Gerhard Friedrich; Grand Rapids, MI: Wm B. Eerdmans Publishing Co., 1964), pp. 69-77.
Derrett, J. Duncan M., 'The Manger at Bethlehem: Light on St. Luke's Technique from Contemporary Jewish Religious Law', in *Studies in the New Testament: Volume 2: Midrash in Action and as a Literary Device* (Leiden: E.J. Brill, 1978), pp. 39-47.
—'The Manger: Ritual Law and Soteriology', in *Studies in the New Testament: Volume 2: Midrash in Action and as a Literary Device* (Leiden: E.J. Brill, 1978), pp. 48-53.
Detweiler, Robert, 'What is a sacred text?', in *Reader-Response Approaches to Biblical and Secular Texts* (Semeia, 31; Decatur, IL: Scholars Press, 1985), pp. 213-30.
Devall, Bill, *Simple in Means, Rich in Ends: Practising Deep Ecology* (London: Green Print, 1990).
Dillon, Richard J., *From Eyewitnesses to Ministers of the Word: Tradition and Composition in Luke 24* (Rome: Biblical Institute, 1978).
DiMento, Joseph F.C. and Pamela M. Doughman (ed.), *Climate Change: What it Means for Us, our Children, and our Grandchildren* (Cambridge, MA: Massachusetts Institute of Technology Press, 2007).
Donahue, John R., 'Tax Collectors and Sinners: An Attempt at Identification', *CBQ* 33 (1971), pp. 39-61.
Douglas, Mary T., *Purity and Danger: An Analysis of Concepts of Pollution and Taboo* (New York: Praeger, 1966).
Dowling, Elizabeth V., *Taking Away the Pound: Women, Theology and the Parable of the Pounds in the Gospel of Luke* (London: T. & T. Clark, 2007).
Draper, Jonathan A. (ed.), *Orality, Literacy, and Colonialism in Antiquity* (Atlanta: Society of Biblical Literature, 2004).

Duling, Dennis, *The New Testament: An Introduction* (New York: Harcourt, Brace, Jovanovic, 1993).

Dyer, Keith D., 'When is the End Not the End? The Fate of Earth in Biblical Eschatology (Mark 13)', in *The Earth Story in the New Testament* (ed. N. Habel and V. Balabanski; London: Sheffield Academic Press, 2002), pp. 44-56.

Eliot, T.S., *Selected Essays, 1917–1932* (NY: Harcourt, Brace & Company, 1932).

Elliott, John H. 'Temple versus Household in Luke–Acts: A Contrast in Social Institutions', in *The Social World of Luke–Acts. Models for Interpretation* (ed. Jerome H. Neyrey; Peabody, MA: Hendrickson Publishers, 1991), pp. 211-40.

Ellis, E. Earle, *The Gospel of Luke* (London: Marhsall, Morgan & Scott, revised edn, 1974).

Elvey, Anne, *An Ecological Feminist Reading of the Gospel of Luke: A Gestational Paradigm* (Lewiston, NY: The Edwin Mellen Press, 2005).

—'Earthing the Text?: On the Status of the Biblical Text in Ecological Perspective', *ABR* 52 (2004), pp. 64-79.

—'Storing up Death, Storing up Life: An Earth Story in Luke 12.13-34', in *The Earth Story in the New Testament* (ed. N. Habel and V. Balabanski; London: Sheffield Academic Press, 2002), pp. 95-107.

Ernst, Josef, *Das Evangelium nach Lukas* (Regensburg: Verlag Friedrich Pustet, 1993).

Evans, Christopher Francis, *Saint Luke* (London: SCM Press, 1990).

Fawcett, S. Vernon, 'Manger', *IDB*, III (ed George Arthur Buttrick; Nashville, TN: Abingdon Press, 1962), p. 257.

Fishbane, Michael, *Biblical Interpretation in Ancient Israel* (Oxford: Clarendon, 1985).

Fitzmyer, Joseph A., *The Gospel According to Luke I–IX* (Garden City, NY: Doubleday & Company, Inc., 1981).

—*The Gospel According to Luke X–XXIV* (Garden City, NY: Doubleday & Company, Inc., 1981).

Foerster, Werner, 'ὄρος', *TDNT*, V (ed. Gerhard Kittel and Gerhard Friedrich; Grand Rapids, MI: Wm B. Eerdmans Publishing Co., 1964), pp. 475-87.

Ford, Josephine M., *My Enemy is my Guest: Jesus and Violence in Luke* (Maryknoll, NY: Orbis, 1984).

Foster, S.M., 'Analysis of Spatial Patterns in Buildings (Access Analysis) as an Insight into the Social Structure: Examples from the Scottish Atlantic Iron Age', *Antiquity* 63 (1989), pp. 40-50.

Freyne, Sean, *Jesus, a Jewish Galilean: A New Reading of the Jesus-Story* (London: T. & T. Clark International, 2004).

Gager, John G., 'Where Does Luke's Anti-Judaism Come From?', *AnnStorEseg* 24 (2007), pp. 31-35.

Garland, David E., 'Swaddling'. *ISBE*, IV (ed. Geoffrey W. Bromiley; Grand Rapids: Wm B. Eerdmans, 1995), p. 670.

Gerhard Delling, 'πληρόω', *TDNT*, VI (ed. Gerhard Kittel and Gerhard Friedrich; Grand Rapids, MI: Wm B. Eerdmans Publishing Co., 1964), pp. 286-311.

Green, Joel B., *The Gospel of Luke* (Grand Rapids, MI: Wm B. Eerdmans Publishing Co., 1997).

Gregory, Andrew, 'The Reception of Luke and Acts and the Unity of Luke–Acts', *JSNT* 29 (2007), pp. 459-72.

Guijarro, Santiago, 'The Family in First-Century Galilee', in *Constructing Early Christian Families: Family as Social Reality and Metaphor* (ed. Halvor Moxnes; London: Routledge, 1997), pp. 42-65.

Habel, Norman, *An Inconvenient Text; Is Green Reading of the Bible Possible?* (Adelaide, SA: ATF Press, 2009).
—*The Birth, the Curse and the Greening of Earth: An Ecological Reading of Genesis 1-11* (Sheffield: Sheffield Phoenix Press, 2011).
Habel, Norman (ed.), *Readings from the Perspective of the Earth* (Sheffield: Sheffield Press, 2000).
Habel, Norman and Peter Trudinger (eds.), *Exploring Ecological Hermeneutics* (Atlanta, GA: Society of Biblical Literature, 2008).
Halliday, Michael Alexander Kirkwood, *Language as Social Semiotic: The Social Interpretation of Language and Meaning* (London: Edward Arnold, 1978).
Hallman, David G. (ed.), *Ecotheology: Voices from South and North* (New York: Orbis Books, 1994).
Hamm, Dennis M., 'The Freeing of the Bent Woman and the Restoration of Israel: Luke 13:10-17 as Narrative Theology,' *JSNT* 10 (1987), pp. 23-44.
Hanson, K.C., 'All in the Family: Kinship in Agrarian Roman Palestine', in *The Social World of the New Testament: Insights and Models* (ed. Jerome H. Neyrey and Eric C. Stewart; Peabody, MA: Hendrickson Publishers, 2008), pp. 25-46.
Hartsock, Chad, *Sight and Blindness in Luke–Acts: The Use of Physical Features in Characterization* (Leiden: Brill, 2008).
Hayes, John. H. (ed.), *DBI*, I (Nashville, TN: Abingdon Press, 1999).
Hays, Richard B. and Joel B. Green, 'The Use of the Old Testament by New Testament Writers', in *Hearing the New Testament: Strategies for Interpretation* (ed. Joel B. Green; Grand Rapids, MI: Wm B. Eerdmans Publishing Co., 2010), pp. 122-39.
Heil, John P., *The Meal Scenes in Luke–Acts: An Audience-Oriented Approach* (Atlanta, GA: The Society of Biblical Literature, 1999).
Hengel, Martin, 'φάτνη', *TDNT*, IX (ed. Gerhard Kittel and Gerhard Friedrich; Grand Rapids, MI: Wm B. Eerdmans Publishing Co., 1964), pp. 49-55.
Herr, L.G., 'Stall', *ISBE*, IV (ed. Geoffrey W. Bromiley; Grand Rapids, MI: Wm B. Eerdmans Publishing Co., 1995), pp. 609-610.
Holgate, David A., *Prodigality, Liberality and Meanness in the Parable of the Prodigal Son: A Greco-Roman Perspective on Luke 15.11-32* (Sheffield: Sheffield Academic Press, 1999).
Horsley, Richard A., *Archaeology, History, and Society in Galilee: The Social Context of Jesus and the Rabbis* (Valley Forge, PA: Trinity Press International, 1996).
House, Paul R., *Beyond Form Criticism: Essays in Old Testament Literary Criticism* (Winona Lake, WI: Eisenbrauns, 1992).
Hur, J., *A Dynamic Reading of the Holy Spirit in Luke–Acts* (Sheffield: Sheffield Academic Press, 2001).
Irudhayasamy, Raymond Joseph, *A Prophet in the Making: A Christological Study on Lk 4, 16-30: In the Background of the Isaianic Mixed Citation and the Elijah-Elisha References* (Frankfurt: Peter Lang, 2002).
Jenson, Robert W., 'Scripture's Authority in the Church', in *The Art of Reading Scripture* (ed. Ellen F. Davis and Richard B. Hays; Grand Rapids, MI: Wm B. Eerdmans Publishing Co., 2003), pp. 27-37.
Johnson, Luke Timothy, *The Gospel of Luke* (Collegeville, MN: The Liturgical Press, 1991).
Joy, Morny and Kathleen O'Grady and Judith L. Poxon (ed.), *French Feminists on Religion: A Reader* (London: Routledge, 2002).
Kähler, Martin, *The So-Called Historical Jesus and the Historic Biblical Christ* (Philadelphia, PA: Fortress, 1964).

Kamp, Kathryn A., 'Towards an Archaeology of Architecture: Clues from a Modern Syrian Village', *Journal of Anthropological Research* 49 (1993), pp. 293-317.
Karris, Robert J., *Eating Your Way through Luke's Gospel* (Collegeville, MN: Liturgical Press, 2006).
—'The Gospel According to Luke', *NJBC* (ed. Raymond E. Brown, *et al.*; London: Chapman, 1991), pp. 675-721.
—*Luke: Artist and Theologian: Luke's Passion Account as Literature* (New York: Paulist Press, 1985).
—'Missionary Communities: A New Paradigm for the Study of Luke–Acts', *CBQ* 41 (1979), pp. 80-97.
—'Women and Discipleship in Luke', *CBQ* 56 (1994), pp. 1-20.
Karris, Robert J. (ed.), *Works of St. Bonaventure: Commentary on the Gospel of Luke. Chapters 1-8* (Saint Bonaventure, NY: Franciscan Institute Publications, 2001).
—*Works of St. Bonaventure: Commentary on the Gospel of Luke. Chapters 9-16* (Saint Bonaventure, NY: Franciscan Institute Publications, 2003).
Kasper, Walter, *Jesus the Christ* (New York: Paulist Press, 1976).
Keitzar, Renethy, 'Creation and Restoration: Three Biblical Reflections', in *Ecotheology: Voices from South and North* (ed. David G. Hallman; New York: Orbis Books, 1994), pp. 52-64.
Kitzberger, Ingrid R. (ed.), *The Personal Voice in Biblical Interpretation*. (London: Routledge, 1999).
Klassen, William, 'The authenticity of the command: "Love your Enemies"', in *Authenticating the Words of Jesus* (ed. B.D. Chilton and C.A. Evans; Leiden: E. Brill, 1999), pp. 385-407.
—*Love of Enemies: The Way to Peace* (Minneapolis, MN: Fortress Press, 1984).
Kleine, Heribert, 'ὄρος', *EDNT*, II (ed. Horst Balz and Gerhard Schneider; Grand Rapids, MI: Wm B. Eerdmans Publishing Co., 1991), pp. 533-34.
Kodell, Jerome, 'The Word of God Grew: The Ecclesial Tendency of *Logos* in Acts 1:7; 12:24; 19:20', *Biblica* 55 (1974), pp. 505-19.
Kristeva, Julia, *Desire in Language: A Semiotic Approach to Literature and Art* (ed. L.S. Roudiez; New York: Columbia University, 1980).
—*Revolution in Poetic Language* (New York: Columbia University, 1984).
Landi, Sheila and Rosalind M. Hall, 'The Discovery and Conservation of an Ancient Egyptian Linen Tunic', *Studies in Conservation* 24 (1979), pp. 141-52.
Landsberger, Henry (ed.), *Rural Protest: Peasant Movements and Social Change* (New York: Barnes & Noble, 1973).
LaVerdiere, Eugene, *Dining in the Kingdom of God: The Origins of the Eucharist according to Luke* (Chicago, IN: Liturgy Training Publications, 1994).
Lenski, Gerhard E., *Power and Privilege: A Theory of Social Stratification* (New York, NY: McGraw-Hill, 1966).
Lenski, Gerhard E., and Jeanne Lenski, *Human Societies: An Introduction to Macrosociology* (New York, NY: McGraw-Hill, 1974).
Léon-Dufour, Xavier, 'Passion (Récits de la)', *Dictionnaire de la Bible, Supplément* 6 (1960), pp. 1419-92.
Levine, Amy-Jill, 'Biblical Views: The Many Faces of the Good Samaritan—Most Wrong', *Biblical Archaeology Review* 38 (2012), pp. 24, 68.
Levine, Amy-Jill and Marianne Blickenstaff (eds.), *A Feminist Companion to Luke* (London: Sheffield Academic Press, 2002).

Longenecker, Bruce W., 'The Story of the Samaritan and the Innkeeper (Luke 10:30-35): A Study in Character Rehabilitation', *BibInt* 17 (2009), pp. 422-47.

Maddox, Robert, *The Purpose of Luke–Acts* (Göttingen: Vandenhoeck & Ruprecht, 1982).

Malbon, Elizabeth Struthers, *Mark's Jesus: Characterization as Narrative Christology* (Waco, TX: Baylor University Press, 2009).

Malina, Bruce J. and Richard L. Rohrbaugh, *Social-Science Commentary on the Synoptic Gospels* (Minneapolis, MN: Fortress Press, 1992).

Marlow, Hilary, 'The Other Prophet! The Voice of the Earth in the Book of Amos', in *Exploring Ecological Hermeneutics* (ed. Norman C. Habel and Peter Trudinger; Atlanta, GA: Society of Biblical Literature, 2008), pp. 75-84.

Marshall, I. Howard, *The Gospel of Luke: A Commentary on the Greek Text* (Grand Rapids, MI: Wm B. Eerdmans Publishing Co., 1978).

Marsh-Letts, Glennda Susan, 'Ancient Egyptian Linen: The Role of Natron and other Salts in the Preservation and Conservation of Archaeological Textiles—A Pilot Study', *BA (Hon) Thesis* (Sydney: University of Western Sydney, 2002).

Martin, Dale B., *The Corinthian Body* (Yale, CN: Yale University Press, 1995).

Martin, Thomas W., 'What Makes Glory Glorious? Reading Luke's Account of the Transfiguration over against Triumphalism', *JSNT* 29 (2006), pp. 3-26.

McDonnell, Killian, 'Jesus' Baptism in the Jordan', *TS* 56 (1995), pp. 209-36.

Metzger, Bruce M., *A Textual Commentary on the Greek New Testament: A Companion Volume to the United Bible Society's Greek New Testament*. Third Edition (London: United Bible Societies, 1971).

Metzger, James A., *Consumption and Wealth in Luke's Travel Narrative* (Leiden: Brill, 2007).

Moessner, David, *Lord of the Banquet: The Literary and Theological Significance of the Lukan Travel Narrative* (Minneapolis, MN: Fortress Press, 1989).

Moi, Toril (ed.), *The Kristeva Reader* (Oxford: Basil Blackwell Ltd, 1986).

Moltmann-Wendell, Elisabeth, *The Women Around Jesus* (London: SCM Press, 1982).

Moxnes, Halvor (ed.), *Constructing Early Christian Families: Family as Social Reality and Metaphor* (London: Routledge, 1997).

Napier, B. Davie, 'Sheep', *IDB*, IV (ed. George Arthur Buttrick; Nashville, TN: Abingdon Press, 1962), pp. 315-16.

Neagoe, Alexandru, *The Trial of the Gospel: An Apologetic Reading of Luke's Trial Narratives* (Cambridge, MA: Cambridge University Press, 2002).

Neusner, Jacob, *The Idea of Purity in Ancient Judaism* (Leiden: Brill, 1973).

Neyrey, Jerome H., 'The Absence of Jesus' Emotions: The Lucan Redaction of Lk 22:39-46', *Biblica* 61 (1980), pp. 153-71.

Neyrey, Jerome H. (ed.), *The Social World of Luke–Acts: Models for Interpretation* (Peabody, MA: Hendrickson Publishers, 1991).

Neyrey, Jerome H. and Eric C. Stewart (ed.), *The Social World of the New Testament: Insights and Models* (Peabody, MA: Hendrickson Publishers, 2008).

Nolland, John, *Luke 1–9.20* (Dallas: Word Books, 1989).

O'Day, Gail R., 'Intertextuality', *DBI*, I (ed. John. H. Hayes; Nashville, TN: Abingdon Press, 1999), pp. 546-48.

—'Jeremiah 9.22-23 and 1 Corinthians 1.26-31: A study in Intertextuality', *JBL* 109 (1990), pp. 259-67.

O'Toole, Robert F., *Luke's Presentation of Jesus: A Christology* (Rome: Editice Pontificio Istituto Biblico, 2008).

Oakman, Douglas E., 'The Countryside in Luke–Acts', in *The Social World of Luke–Acts: Models for Interpretation* (ed. Jerome H. Neyrey; Peabody, MA: Hendrickson Publishers, 1991), pp. 151-80.
—'Was Jesus a Peasant? Implications for Reading the Jesus Tradition (Luke 10:30-35)', in *The Social World of the New Testament: Insights and Models* (ed. Jerome H. Neyrey and Eric C. Stewart; Peabody, MA: Hendrickson Publishers, 2008), pp. 125-40.
Osiek, Carolyn and David L. Balch, *Families in the New Testament World: Households and House Churches* (Louisville, KY: Westminster John Knox Press, 1997).
Patte, Daniel, 'The Guarded Personal Voice of a Male European-American Biblical Scholar', in *The Personal Voice in Biblical Interpretation* (ed. I.R. Kitzberger; London and New York: Routledge, 1999), pp. 12-23.
Pilch, John J., 'Healing in Luke–Acts', in *The Social World of the New Testament: Insights and Models* (ed. Jerome H. Neyrey and Eric C. Stewart; Peabody, MA: Hendrickson Publishers, 2008), pp. 201-20.
Pilch, John J. and Bruce Malina (ed.), *Handbook of Biblical Social Values* (Peabody, MA: Hendrickson Publishers, 1993).
Piper, John,'Love your enemies'. *Jesus' Love Command in the Synoptic Gospels and in the Early Christian Paraenesis: A History of the Tradition and Interpretation of its Uses* (New York: Cambridge University Press, 1979).
Prior, Michael, *Jesus the Liberator: Nazareth Liberation Theology (Lk, 16-30)* (Sheffield: Sheffield Press, 1995).
Quasten, Johannes, 'A Pythagorean Idea in Jerome', *American Journal of Philology* 63 (1942), pp. 207-15.
Ravens, David, *Luke and the Restoration of Israel* (Sheffield: Sheffield Academic Press, 1995).
Reid, Barbara E., '"Do You See This Woman?"': A Liberative Look at Luke 7.36-50 and Strategies for Reading Other Lukan Stories against the Grain', in *A Feminist Companion to Luke* (ed. Amy-Jill Levine and Marianne Blickenstaff; London: Sheffield Academic Press, 2002), pp. 106-20.
Rigato, Maria-Luisa, '"'Remember'…Then They Remembered": Luke 24.6-8,' in *A Feminist Companion to Luke* (ed. Amy-Jill Levine and Marianne Blickenstaff; London: Sheffield Academic Press, 2002), pp. 269-80.
Rindge, Matthew S., *Jesus' Parable of the Rich Fool: Luke 12:13-34 among Ancient Conversations on Death and Possessions* (Atlanta, GA: Society of Biblical Literature, 2011).
Robbins, Vernon K., 'The Social Location of the Implied Author of Luke–Acts', in *The Social World of Luke–Acts: Models for Interpretation* (ed. Jerome H. Neyrey; Peabody, MA: Hendrickson Publishers, 1991), pp. 305-32.
Rohrbaugh, Richard L., 'The Pre-industrial City in Luke–Acts', in *The Social World of Luke–Acts: Models for Interpretation* (ed. Jerome H. Neyrey; Peabody, MA: Hendrickson Publishers, 1991), pp. 125-50.
—'The Social Location of the Marcan Audience', *BTB* 23 (1993), pp. 114-27.
—'The Social Location of the Markan Audience', in *The Social World of the New Testament: Insights and Models* (ed. Jerome H. Neyrey and Eric C. Stewart; Peabody, MA: Hendrickson Publishers, 2008), pp. 143-62.
Ross, James F., 'Salt', *IDB*, IV (ed. George A. Buttrick; Nashville, TN: Abingdon Press, 1962), pp. 167-68.
Roth, S. John, *The Blind, the Lame, and the Poor* (Sheffield: Sheffield Academic Press, 1997).

Rowe, C. Kavin, *Early Narrative Christology: The Lord in the Gospel of Luke* (Berlin: de Gruyter, 2006).
—'History, Hermeneutics and the Unity of Luke–Acts', *JSNT* 28 (2005), pp. 131-57.
—'Literary Unity and Reception History: Reading Luke–Acts as Luke and Acts', JSNT 29 (2007), pp. 449-57.
Sand, Alexander, 'σάρξ', *EDNT*, III (ed. Horst Balz and Gerhard Schneider; Grand Rapids, MI: Wm B. Eerdmans Publishing Co., 1991), pp. 230-33.
Schelkle, Karl Hermann, 'σωματικός', *EDNT*, III (ed. Horst Balz and Gerhard Schneider; Grand Rapids, MI: Wm B. Eerdmans Publishing Co., 1991), p. 325
Schneider, Gerhard, 'κτῆνος', *EDNT*, II (ed. Horst Balz and Gerhard Schneider; Grand Rapids, MI: Wm B. Eerdmans Publishing Co., 1991), pp. 324-25.
Schneiders, Sandra, *Beyond Patching: Faith and Feminism in the Catholic Church* (New York: Paulist Press, 1991).
Schofield, Alison, *From Qumran to the Yaḥad. A New Paradigm of Textual Development for the Community Rule* (Leiden: Brill, 2009).
Schüssler Fiorenza, Elisabeth, *In Memory of Her: A Feminist Theological Reconstruction of Christian Origins* (New York: Crossroad, 1983).
—*Jesus: Miriam's Child, Sophia's Prophet: Critical Issues in Feminist Christology* (London: SCM Press, 1993).
Schweizer, Eduard, 'σάρξ', *TDNT*, VII (ed. Gerhard Kittel and Gerhard Friedrich; Grand Rapids, MI: Wm B. Eerdmans Publishing Co., 1964), pp. 98-151.
—'σῶμα', *TDNT*, VII (ed. Gerhard Kittel and Gerhard Friedrich; Grand Rapids, MI: Wm B. Eerdmans Publishing Co., 1964), pp 1024-1044.
Seccombe, David Peter, *Possessions and the Poor in Luke–Acts* (Linz: A. Fuchs, 1982).
Seeseman, Heinrich, 'πατέω', *TDNT*, V (ed. Gerhard Kittel and Gerhard Friedrich; Grand Rapids, MI: Wm B. Eerdmans Publishing Co., 1964), pp. 940-45.
Segovia, Fernando F., 'My Personal Voice: The Making of a Postcolonial Critic', in *The Personal Voice in Biblical Interpretation* (ed. Ingrid R. Kitzberger; London: Routledge, 1999), pp. 25-37.
—'The Text as Other: Towards a Hispanic American Hermeneutic', in *Text & Experience: Towards a Cultural Exegesis of the Bible* (ed. D. Smith-Christopher; Sheffield: Sheffield Academic Press, 1995), pp. 276-98.
—'Towards a Hermeneutics of the Diaspora: A Hermeneutics of Otherness and Engagement', in *Reading from this Place. Volume 1: Social Location and Biblical Interpretation in the United States* (ed. F.F. Segovia and M.A. Tolbert; Minneapolis, MN: Fortress, 1995), pp. 57-73.
—'Towards Intercultural Criticism: A Reading Strategy from the Diaspora', in *Reading from this Place. Volume 2: Social Location and Biblical Interpretation in Global Perspective* (ed. F.F. Segovia and M.A. Tolbert; Minneapolis, MN: Fortress, 1995), pp. 303-30.
Seim, Turid Karlsen, *The Double Message* (Nashville, TN: Abingdon Press, 1994).
—'The Virgin Mother: Mary and Ascetic Discipleship in Luke', in *A Feminist Companion to Luke* (ed. Amy-Jill Levine and Marianne Blickenstaff; London: Sheffield Academic Press, 2002), pp. 89-105.
Senior, Donald, *The Passion of Jesus in the Gospel of Luke* (Wilmington, DE: Glazier, 1989).
Shellard, Barbara, *New Light on Luke: Its Purpose, Sources and Literary Context* (Sheffield: Sheffield Academic Press, 2002).

Small, Jocelyn Penny, *Wax Tablets of the Mind: Cognitive Studies of Memory and Literacy in Classical Antiquity* (Abingdon, Oxford: Routledge, 1997).

Smith-Christopher, Daniel L. (ed.), *Text & Experience: Towards a Cultural Exegesis of the Bible* (Sheffield: Sheffield Academic Press, 1995).

Soards, Marion L., *The Passion According to Luke: The Special Material of Luke 22* (Sheffield: Sheffield Academic Press, 1987).

Spencer, Patrick E., 'The Unity of Luke–Acts: A Four-Bolted Hermeneutical Hinge', *CurrBibRes* 5 (2007), pp. 341-66.

Sroka, Peter, 'Kostbare Faserstoffe aus der Antike: handelt es sich beim biblischen Byssus um Muschelseide?', ('Precious Fibre used in Antiquity: Is the Biblical Byssus Shell Silk?'), *Restauro: Zeitschrift für Kunsttechniken, Restaurierung und Museumsfragen* 101 (1995), pp. 338-42.

Stinespring, William Franklin, 'Temple, Jerusalem', *IDB*, IV (ed. George A. Buttrick; Nashville, TN: Abingdon Press, 1962), pp. 534-60.

Stock, Augustine, 'Chiastic Awareness and Education in Antiquity', *BTB* 14 (1984), pp. 23-27.

Strelan, Rick, *Luke the Priest: The Authority of the Author of the Third Gospel* (Aldershot, Hants.: Ashgate, 2008).

Tannehill, Robert C., *Luke* (Nashville, TN: Abingdon Press, 1996).

—*The Narrative Unity of Luke–Acts: A Literary Interpretation. Volume 1: The Gospel according to Luke* (Philadelphia, PA: Fortress Press, 1986).

Taylor, Vincent, *Gospel According to St. Mark: The Greek Text* (London: Macmillan & Co. Ltd, 1953).

Telford, William R., *The Barren Temple and the Withered Tree* (Sheffield: Sheffield Press, 1980).

Trainor, Michael, *According to Luke: Insights for Contemporary Pastoral Practice* (North Blackburn, Vic: Collins Dove, 1992).

—'A Footstool or a Throne? Luke's attitude to Earth (ge) in Acts 7', in *The Earth Story in the New Testament* (ed. N. Habel and V. Balabanski; London: Sheffield Academic Press, 2002), pp. 122-36.

—'"... And on Earth, Peace ..." (Lk 2:14): Luke's Perspectives on the Earth', in *Readings from the Perspective of the Earth. Volume 2* (ed. N. Habel; London: Sheffield Academic Press, 2000), pp. 174-92.

—'Five Ways Australian Christians use the Bible', *Reo: A Journal of Theology and Ministry* 8 (1998), pp. 7-17.

—*The Quest for Home: The Household in Mark's Community* (Collegeville, MN: The Liturgical Press, 2001).

Trever, John C., 'Mustard', *IDB*, III (ed. George A. Buttrick; Nashville, TN: Abingdon Press, 1962), pp. 476-77.

Tyson, Joseph B., *Luke, Judaism, and The Scholars: Critical Approaches to Luke–Acts* (Columbia, SC: University of South Carolina Press, 1999).

Vaux, Roland de, *Archaeology and the Dead Sea Scrolls* (Oxford: Oxford University Press, 1973).

Voelz, James W., 'Multiple Signs, Levels of Meaning and Self as Text: Elements of Intertextuality', in *Intertextuality and the Bible* (Semeia, 69/70; Atlanta, GA: Scholars Press, 1995), pp. 149-64.

von Rad, Gerhard, 'The OT View of Satan', *TDNT*, II (ed. Gerhard Kittel and Gerhard Friedrich; Grand Rapids, MI: Wm B. Eerdmans Publishing Co., 1964), pp. 73-75.

Wainwright, Elaine, *Shall We Look for Another: A Feminist Rereading of the Matthean Jesus* (Maryknoll, NY: Orbis Books, 1998).
Waschmann, Shelly, 'The Galilee Boat: 2000-Year-Old Hull Recovered Intact', *BAR* 14 (1988), pp. 18-33.
Weiss, Konrad, 'διαφέρω', *TDNT*, IX (ed. Gerhard Kittel and Gerhard Friedrich; Grand Rapids, MI: Wm B. Eerdmans Publishing Co., 1964), pp. 62-64.
Wiles, Virginia, 'On Transforming New Testament Theology: (Re)Claiming Subjectivity', in *Putting Body & Soul Together: Essays in Honor of Robin Scroggs*, (ed. Virginia Wiles, Alexandra Brown and Graydon F. Snyder; Valley Forge, PA: Trinity Press International, 1997), pp. 311-35.
Wiles, Virginia, Alexandra Brown and Graydon F. Snyder (ed.), *Putting Body & Soul Together: Essays in Honor of Robin Scroggs* (Valley Forge, PA: Trinity Press International, 1997).
Witetschek, Stephen, 'The Stigma of a Glutton and Drunkard, Q 7,34 in Historical and Sociological Perspective', *EphTheoLov* 83 (2007), pp. 135-54.
Woods, Edward J., *The 'Finger of God' and Pneumatology in Luke–Acts* (Sheffield: Sheffield Academic Press, 2001).
Worthington, Mark and Denis Edwards (ed.), *Biodiversity and Ecology as Interdisciplinary Challenge* (Adelaide: ATF, 2004).
Zerbe, Gordon, 'Ecology According to the New Testament', *Direction* 21 (1992), pp. 15-26.
Ziccardi, Costantino Antonio, *The Relationship of Jesus and the Kingdom of God According to Luke–Acts* (Roma: Editrice Pontificia Università Gregoriana, 2008).

Index of References

First Testament

Genesis
1	71
1.1-24	11
1.2-5	76
1.2	73, 104
1.26-28	11, 188
2.4-7	12
8.8	104
18.6	198
49.25	181

Exodus
20.24	86
26.4	86

Leviticus
13.47-48	86
13	223
14	223
25	124

Numbers
5.2-3	223
10.35-36	70
19.2	248
22.40	86

Deuteronomy
5.13	195
6.13	108
6.16	106, 109
32.11	104, 108
21.3	248
21.18-22	148

Judges
6.19	198

1 Samuel
1.24	198
6.3-20	70
6.7	248
6.36	70
14.32	86

2 Samuel
8.6	72
8.14	72

1 Kings
2.33	72
5-8	70
6.14-18	70
6.18	70
6.29	70
7.15-22	70
7.15	70
7.19	70
7.21	70
7.23-26	70
7.39	70
7.44	70

2 Kings
3.4	86

1 Chronicles
11.14	72

2 Chronicles
2–7	70
3.15	70

1 Maccabees
8.14	217
15.23	278

2 Maccabees
8.12	261
2.23	278

Job
1.6	107
31.20	86

Psalms
8.5-8	188
91.12	108

Proverbs
31.22	217

Wisdom
7.4-5	84, 248

Isaiah
1.3	195
7.21-22	86
9.6-7	90
9.7	72
11.6-9	249
25.6-8	282
32.17-20	90
40.3	99, 100
40.3-5	248
40.5	101
40.31	108
53.7	277
56.7	253
58.6	111
61.1	111

Jeremiah
4.28	13
7.14-26	261
7.30-34	261

12.11	13	34.3	86	Micah		
14.18	80	40-43	70	3.12	261	
16.1-9	261					
17.27	261	Joel		Zephaniah		
19.10-15	261	2.30-31	282	1.4-13	261	
		3.1-5	104	1.15	282	
Ezekiel						
16.4	81	Amos		Zechariah		
27.18-19	86	8.9	282	1.5-7	279	
				9.9	248	

SECOND TESTAMENT

Matthew		1.1b	64	1.57-79	66, 75	
1.1-17	105	1.2	52, 283	1.57-60	118	
3.1-12	99	1.3	40, 65,	1.58	76	
5.39	139		294, 295	1.60	76	
13.31-32	197	1.4	40, 67,	1.63	76	
			91, 268	1.64	76	
Mark		1.5–2.52	66-95	1.67-80	76	
1.2-4	99	1.6	68	1.69-73	76	
1.3	99, 220	1.7	68	1.74-75	76	
1.9-12	102	1.8-23	118	1.76	73	
2.15	134	1.9	68, 69	1.77	76	
4.8	152	1.10	69	1.77	76	
6.30-44	157	1.20	90	1.79	76, 77	
9.18-26	156	1.24-25	72, 92	1.80	77	
10.22	231	1.24	118	1.63	71	
10.46-52	233	1.26-38	22, 66, 92	1.67-80	76	
11.1–13.37	246	1.26	77	1.79	109	
11.15-26	259, 260	1.28-29	119	1.80	66	
13	260, 300	1.29	72	2	7	
13.1-9	152	1.31	72, 73,	2.1-20	10, 66,	
13.28-29	259		118		76, 78	
14.3-9	149	1.32	73, 162	2.1-7	75	
14.32-42	272	1.33	129	2.1-6	78	
14.36	172	1.34	118	2.1-3	22, 134	
14.40	272	1.35	72, 73	2.1	107, 276	
14.65	274	1.36	118	2.3	98	
15.22-25	281	1.38	66, 73,	2.6-7	118	
			119, 224	2.7	78, 79,	
Luke		1.39-56	66, 92		81, 118,	
1.1–2.52	9, 40, 64-	1.39	75, 77		159, 195,	
	95, 298	1.41	75		216	
1.1-4	6, 14, 20,	1.42	75	2.8-12	78	
	21, 22,	1.44	75	2.8	85	
	24-27,	1.45	75	2.10-14	85	
	64, 92	1.46-55	75, 166	2.12	79, 95,	
1.1a	64	1.56	75, 93		118, 195	

Luke (cont.)
2.13-20
2.14
2.15
2.16
2.19
2.21-39
2.22-38
2.13-14
2.14
2.21
2.22-52
2.29
2.29-32
2.30-31
2.37
2.40
2.41-51
2.46-49
2.51
2.48
2.49
3.1
3.1–4.30
3.1-20
3.1-18
3.1-6
3.1-2
3.2–4.18
3.2
3.3
3.4-6
3.4
3.5
3.6
3.7-18
3.8
3.12-13
3.13
3.20
3.21-22
3.21

78
86, 87, 88, 109, 249
85, 90
79, 118, 195
90, 119, 224
66
71
194
7, 73, 154
90
90, 91
109
166
91
118
66
66, 71
118
92
91
91
276
9, 96, 97, 114, 115, 298
66, 77, 98, 115
99
118
96
97
97, 117
98
99
99
100
101
101
251
134
239
101
103, 115
136

3.22
3.21–4.30
3.21–4.13
3.21-22

3.22
3.23-38

3.23
3.38
3.27
3.37
4–9

4.1-13

4.1
4.2
4.3
4.4
4.5
4.6-7
4.9-11
4.11
4.13
4.14–7.23

4.14-37
4.14-15
4.16-30

4.16-22
4.16-21
4.18
4.18-19

4.21
4.22-30
4.23-30
4.31–9.50
4.31–7.50
4.32
4.34
4.35-41

103, 162
66
10
66, 89, 96, 102, 118
88
66, 105, 118
105
148
105, 115
298
111, 118, 119, 120, 123, 124
66, 96, 106, 115, 133, 157, 180, 298
102
136
106, 107
107
107
108
108
106
109
9, 118, 125, 130
126
96, 110
96, 97, 110, 115, 166
89, 296
118
111
110, 112, 153
113
114
126
118, 299
119
127
127
154

4.35
4.36
4.37

4.38-41
4.42-44
4.42

5–9
5
5.1–6.16
5.1-11

5.1-3
5.1-2
5.3
5.4-5
5.4
5.6-9
5.6
5.7
5.8
5.10

5.11

5.12-32
5.13
5.15
5.16
5.24
5.27-32
5.29
5.32
5.33-35
5.38-39
6.4
6.7
6.12-16
6.12

6.17-49
6.17
6.19
6.20-49
6.20-26
6.27-36

229
127
128, 144, 299
128, 225
129
136, 144, 299
136
130
130, 131
22, 131, 136
22
144, 299
144, 299
22, 132
144, 299
299
22
22, 23
23
23, 132, 133
133, 135, 144, 198, 299
133
138, 229
299
134
299
134
134, 144
135
135
135
299
276
136, 161
136, 144, 145, 299
137
144, 299
229
138, 139
113, 138
124, 138, 144

Index of References

6.27-30	140		165, 225,	9.58–10.16	169
6.29	273		299	10.1	166
6.29-49	144	8.25	154	10.2-3	170
6.29-34	141, 142	8.26-39	155, 164,	10.3	171
6.35	73, 141, 174		174, 196, 214, 291	10.4	171
				10.8-12	171
6.36	213	8.26	299	10.9	225
6.35-36	141	8.27	299	10.11	225
6.37-49	138	8.28	73	10.13-16	172
6.43	299	8.33	299	10.17-29	172
6.44	299	8.34	299	10.21	172, 174, 178
6.49	299	8.35	299		
7–9	163	8.37	299	10.22	173. 178
7.1-23	142, 143	8.40-56	156	10.29	173
7.13	141, 213	8.44	82, 229	10.23-24	173
7.14	229	9	159	10.25-37	140
7.17	128, 144, 299	9.1-17	157	10.30-37	173
		9.3-5	171	10.33	141, 174, 213
7.20	126	9.3	299		
7.21-23	126, 153	9.10-12	158	10.34-35	174
7.23	126	9.12	299	10.34	214, 300
7.24–9.50	9, 125, 144, 146, 147	9.13-14	159, 160	10.37	175
		9.13	299	10.38	166, 176
		9.16	299	10.39-42	175, 176
7.24-35	148	9.17	161	10.40	176, 177
7.24	299	9.18-36	161	10.41-42	177
7.31-34	163	9.23	225	11.1-4	178, 179, 180
7.33-35	149	9.25	296, 299		
7.33	299	9.28-36	285	11.3	300
7.35	212	9.28	136	11.5	300
7.36-50	178, 203	9.29	299	11.5-28	180, 181
7.36–8.3	149, 150, 151	9.32	161	11.14–12.12	198
		9.34	73, 299	11.27	181
7.37	299	9.35	162, 299	11.28	181
7.39	163	9.37-50	162, 163	11.29–12.12	181, 182
7.46	299	9.42	225	11.50	296
7.47-50	151	9.51–19.27	9, 29, 77, 167, 168, 299	11.53	166
8.1	283			12.1	183
8.4-39	152			12.2-12	182, 183
8.4-8	197	9.51–13.22	169, 198	12.13-48	182, 183, 184, 185
8.5-8	170	9.51–11.13	198		
8.5	299	9.51-56	140, 169	12.13-34	198, 207
8.8	299	9.51	146, 169	12.14	182
8.11-25	153	9.53	166, 169, 223	12.15	183
8.11	299			12.16	173, 185
8.15	299	9.56-62	166	12.17	185, 186
8.21	208	9.56	169	12.19	186
8.22-25	291	9.58	170	12.20-21	186
8.24	6, 154,	9.62	170	12.22–13.5	187

Luke (cont.)		15.1-32	208, 209,	17.33	227, 231		
12.22-24	187		210, 211,	17.37	227		
12.23	300		212, 220,	18.1-17	228, 229		
12.24	156, 188		239	18.15	229		
12.30	296	15.1	204	18.16	230		
12.31-42	189	15.2	209	18.18-37	230, 231		
12.35-48	198	15.3-7	210	18.19-21	178		
12.41-13.5	190	15.7-10	211	18.24-30	232		
12.42	300	15.8	214	18.31-33	233		
12.49-53	198	15.11	173	18.35-43	114		
12.54-13.5	198	15.15-20	212	18.35	166		
13.6-21	190, 191	15.15-16	222	18.36-39	234		
13.6-20	198	15.17	300	18.38-43	233		
13.6-9	199, 205	15.20	141, 213	18.41-42	235		
13.6	300	15.23	300	19.1-10	236, 237,		
13.7-9	191, 192	15.27	300		238		
13.7	201, 300	15.29-32	233	19.1	166		
13.10-17	192, 205	15.30	203, 204,	19.3-5	244		
13.11	193		300	19.4-5	243		
13.12-13	194, 195	16.1-18	214	19.5	268		
13.15-16	195	16.1	173, 204,	19.7	285		
13.15	196, 205,		215	19.9-10	239		
	214, 300	16.2-17	215, 216	19.11-27	239, 240,		
13.17	196	16.14	204		241		
13.18-21	196	16.19-31	83, 216,	19.12	173		
13.21-22	197		221	19.21-31	217		
13.23–17.10	202, 220	16.19	173	19.25-26	242		
13.23-35	202, 203	16.21	218	19.28–21.38	9, 245,		
13.29	202	16.24	300		246, 247,		
13.31	166	17.1-10	218, 219		300		
13.33	166	17.1	204	19.28-36	247, 248		
14.1-6	204, 205,	17.2	300	19.28	166		
	206	17.3	182	19.29	263		
14.1	204	17.5	204	19.29-30	263		
14.7-28	206	17.6	300	19.31	248		
14.2-6	220	17.7	300	19.35-36	264		
14.2	173	17.10	221	19.36	248		
14.5	300	17.11–19.27	223, 242	19.37-38	249		
14.11	206	17.11-17	140	19.38	73, 89,		
14.13	206	17.11	166		250, 282		
14.15	204, 300	17.12-19	223	19.39-40	251		
14.16	173	17.12	285	19.41-44	251, 252		
14.21	207	17.13-14	224	19.45-20.26	252		
14.23	206, 207	17.16	224	19.45	71		
14.24	207	17.19	224	19.46-47	253		
14.25	204	17.20-37	225, 226,	20.1-18	253		
14.29-32	207		227, 228	20.1	71		
14.33-35	207, 208,	17.22-37	263	20.9	173		
	209	17.21	230	20.18-25	254		

20.27–21.4	255	23.26	292	10.36	109
20.46	182	23.27-31	278	13.43	262
21.1–24.53	9, 265, 266, 267	23.28-31	279	16.17	73
		23.33-34	281	17.24	296
21.3-4	256	23.33	292	23.30	276
21.5-33	256, 257	23.39-43	280, 281	23.35	276
21.21	225	23.44-53	282	25.2	276
21.5	71	23.45	71	25.11	276
21.20-24	261	23.46-56	283	25.16	276
21.25-28	263	23.53	82, 83	25.18	276
21.23-33	258	23.56	284		
21.28-32	259	24	83	*Romans*	
21.29-30	263	24.1-53	284, 301	4.25	266
21.34-38	260	24.5-8	285	5.8-10	266
21.34	182	24.5	288	6.3	266
21.36	182	24.6	49	8.15	172
21.37-38	261, 263	24.8	49		
21.37	263	24.9	288	*1 Corinthians*	
22.1–23.56	301	24.10-35	286	7.10-11	266
22.1-53	267	24.12	82, 83, 286	11.23-25	266
22.7-38	268, 271			15.3-5	266
22.7-30	269	24.22-24	287		
22.19	270, 271	24.25-49	288	*2 Corinthians*	
22.21-27	271	24.25-27	49	3.14	266
22.36	271	24.32	49		
22.38	271	24.37-53	289	*Galatians*	
22.39-53	272	24.39	229	4.6	172
22.39-46	137	24.45-47	49	2.20	266
22.43-44	273	24.50-53	166	3.1	266
22.45	272	24.53	71, 290		
22.47-51	138, 273			*Philippians*	
22.51	229	*Acts*		2.8	266
22.54–23.26	274, 275	1.10	285	3.10	266
22.65	275	2.41	262		
22.66-71	276	2.42	294	*1 Thessalonians*	
23.1-12	276	6.7	262	4.15	267
23.2	276	7.48	73		
23.11	82	8.4-25	140	*1 Peter*	
23.13-25	278	10.30	277	3.16	140
23.14	276				

Index of Authors

Aichele, George 41, 55, 327
Alexander, Loveday C. 24, 45, 175, 305
Allison, Dale C. 52, 305
Anderson, Janice C. 53, 305
Anthony, Peter 9, 305

Bailey, Kenneth 168, 305
Balabanski, Veronica 170, 185, 259, 305, 308, 314
Balch, David L. 50, 312,
Ballard, Mary W. 82, 307,
Balz, Horst 101, 103, 107, 136, 174, 310, 313
Barthes, Roland 42, 54, 305
Barzilai, Shuli 51, 305
Bauckham, Richard 3, 11, 12, 129, 130, 133, 155, 171, 183, 188, 195, 305
Beal, Timothy K. 55, 305
Ben-Dor, Immanuel 150, 305
Bertram, Georg 173, 305
Bird, Michael F. 168, 306
Blickenstaff, Marianne 93, 149, 175, 271, 279, 305-307, 310, 312, 313
Bock, Darrell L. 170, 306
Bohmer, Harald 82, 306
Booth, Ken 16, 306
Borgman, Paul 168, 306
Botha, Pieter J.J. 48, 306
Bovon, François 21, 26, 65, 87, 91, 92, 138, 306
Bradley, Keith 30, 306
Breck, John 50, 306
Brown, Alexandra 53, 315
Brown, Colin 122, 306
Brown, Raymond E. 21, 79, 80, 82, 87, 88, 273, 274, 277, 278, 282, 306, 310,
Buttrick, George A. 70, 80, 86, 150, 307, 308, 311, 312, 314
Byrne, Brendan 133, 167, 306

Cadbury, Henry J. 21, 26, 306
Cadwallader, Alan 15, 170, 254, 282, 306
Cargill, Robert R. 100, 306
Carney, Thomas F. 27, 31, 33-36, 306
Carter, Warren 175, 178, 306
Cartledge, Paul 30, 306
Casey, Maurice 161, 307
Chilton, B.D. 140, 310
Cockburn, Eve 82, 307
Collins, John N. 150, 307
Conzelmann, Hans 21, 307
Cosgrove, Charles H. 237, 307
Crossan, John Dominic 27, 52, 307
Culler, Jonathan D. 42, 54, 307

D'Angelo, Mary Rose 149, 274, 307
Davies, Gwynne Henton 70, 307
Davis, Ellen F. 12, 23, 305, 307, 309
Debrunner, Albert 74, 307
Delling, Gerhard 65, 308
Derrett, J. Duncan M. 84, 307
Detweiler, Robert 23, 307
Devall, Bill 307
Dillon, Richard J. 21, 284, 307
DiMento, Joseph F.C. 3, 307
Donahue, John R. 134, 307
Doughman, Pamela M. 3, 307
Douglas, Mary T. 29, 307
Dowling, Elizabeth V. 241, 307
Draper, Jonathan A. 48, 306, 307
Duling, Dennis 27, 308
Dyer, Keith D. 259, 263, 308

Edwards, Denis 15, 282, 306, 315
Eliot, T.S. 45-48, 55, 297, 308
Elliott, John H. 26, 308
Ellis, E. Earle 8, 308
Elvey, Anne 30, 68, 74, 81, 82, 90, 110, 181, 185, 193, 198, 237, 308

Ernst, Josef 8, 308
Evans, C.A. 140, 310
Evans, Christopher Francis 8, 308
Fawcett, S. Vernon 80, 308
Fewell, D.N. 55, 305

Fishbane, Michael 41, 308
Fitzmyer, Joseph A. 8, 21, 24-26, 65, 69, 98, 100, 103, 104, 111, 138, 152, 166, 191, 208, 214-17, 224, 237, 241, 248, 255, 266, 272, 279, 285, 286, 308
Foerster, Werner 137, 308
Ford, Josephine M. 140, 308
Foster, S.M. 50, 308
Freyne, Sean 20, 33, 36, 98, 131, 152, 189, 231, 308
Friedrich, Gerhard 65, 74, 83, 101, 107, 121, 137, 173, 182, 188, 206, 305, 307-309, 313-15

Gager, John G. 262, 308
Garland, David E. 81, 308
Green, Joel B. 9, 13, 27, 43, 45, 66, 67, 69, 98, 103, 105, 113, 126, 127, 134, 140, 141, 150, 166, 167, 175, 176, 180, 183, 198, 205, 208, 214, 215, 218, 226, 229, 232, 241, 247, 251, 271, 279, 286, 305, 308, 309
Gregory, Andrew 168, 308
Guijarro, Santiago 50, 79, 308

Habel, Norman 7, 11-13, 15, 170, 185, 259, 306, 308, 309, 311, 314,
Hall, Rosalind M. 82, 310
Halliday, Michael Alexander Kirkwood 57, 309
Hallman, David G. 190, 309, 310
Hamm, Dennis M. 193, 309
Hanson, K.C. 30, 309
Hartsock, Chad 114, 309
Hayes, John H. 42, 309, 311
Hays, Richard B. 12, 23, 43, 305, 307, 309
Heil, John P. 123, 309
Hengel, Martin 83, 309
Herr, L.G. 83, 309
Holgate, David A. 130, 184, 309
Horsley, Richard A. 7, 29, 48-50, 309
House, Paul R. 57, 309

Hur, Ju 16, 110, 309

Irudhayasamy, Raymond Joseph 111, 309

Jenson, Robert W. 23, 309
Johnson, Luke Timothy 21, 64, 84, 86, 92, 109, 151, 167-69, 217, 219, 227-29, 238, 240, 241, 256, 261, 279, 286, 309
Joy, Morny 41, 42, 309

Kähler, Martin 265, 309
Kamp, Kathryn A. 50, 310
Karadag, Recep 82, 306
Karris, Robert J. 6, 21, 79, 93, 104, 105, 123, 124, 126, 134, 138, 149, 150, 152, 163, 188, 310
Kasper, Walter 129, 130, 310
Keitzar, Renethy 120, 310
Kittel, Gerhard 65, 74, 83, 101, 107, 121, 137, 173, 182, 188, 206, 305, 307-309, 313-15
Kitzberger, Ingrid R. 52, 53, 310
Klassen, William, 140, 310
Kleine, Heribert 136, 310
Kodell, Jerome 74, 310
Kristeva, Julia 41, 42, 45, 47, 48, 51-55, 297, 305, 310

Landi, Sheila 82, 310
Landsberger, Henry 28, 310
LaVerdiere, Eugene 134, 310
Lenski, Gerhard E. 27, 310
Lenski, Jeanne 27, 310
Leon-Dufour, Xavier 291, 310
Levine, Amy-Jill 93, 149, 174, 175, 271, 279, 305-307, 310, 312, 313
Longenecker, Bruce W. 174, 311

Maddox, Robert 21, 311
Malbon, Elizabeth Struthers 59, 60, 311
Malina, Bruce J. 29, 68, 75, 79, 83, 88, 127, 183, 185, 186, 203, 206, 240, 311, 312
Marlow, Hilary 13, 311
Marshall, I. Howard 8, 285, 311
Marsh-Letts, Glennda Susan 82, 311
Martin, Dale B. 122, 311
Martin, Thomas W. 161, 311

McDonnell, Killian 103, 104, 105, 311
Metzger, Bruce M. 151, 285, 311
Metzger, James A. 184, 311
Moessner, David 168, 311
Moi, Toril 51, 52, 311
Moltmann-Wendell, Elisabeth 175, 311
Moxnes, Halvor 50, 308, 311

Napier, B. Davie 86, 311
Neagoe, Alexandru 268, 311
Neusner, Jacob 29, 311
Neyrey, Jerome H. 22, 26, 27, 29, 30, 193, 272, 308, 309, 311, 312
Nolland, John 111, 311

O'Day, Gail R. 41, 42, 44, 46-48, 311
O'Grady, Kathleen 41, 309
O'Toole, Robert F. 82, 91, 148, 311
Oakman, Douglas E. 21, 26, 28, 31, 77, 86, 295, 312
Osiek, Carolyn 50, 312

Patte, Daniel, 53, 312
Phillips, Gary Allen 42, 55, 305
Pilch, John J. 193, 240, 312
Piper, John 140, 312
Poxon, Judith L. 41, 319
Prior, Michael 111, 312

Quasten, Johannes 83, 312

Rad, Gerhard von 107, 314
Ravens, David 252, 312
Reid, Barbara E. 106, 312
Rigato, Maria-Luisa 271, 312
Rindge, Matthew S. 184, 186, 312
Robbins, Vernon K. 26, 312
Rohrbaugh, Richard L. 26-29, 32, 34, 39, 311, 312
Ross, James F. 208, 312
Roth, S. John 126, 312
Roudiez, L.S. 51, 310
Rowe, C. Kavin 168, 176, 313

Sand, Alexander 101, 313
Schelkle, Karl Hermann 103, 313
Schneider, Gerhard 101, 103, 107, 136, 174, 310, 313
Schneiders, Sandra 57, 58, 313

Schofield, Alison 100, 313
Schüssler Fiorenza, Elisabeth 57, 129, 313
Schweizer, Eduard 101, 121, 122, 313
Seccombe, David Peter 138, 313
Segovia, Fernando F. 53, 313
Seim, Turid Karlsen 279, 288, 313
Senior, Donald 271, 272, 277, 278, 313
Shellard, Barbara 21, 313
Small, Jocelyn Penny 72, 314
Smith-Christopher, Daniel L. 53, 37, 313, 314
Snyder, Graydon F. 53, 315,
Soards, Marion L. 266, 268, 271, 276, 314
Spencer, Patrick E. 168, 314
Sroka, Peter 82, 314
Staley, Jeffrey L. 53, 305
Stewart, Eric C. 22, 27, 29, 30, 193, 309, 311, 312
Stinespring, William Franklin 70, 71, 314
Stock, Augustine 50, 314
Strelan, Rick 262, 314

Tannehill, Robert C. 9, 21, 111, 284, 314
Taylor, Vincent 260, 314
Telford, William R. 260, 314
Trainor, Michael 6, 7, 15, 24, 50, 86, 134, 296, 314
Trever, John C. 197, 314
Trudinger, Peter 13, 309, 311
Tyson, Joseph B. 252, 314

Vaux, Roland de 100, 314
Voelz, James W. 54, 314

Wainwright, Elaine 46, 57, 315
Waschmann, Shelly 132, 315
Weiss, Konrad 188, 315
Wiles, Virginia 52, 53, 315
Witetschek, Stephen 148, 315
Woods, Edward J. 180, 181, 315
Worthington, Mark 282, 306, 315

Zerbe, Gordon 129, 315
Ziccardi, Costantino Antonio 129, 315

www.ingramcontent.com/pod-product-compliance
Lightning Source LLC
Chambersburg PA
CBHW071328190426
43193CB00041B/963